More praise for
THE RED AND THE WHITE

"While the Marias Massacre and the conflicts of Northern Rockies settlement are well known in the pantheon of the American West, Graybill eloquently redefines our understanding of both when he extends
the Clarke family history beyond the confines of the 19th and 20th
centuries to the present. . . . Graybill's saga is Shakespearean in its tragedy and Biblical in its parable of how the Indian tribes have endured a
diaspora of such magnitude. . . . [The] Clarke family chose a purpose-
ful, meaningful life, offering up, for all of us, a shining example of the
power and strength of the human spirit."   —J. Stuart Rosebrook,
True West

"Graybill . . . has written a gripping Western saga. But more, he has
plumbed the depth of racial and generational conflict by means of previously unexamined archival material and interviews with descendants
on both sides. . . . Western history buffs and general readers alike cannot fail to profit from a careful reading of its pages—dramatic, heartbreaking and wise."   —Gaylord Dold, *Wichita Eagle*

"[The Clarke family's] experiences provide fascinating insights into
race relations on the evolving frontier. . . . Graybill's book is highly
recommended for all readers interested in the 19th-century West."
     —*Library Journal*

"*The Red and the White* astutely tracks the enduring footprints of an
Indian-white family whose dramatic story symbolizes the challenges
faced by mixed-race pioneers on the explosive racial frontier of America's Wild West. Depicting the haunting brutality and tragic complex-
ity of a forgotten massacre, Graybill reveals vividly the true colors of
American history."   —Yunte Huang, author of *Charlie Chan*

"Through the intimate history of a native-white family, Graybill tells a vivid and absorbing story of war, dispossession, and survival, the tragic consequences of U.S. expansion into western North America. This is our history as we rarely see it but as so many lived it."
—Claudio Saunt, Richard B. Russell Professor in American History and codirector of the Institute of Native American Studies, University of Georgia

"With meticulous research and a keen eye for the grand sweep of time and space in the West, Andrew Graybill tells the story of a forgotten massacre that blows apart stereotypes of the nineteenth-century frontier. He brings to life a remarkable family that lived at the intersection of worlds, where the fur trade and intermarriage blurred the distinction between American Indians and white Americans."
—T. J. Stiles, author of *The First Tycoon*, winner of the Pulitzer Prize and the National Book Award

"This three-generation biography provides a lens through which to view the social history of Montana and of Indian-white relations during more than a century of the American saga. It is a story of both tragedy and triumph, told with sensitivity and power."
—James M. McPherson, author of *Battle Cry of Freedom*, winner of the Pulitzer Prize

"Andrew Graybill has provided us with an absorbing and intimate story of the unexpected ways race works in the American West. His wonderfully detailed and beautifully contextualized history of three generations of the Clarke family offers a surprising story about Indian and white and mixed-blood lives." —Anne Hyde, author of *Empires, Nations, and Families*

"Andrew Graybill's *The Red and the White* makes a deeply meaningful contribution to our understanding of interracial encounters in the

American past. He creates a finely textured, ground-level view of the struggles and achievements of people obliged to live 'in between.' This is family history, ethnohistory, and narrative history of a very high order."   —John Demos, author of *The Unredeemed Captive*

"In captivating detail, Graybill reconstructs five generations of an extraordinary mixed-race family. In the process he explodes the myth of the tragic half-breed caught between Indian and white worlds."
          —Margaret Jacobs, author of *White Mother to a Dark Race*

THE RED
and
THE WHITE

ALSO BY ANDREW R. GRAYBILL

Policing the Great Plains: Rangers, Mounties,
and the North American Frontier, 1875–1910

Bridging National Borders in North America:
Transnational and Comparative Histories
(co-editor, with Benjamin H. Johnson)

THE RED
and
THE WHITE

*A Family Saga of the
American West*

ANDREW R. GRAYBILL

LIVERIGHT PUBLISHING CORPORATION
A DIVISION OF W. W. NORTON & COMPANY
New York   London

For information about permission to reproduce selections from this book,
write to Permissions, W. W. Norton & Company, Inc.,
500 Fifth Avenue, New York, NY 10110

For information about special discounts for bulk purchases, please contact
W. W. Norton Special Sales at specialsales@wwnorton.com or 800-233-4830

Manufacturing by RR Donnelley, Harrisonburg
Book design by Helene Berinsky
Production manager: Devon Zahn

Library of Congress Cataloging-in-Publication Data

Graybill, Andrew R., 1971–
The red and the white : a family saga of the American West / Andrew R. Graybill. —
First Edition.
pages cm
Includes bibliographical references and index.
ISBN 978-0-87140-445-9 (hardcover)
1. Marias Massacre, Mont., 1870. 2. Interracial marriage—West (U.S.)—History—19th
century. 3. Whites—West (U.S.)—Relations with Indians. 4. Clarke, Malcolm, 1817–1869.
5. Clarke, Malcolm, 1817–1869—Family. 6. Clark family. 7. Piegan Indians. I. Title.
E83.866.G73 2013
978'.02—dc23
                                        2013011167

ISBN 978-0-87140-857-0 pbk.

Liveright Publishing Corporation, 500 Fifth Avenue, New York, NY 10110
www.wwnorton.com

W. W. Norton & Company Ltd., Castle House, 75/76 Wells Street, London W1T 3QT

1 2 3 4 5 6 7 8 9 0

For my wife, Jennifer,
and especially our children,
Fiona and Gavin
You will never know how much, unless and until . . .

"... you will mix with us by marriage,
your blood will run in our veins,
and will spread with us over this great island."

—*Thomas Jefferson to Indian correspondents, 1808*

Contents

Acknowledgments

Although it has taken me far longer to complete than I originally anticipated, I have loved writing this book, and I hope that my fascination with the Clarkes shows on every page. As I have told friends and colleagues on numerous occasions, the raw material for the book is a historian's dream; I leave it to the reader to determine whether I have done it justice.

Many, many people helped me along the way, and I welcome this opportunity to acknowledge their assistance, beginning, appropriately, with Joyce Clarke Turvey. Joyce fielded a telephone call from me in June 2006 in which I told her of my preoccupation with her family's history and asked whether she would be willing to help me with my research. She has, time and again, by sitting for interviews, generously providing me with invaluable photos and family memorabilia, and giving me broad latitude in writing the story of the Clarkes. I owe her a tremendous debt, one that I hope is repaid—at least partially—with the completion of this book, which she has waited on most patiently. Joyce's daughter, Dana Turvey, herself a writer, stepped in at a key moment in the later stages.

Of course, I might never have found Joyce—or at least not so early on—without the help of Kirby Lambert at the Montana Historical Society, who first put us in touch. I met Kirby and his colleagues at the MHS during a glorious one-month stay in Helena as the James H. Bradley Fellow, generously underwritten by the MHS to use its superb collections. I remain incredibly grateful for the expert assistance and tremendous personal kindness shown to me by Rich Aarstad, Ellie Arguimbau, Ellen Baumler, Jodi Foley, Kate Hampton, Becca Kohl, Martha Kohl, Molly Kruckenberg, Jeff Malcolmson, Lory Morrow, George Oberst, and Brian Shovers. It was a special treat to work with Molly Holz, editor of *Montana: The Magazine of Western History*, on an article about Helen P. Clarke that developed from my research at the MHS (and which appears in this book in different form). Thanks also to her assistant editor, Christy Goll, and the other members of Molly's staff. I feel privileged to have met Dave Walter before his untimely death in 2006.

Other Montanans showed me wonderful hospitality as well, none more than a handful of individuals on the Blackfeet Indian Reservation who consented to be interviewed about Piegan history and culture. My book is far better for the insights provided by Darrell Robes Kipp, Carol Murray, Darrell Norman, Marvin Weatherwax, and Lea Whitford. Thanks also to Donald Pepion, who grew up on the reservation but now lives in the Southwest, for visiting the University of Nebraska to present his own research on the Marias Massacre and to sit for an interview with me. I am grateful also to the following Treasure State residents: Stan Hayne, for speaking with me about his study of the Marias Massacre site; Lyndel Meikle, park ranger at the Grant-Korhs Ranch National Historic Site, for information on Johnny Grant; Bob Morgan, former curator of collections at the MHS, who corresponded with me about his relationship with John Clarke; Ripley Schemm, for hosting me on an early visit to Missoula and introducing me to Lois Welch (and to Ripley's niece, Ariadne Schemm, for putting me in touch with her aunt); to Charles M. Stone, for sharing his knowledge about the Bar X Six Ranch; Dick

Thoroughman, for information about Fort Shaw; and especially Mary Scriver, editor of an indispensable blog about Montana's past and present (among other subjects), who cheerfully fielded numerous inquiries from me.

I offer my heartfelt thanks to archivists, librarians, and volunteers at a range of institutions: the American Antiquarian Society, especially Ashley Cataldo; the Archdiocese of Milwaukee, especially Shelly Solberg; the Bridgeman Art Library, especially Kajette Solomon; the C. M. Russell Museum; the Cumberland County (Pennsylvania) Historical Society, especially Barbara Landis and John Slonaker; Fort Union National Historic Site; the Gallaudet University Library, Deaf Collections and Archives, especially Michael Olson; the Glacier County (Montana) Historical Society; the Glenbow-Alberta Institute, especially Jim Bowman and Doug Cass; Historic Fort Snelling, especially Nancy Cass, Matthew Cassaday, and Tom Lalim; the Joslyn Museum, especially Anne Crouchley; the Milwaukee Public Library, especially Audrey Barbakoff and Jennifer Heidel; the Minnesota Historical Society, especially Eileen McCormick and Eric Mortenson; the Missouri History Museum, especially Jaime Bourassa and Amanda Claunch; the Montana State University Library, Merrill G. Burlingame Special Collections; the Museum of Nebraska Art, especially Gina Garden; the National Anthropological Archives, especially Daisy Njoku; the National Archives and Records Administration in Washington, D.C., especially Mary Frances Ronan and Barbara Rust, and the NARA regional branches in Fort Worth and Kansas City, especially Stephen Spence; the North Dakota School for the Deaf, especially Carmen Suminski; the Oklahoma History Center; the Overholser Research Center and Schwinden Library at Fort Benton, especially Bob Doerk, Bruce Druliner, and, most of all, Ken Robison, who answered countless questions and supplied me with critical citations and documents; the Texas General Land Office, especially John Molleston; the Southern Methodist University Libraries; the United States Military Academy Archives, especially Suzanne Christoff and Casey Madrick; the University of Montana Library, K. Ross Toole Archives; and the University of Nebraska Libraries.

Thanks also to Renee Meade, for her help with research on John Clarke; to Bunny McBride, for sharing with me the curatorial materials for her exhibit "Journeys West: The David & Peggy Rockefeller American Indian Art Collection"; to Harry Palmer, for use of his beautiful and haunting photograph of a commemoration at the site of the Marias Massacre; and to Ezra Zeitler, mapmaker extraordinaire. I want also to acknowledge my debt to Stan Gibson, with whom I never met or corresponded, but whose fascination with the Marias Massacre (as well as his indignation at its obscurity) led him to collect a trove of material now housed in Calgary. I am, moreover, deeply grateful to the National Endowment for the Humanities, which provided me with a faculty fellowship that I used to make great progress on the manuscript during the 2010–11 academic year.

I spent nearly a decade at the University of Nebraska-Lincoln, which treated me exceptionally well, measured in no small part by the generous grants in support of this project that I received from the history department and the UNL Office of Research. And I could not have invented better colleagues, among them Lloyd Ambrosius, Barb Bullington, David Cahan, Parks Coble, Vanessa Gorman, Cindy Hilsabeck, Jeannette Jones, Patrick Jones, Jim Le Sueur, Tim Mahoney, Sandra Pershing, Will Thomas, and Ken Winkle. Thanks especially to my fellow westerners at UNL: James Garza, Margaret Jacobs, Doug Seefeldt, and the godfather himself, John Wunder. Perhaps I would have finished the book faster if not for the hours I passed talking shop (read: Cornhusker football) with Pete Maslowski. But I am much the richer for the time I spent as a visitor to 624 Oldfather Hall, and so is this book—Pete read every word of it, making trenchant suggestions throughout. Deb Hope was an exceptionally kind and patient listener. And Tim Borstelmann kept me grounded—and chuckling—while churning out countless reference letters on my behalf. *Grazie mille, amico.*

I have been lucky indeed to find such a welcoming new home in the Clements Department of History at Southern Methodist University in Dallas. Thanks to Jeremy Adams, Kenneth Andrien, Sabri Ates, John Chávez, Dennis Cordell, Ed Countryman, Crista DeLuzio, Melissa Dowling, Jeff Engel, Neil Foley, Kenneth Hamilton, Erin Hochman, Jim Hopkins, Jill Kelly, Tom Knock, Alexis McCrossen, John Mears, Azfar Moin, Dan Orlovsky, Mildred Pinkston, Sharron Pierson, Ling Shiao, and especially Kathleen Wellman, who as chair offered generous financial support to offset some of the costs of book production.

At SMU it is a singular privilege to work at the William P. Clements Center for Southwest Studies, established in 1996 by its visionary founding director, David J. Weber, and serving ever since as an incubator of first-rate research and publication about Texas and the U.S.–Mexico borderlands. I owe special thanks to my wonderful colleagues at the Center, Ruth Ann Elmore and Sherry Smith, and to Andrea Boardman, who retired in 2012 after more than a decade in Dallas Hall.

Fellow scholars and writers from numerous academic disciplines and endeavors have offered me their expert assistance, among them Steve Aron, Bridget Barry, George Black, Susan Burch, Cathleen Cahill, Sarah Carter, Phil Deloria, John Demos, Brian Dippie, Alec Dun, Bill Farr, Brian Frehner, Tom Gannon, James Haley, Rodger Henderson, Tucker Hentz, Michel Hogue, Fred Hoxie, Paul Hutton, Drew Isenberg, Karl Jacoby, Ari Kelman, Fran Kaye, Shepard Krech, David Leonhardt, Carolyn Merchant, Clyde Milner, Gary Moulton, Laura Mielke, Tice Miller, Ken Price, Sam Ratcliffe, John Reiger, Paul Rosier, Claudio Saunt, John Sunder, William Swagerty, Guy Vanderhaeghe, Elliott West, Laura White, Andy Wilson, David Wishart, Steve Witte, and Don Worster. And a very special thanks to the five hardy souls who so generously read the entire manuscript, saving me from errors big and small (those that remain are squarely on me): Anne Hyde, Ben Johnson, Ken Robison, Sherry Smith, and

Lesley Wischmann. Nick Guyatt, mensch that he is, read it *several* times, and often in piecemeal installments—I know of few better historians, and no finer critics. Thanks also to Kelly Lytle Hernandez, for the invitation to present my work at UCLA, and to Gregg Cantrell and Stephanie Cole, for a similar opportunity at a meeting of the Dallas Area Social Historians (DASH). I am grateful, too, for the attentiveness and consideration of audience members at a variety of conferences and lectures.

Thanks to my good friends Jacob Buchdahl, Josh Galper, David Leonhardt, Greg Raskin, and Brett Zbar, for twenty-three years of "humiliating acts of loving kindness" (not to mention unswerving loyalty).

One of the great pleasures of writing this book has been the opportunity to work again with Bob Weil. Many years ago I was Bob's editorial assistant at St. Martin's Press, and in the short time I spent in the Flatiron Building I learned a lifetime's worth about the business of publishing, from bellybands to tip ins and so much in between. Still more important, however, were the standards Bob set for intellectual commitment and professional conduct, which I have tried ever since to emulate. These lessons have served me in ways I could not possibly have imagined when I was in my midtwenties, and I am thus as grateful for Bob's mentorship as for his unrivaled editorial ability, which has improved this book in more ways than I can count. Thanks also to his terrific assistants, past and present, who have worked with me in bringing this project to completion: Phil Marino, Tom Mayer, Will Menaker, and Lucas Wittman. I am deeply indebted to the copyeditor Otto Sonntag, for his inaugural foray into Montana history.

Of course, I owe the most to my family, starting with my parents, who impressed upon me when I was young the idea that I should choose a path that interested me, and then made that possible in every imaginable way; I have come to understand just how rare and generous a gift that was. My sister, Lisa, inspires me with her activism even as she keeps me in my proverbial shoes. And one of the many benefits in marrying Jennifer Ebinger in 1999 was becoming a part of her family: hugs to Chuck, Lynn, Brad, and Margaret, as well as the wider Ebinger and Makkonen clans. And a sad goodbye to my wonderful sister-in-law, Sara Ebinger, who passed away most unexpectedly just as this book was going to press.

Compelling as I have found the history of the Clarkes, I doubt that the subject would have appealed to me nearly as much if I were not a father and husband myself. My wife, Jennifer, and our children, Fiona and Gavin, are the best parts of every day, the ones who give my life meaning, purpose, and direction. I do not have the words to adequately express my love for them, so perhaps it is best to leave those things—which are so indelibly felt—largely unsaid.

THE RED
and
THE WHITE

Clarke Family Tree

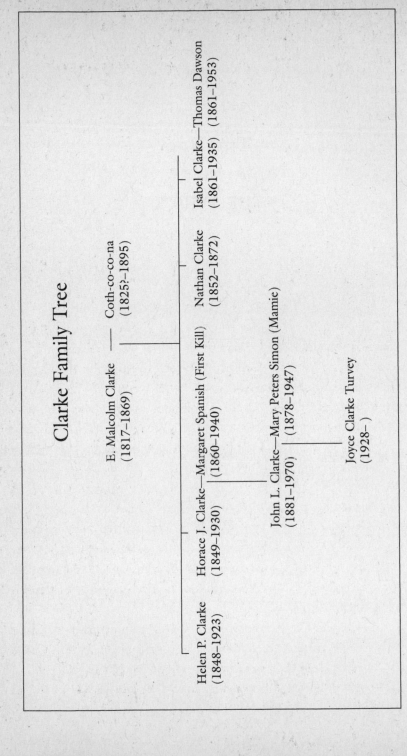

Prologue

This book is the fruit of what seemed at first a dispiriting after-noon in June 2006. I had spent several weeks that summer in Helena at the Montana Historical Society investigating the Cypress Hills Massacre, an obscure yet notorious 1873 event in which a mixed group of American and Canadian wolf hunters butchered nearly two dozen Assiniboine Indians in southern Alberta.[1] That slaughter, I believed, could help explain why the U.S.–Canada border became more rigid ever after.

Sometime around the middle of my stay in Montana, however, I grew bored with this story—never a good sign in the early going of a new project—and so one day I decided to step away from my research and see what other collections the MHS might hold. After all, I had long heard the society's archives described in rapturous terms by colleagues who insisted that it was among the best reposi-tories west of the Mississippi.

In choosing where to look first, I thought immediately of James Welch's masterpiece, *Fools Crow*, a historical novel about a small band of Blackfeet Indians in Montana experiencing the invasion of their country by white newcomers during the late 1860s. I had just taught the book in a course on the North American West at the University of Nebraska, and my students had admired it greatly, just as I had when first reading it nearly a decade before. I still consider it the best tool for capturing the perspective of native peoples themselves during the so-called Indian Wars of the Reconstruction era.

One of the incidents upon which the novel hinges is the killing of a character named Malcolm Clarke, a white fur trader married to a Piegan Blackfeet woman; his sensational murder—at his ranch, as his family looked on—sets in motion a series of tragic events culminating in the Marias (or Baker) Massacre of 23 January 1870.[2] Though largely forgotten now, much like the brutal episode in the Cypress Hills, the slaughter was enormously controversial at the time, because of the high number of Indian deaths and the fact that many of the victims were suffering from smallpox, thus utterly defenseless against the bitter cold as well as the bullets of the Second U.S. Cavalry. Given these circumstances, the Marias Massacre easily belongs in any conversation about the worst atrocities committed by American military forces against native peoples, from Sand Creek in 1864 to Wounded Knee in 1890.

With memories of *Fools Crow* still resonant, I resolved to find out whether Malcolm Clarke had actually existed or whether Welch had invented him as a literary device to move the story along. A brief search of the library's online catalog turned up a microfilm reel, and with help from an MHS staff member I soon located a vertical file as well, both containing tantalizing biographical information about Clarke.

Malcolm Clarke was indeed a real person, and his murder was precisely the watershed event Welch described.* But Clarke was even more important than *Fools Crow* led me to believe. As I quickly ascertained, Clarke was one of the earliest and most consequential white

---

*The spelling of the family surname was wildly inconsistent throughout the nineteenth century, alternating between "Clark" and "Clarke" until the latter became the widely accepted version.

pioneers in Montana, having arrived on the Upper Missouri aroun. 1840, just as the fur trade in Montana entered its heyday. His killing was so significant that I found an abundance of historical accounts that touched on the event, including newspaper articles that recalled the murder many decades later and described its lasting repercussions. Clarke's descendants had also been quite prominent, and their stories and secrets were housed at the MHS, too. By the close of that summer day, I had abandoned my work on the Cypress Hills Massacre and have been preoccupied—maybe even a little obsessed—with the Clarkes ever since.

Still, the timing of my discovery was ironic. I had been looking for the Clarkes—or, rather, any racially blended family like them—for more than two years, but just a few months earlier had abandoned the investigation. Previously, I had become keenly interested in nineteenth-century North Americans of mixed ancestry while researching my first book, in which I encountered the Métis, individuals in the U.S.–Canada borderlands who were eventually recognized by the Canadian government as a separate indigenous group, neither red nor white but a distinct people in between.

Though similar people had, of course, lived in the United States, especially in places where the fur trade had flourished, they remained largely invisible in the archival record (and thus in the relevant secondary literature) because of the binary U.S racial formulation that classifies such persons as either white or Indian. Despite the paucity of historical documentation, I wondered how these mixed-race peoples had navigated their incorporation into the United States as the nation absorbed the trans-Mississippi West—their last redoubt—in the years following the Civil War. But in time I grew frustrated by the relative absence of source material and moved on to other book ideas. Then I found the Clarkes that afternoon in Helena.[3]

Having discovered them, however, I was surprised that they did not conform to my expectations about peoples of mixed ancestry. This was perhaps because of my passing familiarity with the life of

(1843–1918), one of the best-known mixed-blood
⸱ᴄᴐ   ɔf the nineteenth century. Like the children born to
       ᴄlarke and his Blackfeet wife, Coth-co-co-na, Bent had a
       vho was Indian (a Cheyenne named Owl Woman) and a
       vho was a prominent white trader (William Bent). George
led a remarkable life, serving in the Confederate army and surviving
the murderous work of the Colorado militia at Sand Creek, an event
that left him embittered with white Americans. Although in later
years he worked closely with Anglo scholars like George Bird Grinnell to record the history of his mother's people, Bent felt like an
alien, stranded uncomfortably between these two worlds—one red,
one white—for the rest of his days, retreating into alcoholism before
dying penniless in the Spanish influenza pandemic near the close of
World War I.[4]

Given the despairing arc of George Bent's life, I imagined that
the Clarkes—especially in their later generations—would have similarly tragic stories, and assumed that their lives would reveal the same
social dislocations and pathologies that Bent and his kin struggled to
overcome. To be sure, the Clarkes suffered their share of pain and
calamity. And yet in the course of my research I found that race was
not necessarily the intractable issue for the Clarkes that it had been
for George Bent, or especially his younger brother Charles, who, following the Sand Creek Massacre, renounced his Anglo heritage and
plundered whites with other Cheyennes until he was killed by Kaw
government scouts in 1867, when he was just twenty-two.[5]

While the tale of the Bents could have served as inspiration for
one of the novelist Cormac McCarthy's darker tales, this was not the
case with the Clarkes. In fact, race was the very attribute that gained
one family member a job with the U.S. Indian Service, and it was
the source of creative inspiration that helped another achieve enduring artistic fame. Moreover, at different moments, other variables—
gender, economic status, disability—proved much more important
in shaping their personal choices and possibilities.

The Clarkes thus offer a rich historical lens through which to view the shifting grounds of race in the West and the wider nation during the mid-nineteenth century. They are also ideal in another sense: their individual stories are enormously compelling, for both the historian and the general reader. This book is built around five extraordinary members of the family, drawn from three generations.[6]

The narrative begins with the wedding of Coth-co-co-na and Malcolm Clarke in 1844, explaining how a marriage that seems so unusual to us—between the teenaged daughter of a prominent Indian warrior and a white American nearly a decade her senior—was actually quite common on the Upper Missouri. This chapter is thus a story about the fur trade, in part, but also about the incorporation of the trans-Mississippi West into the political and economic fabric of the United States in the first decades of the nineteenth century.

Clarke, who like so many young men of the time had come west in search of adventure and wealth, is the subject of chapter 2. Through a combination of cunning, ability, and perseverance, he achieved levels of wealth and prominence that eluded all but the most successful fur traders, which—along with his personal courage—earned him lasting fame among white residents of the territory. And yet Clarke, who as a youth was expelled from West Point for fighting, never fully tamed his quick temper or his penchant for aggression. Bloodshed thus ran through his life like a crimson thread, from killings he committed to the violence that led to his own death at the age of fifty-two.

This multigenerational family story continues with Horace and Helen Clarke, two of the four children born to Malcolm and Coth-co-co-na. Both struggled to find their places in Montana after their father's slaying and the Marias Massacre. Though nursing a deep antipathy to the Piegans because of his father's murder, Horace lived among them in the years after 1870, marrying a full-blooded Indian woman named Margaret First Kill and establishing a homestead and small ranch in the northern Montana hamlet of Midvale, later renamed East Glacier Park. He moved fluidly between white

and native society, defending reservation-bound Piegans against
rapacious Indian agents and serving as an occasional intermediary
on behalf of the federal government. In the early twentieth century
Horace sold a sizable portion of his land to the Great Northern Railway, which then built the luxurious Glacier Park Lodge and golf
resort, still in operation today.

Helen's journey proved far more arduous than that of her brother.
After her father's murder, she left Montana to join Malcolm's family
in the Midwest. She then enjoyed a brief but highly acclaimed stage
career in New York and Europe, where she starred in several produc-
tions with the famous French actress Sarah Bernhardt. Drawn ineluc-
tably back to her native land, Helen returned to Montana and served
for eight years as the superintendent of schools for Lewis and Clark
County; that made her the first woman to hold elective office in the
history of the territory. In 1890 she assumed an even more unusual
post for a woman, accepting a position as one of the nation's first
female allotment agents. In this capacity she moved to Indian Territory and participated in the breakup of the Ponca and the Otoe Reservations, among others. And yet in the end, despite having spent
most of her adult life in the white world and assisting in the dispossession of indigenous peoples, Helen selected her own allotment on
the Blackfeet Reservation, where she lived with her brother Horace
until her death in 1923.

The book concludes with the story of Horace's son, John. Born
in 1881, twelve years after the murder of a grandfather he never
knew, John contracted scarlet fever as an infant and was rendered
deaf and mute. In spite of his deafness, he became a renowned sculptor of western wildlife; he captured the attention of Montana luminaries like the famed cowboy artist Charlie Russell and attracted
such deep-pocketed patrons as John D. Rockefeller Jr. Yet for all
his acclaim and widespread acceptance by non-Indians, Clarke rarely
left the reservation, choosing instead to live there with his wife and
adopted daughter, both of whom were white. In 2003, more than

three decades after his death, Clarke was inducted into the Gallery of Outstanding Montanans, a hall of fame celebrating notable residents of the Treasure State.

In the end, I came to appreciate my great fortune in stumbling upon the history of the Clarke family, which offers keen insight into the lives of people who were both red and white, and thus contemptuously dismissed in their own time and often since as "half-breeds." If their experiences were typical in many ways of mixed-blood families in the Rocky Mountain West of the nineteenth and twentieth centuries, their lives were nevertheless extraordinary, and the Clarkes are still well known throughout Big Sky Country, with their names literally etched into the geography of northern Montana. They are remembered, too, for their tragic association with the darkest day in Piegan history. This book, then, is the story of their journey through the complex landscape of race in America, with particular attention to what they gained—and what they lost, irretrievably—along the way.

I

Cutting Off Head Woman

Sometime in 1844 a young Piegan woman married a white trader employed by the American Fur Company (AFC). The bride was about nineteen, slightly beyond the typical age of first marriage for women of her tribe but nearly a decade younger than her new husband. Little else about the wedding is known for certain, and even the date is merely an educated guess handed down through generations.

The couple probably wed at Fort McKenzie, a key AFC post in what is now north-central Montana. Located on the north bank of the Missouri River—the broad riparian thoroughfare that threads across the upper reaches of the Great Plains before tumbling into the Mississippi—the small stockade was dwarfed by steep bluffs that thrust upward from the south bank and ended at the water's edge. If the scenery was dramatic, however, the ceremony was much less so, consisting perhaps of a simple exchange of horses between the groom and the bride's family.

The woman's name was Coth-co-co-na, meaning "Cutting Off Head Woman," a moniker conjuring up her indispensable role in dressing animal skins. At the time of her wedding, the fur trade was the dominant economic pursuit of her people, the Piegans, one of the three groups of the so-called Blackfoot Confederacy. Her father, Under Bull, was a reputable warrior, and it was he who selected her husband. He chose well, for Malcolm Clarke, though he had been on the Upper Missouri for only a short time, was already one of the AFC's most successful traders, endowed with irresistible charm and ruthless business acumen. Clarke was also remarkably handsome: just shy of six feet, with brown eyes, soft auburn hair, and a dark beard.

By most objective measures, their union appears unlikely, even extraordinary, given the vast chasm between husband and wife in terms of race, language, custom, and experience. After all, Coth-co-co-na had lived her entire life within the shadows cast by the Rocky Mountains, whereas Malcolm Clarke was born in Indiana and raised in Ohio, and he had spent two years at the U.S. Military Academy before coming west in his midtwenties. Moreover, the first meeting between their peoples four decades earlier had ended in a spasm of violence that left two Piegans dead and their tribesmen bearing a powerful grudge against the white invaders.

And yet, despite the seeming improbability of a partnership like theirs, such marriages were in fact quite common throughout fur country and had occurred wherever the trade in animal skins flourished in North America, dating back as far as the seventeenth century. Nearly all of Malcolm Clarke's AFC associates had Indian wives, a circumstance that provoked condemnation from white Americans in the East both for the transgression of racial boundaries and for the sense that these nuptials—as the gift exchanges that accompanied them suggested—were, in effect, business transactions meant only to facilitate the fur trade, devoid of love and commitment and lacking religious consecration. Although the economic benefits were undeniable, especially for the groom and his in-laws, many of these unions were built upon genuine affection. So it was with Coth-co-co-na and Malcolm Clarke.

In order to understand their marriage and the world they made, a world that, according to a family friend, "mingles the best of the

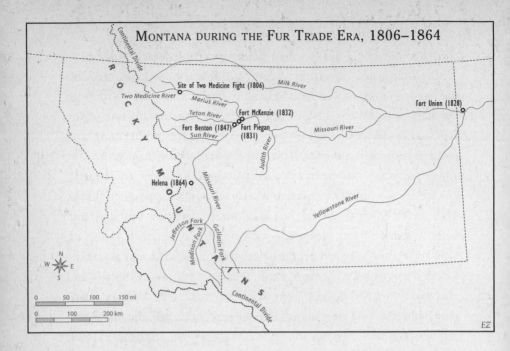

Continental Divide

ROCKY

Site of Two Medicine Fight (1806)

Milk River

Two Medicine River

Marias River

Fort Union (1828)

Teton River

Fort McKenzie (1832)

M

Fort Benton (1847)

Fort Piegan
(1831)

Missouri River

O

Sun River

U

Judith River

Helena (1864)

N

Missouri River

T

Yellowstone River

A

Jefferson Fork

Gallatin Fork

I

N

Madison Fork

S

Continental Divide

N
W   E
S

0   50   100   150 mi

0   100   200 km

EZ

white race and the red," one must start with the broader history of the period, beginning on an unseasonably warm day in New Orleans some forty years before that humble wedding ceremony at Fort McKenzie.

One Land, Two Worlds

Though it was nearly Christmas, 20 December 1803 was a beautiful day in New Orleans, with ample sunshine and moderate temperatures more typical of late spring than the onset of winter. The pleasant weather, however, did not lift the spirits of Pierre Clément de Laussat, the French governor of Louisiana. His duty that morning was the sad one of transferring control of the colony to the United States, which had purchased Louisiana from France earlier that year. Laussat had held his office for only nine months.

At ten-thirty the governor joined a small crowd that had assembled at his stately home near the east gate of the city, on the sprawling plantation owned by Marquis Bernard de Marigny. Among the group that morning were government officials, military officers, and French citizens, who accompanied Laussat on the half-mile walk to the Place d'Armes in the Vieux Carré. After meeting with the American commissioners and handing over the key to the city, Laussat and his companions retired to a balcony overlooking the great, crescent-shaped curve of the Mississippi River at its majestic terminus. There they watched solemnly as below them a French officer lowered the *tricolore* for the last time. As the governor recorded in his journal, "more than one tear was shed at the moment when the flag disappeared from that shore."[1]

The handover that day was the culmination of momentous events on both sides of the Atlantic. In 1801, as first consul, Napoleon had dispatched an enormous military expedition to quell a slave uprising on the island of Saint-Domingue, a French outpost in the Caribbean (now the independent nation of Haiti). Yet after two years of brutal fighting and the loss of 24,000 troops, including his own brother-in-law, who like so many other Frenchmen had succumbed to yellow fever, Napoleon tired of the effort altogether and uttered famously in January 1803, "Damn sugar, damn coffee, damn colonies."[2]

Thomas Jefferson, then in his first term as U.S. president, was only too pleased to assist Napoleon in liquidating his overseas possessions. As it happened, in 1801 American emissaries had tried unsuccessfully to negotiate the French sale of New Orleans, long coveted for its strategic position near the mouth of the Mississippi River and its easy access to the Gulf of Mexico. Jefferson's officials were thus delighted when in April 1803 Napoleon offered far more, a huge domain stretching deep into the continent's interior, containing all or parts of fifteen future U.S. states. And the asking price of $15 million was a veritable bargain, working out to about three cents per acre.

If the Louisiana Purchase was the greatest achievement of Jefferson's presidency, it was also its most controversial, given the dubious constitutional authority permitting such a transaction. Jefferson forged ahead, however, spurred by his aspiration to make the United States an "empire of liberty," a dream that hinged upon the acquisition of sufficient space to guarantee that it remained an agrarian nation populated by yeoman farmers, whom Jefferson considered "the chosen people of God." With the Louisiana Purchase, the president believed he had acquired enough land for hundreds of generations of American settlers and, at the same time, dealt a crucial blow to European imperial ambitions in North America.[3]

As reflected by the sobs—many of them not even muffled—that Lassaut heard on that bright December morning in New Orleans, not everyone shared Jefferson's enthusiasm for the American acquisition. And yet while the French were despondent, members of a much larger group—the native peoples of the territory—remained uninformed, though presumably most of them would have looked upon the transfer with scorn or amusement rather than concern. After all, it was one thing to claim land but quite another to possess it, as countless Europeans had discovered during their imperial misadventures in North America. The Indians would have their own say about these matters.

In time the new owners of the Louisiana Territory came to understand that few groups were more stubbornly resistant to American expansion than the Blackfeet, who lived at the opposite extreme of the Mississippi-Missouri river system, some 3,700 miles upstream from New Orleans. By the early nineteenth century, they—and not the French or the Americans—were in full control of the northwestern Plains, jealously guarding against the incursions of all outsiders, native, white, or otherwise.

Nevertheless, even as the *tricolore* came down in the Place d'Armes in the waning days of 1803, plans were already underway in Washington, D.C., to explore and eventually absorb this infinite wilderness, which, in Jefferson's eyes, held the promise of perpetual renewal for the nascent United States. In short order, Americans would make their way across the continent and enter the orbit of the Blackfeet, first as a mere trickle and later as a flood. This encounter between two disparate peoples, by turns violent and cooperative, would shape the history of the West and the larger nation that claimed it.

AT THE TIME of the Louisiana Purchase, St. Louis was a modest but ambitious village of about one thousand residents. Established in 1764 by a New Orleans trader named Pierre Laclède Liguest, the site on the west bank of the Mississippi had much to recommend it, including its position on a high bluff and especially its nearness to the confluence of the Missouri River, just ten miles upstream. Though attracting a diverse group of travelers and traders from its earliest days, the settlement retained its French character well into the nineteenth century, in language, religion, and especially architecture, marked by the white lime application disguising the "meanness" of its many buildings fashioned from mud or stone.[4] For all of its Old World attributes, however, St. Louis took on singular importance for the young American republic when it served as the "gateway to the West" for Jefferson's Corps of Discovery, which shoved off from its environs on 14 May 1804, bound for the Pacific Ocean.

The expedition consisted of approximately three dozen men packed into a keelboat and two pirogues (modest, flat-bottomed craft agile in shallow waters), led by Meriwether Lewis and William Clark. While the two commanders acted as equals, it was the younger Lewis who was officially in charge. Born in 1774 in Albemarle County, Virginia, the mercurial Lewis had spent most of his life as a soldier, in the process gaining valuable experience with frontier conditions and native peoples. He was thus an obvious choice for Thomas Jefferson, who knew him well, having appointed him as his private secretary in 1801 shortly after assuming the presidency. Lewis in turn tapped another Virginian, the redheaded William Clark, whom he had met in the military.[5]

If small in size, the Corps of Discovery was invested with enormous responsibility: namely, to chart the lands Jefferson had bought
from Napoleon while binding them to the United States, safe from
any imperial designs entertained by the Spanish (to the south) or the
British (to the north). To that end, Lewis and Clark sought to make
contact with the many indigenous peoples of the region, hoping to
win their loyalty on behalf of the fledgling nation to the east. With
such diplomacy in mind, the expedition lugged along a variety of
gift items: clothes and blankets, guns and ammunition, liquor and
tobacco, and, most memorable of all, Indian peace medals specially
produced by the U.S. Mint.

Given the importance of establishing amicable relations with the
native peoples of the trans-Missouri West, it is not surprising that
encounters with Indians receive extensive treatment in the detailed
journals kept by Lewis and Clark and stand out as some of the most
enduring episodes of the journey. Take, for instance, the five months
the expedition spent among the Mandans in present-day North
Dakota during the hyperborean winter of 1804–05. Beyond spreading word of U.S. sovereignty and promoting peace among rival tribes
of the area, the corps enlisted there the French-Canadian interpreter
Toussaint Charbonneau and his young Shoshone wife, Sacagawea,
who became one of the most famous Indians in American history.[6]

Yet for all the indigenous peoples they contacted during their
epic voyage, there was one tribe the Corps of Discovery worked
strenuously to avoid: the Siksikau, as they called themselves, a term
meaning "black foot" or "black feet," which probably referred to
their moccasins, because they were either painted black or discol-
ored by the prairie fires that frequently swept the Plains. Though
divided into three groups who remained politically distinct—the Sik-
sikas proper (or Blackfoot), the Kainahs (or Bloods), also known as
the "many chiefs," and the Piegans (or Pikunis), meaning "scabby
robes"—all members of the Blackfoot Confederacy spoke one language, shared common customs, and faced off against the same

adversaries. Together, they controlled a vast swath of territory east of the Rocky Mountains, stretching south from the Saskatchewan River in Canada all the way to the Teton Range, in what is now northwestern Wyoming. And they were reflexively hostile to interlopers, whom they perceived as a threat to both their horse herds and their access to buffalo.[7]

The expedition avoided the Blackfeet on the outbound portion of its trip across present-day Montana during the summer of 1805. The Americans were not so fortunate the next year when they traversed the same area on the way home, for Lewis had an accidental run-in with a small group of Piegans just south of the forty-ninth parallel, which now marks the U.S.–Canada border. That meeting sparked the only episode of lethal native-white violence during the entire twenty-eight-month odyssey of the Corps of Discovery, but its impact set an ominous tone for U.S.-Blackfeet relations for decades to come.

IN THE SMALL CAMP on the banks of the Two Medicine River, 26 July 1806 dawned cloudy. Captain Meriwether Lewis had hoped to use his sextant that morning to fix the longitude, but overcast skies and intermittent rain made such work impossible. Instead, he and his small group moved on from "Camp Disappointment," as Lewis ruefully named the site. As they traveled in a southeasterly course down the valley of the Two Medicine, the mood of Lewis brightened a bit as he took note of a species of cottonwood tree he had never before glimpsed on the Missouri River or its tributaries. But he did not pause for long; Lewis was homeward bound, and he was eager to return to the welcoming confines of St. Louis before summer turned into fall, no mean feat given that the city—and thus the finish line for the Corps of Discovery—lay 2,300 miles downriver.

Lewis was on his own that day, save for his three companions: George Drouillard, a half-French, half-Shawnee interpreter widely regarded as the best hunter on the expedition; and the brothers Joseph and Reuben Field, dependable Virginians who had been among the earliest enlistees in the Corps of Discovery. Three weeks earlier, Lewis and his co-captain, William Clark, had divided their command in order to explore uncharted areas they had passed through the year before. Clark took his group south to investigate the Yellowstone River, while Lewis and nine men headed in the opposite direction to scout the headwaters of the Marias.

Since then, Lewis had suffered one frustration after another, including the loss of several horses to Indian thieves. In order to make better time, he sent six of his men downriver and led Drouillard and the Field brothers northwest. But more irritations awaited him: the failed astronomical readings and especially his discovery that the Marias, which he had named for his cousin Maria Wood, did not extend as far north as he had hoped. This meant less territory that he could claim on Jefferson's behalf as part of the Louisiana Purchase.

Later on that summer afternoon, Lewis's displeasure gave way to apprehension. Cresting a small hill, he spotted a herd of thirty ponies about a mile away, tended by eight Indians. Worried that flight might signal weakness and perhaps spur the natives to attack, Lewis instead rode out to meet them. At first, he took the Indians to be Hidatsas, perhaps because three days earlier Drouillard had discovered a recently abandoned Indian camp that Lewis supposed to have belonged to members of that tribe. In fact, the Indians Lewis had stumbled upon were Piegans. His fear ebbed a bit when the Indians drew close, for he noticed that they were not adult men but rather boys in their early teens. As it happened, the Piegans were probably just as surprised by this chance encounter, although they may have regarded it as some sort of supernatural test on their road to becoming warriors.

As he had done on other such occasions, Lewis offered gifts to the Indians, including an American flag, a handkerchief, and a peace medal. Communicating in the sign language common on the Plains, he invited the Piegans to camp with them that night. Together, the group rode down a steep bluff and found a good spot close to the river. Lewis and Drouillard accepted the Piegans' invitation to share one of their teepees, while the Field brothers bedded down just outside near the fire. With Drouillard's help, Lewis conversed with the Indians late into the evening, and he shared his pipe and tobacco with them. In the course of their discussion, Lewis learned that the Indians traded with the British Hudson's Bay Company at a post on the Saskatchewan, where they had acquired guns, ammunition, and liquor in exchange for animal skins. In turn, Lewis explained that he had come to establish relations with all the Indians of the region, and to facilitate peace among them. Despite their apparent friendliness, Lewis remained uneasy about the presence of the natives, and so took the first watch. At around eleven-thirty, with the Indians fast asleep, he retired.

Lewis awoke the next morning to a commotion that confirmed his worst premonitions. At dawn one of the Piegans attempted to steal the rifles of the Field brothers, who darted off after the thief. When they caught up with the boy, who was known as Side Hill Calf, Reuben stabbed him in the heart with a knife; the injured youth lurched forward a few steps before falling dead. Thwarted in their bid to capture the Americans' firearms, the Piegans then turned their attention to the white men's horses. Lewis grabbed his rifle and pursued two of the Indians; when one of them turned to attack, Lewis shot the boy in the stomach. Though fatally wounded, the young man raised himself onto one elbow and snapped off a bullet, narrowly missing Lewis's head. Having seen two of their number killed, the six remaining Indians rode away. For their part, the Americans quickly struck the campsite and gathered up their own belongings as well as those of the Indians, although Lewis "left the medal about the neck of the dead man [Side Hill Calf] that they might be informed who we were."[8]

The surviving Piegans carried word of the clash back to their friends and relatives, who were camped in the foothills of the Rocky Mountains. The Indians hastily assembled a war party that chased the Americans, but to no avail, given that Lewis enjoyed a head start of more than a day. In teepees throughout Blackfeet country that fall and winter, the skirmish was no doubt a central topic of conversation, and in time the story of the Two Medicine fight became a part of tribal lore, carrying the unmistakable lesson that white men were brutal and duplicitous.[9]

Surely the tale was heard by Coth-co-co-na sometime in the early 1830s, as it was by most Blackfeet children born during the early nineteenth century. By that time, however, the relationship between the white race and the red had undergone a total metamorphosis.

IN THEIR OWN ACCOUNT of that portentous 1806 meeting with the Corps of Discovery, Piegans of today, more than two centuries later, describe it as a collision of "two worlds at Two Medicine." There is much truth in that telling, for it captures the yawning gulf between the natives and the newcomers. By another metric, however, the Blackfeet and the Americans were in fact quite similar: both belonged to dynamic, expansive societies that at the start of the nineteenth century were brimming with ambition and confidence. Little wonder, then, that their early interactions generated such friction.

Beginning around 1800 the fledgling United States began a transformation that remade it as a nascent industrial power, and frontier absorption served as a catalyst for these developments.[10] For more than a century Americans had pushed outward from their beachheads on the Atlantic coast in search of fertile territory, but that process slowed considerably at the end of the Seven Years' War (1756–63) when the British retarded colonial migration beyond the crest of the Appalachian Mountains, hoping that the careful management of intending settlers would curb whites' encroachment on Indian lands. Some colonists ignored these prohibitions altogether, including Daniel Boone, who famously led a group of pioneers through the Cumberland Gap and into the new backcountry of present-day Kentucky in March 1775, one month before the American Revolution erupted at Lexington and Concord.[11]

In the wake of the British defeat, citizens of the new republic clamored for their government to reverse the English policy and throw open the Ohio Valley, where land grants had been promised to veterans in lieu of payment for their military service during the revolution. Bowing to these pressures, Congress in 1784 tasked one of its members, the thirty-one-year-old Thomas Jefferson, with the responsibility of developing a plan for the survey and settlement of the region. The brilliant Virginian proposed a grid system of adjacent townships, which would ensure orderly and egalitarian distribution of the public lands; three years later, Congress ratified these guidelines as the Northwest Ordinance. This legislation provided the framework for integrating territory acquired from the region's native peoples through war or diplomacy, a process that gained particular momentum in the aftermath of the U.S. victory at the Battle of Fallen Timbers in 1794, which secured most of contemporary southern Ohio for the Americans.

Thus unleashed, whites poured across the Ohio River into the Northwest Territory (present-day Ohio, Indiana, Illinois, Michigan, and Wisconsin, and part of what is now Minnesota). Between 1790 and 1820 the population of this "first American West" mushroomed from ten thousand residents to more than two million, equal to one-fifth of the nation's population. It was this migration, of course, that motivated Jefferson's purchase of Louisiana, given his concerns about sufficient farmland for future generations.

To be sure, the Indians of the region were not about to surrender their patrimony to the invaders, and they found a strange bedfellow in Great Britain. Though defeated by the Americans in 1783, the British retained some of their trading establishments and military posts in the Ohio Valley, from which they now provisioned native insurgents. The Northwest was thus roiled intermittently by Indian-white violence for much of the next two decades, helping to precipitate the War of 1812, between England and the United States.[12] The American conquest of the territory was achieved only in October 1813 at the Battle of the Thames in Canada, when General William Henry Harrison—described by one biographer as "Mr. Jefferson's Hammer"—crushed a British force and its Indian allies, commanded by the famed Shawnee military leader Tecumseh. Harrison rode his reputation as an Indian fighter all the way to the White House in 1840, though "Tippecanoe" died just one month into his term.[13]

It would be hard to overstate the importance of the incorporation of the Northwest to the growth of the United States during the early republic. The Ohio River was a pivotal east–west waterway, stretching from western Pennsylvania to the border between Illinois and Missouri, where it met the Mississippi River. Farmers in the trans-Appalachian West now had a perfect route for sending their harvests of corn and wheat downriver to New Orleans. But Americans were not content to settle for the natural routes of passage offered by mere geography; they therefore embarked on what some historians have called a "transportation revolution," which saw the frenzied construction of roads and railways as well as the advent of the steamboat, which facilitated upriver travel.[14]

The crowning achievement of the age, however, was the 363-mile Erie Canal, an astonishing feat of engineering begun in 1817 and finished just eight years later. In linking the Great Lakes to the Hudson River, the project united the agricultural heart of the nation to New York City, its most vital seaport, and in short order that easy access to the bounty of the Old Northwest made New York the Empire State. To celebrate its completion, Governor DeWitt Clinton, who had staked his reputation on the success of the venture, "wedded the waters" on 26 October 1825 by pouring a keg drawn from Lake Erie into the Atlantic Ocean. At once thrilled and humbled by the achievement, he asked that "the God of Heavens and the Earth smile most propitiously on the work, and render it subservient to the best interests of the human race."[15]

IN A WEST even beyond the West, the Blackfeet held a different world-view. Like DeWitt Clinton and his fellow Americans, they believed that their Creator, whom they called Napi (Old Man), took a special interest in them.[16] To early white explorers like Meriwether Lewis and even rival native groups of the northern Plains, it surely seemed that the territory inhabited by the Blackfeet was a gift from a benevolent higher being. It was magnificent country. Rolling hills swept the landscape, verdant from late spring to the end of summer, becoming dun-colored as the weather turned cold. Fast-running tributaries knifed through forests and prairies before emptying into the Saskatchewan and Missouri Rivers. And looming on the western horizon were the tremendous Rocky Mountains, known to the Blackfeet as *Mistakis*: "the backbone of the world."

The opportunities and limitations presented by the environment determined the rhythms of Blackfeet daily life, especially the quest for sustenance. Napi, they believed, had shown his people how to gather and prepare a wide variety of plants, chief among them the prairie turnip, the fruit of the red willow, and a range of berries. The most important nonmeat food for the Blackfeet was the camas root, gathered when it bloomed during a short window in the early summer and then roasted in an enclosed pit. Eager children would huddle at the edge of the fire, waiting for an adult to remove the grass covering so that they could taste the syrup that oozed out onto branches and leaves. Women then laid the roots in the sun to dry before storing them in parfleche sacks for later use.[17]

The lifeblood of Blackfeet existence, however, was the bison, to such an extent that the Indians structured their entire lives around the movements of this enormous, shaggy beast. For much of the year, the Blackfeet broke into smaller bands composed of several family groups, following the undulations of the herds throughout the spring, summer, and fall. This meant almost constant motion for the Indians, who before the arrival of the horse relied on dogs to haul their belongings across the immense spaces of the northern Plains. With the end of autumn, the bison took to the river valleys and the Blackfeet did likewise, pitching their winter camps near dependable sources of wood and water to wait out the snow and wind that pummeled the tablelands above them.[18]

Before they had horses, the Blackfeet used several ingenious methods to kill bison. One of these was the surround, in which Indians on foot drove a group of buffalo into a corral constructed of rocks, logs, or brush, and then shot them with bows. Particularly effective was the *piskun*, or buffalo jump: stampeded animals plunged over the precipice and either died on impact or from the hail of rocks and arrows showered upon them by Indians waiting at the bottom of the cliff. Whatever the technique, the Blackfeet then divided up the spoils among members of the band; the hump and tongue were deemed the choicest parts. As an indication of the importance of buffalo meat to the Blackfeet, the Indians called it *nita'piwaskin*, or "real food," suggesting that anything else was counterfeit.[19]

Of course, the bison was more than food to the Blackfeet, and women made use of virtually the entire animal, from the horns (which became spoons and ladles) to the tail (fashioned into a flyswatter). From an early age, Coth-co-co-na would have learned how to use the parts in between to meet multiple additional needs: dressed skins, with the hair left on, served as winter robes; tanned hides stitched together made lodges; hooves became glue; ribs provided a variety of scraping tools; scapulas lashed to sticks with tendon or sinew made axes and hoes; and skin from the hind legs furnished moccasins and leggings. In short, the bison was a walking commissary for the Indians, and with the gift of its many products the Blackfeet crafted a hard but satisfying existence that endured for generations.[20]

And yet, as with the American colonies to the east, sweep-

George Catlin, *Buffalo Hunt, Chase—No. 6*. Lithograph, ca. 1844. Horses gave Plains Indian peoples increased mobility and greatly facilitated the bison hunt. Courtesy of the Museum of Nebraska Art.

ing changes had begun to transform the Blackfeet world of Coth-co-co-na's ancestors starting in the mid-eighteenth century. The first and most important of these was the arrival of horses, which appeared among the Blackfeet around 1730, acquired by theft from their bitter rivals, the Shoshones. One elderly Indian man remembered that the strange new animal "put us in mind of a Stag that had lost his horns . . . [and] he was a slave to Man, like the dog." They came to call the animal *ponokaomita*, or "elk dog."[21] In short order, horses revolutionized the life and culture of the Blackfeet (and other Plains tribes, for that matter), because with them the Indians "had conquered their oldest enemy, which was distance."[22] Horses were infinitely more efficient than dogs in lugging camps from one location to the next, and mounted hunters could find, pursue, and kill bison with a degree of ease previously unimaginable. By 1830, the earliest year for which such estimates are available, the Piegans possessed an average of ten horses per lodge, while the Bloods and Blackfoot had about five each.[23]

The second element that irrevocably altered Blackfeet life was the gun. The Piegans obtained firearms at about the same time they got their first horses, in the late 1720s or early 1730s. Having suffered for years at the hands of the Shoshones, the Piegans reached out for help from their then allies, the Crees and the Assiniboines, who supplied them with muzzle-loaders. Shortly thereafter the Piegans faced the Shoshones in battle, with ten weapons concealed among them. At a set time the chosen warriors discharged their guns, killing or wounding every Shoshone at whom they had aimed. Armed only with short stone clubs, the overmatched Shoshones eventually fled, and the Piegans and their allies celebrated the next day by presenting each rifleman with a scalp torn from the head of one of the fallen enemy.[24]

Despite all the advantages they conferred, such technological advances had a steep downside. For one thing, guns required ammunition, for which the Indians depended upon Europeans. Moreover, in contrast to conditions on the southern Plains, where milder temperatures and better feed allowed groups like the Comanches to amass substantial herds, conditions at the opposite end of the grasslands were harsher and therefore made it difficult to sustain horses. As a result of their scarcity among northern tribes, horses became a form of currency for groups like the Blackfeet, for whom equine wealth equaled social capital. This new measure of status eroded the egalitarianism of northern peoples, including the Blackfeet, as the number and quality of a man's steeds became key factors in determining his political and marital prospects. And since the surest way to gain additional horses and to win recognition for bravery was to steal mounts from enemies, a cycle of near-constant raiding and warfare on the northern Plains thus began in the mid-eighteenth century, made more lethal by the proliferation of guns. Women sometimes constituted 65–75 percent of northern tribes because their men fell so often in battle.[25] As a girl,

Coth-co-co-na surely witnessed the terrible aftermath of such violence, marked by the elaborate mourning rituals through which Blackfeet women grieved deceased husbands and sons (but not daughters): the bereaved cut their hair short, lacerated their calves, and sometimes amputated several fingers at the joints.[26]

The Piegans bore the brunt of these assaults because of their exposed position at the southern edge of Blackfeet territory, where they were sandwiched between the confederacy's chief rivals: the Shoshones to the southwest and the Crows to the southeast. This prime country was more temperate than the northern lands of their Blood and Blackfoot kinsmen and boasted the "superb winter sanctuary" of the Marias River. Thus the Piegans—with an early nineteenth-century population of approximately 2,800 (350 lodges with 8 persons per lodge)—dwarfed both the Blackfoot (1,600) and the Bloods (800), and they were far wealthier in horses.[27] And yet because of their vulnerability, the Piegans according to one observer led a more "precarious and watchful life," with the result that "from their boyhood [they] are taught the use of arms, and to be good warriors, they become more martial and more moral than the others, and many of them have a chivalrous bearing, ready for any enterprise."[28]

Piegan men certainly looked the part: brave, fearsome, and seemingly invincible. Though one early

George Catlin, *Blackfoot Indian Pe-Toh-Pee-Kiss, The Eagle Ribs.* Lithograph. According to Catlin, Eagle Ribs "boasts of eight scalps, which he says he has taken from the heads of trappers and traders with his own hand." Courtesy of the Bridgeman Art Library.

visitor found the typical Blackfeet costume of tanned shirt and leg-gings largely unremarkable for the region, he came away haunted by the Piegan warriors' crimson colored faces, an effect created by the application of vermilion, sometimes accentuated with a stripe of bluish ore running down the forehead, across the bridge of the nose, and ending at the chin.[29] Another traveler considered the Black-feet gaudy but no less intimidating, writing breathlessly of these "wild red knights of the prairie" and the awesome spectacle they presented when mounted for a raiding expedition. This, of course, was to say nothing of their adornments, which sometimes consisted of scalps sawed from the heads of their enemies—natives or even the occasional white man who had ventured boldly, if unwisely, into Piegan territory.[30]

According to Blackfeet belief, before he left them, Napi had marked off the ground he reserved for the tribe and said, "When people come to cross the line, take your bows and arrows, your lances and your battle axes, and give them battle and keep them out. If they gain a footing, trouble will come to you."[31] The Blackfeet listened, and so they fought off not only the Shoshones but also the Flat-heads and the Kutenais, and eventually even their former allies, the Crees and the Assiniboines. By the close of the eighteenth century, the Blackfeet—with their unwavering vigilance and pugnacity—were ascendant, dominating their rivals and establishing full control of the northwestern Plains. But they soon faced new opponents, men more powerful than any of their previous enemies, who came not for their horses or even to make captives of their women and children; rather, the outsiders sought *ksisskstaki*, the beaver. One such man was an expelled West Point cadet named Malcolm Clarke.

When Worlds Collide

The Hidatsa Indians tell a story about the first white men to visit the upper reaches of the Great Plains sometime in the late 1630s or

early 1640s. According to the tale, two Frenchmen—known thereafter as Long Beard and Little Beard—appeared among them on a late
summer evening, stopping at a village near the spot where the Little
Knife River meets the Missouri in what is now central North Dakota.
Long Beard changed the course of the tribe's history that day when,
spotting a beaver at the water's edge, he summoned an enormous
blast from his "thunder stick," which tore a fist-sized chunk from the
animal's back. Looking on with a mixture of fear and awe, the Hidatsas conducted the two men back to their camp, where the strange
visitors promised riches for the Indians if they agreed to help the
men and their friends hunt beaver. The next morning the Indians
led the Frenchmen to a cluster of nearby beaver hutches, where the
natives promptly slaughtered fifty-two of the animals, using clubs
and stakes.[32]

Long Beard and Little Beard, the latter remembered chiefly for
his lecherous sideways glances at the native women, became the vanguard of a westward thrust that had begun earlier in the seventeenth
century, when Samuel de Champlain founded Quebec at the narrows
of the St. Lawrence River. Thereafter stout, indefatigable voyageurs
pushed relentlessly into the continental interior of New France, first
to the Great Lakes and then onto the prairies and parklands beyond.
They came in search of *Castor canadensis,* the North American species of beaver, which could grow up to four feet long and weigh in
excess of a hundred pounds (though they averaged about half that
size). Although the animal was famous for its massive incisors and
equally impressive tail, hunters prized it rather for its soft undercoat,
from which European manufacturers fashioned hats that dominated
the haberdashery market for nearly two hundred years.[33]

Not to be outdone, the English announced their intent to com-
pete with the French, on 2 May 1670, when King Charles II established the Hudson's Bay Company (HBC) by royal charter, granting
the enterprise full control of all the lands drained by Hudson's Bay
(roughly all of present-day western Canada). The HBC developed

an ingenious factory system that helped England dominate the fur trade throughout Rupert's Land, the name given the area in honor of the king's cousin, who became the company's first governor. Various Indian peoples visited these HBC posts, built at the mouths of key rivers and their tributaries, where they exchanged packs of beaver pelts and other animal skins for guns, tools, liquor, and additional goods, including the ubiquitous HBC blanket, recognizable even today by its stripes of green, red, yellow, and blue.[34]

Given the HBC's supremacy in the region, it is not surprising that it was a Bayman who made the first known contact between the Blackfeet and white people, whom the confederacy referred to generically as *napikwans*, meaning "old man persons," perhaps because the technological wonders brought by the pale-faced outsiders rivaled those of the Creator himself.[35] In the summer of 1754, Anthony Henday, a fearless and hard-driving Scot hired by the HBC despite his reputation for smuggling, set out from York Factory, on the southwestern shore of Hudson's Bay, bound for the interior. That fall he met with a Siksika chief in the hopes of establishing a relationship with the Blackfeet, but the headman demurred, explaining that the journey to the English outpost was simply too far.[36] Though unsuccessful, Henday's efforts paved the way for David Thompson, a Welsh trader and cartographer who spent the winter of 1786–87 in a Piegan camp at the base of the Rockies and persuaded his hosts to trade with the HBC.

While the Piegans (and the Blackfeet generally) developed more cordial relations with British and later Canadian traders, whom they called "Northern White Men," they hated the "Big Knives" (Americans) who began trickling into their country at the start of the nineteenth century, about two decades before Coth-co-co-na's birth.[37] This enmity had a pair of root causes: lingering bitterness over the Two Medicine fight, but also the methods employed by American fur trappers. In contrast to the HBC and its chief competitor, the North West Company (NWC), both of which established outposts on the margins of Indian country and let natives come to them for trade, Americans went directly to the rivers and streams in the heart of Blackfeet territory to set their own traps.[38] The harrowing tale of John Colter, a veteran of the Lewis and Clark expedition, gives some sense of the Piegan response to early American intruders.

BORN IN VIRGINIA about 1775, John Colter enlisted as a private in the Corps of Discovery just prior to his thirtieth birthday. It testified to his backcountry savvy that contemporaries likened him to another frontiersman of the Upper South, Daniel Boone. Colter's skills proved invaluable to Lewis and Clark, who relied heavily on his marksmanship to furnish the corps with game: deer, elk, buffalo, turkey, rabbit . . . most anything he sighted down the barrel of his musket. As Colter earned the trust of his captains, they assigned him to some of the expedition's most arduous tasks, including the establishment of Fort Clatsop, the post near the mouth of the Columbia River where the corps endured illness, malaise, and near-constant rainfall during the miserable winter of 1805–06.[39]

On the return voyage down the Missouri, the members of the expedition encountered the first white people they had seen in almost a year and a half when they came across the camp of two trappers in present-day North Dakota. Hailing originally from Illinois, the men had come west in search of beaver. Though they had had little success, their stories and especially the lure of earning quite a bit more than the five dollars per month he had been paid for his services to the Corps of Discovery led Colter to ask Clark for his discharge. With some reluctance, Clark assented, and so in mid-August 1806 Colter and his companions headed back upriver, where they spent the winter trapping in the valley of the Yellowstone. By spring, however, having tired of Indian attacks as well as the disagreeable company of his new friends, Colter headed down the Yellowstone to deliver his haul to market.[40]

At the mouth of the Platte River, Colter met by chance another group of fur trappers bound for the Upper Missouri. Led by Manuel Lisa, an intrepid Spaniard operating out of St. Louis, the forty-man party was the first major fur expedition to follow in the wake of the Corps of Discovery. As it happened, Lisa's men included three of Colter's compatriots from the Lewis and Clark expedition: John Potts, Peter Weiser, and George Drouillard, the interpreter who had been with Lewis at the Two Medicine fight with the Piegans. Urged on by his old friends, Colter once again abandoned his plans to return to the East, opting instead to seek his fortune in animal skins.[41]

Once in the upcountry that winter, Lisa oversaw the construction of Fort Raymond (usually known as Fort Manuel or Lisa's Fort) at the confluence of the Bighorn and Yellowstone Rivers, in what is now eastern Montana. From there the trappers fanned out to tap the region's wealth, ever mindful of Blackfeet hostility but usually avoiding disaster. Colter's luck, however, ran out in the spring of 1808 when he and Potts traveled west to the Jefferson River, newly named for the president. Though they took standard precautions—setting their traps at night and collecting them at dawn, remaining out of sight during daytime—an enormous Piegan war party nevertheless discovered them early one morning. Seeing that escape was impossible, Colter steered their canoe to the river's edge, where an Indian seized Potts's rifle. When Colter snatched it back and returned it to Potts, his frightened companion quickly squeezed off a shot, killing one of the natives before the others riddled Potts with arrows. Colter faced a far different fate.

The Piegans stripped their captive naked and began a spirited discussion about how best to dispatch him. At some point, a chief approached Colter and asked him in Blackfeet whether he could run fast. Colter knew the language and the customs, so he said that he was slow-footed, even though his fellow trappers thought him rather fleet. The chief then led Colter—still stark naked—about three or four hundred yards out onto the prairie and ordered the American to save himself if he could. With that, the headman let out a whoop and Colter broke into a dead sprint toward the Madison River, six miles distant across a plain studded with prickly pear. With blood flowing from his nostrils from sheer exertion, Colter outran all but one of the Piegans, whom he dramatically killed by wresting away the Indian's spear and running it through him.

When he reached the Madison, Colter hurled himself into the water and looked around frantically for a place to hide. He found a perfect spot among a pile of driftwood that had collected at the head of a small island. There he remained for the rest of the day, even as the furious Piegans passed directly overhead, close enough for him to touch. At dusk, after he was confident that the Indians had abandoned the chase, Colter swam to a point downstream and then traveled overland throughout the night. Hungry, exhausted, and shredded by thorns and brambles, he covered three hundred miles in seven days, arriving back at Fort Manuel with a story that won him instant fame among his fellow mountain men. Amazingly, Colter continued to trap in Blackfeet country for two more years and survived another close encounter with the Piegans later in 1808 when he returned, unsuccessfully, to try and reclaim the traps he and Potts had left behind.[42]

Colter's narrow escape did not douse Americans' enthusiasm for trapping in Blackfeet country, which Manuel Lisa sought to dominate through his fledging Missouri Fur Company (MFC).[43] With beaver populations on the lower reaches of the river already in decline, the Spaniard and his men (Colter and Drouillard among them) headed for the Three Forks of the Missouri River, right in the heart of the Piegans' chief hunting grounds. From the start the Blackfeet laid siege to the trappers, for they were enraged at the invasion, as well as by Lisa's history of trading with the Crows, their bitter enemies. The Indian harassment became so intense that, after yet another close call, even the fearless Colter decided to leave the area for good early in 1810. He returned to St. Louis to settle his accounts, and then moved sixty miles west to the mouth of Big Boeuf Creek, where he lived until his death of jaundice in 1813.

Colter's friend George Drouillard was not so fortunate. Later in the spring of 1810 he was caught setting traps by a group of Blackfeet. One of the men who discovered his body a short time later noted that the Indians had taken their frustrations out on him: Drouillard's "head was cut off, his entrails torn out and his body hacked to pieces."[44] The MFC limped along for the rest of the decade, but folded for good in the wake of two calamities: Lisa's death in 1820, and the slaughter of a seven-man trading party the following year by a group of Bloods, who made off with $15,000 in property.

Despite these most unpromising beginnings, within a decade the Americans would be entrenched in Blackfeet country, economically, to be sure, but also in far more intimate ways unimaginable to the first wave of U.S.-based trappers.

IN THE YEARS following the American Revolution, New York became one of the most heavily trafficked seaports in the world, famous for the village of ships bobbing just offshore. The scene along the docks was unforgettable, as "bowsprits and jib booms projected nearly to the buildings across [South] street that housed the businesses of merchants, ship chandlers, sailmakers, and figurehead carvers, as well as boarding houses, saloons, and brothels."[45] In the summer of 1810, this maritime tableau included the *Tonquin*, a ninety-four-foot merchant vessel outfitted with ten guns and commanded by a young navy lieutenant named Jonathan Thorn. On the morning of 8 September, Thorn eased the ship from its moorings and headed out bound for the Pacific Ocean, where his employer, John Jacob Astor, dreamed of establishing a fur-trading empire at the mouth of the Columbia River.

In contrast to Manuel Lisa, who was nine years younger and had a dark complexion that reflected his Spanish ancestry, Astor was a pale-faced German, born in the Black Forest town of Walldorf in 1763. And if Lisa gravitated to the fur trade quite naturally, given his New Orleans roots, Astor's entry into the business came rather by accident. Shortly after his twentieth birthday, just as the Revolutionary War was ending, the nearly destitute young man set sail for the United States hoping to sell some musical instruments to get his start in America. On the transatlantic crossing, however, Astor fell in with a group of HBC employees, and by the time he disembarked at Baltimore the young German was so enthralled that he decided to try his own hand in the industry. Astor's rise was meteoric; in the words of one historian, "by the end of the century he had become the leading fur merchant of the United States and probably the leading authority in the world upon that business." He founded the American Fur Company (AFC) in 1808, the same year that Colter made his legendary run.[46]

As it turned out, Astor's hopes of controlling the fur trade of the Pacific Northwest came to naught. For one thing, the voyage of the *Tonquin*, which Astor had underwritten at a cost of $400,000, was ill-fated from the start. Captain Thorn proved insufferable to his crew and the AFC employees on board as well as to some of the Indians with whom he traded after arriving in the Northwest. In June 1811 Thorn assaulted a Nootka chief on Vancouver Island, angered by the headman's resolute bargaining. The Indians took their revenge several days later, slaughtering Thorn and most of the crew, though one survivor managed to ignite the ship's magazine, killing as many as two hundred Indians. Astoria, the outpost Thorn had established at the mouth of the Columbia, did not fare much better, because the British seized it during the War of 1812. Thereafter Astor focused his efforts on the Great Lakes trade. But by the time Lisa's MFC went under, in 1821, Astor had come to the same conclusion reached earlier by the Spaniard: namely, that the mother lode for beaver skins was inconveniently located in the Upper Missouri watershed.[47]

To make inroads there, Astor needed first to establish a position in St. Louis, which after the War of 1812 had become the dominant city in the American West, described by one historian as "a regional emporium and the central headquarters of the national quest for empire."[48] Its population grew accordingly, from little more than 1,500 residents in 1810 to nearly 5,000 by 1830, a mix of American migrants and the foreign-born, mostly Irish and Germans. To get a foothold there, in 1822 Astor created the AFC's Western Department by absorbing a local firm; four years later he bought up another St. Louis outfit, Bernard Pratte & Company, which then assumed control of the Western Department.[49] This transaction also netted Astor the services of Pierre Chouteau Jr. (known as Cadet), a visionary whose practices would eventually transform the industry. But the pivotal acquisition for the AFC was the Columbia Fur Company, run by Kenneth McKenzie, an indomitable and experienced Scotsman who had come to St. Louis by way of the Canadian fur trade.

McKenzie had resisted the initial overtures of the AFC, but the determined Astor dispatched his principal agent, Ramsay Crooks, in the hope that a face-to-face meeting with a fellow Scot might close the deal. Two bargaining sessions in the spring of 1827 went nowhere; in July, however, Crooks wrote Astor triumphantly that after "endless negociation" he had finally swayed McKenzie. The deal was a boon for both parties. McKenzie got to bring along his best men from the CFC and was installed as the head of the AFC's Upper Missouri Outfit, with total discretion in running the company's affairs in the region. Astor, in turn, obtained the services of one of the true geniuses in the industry, a man who possessed not only business savvy but tremendous personal charisma as well. The AFC also acquired the company's network of posts throughout the northern Plains.[50]

McKenzie, however, believed that the AFC needed a new fort, too, situated at a strategic point that would allow him both to trade with native peoples and to control access to the headwaters of the

After Karl Bodmer, *Fort Union on the Missouri*, ca. 1833. Bodmer's painting shows a group of Blackfeet arriving at Fort Union to trade. Note the enormous plain spreading out beyond the fort, ideal for accommodating large Indian encampments. Courtesy of the Joslyn Museum of Art, Omaha.

Missouri. He chose brilliantly, building Fort Union on the north side of the Missouri River near its confluence with the Yellowstone. From this spot on the present-day border between Montana and North Dakota, McKenzie could cultivate native peoples of the northern Plains while surveying all river traffic entering or exiting the vast drainage that stretched along the front range of the Rockies from the forty-ninth parallel to what is now central Wyoming.

Construction on the post began in 1828, with cottonwood the principal building material. The fort was designed as a rectangle rather than a square, 198 feet long from north to south and 178 feet wide, with bastions in the northeastern and southwestern corners to provide defense in the event of an Indian attack. The main gate was on the south side, facing the river below, and stretching to the north and east was a rolling plain, perfect for accommodating hundreds of Indian lodges when the natives came to trade.[51] Inside the walls were employees' quarters, storerooms for food and trade goods, and craft shops for the blacksmith and tinner. One structure, however, stood out from the rest. At the north end of the fort was the bourgeois house, the home of the field agent and his chief clerk. Considering the rather coarse surroundings, the building was fit for royalty, appropriately enough, since McKenzie, who served as bourgeois from the fort's inception to his (temporary) retirement in 1837, was known to all as "the King of the Missouri." He certainly played the part, dressing always in uniform and acting as the gracious host whenever artists, explorers, scientists, or European noblemen paid a visit.

One of McKenzie's most notable guests was the painter George Catlin, who spent part of the summer of 1832 at Fort Union. As a young man, the Pennsylvania-born artist had become obsessed with the idea of native peoples as a "vanishing race," and thus he set to work producing an Indian gallery of canvases meant to capture their portraits and customs before they became extinct. During Catlin's stay at Fort Union, McKenzie lent his guest one of the bastions as a studio, where—using a cool brass cannon as a workbench—he painted multiple Indian visitors. Catlin was just as intrigued by McKenzie himself, enchanted by his hospitality. In describing the banquet table, Catlin wrote that it "groans under the luxuries of the country; with buffalo meat and tongues, with beavers' tails and marrow-fat; but *sans* coffee, *sans* bread and butter . . . and good wine, also; for a bottle of Madeira and one of excellent Port are set in a pail of ice every day, and exhausted at dinner."[52]

SOMETIME IN THE EARLY 1830s Kenneth McKenzie sat for a portrait.[53] It provides a striking image of Fort Union's powerful bourgeois. The artist depicted McKenzie clad in his typical formal attire: a starched white shirt underneath a black overcoat, with a knotted cravat around his neck. But the painter captured the essence of the man in rendering his face: square-jawed, straight-lipped, and with a gaze best described as menacing. McKenzie was ruthless in his quest to dominate the Upper Missouri, and he soon turned Fort Union into the AFC's most lucrative post. Trade was brisk from the beginning. For instance, the post processed more than 14,000 buffalo robes in 1830, which surely kept teams of men busy on the robe press, an enormous contraption just outside the front gate that squeezed buffalo skins into hundred-pound bundles. Under the guidance of its despotic king, within two years Fort Union's sales and inventory were easily the largest of the half-dozen major AFC posts in the region.[54]

Still, for the ambitious McKenzie, developing remunerative trading relations with the Crows, Assiniboines, Crees, and Ojibwas was not enough, and thus like so many fur hunters before him, the king turned his eyes westward to Blackfeet country. Mindful of past failures, he opted for a different strategy, organizing a small party in the winter of 1830–31 to seek out the Piegans in their own country and treat for peace. Led by a French Canadian named Jacob Berger, who had been on the Upper Missouri since 1826 and who spoke fluent Blackfeet, the group headed up the Marias River on dogsleds. For their part, the other men at Fort Union thought Berger's prospects dismal, naming the expedition the "forlorn hope." Nonetheless, after about five weeks, Berger and his anxious detachment came across a band of seventeen Piegans, who conducted them to their chief's camp. Berger succeeded in persuading a hundred or so Indians to accompany him to Fort Union, where a jubilant McKenzie greeted the natives with pomp and lavished presents upon them. Before they left, the Piegans consented to let the AFC build a post in their territory.[55]

For this tricky mission, McKenzie selected James Kipp, an impos-

Interior, Fort Union, 1866. This photograph shows the bourgeois house at the end of the fur trade era. Kenneth McKenzie and his successors lived here in grand style and entertained notable visitors like George Catlin and John James Audubon. Courtesy of the Montana Historical Society.

sibly long-faced Canadian with a deep fondness for alcohol and extensive experience in the fur trade. In the spring of 1831 Kipp shoved off from the landing at Fort Union in charge of nearly four dozen men and a fifty-ton keelboat stocked with trade items. The 500-mile trip was grueling: a keelboat (the same vessel used by the Corps of Discovery) normally progressed upstream by "cordeling," a muscle-straining process in which crewmen on either bank towed the boat by a line attached to the mast, making about fifteen to thirty miles per day.[56] Kipp chose a spot at the mouth of the Marias, and the day after his arrival hundreds of Piegans appeared, eager to begin trading; he persuaded the Indians to come back in seventy-five days, the time he needed to build the outpost. The Indians returned at the appointed hour to find Fort Piegan, as Kipp named it, open for business. Kipp then took in almost 6,500 pounds of beaver skins (worth an estimated $46,000), "a transaction rarely equaled in the annals of the fur trade."[57]

When Kipp headed back downriver in April 1832 to deliver his haul and report to McKenzie, some jealous Bloods or Assiniboines torched the fort. McKenzie was not so easily deterred; that fall he sent another of his associates, David Mitchell, to reestablish the AFC presence in Piegan country. Mitchell selected a location about six miles upstream from the site of Kipp's post and named the new fort after his boss. In time, Fort McKenzie became Union's most productive satellite, especially in its delivery of bison robes, which in the early 1830s supplanted beaver skins as the cornerstone of the far western fur trade, because of changing fashions in Europe and eastern North America, where hats made from beaver hair lost their popularity. Fort McKenzie took in two hundred packs of buffalo

Portrait of Kenneth McKenzie (photograph of a painting, 1910). This image shows "the King of the Missouri" at the height of his power during the 1830s. Courtesy of the Missouri History Museum, St. Louis.

robes in 1834 (ten robes per pack), and ten times that amount by the end of the decade.[58]

The lucrative business of fur trading was remarkable to behold, and it fascinated visitors to the Upper Missouri like Prince Maximilian of Wied, a middle-aged German noble who arrived at Fort Union in 1833 accompanied by the Swiss artist Karl Bodmer. After two weeks enjoying McKenzie's hospitality, the prince headed upriver to see the Blackfeet in their own country. He was not disappointed, for a large Piegan trading party showed up at Fort McKenzie shortly after his arrival in mid-August. As Maximilian recorded, Mitchell, the fort's bourgeois, raised a flag in the courtyard and fired off a cannonade to signal the Indians, who emerged from their lodges half an hour later and approached the fort dressed in their finest costume. Four chiefs and several dozen warriors entered the post, exchanging gifts with Mitchell and then sitting down in a circle to pass the pipe and drink whiskey. After several hours of pleasantries, the chiefs left, returning with beaver skins and buffalo robes as well as little kegs that Mitchell dutifully filled with alcohol. Trading extended late into the night, and many of the Indians and lower-level post employees became drunk and unruly. For his part, Maximilian was delighted to trade liquor for "a very tame, live she-bear" brought to the fort by an elderly Piegan man.[59]

ON 13 NOVEMBER 1833, an enormous Leonid meteor shower lit up the night sky over North America, from the Rocky Mountains to the Atlantic Ocean. It was a truly national event, remembered years later by people who had witnessed it from various points throughout the country. The abolitionist Frederick Douglass, who at the time was a teenaged slave on a Maryland farm, recalled that "the air seemed filled with bright descending messengers from the sky."[60] Near Kirtland, Ohio, the Mormon leader Joseph Smith was roused at four in the morning by one of his followers to behold the sight, which he interpreted "as a sure sign that the coming of Christ is clost [*sic*] at hand."[61] And a young odd-jobber named Abraham Lincoln watched the spectacle from the window of his boardinghouse in New Salem, Illinois. Years later as president, during one of the darkest hours of the Civil War, Lincoln supposedly used his memory of the incident to reassure anxious listeners that "the world did not come to an end then, nor will the Union now."[62]

Indians of the northern Great Plains were not so sanguine on that autumn night. As described by Alexander Culbertson, an AFC clerk who had escorted Prince Maximilian upriver earlier that summer, the natives at Fort McKenzie regarded the celestial display, which included a total eclipse of the sun, "as forerunners of some great catastrophe."[63] Little did they know that disaster was already upon them. Having embraced the trade goods brought by the *napikwans*, the Blackfeet began to spurn the old ways. Whereas such items had once been the rarest of luxuries, by the time the stars fell on that November evening, Culbertson noted that the average lodge possessed "one gun, an axe, a kettle, and ten knives." Though such objects made life easier, they also eroded the Indians' autonomy by creating economic dependence upon the outsiders.[64]

Other ominous signs indicated that the Piegan world was changing as rapidly and dramatically as it had a century before, with the advent of the horse and gun. On 16 June 1832 the *Yellow Stone*, the first steamboat to travel so far up the Missouri, reached Fort Union, carrying George Catlin among others. The Piegan reaction to "the fire boat that walks on the water," as some Indians called the vessel, must have been similar to that which Catlin observed among other native peoples during the upstream voyage.[65] Of those Indians, the artist noted that "some of them laid their faces to the ground, and cried to the Great Spirit—some shot their horses and dogs, and sacrificed them . . . some deserted their villages and ran to the tops of the bluffs some miles distant."[66] The AFC's use of steamboats, urged by McKenzie and endorsed by Chouteau, facilitated the movement of more goods and *napikwans* into Blackfeet country while degrading the river valleys of the Missouri and its tributaries, as the *Yellow Stone* and each of its brethren devoured an astonishing twenty-five to thirty cords of wood for every twenty-four running-hours.[67]

Even worse, AFC steamboats brought vast quantities of spirits to the Upper Missouri. Like other native peoples of the northern Plains, the Blackfeet had never tasted liquor until traders brought it among them in the late eighteenth century. Having no word for it in their own language, they called it *napiohke* ("white man's water") and refused initially to pay for it, since the lakes and rivers of their country provided all the liquid refreshment they needed.[68] Nevertheless, it was soon entrenched among them, used by British, Canadian, and American outfits alike to lubricate the trading process. McKenzie even constructed an illegal still at Fort Union in 1833, though it was short-lived. Spiked sometimes with ingredients like strychnine or gunpowder to heighten its effects, whiskey wreaked havoc in Indian communities.

At the time there was growing concern about the consumption of alcohol more generally in the United States, anxiety that led to the establishment of the American Temperance Society in 1826. Reformers of the period, including the evangelical leaders Charles Grandison Finney and Lyman Ward Beecher, emphasized the evils of drinking, and the Whigs, formed in the 1830s as the opposition to Andrew Jackson's Democratic Party, incorporated abstinence into their political platform, although temperance did not become the law of the land, for a brief period, until a century later.[69] It was a different story beyond the Mississippi, where U.S. officials were so concerned about liquor's pernicious influence among the western tribes that the government passed a strict prohibition law in 1834. No matter, because the aptly named Andrew Drips, the Indian agent for the Upper Missouri, turned a blind eye to the AFC's extensive smuggling operations.[70]

And yet of all the dangerous imports—from guns to liquor—

brought to the northern Plains, it was a microbial agent, invisible to the human eye, that left the most devastating impact. In the summer of 1837 an AFC steamboat, the *St. Peters,* arrived on the Upper Missouri carrying passengers infected with smallpox. Although the disease had raged among area tribes in 1781, most of the natives had no immunity to the affliction and thus died in staggering numbers. Learning of the outbreak at Fort Union, Culbertson tried vainly to keep away a keelboat headed upriver to Fort McKenzie with passengers and cargo from the larger post. But a camp of some five hundred Piegan and Blood lodges insisted upon the delivery of the trade items once the vessel arrived. Within days the disease spread like a prairie fire throughout Blackfeet country, and no Indians visited the fort for two months. Around 1 October, Culbertson, who himself had fallen ill, traveled from Fort McKenzie to the Three Forks to see how the Piegans had fared. He smelled the camp before he saw it: sixty lodges, littered all about with the decaying bodies of people, horses, and dogs. When the epidemic finally burned out later that fall, more than six thousand Blackfeet had perished.[71] For all the riches it brought to some native peoples, the fur trade immiserated many more, and few groups suffered as much as the Blackfeet.

Coth-co-co-na

On a stifling morning in late August 1833, near the middle of his monthlong stay at Fort McKenzie, Prince Maximilian was jolted from his slumber by a post employee and urged to take arms. Ascending the ramparts and wielding a double-barreled shotgun, Maximilian beheld an astonishing scene unfolding below: hundreds of Cree and Assiniboine warriors, whom he described as "a red line . . . of fighters," had descended on a small camp of about twenty Piegan lodges pitched in the shadows of the fort. Since the Piegans had caroused late the night before, passing the cup and pipe while marveling at the

After Karl Bodmer, *Fort MacKenzie, August 28th 1833*, ca. 1833. Bodmer personally witnessed this fight between the Piegans and a joint force of Crees and Assiniboines during his visit to the Upper Missouri with Prince Maximilian of Wied.
Courtesy of the Joslyn Museum of Art, Omaha.

sounds of Karl Bodmer's music box, they were slow in mounting a
defense. Their attackers showed no quarter, indiscriminately shooting and stabbing men, women, and children, all of which the prince
observed from inside the compound.

   Riveting though the battle was, it was sadly typical of the day,
as Indians competed bitterly with one another for the spoils of the
American trade, not to mention horses and captives stolen from
native rivals. The prince regarded the spectacle with a mixture of
fascination and horror; he was struck especially by the activity surrounding White Buffalo, a highly respected Piegan warrior who in
the early going had suffered a head wound so severe that "his brain
seemed to be protruding into his hair." To dull his agony, several
native women plied him with whiskey and in short order he was

"completely stone drunk." The battle raged all afternoon just outside the walls, but with help from the post's employees as well as
many additional Piegans who hurried to the fort from their main
camp nearby, the Indians drove off the war party, though not before
losing several dozen of their people.[72]

Somewhere in the maelstrom, perhaps, was a young Piegan girl.[73]
The terror she would have felt that late summer morning is easy
to imagine, since Bodmer painted a tableau of the struggle. The
watercolor depicts utter chaos: wisps of gun smoke, a rearing horse,
and pockets of furious hand-to-hand combat. After the battle an old
Piegan medicine man named Distant Bear thanked Bodmer pro-
fusely, insisting that no bullets had cut him down because Bodmer
had made his portrait a few days earlier, which had worked as good
medicine. The little girl, however, probably felt no such assurances
amid the fighting all around her—maybe she took cover inside the
fort with other Piegans, or found a hiding spot among the trees or in
the wreckage of a lodge. She might even have seen a group of Piegan
women and children exact their revenge on the body of a fallen Cree
warrior, taking his scalp, smashing his limbs, and splitting his head
in two. If so, it would not be the last time she bore witness to such
violence.

LITTLE IS KNOWN for certain about the girl except that her name was
Coth-co-co-na and that her parents were a Piegan warrior named
Under Bull and his wife, Black Bear. Coth-co-co-na was probably
born around 1825, the same year that the Erie Canal joined the
Great Lakes to the Hudson River, and that John Quincy Adams
assumed the presidency after prevailing in a bitter electoral struggle
against Andrew Jackson. However, like most native people of the
time and place, Coth-co-co-na is almost entirely absent from written historical records, appearing in a letter here, a census record
there, maybe a pioneer reminiscence of the frontier era. Still, it

is possible to sketch the contours of her early existence given the rhythms of Piegan life during the first few decades of the nineteenth century.[74]

Shortly after Coth-co-co-na's birth, Under Bull called upon a person of distinction within the tribe to choose a name for his child, building his guest a sweat lodge and bestowing presents upon him, waiting for the namer to suggest a handful of monikers from which he, as the father, chose.[75] Thereafter Under Bull was probably a more distant figure in Coth-co-co-na's world. If she had brothers, he spent more time with them, teaching the boys how to hunt and fight. On almost all matters Coth-co-co-na would have looked to Black Bear and other female relatives for guidance. And she knew hard work from a young age: gathering berries, collecting wood, carrying water, mending clothes, stitching lodges, and building travois.[76]

When she was a bit older, her mother (or, in her absence, another female relative) taught Coth-co-co-na the most important skill known to Blackfeet women—tanning a buffalo hide. Such expertise was necessary, of course, for basic survival; after all, bison skins gave the Indians clothing and shelter and brought them trade goods from the *napikwans*. Tanning was also important as a marital prerequisite, for Blackfeet men relied upon their wives to dress the animals they killed. So critical was the work of Indian women that, as the robe trade increased, so did the practice of polygyny, whereby native men acquired additional spouses, and at increasingly younger ages, in order to meet their growing labor needs.

Dressing a buffalo hide was a messy and backbreaking task, as Coth-co-co-na learned. Once she tore the skin from an animal's body, a native woman "fleshed" the hide by staking it to the ground (hair side down) with wooden pegs and scraping away any bits of tissue, fat, or dried blood, an exhausting and time-consuming process. She then left the skin to bleach in the sun for several days before scraping it again to achieve a uniform thickness. Finally, she applied a mixture of brains and fat to soften the hide before smoothing it out with strokes from a rough stone. It took two full days of work to tan a single robe.[77]

As in earlier native-white encounters throughout North America, some newcomers to the Upper Missouri were appalled by the division of labor among the Blackfeet, believing that men's hunting was a form of leisure or sport while their wives were treated like drudges and forced to do the heavy lifting required for the trade in animal skins.[78] Although life for Piegan women was undeniably hard—beyond tanning hides and preparing food they were also responsible for child rearing—the prejudice and chauvinism of most European and American outsiders make such accounts problematic at best. And it is worth noting that some later observers emphasized the essential role of Piegan women in religious and ceremonial rites.[79]

As Coth-co-co-na reached puberty, Black Bear instructed her daughter on the rituals of courtship and marriage.[80] Thereafter the husband enjoyed almost total control over his wife or wives. To impress upon her daughter the importance of a woman's marital conduct, Black Bear might have held up to Coth-co-co-na the powerful example set by a medicine woman. This individual was the chief figure in the annual Sun Dance, the tribe's most important religious ceremony. In order to qualify, a woman had to possess unimpeachable character, marked especially by unwavering devotion to her husband.[81] And yet for Coth-co-co-na and other girls of marrying age, it was likely the punishment for female adultery that made the stronger impression. As Prince Maximilian recorded in his journal, "[Men] punish the infidelity of their women swiftly and severely; they cut off their noses; and one saw many such horribly disfigured faces among the Piegans."[82] Surely Coth-co-co-na took note of them.

Despite Black Bear's prominent role in raising Coth-co-co-na and preparing her for marriage, it was Under Bull who ultimately chose a suitable husband for their daughter once she reached her teens. And like many other prominent Blackfeet men in the 1830s and 1840s, he did not select a young and distinguished Piegan warrior for his son-in-law, but opted instead for a fur trader named Malcolm Clarke, whom the Indians called Ne-so-ke-i-u, or Four Bears.

UNDER BULL'S DECISION to marry his daughter to a white man can be understood only in the context of the refashioned social conditions brought about by the advent of the fur trade in Blackfeet country. Intermarriage between white men and native women was found everywhere throughout the continent where Europeans and their descendants sought animal skins, from the valley of the St. Lawrence to the far Southwest, from the Great Lakes to the Rocky Mountains.[83] Such arrangements *à la façon du pays*—"according to the custom of the country"—were especially common among HBC and NWC employees and reflected indigenous ceremonial practices as well as the natives' own social and economic imperatives.

By comparison, those who settled the American colonies largely resisted intermarriage, both because white women were present in many such locales right from the start and because early interaction between natives and newcomers often led to violent conflict. In the lands that became the eastern United States, removal or extermination was thus as likely an outcome as any sort of cultural exchange or interpenetration.[84] And yet around the turn of the nineteenth century, some westering Americans warmed to the concept of intermarriage. They had an unlikely champion in Thomas Jefferson, who during his presidency viewed such unions as the key to peaceful frontier absorption as well as the eventual assimilation of Indians into mainstream Anglo-American society. He exhorted a group of Delawares and Mohicans in 1808, "[Y]ou will unite yourselves with us . . . and form one people with us, and we shall all be Americans; you will mix with us by marriage, your blood will run in our veins, and will spread with us over this great island."[85]

Jefferson's enthusiasm for such liaisons stood in stark contrast to his vehement opposition to white romantic relationships with blacks, who he believed should be placed "beyond the reach of mixture" (this despite his own thirty-eight-year affair with his slave Sally Hemings, who bore him seven children).[86] While Jefferson intimated that African Americans were racially inferior, according to one biographer his comparatively progressive views about Indians stemmed from an "an authentic admiration mingled with a truly poignant sense of tragedy about their fate as a people."[87] Even so, official attempts to promote native-white intermarriage failed at both the state and the federal levels in the late eighteenth and early nineteenth centuries, defeated by intense and near unanimous hostility from white lawmakers.[88]

Despite the routine nature of intermarriage throughout North America's fur country, it is still worth pondering why Under Bull and other Blackfeet fathers would embrace such a practice. After all, few native groups had so consistently and violently opposed white expansion into their territory. While it was one thing to trade beaver skins and buffalo robes for guns and whiskey, it was quite another to give their daughters in marriage to the *napikwans*, whom the Blackfeet usually found repulsive, with their hairy faces and the sour smell of their unwashed bodies. In the end, just like native groups to their east such as the Mandans, Hidatsas, and Arikaras, the Blackfeet accepted intermarriage with whites because of its extraordinary political and economic benefits.

For one thing, such unions made good business sense. An Indian father who married his daughter to a white man built an invaluable trading relationship with his son-in-law. The marriage secured the native man's access to coveted trade goods, both for his own consumption and for wider distribution among his people, which in turn earned their loyalty and thus enhanced his prospects for a tribal leadership position. The fact of the marriage itself lent a crucial measure of prestige to the man's family. For his part, through intermarriage the trader obtained not only the skins and pelts gathered by his father-in-law but likely the haul of other male family members as well. Moreover, the union integrated the trader into his wife's extended kinship network.[89]

It would be a mistake, however, to assume that these intimate relationships were all about economics. Consider the case of Alexander Culbertson. In the winter of 1840–41 he married Natawista, the teenaged daughter of a Blood headman named Two Suns. Though Culbertson, whom the Blackfeet called Little Beaver, no doubt benefited financially from a close alliance with his wealthy and powerful father-in-law (not to mention Seen From Afar, Natawista's influential brother), Culbertson's intense physical attraction to Natawista led him to seek her hand. So strong were his feelings—supposedly from the moment he first saw her at Fort McKenzie, when she was in her early teens—that he readily agreed to Two Suns' stark preconditions: a delay of marriage until Natawista had grown a bit older, and a renunciation of his other romantic liaisons, which included a previous marriage to a Piegan woman.[90]

Thus in short order, a heady mix of love, sex, power, and especially money had led intermarriage to take hold among the Blackfeet by the 1830s (just as it had elsewhere in fur country). So pervasive was the pattern that fur traders who did not marry Indian women became the exception. Like Alexander Culbertson, Kenneth McKenzie and James Kipp took Indian wives, as did almost all of the white men who lived and worked at Fort Union and its satellites. These marriages usually conformed to the region's rough social hierarchy, so that women from more prominent native families tended to marry upper-level employees like the bourgeois or his clerks, while girls of more modest means found husbands among the *engagés*, the fur posts' rank and file. Although many of these unions broke apart when traders elected to return to the eastern climes of the United States, others, like Culbertson's, lasted for years, suggesting a degree of closeness that some white visitors to the Upper Missouri found inconceivable.[91]

ONE CAN ONLY speculate as to how Coth-co-co-na viewed the arrangement of her 1844 marriage to Malcolm Clarke. Certainly she understood that she had to accede to Under Bull's wishes, but perhaps she nursed some quiet doubts about the union. Maybe there was a young warrior in camp or even a different trader whom she preferred as a husband. Or possibly she ached at the notion of leaving behind her mother, who, by custom, would now visit Coth-co-co-na only during Clarke's absence, for among the Blackfeet it was improper for a married man to speak with his female in-laws.

On the other hand, a Piegan girl who wedded a *napikwan* gained clear advantages. Life at a trading post was easier. No longer would she have to pack and unpack her family's belongings as they moved about on the Plains, and lower-level employees assumed much of her workload, like gathering firewood. As the Swiss artist and traveler Rudolph Friederich Kurz cynically observed during a visit to Fort Union in 1851, "an Indian woman loves her white husband only for what he possesses—because she works less hard, eats better food, is allowed to dress and adorn herself in a better way—of real love there is no question."[92] Kurz, however, was blind to the disincentives of intermarriage for the Indian bride, especially the loss of autonomy in child rearing and the increased exposure to epidemic diseases.[93]

Regardless of her anxieties or expectations regarding marriage to a white man, Coth-co-co-na must have seen attributes in Malcolm Clarke that intrigued her. Not only was he handsome, but he was well connected, too, having come upriver in 1841 with Alexander Culbertson, who assigned him to Fort McKenzie as a clerk. Clarke had quickly made a favorable impression upon the Blackfeet, who initially called him White Lodge Pole, a reference not only to his fair skin but also to his stature and perceived importance (the white lodge pole held in place the teepee where the tribal council met to discuss weighty affairs). Clarke later acquired the name Four Bears

Alexander Culbertson, Natawista, and their son Joe, ca. 1863. Taken during their residence in Peoria, Illinois, after Culbertson's retirement from the AFC, this photograph shows perhaps the most famous intermarried couple on the Upper Missouri during the heyday of the fur trade. Courtesy of the Montana Historical Society.

because of his hunting prowess, having once killed four grizzlies before breakfast.

His reputation, however, was not unalloyed. Even as the Piegans came to call him Four Bears, the name probably carried a whiff of irony. After all, it was common among the Blackfeet to bestow a deliberately contrary moniker; for instance, a band called the Never Laughs was in fact probably quite merry.[94] Thus Clarke's honorific, while seeming to flatter his skill with a rifle, may have been a rebuke for his wanton slaughter of a creature that most Blackfeet held in awe.[95] Death and violence would shadow Malcolm Clarke during the three decades he spent in Blackfeet country.

Since there is no surviving record of Malcolm Clarke's marriage to Coth-co-co-na, one can only surmise that it conformed in

its particulars to the wedding between Alexander Culbertson and
Natawista, which took place at Fort Union in the winter of 1840–41.
Having divorced his first wife and lived alone in the interim, Culbertson had met the terms set by Natawista's father. The union was
solemnized by a simple exchange of nine horses each between Culbertson and his in-laws.[96] Though the bride was just fifteen, their
union was unremarkable for its time and place. Thus began a relationship that endured for thirty years and that perfectly illustrates the
cultural confluence generated by the fur trade: the marriage of an
Indian woman and a white man; their gift exchange on terms set by
the Indians; and in due time, the birth—in this case—of five children
of mixed ancestry.

2

Four Bears

Near the end of his first trip to North America, Charles Dickens made a brief stop at West Point, New York, in June 1842. Though put off by the customs of the local hotel, which forbade spirits and served meals at "rather uncomfortable hours," the English novelist—who had achieved literary celebrity only a few years earlier—wrote rapturously of the little town nestled in the shadows of Bear Mountain and its famous institution of higher learning, the U.S. Military Academy (USMA). As he recorded in *American Notes*, the travelogue of his six-month journey along the East Coast and to the Great Lakes, the school—perched on a high granite bluff overlooking the Hudson River—"could not stand on more appropriate ground, and any ground more beautiful can hardly be." Dickens was no less impressed by the rigorous course of study pursued by the academy's cadets, which he praised as "well devised, and manly."[1]

Established in 1802, the USMA had survived its sputtering origins and the occasional hostility of state and federal politicians to become the key supplier of the young republic's engineers and military leaders. Indeed, around the time of Dickens's visit, James Longstreet, class of 1842, had just graduated; Thomas "Stonewall" Jackson, class of 1846, was settling in; and Ulysses S. Grant, class of 1843, was plodding his way through the curriculum to finish twenty-first in a class of thirty-nine. Because of its reputation and also its egalitarianism (in theory, West Point's doors were open to any young man who obtained a congressional nomination and passed the entrance exam), competition was fierce for the four or five dozen places in each cohort.[2]

With help from his father, Malcolm Clarke had secured one of the coveted spots from Ohio in the class of 1838. But instead of graduating with his peers and winning glory on battlefields from Mexico to Virginia, Clarke became an unwitting member of a different club: nongraduate alumni of the USMA. To be sure, this group counted luminaries of its own, like Edgar Allan Poe, class of 1834, who lasted just a single semester at West Point before deserting in 1831. Apparently, Poe found his courses insuperably boring—not surprising, given that he would come to write some of the most phantasmagorical verse in American literary history—and was unable to drink as he pleased. He managed, nevertheless, to churn out a book of poems during his short stint at the academy, underwritten by subscriptions from his fellow cadets. For Malcolm Clarke, however, it was a keen sense of personal honor that caused trouble at West Point.[3]

Early one morning in March 1835, Lindsay Hagler, a North Carolinian who had matriculated

Malcolm Clarke. By equal turns charming and hot-tempered, Clarke found great success and personal fulfillment in Montana before his life was cut short in August 1869, when he was just fifty-two. Courtesy of the Montana Historical Society.

with the class of 1837 but been held back because of poor academic performance, excoriated Clarke for disturbing his sleep while sweeping their dormitory. A scuffle ensued, but the combatants were soon separated. Others might have let the matter rest, but Clarke seethed, and so several days later he sent a note to Hagler that read in part, "I demand of you, that satisfaction, which no true gentleman will refuse another." When Hagler ridiculed Clarke's proposal to settle their disagreement with a duel, Malcolm opted for another course of action. During roll call on the morning of 11 March, he took a stick and crumpled the unsuspecting southerner with a blow to the head. Only the quick intervention of some bystanders prevented a tragic outcome, as the dazed but livid Hagler rose to defend himself brandishing a dirk.

While USMA brass frowned upon brawling and in some cases even dismissed cadets for the offense, dueling was another matter entirely. Even issuing a challenge was considered a grave breach of conduct. But such recourse seemed only natural to Malcolm Clarke, given his exposure to the practice while growing up. Still, understanding the gravity of the charges against him, he wrote a lengthy letter to the members of the court-martial hearing his case. Clarke did not grovel. Instead, he simply explained that, while he knew he risked expulsion, he had challenged Hagler because "there is another and a higher standard of conduct, which must regulate the actions of a man of honor." The court rejected his defense and expelled him.[4]

But Malcolm Clarke was not finished at West Point, for he was granted a pardon by no less a figure than the commander in chief, President Andrew Jackson. This was not as unlikely as it might have seemed, because Jackson, who had grave misgivings about the elitism engendered by the USMA and was thus happy to meddle in its proceedings, had overturned a number of such expulsions. And yet there can be little doubt that Jackson took a special interest in the case of Malcolm Clarke, whom he knew personally through Clarke's father, who had been stationed in Nashville in the late 1820s. More-over, Old Hickory himself had fought at least a dozen duels in his own day, including one dispute in 1806 in which he had killed his opponent but taken a bullet to the chest, which remained lodged in his body for the rest of his days. Surely, Jackson must have thought, the U.S. Army needed more men with young Clarke's bravado.[5]

Malcolm repaid his benefactor's generosity by engaging in another fight while at West Point in November 1836, and this time he was the one wielding the dagger (in addition to a cowhide whip). On that occasion, however, there was no one to save him. Jackson, who was in the waning days of his second and final term, had renounced his policy of reinstating expelled cadets. In any event, Clarke could hardly lean upon his classroom record for support, given that he ranked forty-seventh out of fifty-one members in his class.[6] He was convicted and expelled, but in absentia, because knowing the inevi-table outcome of the court-martial, Clarke had already set out for perhaps the best place for a failed military man to make himself anew: the West.

Over the next three decades he flourished in the lands beyond the Mississippi, finding ample opportunity for personal fulfillment. After all, the mid-nineteenth-century West was a place where a strong jaw and a steady hand were revered. Thus in time Malcolm Clarke grew into something of a legend, known from the Southwest to the north-ern Plains as a cunning man of unmatched bravery. But the same penchant for violence that had undone him at West Point followed him like a ghost, and in the end, when it tracked him down years later on a warm summer day in Montana, it ensnared those whom he loved best.

A Martial Youth

Malcolm Clarke was born to the martial life, descended from two families with impressive records of military service. His mater-

nal grandfather, Major Thomas Seymour, took a commission in
the Continental army upon his graduation from Yale College in
1777 and commanded a light horse company during the American Revolution. After helping to defeat the British at Saratoga that
autumn, the then captain Seymour accepted the pistols and riding
equipment relinquished by General John Burgoyne. It bespeaks
his prominent role in the battle—one of the most important in the
war, for the rebel victory paved the way for a formal military alliance
between the Americans and the French—that Seymour appears in
John Trumbull's famous painting of the surrender, mounted on
one of the sleek black steeds for which his regiment was known
and feared.[7]

Malcolm's father, Lieutenant Nathan Clarke, served with distinction during the War of 1812.[8] At the conflict's end, the New
England native was stationed as a recruiting officer in Hartford,
Connecticut, where he met and courted Major Seymour's daughter,
Charlotte, who at twenty-one was six years Clarke's junior.[9] The couple wed hurriedly the next summer after Lieutenant Clarke received
orders to join the Fifth U.S. Infantry at Detroit, though the circumstances of the ceremony were inauspicious. At the time, Charlotte
was still recovering from "spotted fever" (probably some variant of a
tick-borne disease) and could not stand without assistance. Still, she
managed to take her vows in a firm voice and immediately afterward
boarded a carriage with her husband for the long, uncomfortable
trip to the interior. Such resolve served her well during the many
years she spent in the Old Northwest.[10]

When Nathan Clarke and his new bride set out for the Great
Lakes in July 1816, peace prevailed in the region for the first time
in more than half a century. Beginning with the Seven Years' War
between France and England, the area had suffered endemic conflict
as European imperial powers, their North American colonists, and
the region's many indigenous groups struggled for control of the
Ohio Valley. It was only after the War of 1812 that relative tranquil-

lity descended upon the Northwest, as the British, who since the end of the American Revolution had supported Indian resistance against U.S. expansion, finally recognized American sovereignty there. White Americans now moved in ever-greater numbers to the present-day states of Ohio, Indiana, Illinois, Michigan, and Wisconsin, while the territory's native peoples looked on with alarm.[11]

It was against this backdrop that units like Lieutenant Clarke's Fifth U.S. Infantry deployed to the Northwest, invested with three key responsibilities: to keep a watchful eye on the British, to protect white settlers from Indian attacks, and to facilitate the business of the fur trade. Detroit was particularly important to federal officials in Washington, given its strategic location on the border with Canada and its excellent access to multiple waterways.[12] As one of their daughters remembered, the Clarkes found much to like about the settlement there, which is somewhat surprising in view of its remote location on the western frontier of the United States as well as the war-weariness of its inhabitants following the recent conflict with England. More than anything else, it was Charlotte's improving health and especially the company of prominent military families like those of John Whistler and Lewis Cass that cheered the young couple during their stay in Michigan.[13]

The Clarkes' Michigan honeymoon lasted less than a year before Nathan was ordered in spring 1817 to make yet another foray deeper into the continental interior. This time the destination was Fort Wayne, Indiana, located some two hundred miles southwest of Detroit and named in honor of General "Mad Anthony" Wayne, a Revolutionary War hero who routed a confederacy of western Indians at the Battle of Fallen Timbers in 1794. Charlotte once again endured a miserable journey, made even more arduous by travel on horseback over pitted roads and by an advanced pregnancy. On 17 July 1817, within a few weeks of their arrival, she gave birth to her first child and only son, whom she christened Egbert Malcolm in honor of her youngest brother.

EXCEPT FOR OCCASIONAL VISITS to the East with his family, young Malcolm passed the first decade of his life in the Northwest, most of it at Fort Snelling, where the Fifth U.S. Infantry was ordered in the summer of 1819 after the closure of Fort Wayne. Perched high on a bluff overlooking the confluence of the Minnesota and Mississippi Rivers in what is now downtown Minneapolis–St. Paul, the diamond-shaped fort was the westernmost outpost in U.S. territory at that time, and resembled "a medieval stone castle."[14] On an inspection tour in 1824, General Winfield Scott came away so impressed with the fort—which boasted thick stone walls, an impregnable round tower, and a lavish, Georgian house for the commandant—that he insisted it bear the name of its chief officer, Colonel Josiah Snelling.

Its beginnings were less grand. The troops arrived late that first summer and, as ordered, simply stopped at the mouth of the Minnesota River, which had not even a proper landing for their watercraft. While the soldiers hacked out a clearing on which to build makeshift cabins, their families used the boats they had taken up the Mississippi River as temporary shelter. The winter was bitterly cold, with heavy snows and lashing winds; adding to the misery was a severe outbreak of scurvy, which struck at the first signs of spring and carried off forty men. But inspired by Snelling's spirited example, the troops got quickly to work building the fort as well as a sawmill upriver at St. Anthony's Falls. For his part, Malcolm's father served as the post's assistant commissary of subsistence, charged with provisioning the three hundred men stationed there.[15]

The time Malcolm spent with his family at the isolated post in Minnesota had a lasting and indelible effect on the boy. For one thing, it was at Fort Snelling where he acquired the outdoor expertise that years later so awed the Blackfeet. His younger sister, Charlotte Ouisconsin Van Cleve, recalled her brother at a very early age became "a ready pupil and prime favorite of Captain Martin Scott, widely known as the veritable Nimrod of those days."[16] The Ver-

Henry Lewis, Fort Snelling, 1858. Malcolm Clarke spent his formative boyhood years at the fort, where his father was stationed with the Fifth U.S. Infantry from 1819 to 1828. Courtesy of the Minnesota Historical Society.

monter's hunting prowess was legendary, his aim so true that a stream in Wisconsin bore the name Bloody Run on account of all the game he slaughtered while stationed in its vicinity. Furthermore, Scott shaped his young protégé into an expert horseman and, critically, a willing duelist, for Scott had once faced off with a rival who had teased him for his humble origins.[17]

At Fort Snelling, Malcolm also developed the code of personal honor that governed his behavior and his relationships with others. He may have come by such a disposition naturally, for his sister remembered that from the time Malcolm was small, "he was very quick to resent anything that looked like an imposition, or an infringement of his rights, it mattered not who was the aggressor." And yet a boyhood spent in a rigid military environment, which placed a premium on fortitude and masculinity, could only nourish such a worldview. Henry Snelling, son of the commandant and one of Malcolm's closest companions, had the bruises to show for it. He recalled, "We were very good friends, but he was very passionate and would get angry with me on the slightest provocation . . . and, as I never would take a blow without returning it, black eyes and bloody noses [were the frequent result]."[18] This tendency to answer all affronts with a closed fist shaped Malcolm Clarke's entire life.

The most important development from Malcolm's time in Minnesota, however, was his exposure to native peoples, whom he saw frequently because of Fort Snelling's location in the middle of a contested borderland between the Dakota Sioux and the Ojibwas.[19] In fact, one of the post's key reasons for being was to mediate the escalating conflict between these two groups, which stretched back decades but had accelerated in the early nineteenth century as migrating Americans pushed the Ojibwas and their allies westward from Michigan and Wisconsin into Minnesota, where they competed for space and game with the Dakotas, who inhabited the watershed of the Upper Mississippi. Both peoples came often to trade at the American Fur Company post directly across the river from the garrison; that kept tensions in the region high.

Although his mother was terrified of the natives, Malcolm evinced sincere interest in them from an early age, captured nicely in a story recounted by his sister. One morning during the winter of 1825–26, the two children attempted to track a wounded wolf that had preyed for some time on their family's livestock and pets but that had escaped the steel trap the siblings had set near the barn. After following the wolf's bloody trail for more than a mile, they were about to give up the chase when they came across an Ojibwa boy, whom Malcolm, speaking in the Indian tongue, promised to reward if he could catch the animal and bring it to them at the fort. The children were delighted when the Indian arrived at the garrison a few hours later with the haggard wolf, and they treated their guest to "a royal breakfast."[20]

Not all encounters with natives yielded such fond memories, however. Indeed, Malcolm, Charlotte, and other children of the post witnessed an infamous episode in the spring of 1827 that haunted the Clarke siblings ever after. In late May a band of Ojibwas pitched their lodges near Fort Snelling, having come to trade maple syrup and other goods with the soldiers. A few days later they were joined in camp by a party of Sioux, the apparent comity a result of the Treaty of Prairie du Chien, a pact signed in 1825 that established discrete hunting grounds for the tribes. The mixed group spent the evening sharing food and passing the pipe, trading stories about hunting and warfare. When the festivities ended around nine o'clock on 28 May, the Sioux bid their hosts goodbye, walked a few paces, but then turned and fired into the teepees, killing two Ojibwas and wounding six others. Charlotte was particularly affected by one of the injured, a young girl just a year or two her senior who lingered in agony for a few days before expiring.[21]

Mortified that such a slaughter should take place in the shadows of his post and with friendly Indians as the victims, Colonel Snelling ordered the capture of the perpetrators, and the next morning two of the guilty were hauled before him. The pair were then tied together and forced to run the gantlet on the prairie near the fort, an exercise in which freedom was assured to those among the condemned who managed to outrun the bullets of a nearby firing squad. Both men were immediately cut down by the Ojibwas, and their bodies dismembered. A few days later, the Sioux delivered the principal offenders, insisting that—in the unlikely event that the Ojibwas declined—they would kill the two men themselves because of the dishonor they had brought upon the Dakotas. The murderers were sentenced to the same fate, but took the news differently: one of them, known as Split Upper Lip, wept and pled for mercy; but the other, a tall and handsome warrior called Little Six, rebuked his companion and calmly gave away his worldly possessions in preparation for death.

As in the first execution, the convicted men were forced to run the gantlet, but this time the children at the fort were heartbroken when they recognized Little Six as one of the accused, for he had become a favorite visitor to the post, often distributing gifts to the youngsters. Six decades later, Charlotte still trembled at the memory of that day, when she watched with horror as the shackled men struck out across the field, headed for a line of trees representing freedom and from which their tribesmen shouted encouragement. She and her peers briefly experienced hope, when, in a stroke of luck, the bullet that struck down Split Upper Lip severed the cord binding him to Little Six, who lurched forward toward safety. "But the [Ojibwas] were cool in their vengeance," and after calmly reloading their rifles they shot him down just before he reached the copse, reducing the children to tears.[22]

As it turned out, the execution itself was merely a prelude to greater horrors. Charlotte vividly recalled that the corpses were dragged to the top of a nearby hill and scalped, with the gory prizes presented as a souvenir to an Ojibwa headman. Indian women and children then descended upon the fallen Sioux, tearing open their bodies and drinking handfuls of blood before leaving the carcasses to rot in the afternoon sun. That night, as the corpses were hurled into the Mississippi, Malcolm and Charlotte lay awake in bed, "awe-struck and

Charlotte Ouisconsin Van Cleve, 1899. Clarke's younger sister, Charlotte, pictured here at the age of eighty, witnessed with her brother the killing of two Sioux Indians forced to run the gantlet at Fort Snelling in 1827. Courtesy of the Minnesota Historical Society.

quiet," lamenting the fate of their cherished Little Six and trying to imagine what the people of New Orleans would make of the desecrated bodies if they managed to float that far downriver.[23]

Notwithstanding such occasional brutality, the eight years the Clarkes spent at Fort Snelling were essentially happy ones. Their stay there ended swiftly, however, in the summer of 1827 when Nathan, by then a captain, and several companies were sent downriver to Wisconsin to quell an insurrection by the Winnebagos. It was the last time the family would ever be together at Fort Snelling. Years later, after many intervening moves, Charlotte relocated to St. Paul and spent much of her adult life there. In her autobiography, she recalled that whenever she passed the spot near the fort (which was eventually engulfed by the Twin Cities) where her family had bidden farewell to their friends in 1827, "a tender, reverential awe steals over me, as when standing by the grave of a friend long buried."[24]

On an April day in 1834, Malcolm and Charlotte Clarke embarked with their father on a trip to the East Coast, a voyage that epitomized the transportation revolution that remade America in the early years of the nineteenth century. The first leg of their journey began at Fort Winnebago and involved an open boat crowded with soldiers and civilians and buffeted by wind and rain as it traveled down the Fox River to Fort Howard, located at the southern end of Green Bay. There the Clarkes boarded a schooner that ferried them across Lake Michigan, through the Straits of Mackinac, down Lake Huron, and up Lake Erie to Buffalo, where they marveled at the sight of Niagara Falls. No less impressive to Charlotte than the "hoary, magnificent" cataract were the modern conveyances they used to complete the last segment of the trip: the new Erie Canal, the Albany and Schenectady Railroad, one of the nation's first lines, and finally a steamboat, which carried them down the Hudson River to West Point.[25]

Though thrilling to the children, the trip was long, requiring more than a month's time. And yet the journey from the Old Northwest to the U.S. Military Academy was simpler for Nathan Clarke than getting his son admitted to the school in the first place. Having received no extended education of his own, Captain Clarke had ascended through the military ranks at a slow and frustrating pace, and he resolved early on that his only boy would not suffer the same disadvantages. Thus he initiated a campaign—which started long before his son had reached sixteen, the minimum age for entry at the USMA—to secure a berth for Malcolm at West Point. Despite Captain Clarke's distinguished record of service in the U.S. Army, he nevertheless faced a daunting task, given the intense competition for the few seats in each class.

Clarke sensed an opportunity to advance his son's candidacy in the summer of 1831 when President Andrew Jackson appointed Lewis Cass as his secretary of war. Clarke knew both men well: he and Cass had been stationed together at Fort Detroit fifteen years earlier, and then in 1828–29 Clarke had served as a recruiting officer in Nashville, Tennessee, where he met Jackson and his adored wife, Rachel, in the heady days between Old Hickory's election and his departure for Washington, D.C. The couple left quite an impression on the Clarke children. Young Charlotte provided one of the most famous and oft-invoked descriptions of the homely Mrs. Jackson, whom she recalled as "a coarse-looking, stout little old woman, whom you might easily mistake for his washerwoman." Doubtless she paled by comparison with her husband, remembered by Charlotte for his "keen, searching eyes, iron-gray hair . . . [and] a face somewhat furrowed by care and time."[26]

In any event, heartened by Cass's appointment, Clarke wrote his old friend in December of 1831 to register Malcolm as an applicant for the class of 1837, but nothing materialized. Clarke tried again in the summer of 1833, to no avail. Driven to desperation, he then took a three-month leave of absence in the spring of 1834 and journeyed

U.S. Military Academy. After his father pulled every conceivable string to have him admitted, Malcolm Clarke had a brief and tumultuous career at West Point, marked by fighting and indifferent academic performance and ending in expulsion. Courtesy of the U.S. Military Academy Archives, Stockbridge Collection.

from his post in Wisconsin to New York in order to lodge a personal appeal. In the end, it took the direct intervention of General Winfield Scott, whom Captain Clarke had met years earlier at Fort Snelling and who was a veteran of the War of 1812 and the Black Hawk War, to place his son in the class of 1838.[27] Malcolm enrolled just a few days shy of his seventeenth birthday. Among his fellow plebes was a handsome French Louisianan named P. G. T. Beauregard, who later graduated third in the class and became notorious when he accepted the surrender of Fort Sumter at the start of the Civil War and led Confederate troops to victory in the First Battle of Bull Run.

Malcolm, of course, enjoyed a much shorter stay at the USMA. Perhaps his only comfort was that his father did not have to endure the debacle of his expulsion. Exhausted by two decades of mili-

tary service and constant relocations throughout the Old Northwest, Nathan in the autumn of 1835 suffered an undisclosed illness
and died the next February at Fort Winnebago, leaving his family
"crushed and desolate." Charlotte was at his side, along with her
fiancé, Horatio Van Cleve, a lieutenant in the Fifth U.S. Infantry
and a West Point graduate, class of 1831. On his deathbed, Nathan
Clarke must have found solace in the belief that his two eldest children had secured the sort of exalted positions in military society that
had eluded him in his own career. And so it was at least with Charlotte, whose husband won renown as a general in the Union Army
during the Civil War and later served as the adjutant general of Minnesota. Malcolm would follow another path.[28]

As NATHAN CLARKE slipped away, momentous events were occur-
ring some one thousand miles to the south, in Texas. The preceding
October a bitter conflict had erupted there between the Mexican
government and the Anglos it had invited to settle in the northern
portion of their republic over the past decade and a half. At first,
federal officials in Mexico City hoped that these newcomers would
provide a buffer between raiding Indians on the southern Plains and
residents of the Mexican interior. Yet the Anglos soon chafed under
Mexican rule, especially after President Antonio López de Santa
Anna attempted to exert greater control over outlying regions of the
country, including the province of Coahuila y Tejas. When Mexican
troops tried to seize the cannon at the small southern Texas hamlet
of Gonzales on 2 October 1835, the Anglo residents drove them off,
sparking the Texas Revolution.[29]

Word of the conflict spread quickly to the United States and
exerted an almost centripetal pull on adventuresome young men
who headed off to join the fray. Many hailed from Tennessee, none
more famous than Davy Crockett. The forty-nine-year-old politician
and frontiersman was already celebrated as a legend in his own time,

much like Buffalo Bill Cody later in the nineteenth century; both were products of relentless self-promotion and the fabrication of tall tales, but they also had legitimate ability in the outdoors. Following a defeat in his bid for reelection to the House of Representatives in 1834, Crockett allegedly told his constituents that they could "go to hell" while he went to Texas.[30] His celebrity reached untold heights when he and the approximately 180 defenders of the Alamo, a small fortified mission in the sleepy town of San Antonio, were killed by Mexican troops on 6 March 1836, following a two-week siege.

Also from the Volunteer State was Crockett's good friend Sam Houston, former governor of Tennessee and one of Andrew Jackson's favorite protégés. Houston had fled Nashville in 1829 following the embarrassing breakup of his short first marriage, hounded by accusations of reprobate personal conduct. After recuperating from his divorce among Cherokee friends in what is now Oklahoma, Houston made his way to Texas in 1832 and soon became involved in the Anglo struggle against Mexico. At a convention organized to declare the independence of Texas held on 2 March 1836, four days before the fall of the Alamo, Houston was named commander in chief of the Texas army. Seven weeks later "the Raven," as the Cherokees called him, brought an unlikely but decisive end to the war by leading his ragtag troops in a rout of Santa Anna's forces at the Battle of San Jacinto in eastern Texas.[31]

As it is for most men who came to Texas during the chaotic period of the revolution and its aftermath, it is difficult to fix with certainty when and how Malcolm Clarke arrived. One thing is sure: he did not see any of the fighting, for at the time that Sam Houston's men swarmed the battlefield at San Jacinto with their cries of "Remember the Alamo!" Clarke was finishing his second year at the USMA.[32] The first indication of his presence in Texas is a payment claim for service in the revolutionary army for a period from August to December 1837, suggesting an arrival sometime in the summer of that year.[33] This seems plausible considering that, after his expulsion,

Clarke probably visited his widowed mother in Cincinnati (a good bet, given the Queen City's location on an obvious river route from West Point to Texas), before making his way down the Mississippi to New Orleans and then across the Gulf of Mexico to Galveston.[34]

Though he was twenty years old and widely traveled, nothing had prepared Malcolm Clarke for what he saw upon his arrival in the new Lone Star Republic. With the end of hostilities, most of the volunteers—heavily armed, shiftless young men—roamed the towns and countryside, and with little to do they turned to gambling, drinking, and much worse. Given this unpromising demographic, President Sam Houston and his military leaders were doubtless pleased to fill the ranks of their professional army with more-seasoned soldiers like Clarke, which perhaps explains how Clarke, despite his late appearance on the scene and total lack of combat experience, was made a captain. Though additional details of his service are unknown (for instance, which company he commanded), he was likely deployed in eastern Texas, protecting the settlements there as well as the state capital at Houston from Indians and desperadoes.

While in Texas, as if out of a scene from a novel, Clarke seems to have encountered his old West Point nemesis, Lindsay Hagler, whose tenure at the USMA had been even shorter than his own (no surprise, perhaps, given Hagler's eighty-nine demerits during the 1834–35 school year; Clarke had less than a third that number).[35] Enlisting as a captain in the Texas army in June 1836, Hagler served through the end of the following year and spent at least some of his time recruiting for the cause in the United States. According to an account offered by Clarke's sister Charlotte, one day the two men found themselves on the same stretch of lonely road, riding in opposite directions. Clarke, who carried two pistols, had fired earlier at a prairie hen, but could not remember which gun he had discharged. Not wanting Hagler to see him fumbling with his weapon, a sure sign of cowardice, Clarke simply placed his hand on one of the revolvers and stared coolly at his enemy. The two passed each other without a word, though Clarke tensed in anticipation of a shot to the back (he expected nothing less from the craven southerner). Hagler remained in Texas and later served three terms in the state's house of representatives, but died in 1846 during a street brawl in the small town of Goliad.[36]

Clarke, however, did not linger in Texas. After mustering out of the army in December 1837, he signed on for a short stint as a private in the Houston Volunteer Guards, a unit composed mostly of outlaws under the command of Reuben Ross, a veteran of the Texas Revolution. Although his military service made him eligible for a land grant in the new republic, by the end of 1838 Clarke had returned to the United States, having determined to fulfill his father's wish that he obtain a commission in the U.S. Army.[37] With the help of a Missouri congressman named John Miller (who may have taken an interest in Malcolm's case because, like Nathan Clarke, Miller was a veteran of the War of 1812), Malcolm received an invitation to interview with the army's board of examiners. Before such a meeting could take place, however, Secretary of War Joel Poinsett wrote Miller an apologetic note on 31 December 1838 to explain that it was all a mistake: Clarke's expulsion from West Point rendered him ineligible for further service.[38]

As the New Year began, Malcolm Clarke surveyed the wreckage of his life: no job, no property, not even a family of his own. Like Sam Houston and Davy Crockett before him, he looked to the West for a new start, but this time he set his sights far beyond Texas.

To the Upper Missouri

In 1843 the painter and naturalist John James Audubon traveled up the Missouri River with his eldest son, Victor, for research that led ultimately to his final published work, *The Viviparous Quadrupeds of North America*. Having just issued the octavo edition of his celebrated *Birds of America* the year before, the fifty-eight-year-old Audubon was at the height of his fame, renowned throughout Europe and the United States for the precision and beauty of his work. With dark eyes, flowing gray hair, and a matted beard, Audubon looked every bit the quintessential U.S. frontiersman. He thus fit in nicely at Fort Union when he and his party arrived in June. Alexander Culbertson gave them a warm welcome there. Over the next two months, the artist hunted, sketched, and even executed portraits of Culbertson and his wife, Natawista, all of which he meticulously described in his journal.

Fort Union and its environs fascinated Audubon; one day in mid-July proved particularly memorable. Following an afternoon meal, the painter watched from the fort as the Culbertsons and several others—including Owen McKenzie, son of the post's legendary former bourgeois, and Lewis Squires, Audubon's New York neighbor and personal secretary—put on Indian dress and rode out onto the prairie. The riders thrilled the audience with a show of equestrian skill, which ended abruptly when a "fine Wolf" trotted into view. All at once, the mounted party gave chase to the animal, each member hoping to claim it as a trophy. Though a crack shot with a gun, McKenzie let fly with an arrow instead and missed, but Culbertson overtook the terrified creature and dropped it with a blast from his musket. The group then ran their horses at full gallop all the way back to the gates of the fort, despite the blazing summer heat. While Audubon was pleased that Squires had held his own with the others, he confessed to his journal that the paint Natawista had applied to his assistant's face gave him the appearance of "a being from the infernal regions."[39]

This was the world Malcolm Clarke discovered when he came upriver in 1841, and it is easy to see how it captivated him so much that he stayed on the Upper Missouri for the next three decades. One associate observed, "This wild and reckless life was suited to his nature. It afforded ample scope for the exercise of all his resources."[40] Moreover, as the friendly but zealous competition between Culbertson and McKenzie suggests, the region was one where men (and even the occasional woman, like Natawista) could prove themselves against each other in sport and sometimes more lethal contests. Most of all, the Upper Missouri gave Malcolm Clarke an opportunity to reinvent himself, to cast off the fetters of eastern society and its stifling social expectations, just as Lewis Squires had done, metaphorically at least, when he went native for an afternoon.

Clarke arrived in the region under circumstances different from Audubon's in virtually every respect. Whereas the eminent painter came seeking inspiration for a grand project, Clarke traveled to the far West as a last resort. Unable to find work in Cincinnati "congenial to his taste," he applied one final time in the spring of 1841 for a position in the army. The answer from the Department of War was unequivocal: "Having had one opportunity of entering the Service of the Country, and forfeited it by your own indiscretion, it could not be considered other than an act of impropriety to other meritorious applicants were your claims now preferred to theirs."[41] In the wake of this disappointment, he turned to one of his father's old military friends, John Craighead Culbertson, who recommended Malcolm to his nephew Alexander for a position in the AFC. Later that year, probably in the summer and surely no later than the fall when the rivers froze over, Clarke made his first appearance on the Upper Missouri.[42]

By contrast with his less refined colleagues in the fur trade, who were mostly uneducated and also renowned for their liquor-fueled unruliness, Clarke had enjoyed a relatively sophisticated upbringing. Distinguished by his stint at West Point, which he rarely failed to mention, Clarke used his background to earn himself useful social capital among the trappers and traders in the AFC. And yet it was his association with Alexander Culbertson that proved definitive. In this respect, the timing of Clarke's arrival was perfect, for just the year before, in 1840, Pierre Chouteau had promoted Culbertson by offering him charge of Forts Union and McKenzie, making the

Karl Bodmer, *Sketch of Fort McKenzie,* ca. 1833. Malcolm Clarke worked at Fort McKenzie for much of his first decade on the Upper Missouri, and it was there that he was most likely married to Coth-co-co-na in 1844. Courtesy of the Overholser Historical Research Center, Fort Benton, Montana.

benevolent Pennsylvanian one of the company's most powerful representatives in fur country. Whether he perceived Clarke's abilities right away or merely acceded to the entreaties of his beloved uncle, Culbertson received the newcomer as an apprentice and installed him as a clerk at Fort McKenzie.

At the time of Clarke's arrival, Fort McKenzie was almost ten years old and still one of the AFC's most productive outposts. Yet it was not quite so grand an edifice as Fort Union. Prince Maximilian of Wied, the German who had visited the fort in 1833, derided McKenzie's construction as "crude and very flimsy." That perhaps reflects the time constraints under which it was assembled and especially the understanding that the Piegans might tire of its presence at any time and put it to the torch, a fact that militated against architectural embellishments. Nevertheless, the fort's setting was spectacular: near the confluence of the Marias and Missouri Rivers, opposite an imposing wall of dark bluffs soaring two hundred feet high.[43]

Like that at all AFC posts, the social organization at Fort McKenzie conformed to a strict hierarchy. As a clerk, Malcolm Clarke found himself near the top of the post's chain of command, below the bourgeois (technically Culbertson, though in his absence one or another high-ranking clerk) but above most everyone else, including interpreters, skilled outdoorsmen, craftsmen, and especially the *engagés* and *voyageurs*, who, quite literally, did the post's heavy lifting. From his position in the upper 10 percent of AFC employees, Clarke could expect to negotiate with Indians, keep the post's inventory, and take the annual returns downriver to Fort Union and beyond, sometimes as far as St. Louis. For his efforts he earned an average of about $375 per year, a little more than half of Culbertson's annual take but close to three times what a lowly *voyageur* made.[44]

IN A SHORT BIOGRAPHY of her father penned many years after his death, Helen Clarke acknowledged, "It would be somewhat singular if a man with as strong characteristics as Malcolm Clarke should pass through life without making enemies."[45] By the time he arrived in Montana, Clarke had amassed quite a collection of antagonists: Lindsay Hagler and another, unnamed cadet at West Point, and, even before his troubled stay at the USMA, a boyhood classmate in Cincinnati whom Malcolm had pummeled for insulting a female classmate.[46] Clarke's violent clash with his fellow trader Alexander Harvey was different, however, for it was born of nobler ideals than simple pride or old-fashioned chivalry. Their battle in August 1845 almost cost Malcolm his lucrative career as a fur trader just as it got underway.

Even in a profession replete with rogues and scoundrels, Alexander Harvey stood out as perhaps the most notorious individual on the Upper Missouri, a judgment rendered by contemporaries and historians alike. Though he looked the part of a "well-built storybook hero," standing more than six feet tall and weighing in excess of 170 pounds (both impressive figures for the day), there was little about him to admire, save for his unquestioned strength and courage.[47] Born in St. Louis in 1808, Harvey in his youth found work in the saddle trade, but "as he happened to be one of those men that can never be convinced, and with whom it was no use to argue unless one wished to get into a fight," he soon ran afoul of his employer.[48] Like other young men of that time and place, Harvey made his way upriver to fur country, arriving in the early 1830s.

Harvey worked for the AFC throughout the decade, stationed primarily at Fort McKenzie, and quickly earned a reputation as "so wicked and troublesome" (especially when drunk, which was often) that in the fall of 1839 Pierre Chouteau ordered Harvey to appear before him in St. Louis the following spring. When Harvey learned of his pending termination, he grumbled, "I will not let Mr. Chouteau wait long on me," and set off in the dead of winter, taking only what he and his dog could carry, on the 2,300-mile overland trek to AFC headquarters. Upon his arrival in St. Louis in March 1840, the astonished Chouteau promptly reengaged him, and thus redeemed, Harvey returned to the Upper Missouri in June.[49] Chouteau's change of heart had disastrous consequences.

During the winter of 1843–44, the AFC trader Francis Chardon turned away a Blackfoot trading party that had come to Fort McKenzie. Angered by the brusque treatment, the Indians killed a company hog as they departed. Chardon immediately dispatched some men to chastise the natives. They, in turn, ambushed their pursuers, killing a black servant, likely a slave, who belonged to Chardon. Indignant at the loss of his property, Chardon conferred with Harvey, who relished the chance to plot a reprisal. When a band of innocent and unsuspecting Piegans visited Fort McKenzie some weeks later, Harvey fired a cannon into the crowd, killing and wounding several Indians. Afterward, Harvey strode among the fallen, finishing off the dying with thrusts from his dagger. The whites celebrated their vengeance with a scalp dance that evening, forcing a handful of captured Indian women to participate in the degradation of their mutilated warriors. It took Alexander Culbertson several years to earn back the trust of the Blackfeet.[50]

Under different circumstances, Malcolm Clarke and Alexander Harvey might have become allies, or at the very least evinced a grudging respect for each other, given their reputations as two of the most fearless men on the Upper Missouri. In fact, the two were bound by violence, for in 1841 they chased down and murdered a native headman of mixed Blood and Gros Ventre ancestry named Kah-ta-Nah, who had committed some infraction at Fort McKenzie. (That neither tribe retaliated afterwards suggests that the Indians may have viewed the killing as justified.)[51] Nevertheless, despite these outward similarities, they were very different men: whereas Clarke's bellicosity was predictable, even banal—his eruptions almost always came in response to an actual or perceived slight—Harvey's behavior was sociopathic. Clarke thus resolved to rid Montana of this threat, driven by loyalty to both Culbertson, whose bottom line Harvey endangered, and the Piegans, his wife's people, whom Harvey had slaughtered for no cause in the so-called Fort McKenzie massacre. He waited more than a year to act.

On 16 August 1845 Harvey rode out from Fort Chardon, an AFC post on the Judith River in central Montana, to meet a passing keelboat headed upstream from Fort Union. On board were Malcolm Clarke and two veterans of the fur trade, Jacob Berger and James Lee. All three men were sworn enemies of Harvey and had plotted his murder for some time. When Harvey boarded the vessel and greeted the men, Clarke replied, "I don't shake hands with such a damned rascal as you," and sent him reeling with a blow from his tomahawk while Berger assaulted him with a rifle butt. Harvey recovered quickly and grabbed hold of Clarke, whom he might have killed had Lee not clouted him with a pistol. Severely wounded and thinking better of taking on three armed men, Harvey staggered off the boat and retreated to Fort Union, where he recuperated before heading off to St. Louis.

What Harvey could not settle with his fists he chose to pursue in court. Once in Missouri he thus appealed to the U.S. district attorney, and in April 1846 a grand jury indicted Berger, Clarke, and Lee on charges of attempted murder. The three men were ordered to leave Indian country immediately. Worried about losing one of their best young traders in Malcolm Clarke, the AFC quickly reassigned five key witnesses to distant parts of the Upper Missouri, placing them beyond the reach of the grand jury's subpoena. The strategy worked, and the district attorney was forced to end the prosecution in April 1847 because of insufficient evidence against the accused.[52]

Meanwhile, having survived this worrisome brush with the law, Clarke became one of the most powerful men in the AFC. In recognition of his value to the company, in the late 1840s Culbertson stationed his protégé at a new post near the mouth of the Marias River, built to replace Fort McKenzie. Situated on a broad, grassy plain on the north bank of the Missouri, Fort Benton, as it came to be called (in honor of Thomas Hart Benton, a Missouri senator and noted proponent of westward expansion), was originally built of logs, but these were replaced in the 1850s with clay dug from the riverbed, giving the structure a rare frontier permanence.[53]

That Culbertson tapped Clarke for this position was no surprise, since Malcolm had excelled in his work right from the start. For instance, during the winter of 1841–42 (his first on the Upper Missouri) Clarke had helped Fort McKenzie take in a record haul of buffalo robes.[54] And Culbertson was not the only white man he impressed. Father Nicolas Point, a Jesuit priest who tried unsuccessfully to establish a permanent mission among the Blackfeet, spent eight months at various AFC posts during 1846–47. The cleric passed much of his time at Fort Lewis (a precursor to Fort Benton), where he met Clarke and even painted his portrait. Point came away deeply moved by Malcolm's "self-sacrificing" character, which he commended to his Jesuit superiors as setting an excellent example for the "savages" while indicating also Clarke's possible receptive-

Fort Benton, ca. 1860s. Soon after its establishment in 1847, Fort Benton supplanted Fort Union as the most profitable AFC post and became the chief entrepôt and transportation hub on the Upper Missouri. Courtesy of the Montana Historical Society.

ness to Catholicism. (Of that there seems to have been little chance; Clarke was baptized as an Episcopalian and, at any rate, showed only marginal interest in formal religious practice outside of the sacraments. He did, however, contribute five dollars to Point's proposed mission.)[55]

Just as essential to his success as a trader was Clarke's reputation among the Blackfeet. Although many thought him an inveterate show-off—hence the derogatory connotations of his Indian name—they admired him, too. For one thing, unlike most high-ranking AFC employees, Clarke spent considerable time, often entire winters, in their camps, where he cultivated personal relationships that facilitated trade. As a result, he earned a wide reputation among natives and whites alike for his expert knowledge of Blackfeet customs and his proficiency in their language (which he spoke along with French and Sioux).[56] Most of all, the Indians were drawn to Clarke because of his charisma. Consider the words of Calf Shirt, a Blood headman esteemed by the Blackfeet but feared and despised by most whites: "What power do you possess? Has the spirit of the Manitou fallen on you? I say to you I hate the white man, but I hate you less than any white man I ever knew."[57] Little wonder that in due time and under Clarke's leadership, Fort Benton supplanted Fort Union as the brightest star in the AFC firmament.

DESPITE HIS TREMENDOUS SUCCESS at Fort Benton and elsewhere throughout the AFC empire, Malcolm Clarke in the spring of 1857 moved his family to Ann Arbor, Michigan, where his sister, Charlotte, was then living.[58] His reasons are unclear, but within just a few months he had become dissatisfied with "this mode of life." He headed back to the Upper Missouri that summer with Coth-co-co-na and their children in tow. His unhappiness in the more densely settled Midwest was predictable. After all, Clarke had spent all but a few of his forty years on the nation's frontiers and had there enjoyed the respect (if not always the affection) of Indians and whites alike.

Clarke's decisions to return to Montana and to keep his family intact were unusual, given that many traders abandoned their Indian spouses, or "country wives," as they were known, when they retired and returned to the United States upon their leaving the fur trade. Such was the case with James Kipp, the legendary AFC fur man, who in 1851, "after apparently wrestling with his conscience for some time," left Earth Woman, his Mandan wife, and moved to Missouri, casting his lot with a white woman to whom he had been concurrently married and with whom he had children.[59] Not so Malcolm Clarke, who, by the admittedly low standards of the time, was an exemplary husband. That could be seen not only in his devotion to

Coth-co-co-na but also in his being "one of the exceptional few who was not addicted to alcohol," no small feat considering the abundance of liquor at trading posts and the attendant dissolution of men like Francis Chardon and Alexander Harvey.[60]

Malcolm Clarke was no less committed to his four children: Helen (b. 1848), Horace (b. 1849), Nathan (b. 1852), and Isabel (b. 1861).[61] Though his work required frequent travel and though, according to Helen, he was "a stern disciplinarian," by all accounts Clarke was an exceptionally loving parent who, like his own father, held high expectations for those who carried the family name. For this reason, Malcolm sent his two eldest children to the East for their education. Though he was able to see them only once a year, Helen recalled that such visits "flashed on us like meteors, bright, beautiful and brilliant."[62] For her part, Coth-co-co-na was nearly undone by the separation. Years later, Horace remembered how, as the mackinaw boat carrying him and Helen slipped from its mooring at the Fort Benton levee, their bereft mother ran down the riverbank, wailing with grief, until she collapsed and could go no farther.[63]

While interracial marriages like the one between Coth-co-co-na and Malcolm Clarke were typical on the Upper Missouri and in other pockets of the Rocky Mountain West where the fur trade still flourished in the mid-nineteenth century, most white Americans of the time condemned such relationships. To be sure, native-white unions did not spawn the same levels of anxiety and outrage as their black-white counterparts, which U.S. states from Maine to Texas prohibited by legal decree. In fact, because of the perceived utility of Indian-white intermarriage, which facilitated westward expansion and economic development, most lawmakers refused to apply such injunctions to these relationships; the one state that did, Tennessee, soon repealed it.[64]

Although not illegal in the United States, native-white intermarriage hardly enjoyed widespread social acceptance. If the so-called squaw man served as the vanguard of American frontier settlement,

he outlived his utility almost as soon as he had shown the proverbial flag. In the eyes of their detractors, by remaining in the wilderness and consorting with Indian peoples, such individuals reverted
to a similarly primitive stage of human development, seen in their
adoption of native speech, dress, customs, and beliefs. Furthermore,
because many of these white men were presumed to hail from the
more squalid ranks of American society (though this was not true of
Malcolm Clarke), it was believed that they in turn corrupted their
Indian hosts through the introduction of alcohol and the modeling of
poor behavior. By this rationale, in the long run squaw men did more
harm than good, for they complicated the urgent work of Christian-
izing and uplifting native peoples, thus retarding the process of white
settlement they had initiated by coming west in the first place.[65]

A more significant problem than their own supposed degeneration
and their adverse effect upon Indians was the children they produced,
who were known commonly as "half-breeds" (sometimes shortened
scornfully to "breeds"), a term found in usage in America as early as
the 1760s.[66] To many observers, mixed-blood offspring combined
the very worst elements inherited from both parents: the laziness
and improvidence characteristic of their lower-class white fathers,
and the superstition and limited aptitude of their Indian mothers.
Furthermore, peoples of mixed native-white ancestry were difficult
to place within the schemes of racial classification that emerged in the
nineteenth century, complicating matters surrounding property and
citizenship. Most of all, the very existence of half-breeds disgusted
white Americans opposed to racial amalgamation.

These prejudices found broad expression in the literature and
popular culture of the day. Take, for instance, the serialization in
1849 of *The Half-Breed*, a novella by Walt Whitman. The title character is a perfidious mixed-blood named Boddo, whose physical
deformities, including a hunched back, serve as an obvious criticism
of Indian-white miscegenation. In the ungainly prose that characterized his earlier writings (and thus made the 1855 publication of

Leaves of Grass so unexpected), Whitman penned this description of his protagonist: "The gazer would have been at some doubt whether to class this strange and hideous creature with the race of Red Men or White—for he was a half-breed, his mother an Indian squaw, and his father some unknown member of the race of the settlers." As the reader learns, Boddo's father had come west to trap and hunt and, while there, succumbed to "the hot blood of young veins" and slept with an Indian girl. Horrified by "the monstrous abortion" he sired, he becomes a monk, remaining in the West in an attempt to mitigate his son's adverse impact on the community. Yet his vigilance comes to naught, for Boddo's duplicity causes the death of a noble full-blooded Indian named Arrow-Tip, whose stoicism and courage reflect his unblemished racial purity.[67]

So long as these mixed communities remained relatively isolated, families like the Clarkes and Culbertsons were insulated against such prejudice. But by the 1860s the sands had shifted perceptibly in places like the Upper Missouri or the Arkansas Valley in southeastern Colorado, where the brothers Charles and William Bent had established an eponymous fort in 1833 and intermarried with the Cheyennes.[68] In both locations and throughout the wider trans-Missouri West, white Americans began to appear in greater numbers in the years following the Mexican-American War, either passing through on the way to California and Oregon or settling somewhere in between. Some of these newcomers were Anglo women, whose advent in colonial settings throughout the English-speaking world usually heralded profound changes in the structures of society, with significant implications for their indigenous counterparts and racially hybrid families. For one thing, white men considered white women preferable to natives and mixed-bloods as marriage partners. For another, with their presence came a heightened attention to establishing and policing gender norms, especially where they intersected with race.[69] Historical accounts suggest that the first white woman would finally arrive on the Upper Missouri by steamboat in 1847.[70]

Though Malcolm Clarke and his intermarried colleagues on the Upper Missouri could not have known it, mixed communities like theirs had not fared well in the course of American history. Time and again, gatherings of native-white families—almost always a result of fur trade interaction—had thrived along the western edges of the United States, where Anglos were scarce and the two-handed grip of civil and social authority was weak. As noted by one scholar, "Had the Americans not come, possibly a line of *metis* or halfbreeds would have existed from Oklahoma to Saskatchewan." But come they did, and often with surprising speed.[71] It had happened in the Great Lakes region over the course of the eighteenth century, just as it did in the Lower Missouri Valley during the early decades of the nineteenth. In each instance, waves of Anglo emigrants overwhelmed these "syncretic societies" and in some cases literally erased their histories, deliberately writing such periods out of the formal accounts of the past as if Clio herself was ashamed that such debased places had ever existed.[72]

Even if unaware of these depressing outcomes, some male heads of interracial families on the Upper Missouri recognized, nevertheless, the clear and present danger to their fragile world. Thus Johnny Grant, a successful rancher and himself a man of mixed ancestry, left Montana's Deer Lodge Valley in 1867 and took his Indian wives and children to the Red River country of southeastern Manitoba.[73] Located at the forks of the Red and Assiniboine Rivers in what is now downtown Winnipeg, the community was home to thousands of mixed-blood peoples, many of whom identified themselves as a separate indigenous group called Métis.[74] A number of their American counterparts found sanctuary there, including the young mixed-blood son of Andrew Dawson, the veteran trader who in 1856 had succeeded his friend Alexander Culbertson as the AFC's chief factor on the Upper Missouri. The boy's guardian wrote Dawson in the spring of 1864 to encourage the trader to retire there, saying of Red River that "it is a very good place for one with an

Indian family to settle."[75] Dawson did not move to Manitoba, but neither did he stay in Montana, opting instead to return with his other mixed-blood sons (but not his Indian wife) to Scotland, the land of his birth, where he died in 1871. Dawson's youngest son, Thomas, eventually returned to Montana, where in February 1891 he married Isabel Clarke, daughter of his father's former partner.[76]

Alone among nearly all of his contemporaries, Malcolm Clarke chose to remain on the Upper Missouri. Perhaps he thought that his corner of the Rockies was simply too remote to experience an influx of white emigrants, or at the very least he hoped that by the time of their arrival any newcomers would have adapted themselves to the mores of the frontier. Maybe he assumed that his class standing would provide sufficient insurance against the intolerance of poorer Anglo settlers. In any event, he surely entertained scant enthusiasm for leaving a place where he had enjoyed such success and lived for so long. Having spent half his fifty-two years on the Upper Missouri, he was hardly inclined to start over at Red River or, even worse, somewhere in the crowded and rapidly urbanizing East. Instead, he resolved that his family would remain in Montana, a fateful if not tragic decision that would cost him his life.

A Frontier Tragedy

The conquistador Hernán Cortés supposedly told Montezuma, ruler of the Aztec Empire in the early sixteenth century, that the Spaniards had a disease of the heart that only gold could cure.[77] Along with healthy doses of missionary and territorial zeal, this lust drove the Spanish to explore every corner of the New World. Although they found little of the precious metal in what is now the American West, nineteenth-century argonauts hit pay dirt. First came the California gold rush, which began when word of the January 1848 discovery at Sutter's Mill leaked out. Over the next decade, more than 350,000 people flocked to the region, using pocketknives, gold pans, sluice boxes, and water cannons to coax some $550 million in gold from the California landscape.[78] The next major find was on the South Platte River in Colorado, which in the years 1859–61 drew another 100,000 migrants to the West.[79] The result was much the same in both places: a select few became rich, many more died or went home with nothing to show for their efforts, and the local Indian peoples suffered terribly from disease, exploitation, and violence. Montana's gold rush would be no different.

Whereas gold fever spread rapidly in California and Colorado, it set in slowly in Montana.[80] In 1856 at Fort Benton, Alexander Culbertson took part in the region's first-known commercial transaction involving gold when he skeptically accepted a bit of gold dust from a mountaineer in exchange for $1,000 worth of goods. In the end, Culbertson got the better end of the deal, for when coined the gold had a value of $1,500.[81] Trace amounts were found over the next several years, but it was an 1862 strike on Grasshopper Creek, about 150 miles southwest of Fort Benton, that set off the stampede. Within months a boomtown called Bannack had sprung up nearby and quickly counted 3,000 inhabitants. Many of the newcomers came west to escape the turmoil of the Civil War, which intensified that September with the Battle of Antietam, a fierce engagement in western Maryland that saw nearly 23,000 combined casualties. The yield from Montana's gold mines grew steadily over the next few years, rising from $600,000 in 1862 to a peak of $18 million in 1865.[82]

The transformation of Montana during the 1860s was breathtaking in speed and reach, reflected in its rapid political evolution. Montana began the decade as part of Nebraska Territory, in 1861 became a piece of the newly established Dakota Territory, and three years later achieved its own territorial status.[83] Its population soared from fewer than seven hundred white people in the area around the time of the Grasshopper Creek gold strike to almost twenty thousand by the end of the 1860s.[84] Such an influx of outsiders had enor-

Lynching tree, Helena, 1870. The rapid influx of white Americans in the 1860s led to
widespread social unrest in Montana and gave rise to the infamous Vigilance Committee,
which lynched more than fifty victims between 1864 and 1870. Courtesy of the Montana
Historical Society.

mous social ramifications, as suggested by the story of the Montana Vigilance Committee. Established in December 1863 in response to a series of robberies and murders in Montana's gold country, the vigilantes lynched twenty-one suspected road agents over the course of six weeks in early 1864. In a clear indication of the lawlessness of the time and place, the committee's third victim, Henry Plummer, was not only the leader of the gang but also the sheriff of Bannack.[85]

Whatever tumult gold-hungry whites might have experienced in those intoxicating days of the Montana rush was minor compared with the changing circumstances facing the approximately seven thousand Blackfeet.[86] Whereas a slow trickle of Americans bled into their country during the fur trade era, the opening years of the 1860s saw, in the words of one modern Piegan scholar, a wave that "simply overwhelmed them, much like water over a rock."[87] Some sense of this startling transformation may be gleaned from an 1859 report by an Indian agent in Blackfeet country. That summer, the official met with several tribal elders, who, in response to the agent's suggestion that the Indians settle down and take up farming in anticipation of rapid American settlement, politely asked him, "If the white men are so numerous, why is it the same ones who come back to the country year after year, with rarely an exception?" In his report, the agent urged authorities in Washington to invite a Blackfeet delegation to the capital so that its members might behold with their own eyes the wonders of American society. Such a visit never took place, but by 1863 it was unnecessary; the Blackfeet no longer had any doubts about the white man's numbers and might.[88]

The swarm of newcomers was not the only dilemma facing the Blackfeet in the early 1860s. For at least a decade, it had been clear to natives and whites alike that the herds of buffalo on the northern Plains—once so numerous that their supply seemed inexhaustible— had begun to dwindle, raising the specter of a subsistence crisis for the Indians. In effect, the natives confronted a simple but horrifying equation: the number of white people was inversely proportional to that of the buffalo, and the trend was accelerating rapidly. The U.S. commissioners had used this fact to their advantage during negotiations that in 1855 led to a historic accord with the Blackfeet, the very last of the Plains tribes to treat with the United States.[89] With Lame Bull's Treaty, as it came to be known, Washington officials hoped to open the northern Plains for settlement and to extend a rail line from St. Paul, Minnesota, to Puget Sound in the recently established Washington Territory.

The commissioners wrote the document to promote peace between the Blackfeet and not only the Americans but also the other native peoples of the area, including the Flatheads, Kutenais, and Nez Perces. In exchange for allowing Americans to traverse and settle in their lands, the Blackfeet were promised $20,000 in annuities for each of the next ten years, as well as agricultural instruction and schools for their children. The Blackfeet quickly soured on the deal, however; whites arrived in droves, but the Great Father did not uphold his pledges, as Indian agents came and went and the delivery of promised goods was sporadic at best. In time, the words spoken by one Blood chief at the 1855 proceedings came to sound like prophecy: "I wish to say that as far as we old men are concerned we want peace and to cease going to war; but I am afraid that we cannot stop our young men."[90]

EVEN AS MONTANA DESCENDED into chaos during the early 1860s, so, too, did Malcolm Clarke's personal and professional lives. If the tumult convulsing the Upper Missouri was the result of terrifyingly swift social change, Clarke's fortunes, on the other hand, were tied, as ever, to his formidable temper and inclination to violence. His victim in the summer of 1863 was Owen McKenzie, the mixed-blood son of an Assiniboine woman and the late Kenneth McKenzie, the legendary AFC trader and founder of Fort Union, who had died two years before. Unlike Clarke's ambush of Alexander Harvey in 1845, his encounter with Owen McKenzie pitted him against one of the most beloved figures in Montana. And this time the consequences would be dire, driving him finally from the business to which he had dedicated almost his entire working life.

The roots of Clarke's quarrel with McKenzie are murky; contemporary accounts speak merely to a longstanding feud between the two. The contours, however, are easy enough to divine. For one thing, McKenzie was almost a decade younger than Clarke but disinclined to yield to his elders. More important were his legendary skills with horse and gun. Indeed, McKenzie was glorified throughout fur country as an indefatigable rider and a crack marksman; stories abounded celebrating his facility in chasing down bison and felling them with his rifle. Few were more taken than Rudolph Friederich Kurz, the Swiss artist who spent two years on the Upper Missouri in the early 1850s. McKenzie appears frequently in the detailed journal Kurz kept, and in one entry the European noted breathlessly, "Owen McKenzie can load and shoot 14 times in one mile."[91] With a man as reflexively competitive as Malcolm Clarke, such fawning surely rankled.

Clarke and McKenzie had faced off at least once prior to their fatal encounter. Thirteen years earlier the two men had bet on a horse race between them. Though McKenzie shattered his clavicle when his steed stepped into a hole and pitched him headlong onto the prairie, the injured rider regained his mount and still managed to win the contest, an outcome that surely drove Clarke to distraction, especially considering the very public nature of his defeat.[92] Clarke took the second and final round, but won scorn instead of laurels.

In late spring 1863 the *Nellie Rogers*, a new 250-ton steamboat, embarked from St. Louis on its maiden voyage to the Upper Missouri. Clarke was on board, along with his fourteen-year-old son, Horace, who was returning from school in the East. Although bound for Fort Benton, the head of navigation on the Missouri, low water forced the boat to stop at the mouth of the Milk River, about two

hundred miles short of its destination, and offload its cargo for overland transportation. Learning of these developments, McKenzie—
who was stationed at Fort Galpin, a nearby post established the year
before by a small outfit competing with the AFC—rode down to
meet the *Nellie Rogers.*

While there is general agreement to this point in the story among
the many accounts, what happened next has been the subject of
strenuous disagreement. Was McKenzie drunk (which would not
have been out of character) or sober? Did he berate Clarke about
some allegedly unpaid debts, or did Clarke act even before McKenzie challenged him? Whatever the case, this much is clear: McKenzie
forced his way onto the boat, and Clarke fired three shots from his
pistol, killing him instantly. Knowing that the younger man's enormous popularity would likely prompt retribution from his friends,
Malcolm and Horace fled on horseback to the safety of Fort Benton.
Afterward, Helen Clarke insisted that the terrors of that nighttime
ride, featuring packs of howling wolves, drew her father and brother
closer for the remainder of Malcolm's life. [93]

Clarke steadfastly claimed self-defense, which may explain why, in
contrast to his near-fatal bludgeoning of Alexander Harvey in 1845,
he faced no legal repercussions for the homicide. However, according to one source, "On the river it was everywhere considered at
the time a cold-blooded murder."[94] Surely it caused Clarke's family members some discomfort, which emerged in Helen's biography
of her father. While she conceded that both men were probably to
blame for the disagreement that culminated in McKenzie's slaying,
she also acknowledged her father's general pugnacity: "His quick
temper very often led him into difficulties. His life was not faultless,
but 'He that is without sin, let him cast the first stone.'"[95]

Clarke's murder of Owen McKenzie led him to quit the fur trade,
perhaps because he feared for his life. But the decision was likely an
easy one anyway, since by the early 1860s the fur business was in
decline, a victim of vanishing bison herds and growing native-white

violence, which eroded the very relationships that had made possible the trade in animal skins. Thus in 1864 Clarke made a strategic move upriver, establishing a horse and cattle ranch at a magnificent gap in the Rockies.[96] The place did not lack for scenery: six decades earlier, Meriwether Lewis had marveled at the 1,200-foot cliffs on either side of the Missouri and thus labeled the pass the Gates of the Mountains. For his part, William Clark had a painful encounter with a cactus that lent it another, less flattering name: the Prickly Pear Valley.[97]

Either way, Malcolm Clarke found it a splendid locale, well watered and complete with sprawling pastures. On it he built an impressive spread, consisting of a cabin, a smokehouse, and a saloon. And his choice of site proved prescient: on 14 July 1864 a group of four ex-Confederate soldiers from Georgia who had failed as miners made one last-ditch attempt to find gold . . . and discovered a placer deposit in what became known as Last Chance Gulch. A camp took root almost immediately, and in time the settlement, known eventually as Helena, was connected by stage to Fort Benton, 130 miles to the northeast. Clarke's ranch thus became a popular way station for travelers, including notable figures like Thomas F. Meagher, the acting territorial governor, who spent a night there in December 1865.[98]

Clarke found great contentment at his new ranch, which housed a growing family. In June 1862 the Jesuit missionary Pierre-Jean De Smet had married him to a young mixed-blood woman called Good Singing (known to her people as Akseniski), the daughter of Isidoro Sandoval, a Hispano fur trader murdered by Alexander Harvey in 1840, and a Piegan woman named Catch-for-Nothing. Such polygyny was not unusual in the mid-nineteenth-century West, especially in the context of the bison robe trade, which—because of the need for additional female labor in processing hides—led Indian men to take multiple wives. Although the practice was less common among white trappers, data from one historical sample suggests that one-third of those who married more than once had at least two wives at some point (the remainder took single spouses sequentially).[99]

The relationship between Malcolm and Good Singing dated to at least the mid-1850s, as the first of the couple's four surviving children, a boy named Isidoro, was born in 1856 or 1857. A daughter, Judith, came along in 1864; the birthdates of two others, Phoebe and Robert Carrol, are unknown. A fifth child was stillborn. How Coth-co-co-na felt about Malcolm's taking a second wife is unknown, but given the frequency of plural marriage within Plains Indian societies, she likely accepted it as a standard family arrangement. The whole family lived together under a single roof.

Despite—or perhaps because of—his bellicose nature as well as his sheer longevity on the Upper Missouri, Clarke came to be idolized during the 1860s as one of the area's most esteemed "old time pioneers." Along with eleven other leading men in the territory, probably all of whom had moved to the region after him, Clarke incorporated the Historical Society of Montana on 2 February 1865. In this role, he took on the responsibility of enshrining for future generations the very history that he and select others had actually lived, especially since the group listed "incidents of the fur trade" as one of its two key areas of interest (the discovery of the territory's mines being the other).[100] Though it had taken him three decades and an extended residence on the frontier, Clarke had finally attained a level of social prominence of which his father would have been proud.

IN THAT SANGUINARY SPRING of 1865, as the Civil War ended with Lee's surrender to Grant at Appomattox, a fresh conflict erupted in Montana Territory. Unlike the contest between the North and the South, this new campaign did not set enormous standing armies against each other in pitched battles; rather, it was a guerrilla war, fought sporadically by small groups of armed men. And in contrast to the political disagreements that spawned the War of the Rebellion, Montana's conflagration was effectively a race war, in which the

Blackfeet, and especially the Piegans, struggled to preserve their land and lifeways from the onrushing tide of white settlers.

Racial enmity, however, was only one factor contributing to the outbreak of hostilities in Montana. Surely many of the newcomers considered native peoples culturally and intellectually inferior, especially those emigrants hailing from the South who had imbibed the racist tenets of herrenvolk democracy, characterized by a dim view of those not belonging to the supposed "master race."[101] Even some of the federal emissaries sent to help the Blackfeet held them in low esteem, including Gad Upson, the Indian agent to the Piegans, who arrived in October 1863 and described his wards as "degraded savages" and insisted that they remained "free and untrammeled from the shackles of an enlightened conscience."[102] Still, it was their fury over native horse theft that drove some whites to commit unspeakable acts of violence.

The American stampede into Blackfeet territory had a mixed effect on Indian horse raids. On one level, federal officials had sought to eradicate the practice, given its central role in promoting conflict between groups of Indian peoples, which destabilized the region and thus made it unsafe for intending settlers. Therefore U.S. commissioners often extracted promises from Indians to abandon raiding as a key component of the treaty-making process. At the same time, the advent of so many whites created a spike in the equine population, and raids on it proved too hard for the Blackfeet to resist. After all, the Americans' promotion of intertribal accord had robbed young Indian men of the surest path to social advancement; after warfare, horse stealing was the next-best thing, and it mattered not to the Indians that the mounts they now stole belonged to whites and not their native enemies. It was just such an event that inaugurated the so-called Piegan War.

On 23 April 1865 a party of Bloods descended upon Fort Benton and made off with about forty horses. White residents retaliated one month later by ambushing a small group of Bloods who had come to

Bull train near Fort Benton, ca. 1860s. White Americans began pushing into the interior of Montana during and after the Civil War, searching for gold and establishing homesteads, all the while encroaching on Piegan lands. Courtesy of the Overholser Historical Research Center, Fort Benton, Montana.

the town on a peaceful visit, killing four Indians. Two days afterward, on 25 May, Calf Shirt—the prominent Blood chief—and a large war party espied a group of about ten woodcutters felling timber a dozen miles above Fort Benton, where the Americans planned to build a new settlement called Ophir. Calf Shirt, who despite his antagonism toward whites had signed Lame Bull's Treaty ten years earlier, allegedly signaled his benevolent intentions to the terrified lumbermen, who responded with gunfire. At that point the Indians fell upon the whites. Though the Americans fought desperately, using the bodies of their slaughtered oxen as breastworks, the Indians killed every last man, stripping the bodies, scalping one of them, and cutting the throat of another from ear to ear.[103]

Such events received little attention in the East, where most residents were still sorting through the unsettling aftermath of the Civil

War. In Montana, on the other hand, Acting Territorial Governor
Meagher moved quickly to extinguish Indian title to native lands
coveted by whites. To that end he convened treaty negotiations with
the Blackfeet in November 1865, and in exchange for additional
annuities he extracted an agreement from the Indians to relinquish
all of their claims south of the Teton River. The Indians consented,
in large part because they had ceased hunting in the ceded area some
time before and thus saw little use in retaining their access to it.

Malcolm Clarke hosted the American delegation at his ranch before
joining them for the trip to Fort Benton.[104] He was clearly valuable to
the commissioners as an interpreter and a long-term acquaintance of
the Blackfeet, but Clarke went also out of self-interest. For one thing,
he believed that his wives and children were entitled to some of the
annuities. More importantly, Clarke wanted to make sure that he, as
a white man married into the tribe, would not lose his land (which,
after all, was part of the proposed concession). He got his wish,
for article 9 guaranteed such individuals, of whom there were very
few, the right to 160 acres, "including so far as practicable their present homestead." Moreover, Clarke was listed as one of five men who
"on account of their long residence, liberality, and valuable faith-
ful services" to the Blackfeet would receive an additional 640 acres
granted in fee simple by the United States.[105] It is difficult to discern
whether this largesse was sincere or rather manipulated by Clarke. Yet
in the end it meant little, as a new round of native-white violence led
the commissioner of Indian affairs to decide against recommending
the ratification of the treaty.

Blackfeet misery intensified during the late 1860s, and it was the
Piegans who suffered the most. In addition to frequent skirmishing
with whites, their native enemies, chiefly the Crows and Gros Ventres,
stepped up their own attacks and in one battle killed Many Horses,
the wealthiest of all Piegan chiefs. The Piegans even turned on one
another, when one night a group of young, drunken warriors killed
and mutilated Little Dog, a headman believed by some Blackfeet to

have become too conciliatory to the Americans. For their part, federal officials responded to the instability in Montana by establishing two army outposts in the area: Camp Cooke, built in 1866 near the mouth of the Judith River; and Fort Shaw, constructed the next year in the Sun River Valley and boasting an infantry regiment of some four hundred soldiers. The United States offered the carrot as well as the stick, attempting to treat for peace in 1868 on essentially the same terms proffered three years earlier (though again, events on the ground prevented approval in Washington), and moving the agency from Fort Benton to a more remote site on the Teton River in an attempt to reduce incidents with hostile whites.[106]

Neither these friendly overtures nor even the threatening presence of the "seizers," as the Blackfeet called the U.S. troops, could forestall the violence, which continued unabated throughout the decade and claimed dozens of lives on both sides of the conflict. For the besieged Piegans, the tragic nadir came in the summer of 1869 when two Indians—including the elderly brother of Mountain Chief, regarded as the leading warrior of the Piegans—were apprehended in Fort Benton by a group of whites, murdered, and then thrown barbarically into the Missouri River. The Piegan response was immediate and so furious that on 18 August General Alfred Sully, recently appointed superintendent for Indian affairs in Montana, reported to his superiors in Washington, "I fear we will have to consider the Blackfeet in a state of war."[107] As evidence Sully referred to an Indian attack just the day before on a ranch twenty-five miles north of Helena.

WITH WARM WEATHER and ample sunshine, 17 August 1869 was a gorgeous day in the Prickly Pear Valley. But there was unease at Malcolm Clarke's homestead. His cattle had been missing for several days, much longer than usual when they wandered off, and so he sent an Indian boy to search for them. Finally, around seven in the

Smokehouse on the Sieben Ranch, 2007. One of the outbuildings on Malcolm Clarke's ranch in the Little Prickly Pear valley, north of Helena, still stands today, nearly 150 years after his murder. Photograph by the author.

evening, Clarke heard the faint sound of tinkling bells and knew that his young herder had located the animals and steered them home. After a brief inspection of the cows, the heartened Clarke rejoined his family inside the house, where he challenged Helen (known as Nellie) to a game of backgammon.[108]

The two had played a round or two when they were startled by the barking of their dogs. By then it was nine o'clock, a late hour indeed for a visiting neighbor, given the distance between ranches in the area. Overcome with curiosity, Nellie quit the game and ran to the back of the house, where she was surprised to see a group of young Indian men speaking with her sisters and Coth-co-co-na. Helen recognized one of them instantly, a handsome warrior in his midtwenties named Ne-tus-che-o, whom the whites called Pete Owl Child. He was also her mother's cousin. Nellie noted with great pleasure and not a little relief that Ne-tus-che-o "threw aside the stoicism of his race" and embraced Horace, giving him an affectionate kiss on the cheek. The men had not always gotten along so well.

Two years earlier, Owl Child had paid a visit to the ranch with his wife and three other family members. During their weeklong stay, the Indians' horses were stolen, along with several belonging to the Clarkes. An inspection of the trail quickly established that white men, and not Indians, were the thieves, a fact as embarrassing to Malcolm Clarke as it was infuriating to Owl Child. Though Clarke's mounts were soon recovered, Ne-tus-che-o's were not, and so a few nights later the Indian guests slipped away without saying goodbye to their hosts, taking with them some horses as well as Clarke's treasured spyglass.

Discovering the theft, Malcolm and Horace set out and soon tracked Owl Child to a nearby Piegan camp. Upon their arrival they spotted Ne-tus-che-o astride Horace's favorite steed. This was too much for Horace to bear; in an instant he wrested the animal away from his cousin and lashed him across the face with a quirt, calling the Indian "a dog." A crowd of warriors quickly surrounded the Clarkes, jeering and threatening father and son until some elders stepped forward and rebuked the young men for their poor treatment of Four Bears. Before leaving with his reclaimed property, Malcolm berated Owl Child, whom he insulted as "an old woman," telling him that he could have forgiven the theft of his horses but not that of the telescope.

The Piegans, however, have a different version of the falling-out between Owl Child and the Clarkes. According to the Indians, on that 1867 visit to the Prickly Pear Malcolm had raped Owl Child's wife while the other men were away on a hunt, prompting Ne-tus-che-o to retaliate with the theft. According to this story, nine months later Owl Child's wife delivered a fair-skinned baby boy with blue eyes and light colored hair, who was either stillborn or smothered in a badger hole by the woman's horrified relatives. In support of this account, some Piegans note even today that, while Owl Child was renowned for his pride and vanity, anger over a mere horse theft—no matter how insulting—would not have precipitated the violence that ensued two years later. And yet in his defense, Malcolm Clarke held women in the highest regard, and throughout his life the targets of his wrath were exclusively men. It is not possible to square these divergent accounts.[109]

Whatever the cause of the enmity between Ne-tus-che-o and the Clarkes, Owl Child's embrace of Horace on that summer night in 1869 suggested that all ill feelings had passed. Nellie joked lightly, "Our horses are again stolen," and Malcolm invited his guests inside for a hastily prepared supper. The young men accepted and filed indoors—Ne-tus-che-o, along with Bear Chief (whom Nellie called Richard the Third because of his resemblance to the fifteenth-century English king), Black Weasel (known also as Shanghai), his brother, and one of Mountain Chief's sons.[110] They said they had come to deliver some stolen horses and also to entice Clarke to come and trade with the Piegans later that year at one of their winter camps.

Though Clarke was reassured by the Indians' apparent good will, the mood at the dinner table was not only odd but even portentous. Nellie's eight-year-old sister, Isabel, told Owl Child how hard her family had taken the news of the murder of Mountain Chief's brother in Fort Benton, but Ne-tus-che-o hushed her, as if he did not want sympathy, even if offered by a little girl. Meanwhile, Black Weasel sat silently through the meal with his face buried in his hands and tears streaming out from between his fingers. When Owl Child explained away the bizarre sight by insisting that his friend's eyes were merely sore, Isabel sent for some water to relieve the Indian's discomfort. Strangest of all was the erratic behavior of Mountain Chief's son, who paced about the house nervously, running his palms over the furniture, fingering the tablecloth, and talking incessantly in an animated voice.

Horace must have sensed that something was amiss, because he searched for his pistol before accompanying Mountain Chief's son to bring in the horses from a nearby pasture. Perplexed by her brother's alarm, Nellie chided him gently: "What is the use of a fire-arm? You are with a friend." Malcolm agreed, and so Horace and the Indian headed out into the darkness. They had traveled about a mile from the house when Horace was startled to hear his companion begin singing a Crow death song. He turned to face the Indian, who fired a pistol, the ball striking just below Horace's nose, passing through his face, and exiting slightly in front of his left ear. Thrown from his saddle but ensnared in the lariat, Horace was dragged across the ground for some distance before his leg slipped loose of its hold, and then he lay still, bleeding uncontrollably from his wound. Two more Indians, who were not part of the group received at the house, emerged from a patch of nearby brush, and upon inspecting Horace guessed that he was dead. Because of Owl Child's kinship ties to the victim, they did not desecrate the body by taking its scalp, and instead hurried back to the ranch.

Though weakened from the loss of blood, Horace managed to drag himself to within a hundred yards of the house, where he collapsed and cried out, "Father! I am shot!" But he heard only the whinnying of horses and the shrieks of his mother and sisters. Moments before, Owl Child and Malcolm had stepped outside to talk, and when the two men appeared at the door yet another Indian—there may have been as many as thirty concealed at various spots on the ranch—bolted from the darkness and shot Clarke in the chest at point-blank range. As the rancher staggered backward, Owl Child delivered the deathblow, powerfully cleaving Clarke's forehead with an ax. Ne-tus-che-o had planned the attack carefully, counting on Piegan rage over the recent atrocity in Fort Benton to shield him from any tribal punishment.

The commotion was so fierce and the screams so feral that they spooked the Indians' horses. In the confusion Nellie, her mother, and an elderly aunt named Black Bear were able to pull Malcolm's body into one of the bedrooms without drawing the notice of the Indians.[111] The women placed the corpse next to Horace, who had staggered inside moments earlier and whose wound Nellie packed with raw tobacco in a frantic effort to stanch the bleeding. While Nellie, Coth-co-co-na, and the rest of the family took shelter behind barred doors, Black Bear went out to confront the attackers. The old woman admonished the Indians, telling them, "The man murdered to-night was your best friend. You have committed a deed so dark, so terrible that the trees will whisper it."[112] Though Ne-tus-che-o insisted to the others that Horace was still alive, his companions were moved by Black Bear's reproach, and so the raiders left, driving off the Clarkes' cattle and destroying their stores of flour, sugar, and other goods.

With the Indians' departure an eerie calm settled upon the ranch. The women clung to each other in total darkness, afraid to light a candle lest any one of the Indians return and finish off the sur-vivors. "A marvelous stillness" covered the house, broken only by the whimpering of the children and the discomfiting sound of Hor-ace's vomiting up the blood he had swallowed. All the while, Hel-en's mind reeled at the thought that the Piegans—"our blood," she called them—could be guilty of such a deed. At daybreak she and Isabel hurried off to seek help, and by late that afternoon several well-wishers had trickled in, including a physician who announced that, miraculously, Horace had suffered no broken bones and would likely make a full recovery. Nellie's relief, however, was tempered by the arrival of her younger brother, Nathan, who had been away from the ranch for several days in search of some missing horses. Upon entering the house, he passed by the prostrate Horace without a word and approached his father's corpse. Nathan, whom Nellie described as "hotheaded," let out a deep groan, and his youthful face took on a dark and worrisome expression as he vowed retribution. He was just seventeen.[113]

Word of Clarke's murder sent shock waves throughout Montana, and in short order the news ricocheted well beyond the territory. Nathaniel Langford, a close friend and later the first superintendent of Yellowstone National Park, wrote, "The Indians loved him, and it was a common saying among the citizens of Helena where I lived that [Malcolm Clarke] was more a friend to the Indians than to the whites, and when the news that he was killed, reached us, it was thought that a general uprising would follow."[114] Within a few days Clarke's sister, Charlotte, received a telegraph at her home in St. Paul. She carried the dispatch upstairs to her mother, who was visiting from Cincinnati. When she read it, the elderly woman broke down, sobbing, "[M]y bright-eyed little boy who loved his *only* mother, as he used to call me so tenderly."[115]

TWO DAYS AFTER the butchery, Malcolm Clarke was buried in the afternoon of 19 August 1869, on a small rise near his ranch house, mourned by numerous friends and admirers. His final resting place was a quiet and peaceful spot, described eloquently by Helen: "Afar off could be seen the rugged crags of the Bear's Tooth, at the base of which the great river runs, and under its shadow so much of joy, so much of sorrow had met and mingled together and wrought so strange a chapter in his life."[116] But the beauty of the grave site belied the great violence that had swirled all around it: the murder of its occupant, of course, but in a wider sense the decades of struggle between and among natives and newcomers for control of the land and its resources.

The modest cemetery had a most unexpected visitor eight years later, after the property had passed out of the Clarkes' hands. In the summer of 1877 General William T. Sherman, whose marauding exploits in Georgia during the Civil War had earned him a reputation far more savage than Malcolm Clarke's, made a tour of the army forts of the West. He spent much of his trip in Montana, where the Nez Perce War—the final episode in the territory's vicious struggle

Grave site of Malcolm Clarke, 2007. After a visit to his father's grave in 1923, Clarke's son Horace commissioned a fence to enclose it, a fitting tribute, as he put it, to "one of the greatest of Montana pioneers and a kind and good father." Photograph by the author.

between Indians and whites—was entering its climactic stage.[117] Traveling north from Helena on his visit, General Sherman stopped to rest at a quiet ranch in the Prickly Pear Valley. After a meal, he took a walk around the property, and in his wanderings he came across an unmarked grave, which he asked about when he returned to the house. Upon learning that in it lay the body of Malcolm Clarke, the general became pensive. He then explained to his host that the dead man had been a classmate of his at West Point, and that many times during the Civil War he had looked through newspapers and military reports, expecting to find mention of his old friend, probably for some gallant act. The trail had gone cold until Sherman's chance discovery in the fastness of the Rocky Mountains.[118]

3

The Man Who Stands Alone
with His Gun

If Horace Clarke's survival was a miracle—shot in the face at close range and then left for dead—the speed of his recovery was nearly as remarkable. In the immediate aftermath of the attack on the Clarke ranch, the family retreated to the security of Helena, where Horace convalesced. But by the early autumn of 1869 he was back on the Little Prickly Pear, managing his father's spread with his younger brother, Nathan, and living with all members of the household save for Helen, who had joined her aunt Charlotte in Minneapolis.[1] Although Horace bore no lasting effects from the shooting, he wore a thick mustache for the rest of his life, perhaps to conceal the entry wound from his assailant's bullet.

Later that fall, rumors of an army campaign against the Piegans began circulating throughout western Montana, and in time they reached Horace's ears. In the waning days of 1869 he traveled sixty miles to Fort Shaw to speak with Colonel Philippe Régis de Trobriand, an aristocratic French émigré and decorated Civil War veteran who oversaw military affairs in the District of Montana. Though he

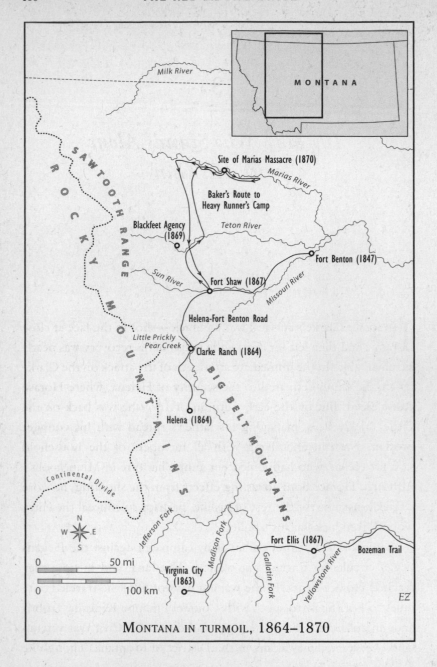

MONTANA

Milk River

Site of Marias Massacre (1870)

Marias River

Baker's Route to
Heavy Runner's Camp

SAWTOOTH

ROCKY RANGE

Blackfeet Agency
(1869)

Teton River

Fort Benton (1847)

Sun River

Fort Shaw (1867)

Missouri River

Helena–Fort Benton Road

Little Prickly
Pear Creek

Clarke Ranch (1864)

BIG BELT MOUNTAINS

MOUNTAINS

Helena (1864)

Continental Divide

N
W   E
S

Jefferson Fork

Madison Fork

Fort Ellis (1867)

Bozeman Trail

0   50 mi

0   100 km

Virginia City
(1863)

Gallatin Fork

Yellowstone River

EZ

MONTANA IN TURMOIL, 1864–1870

Officers' quarters, Fort Shaw, 2007. It was here that Colonel Philippe Régis de Trobriand, the suave but demanding leader of U.S. military forces in Montana, resided during the planning and execution of Major Eugene M. Baker's surprise attack on Heavy Runner's camp. Photograph by the author.

had no formal military experience of his own, Horace volunteered to join the expedition and offered Nathan's services as well.[2] They intended to avenge their father's murder, even if it meant slaughtering their own blood relatives in the process.

As it happened, de Trobriand's bête noire, Lieutenant Colonel Alfred H. Sully, was working furiously to avoid just such an outcome. Thus on New Year's Day 1870, at almost the same moment that Horace visited Fort Shaw, Sully left the post with twenty-five enlisted men, bound for the new Blackfeet agency on the Teton River some thirty-five miles to the northwest. As the superintendent of Indian affairs for Montana Territory, Sully intended to meet with various Blackfeet chiefs about the ongoing violence against whites that enraged young men of the tribe committed. This was no simple parley, however, for Sully carried a set of imposing demands as well, including the surrender of those Piegans indicted for the murder of

Malcolm Clarke and the return of hundreds of horses and mules stolen from whites throughout the preceding summer and fall.

Though skeptical about his prospects with the Indians, the lean, blue-eyed Sully was surely the right man for this delicate assignment. After all, he had extensive experience with native peoples, having served in numerous campaigns against them since the early 1840s, from Florida to California and many places in between. And that he was no racist was suggested by two of his marriages: the first to a Mexican girl he wed while stationed in California and, after her untimely death, the second to a Yankton woman he met in Dakota Territory in the 1860s.[3] Sully was known as a fair and decent man, and he traveled to the Teton River that January day animated by the dim hope of averting additional conflict between the territory's white and Indian residents.

Whatever optimism Sully may have harbored quickly dissipated when he arrived at the agency late that afternoon. Although he had

dispatched a mixed-blood scout to round up as many chiefs as possible, only four had bothered to make the trip: a Blood named Gray Eyes, and three Piegan headmen led by Heavy Runner, known to the military as a dedicated friend to the whites who favored peace. As for the

Lieutenant Colonel Alfred Sully, 1862. An accomplished artist as well as a decorated field commander, Sully sent reports from Montana in the aftermath of the Marias Massacre that earned him the enmity of Generals Phil Sheridan and William T. Sherman. Courtesy of the Montana Historical Society.

other chiefs, the scout explained to Sully that he had found them too drunk to leave their camps.

In his conversations with the chiefs that night and the next morning, Sully expressed his disappointment that so few had shown up and then gave the Indians a stern speech, explaining that the U.S. government was weary of Blackfeet aggression and determined to make war on them if the natives did not cease their raiding and killing. Moreover, in an effort to convey the gravity of the situation, Sully insisted that if the army launched a military campaign against the Blackfeet, U.S. troops would pursue the Indians across the so-called Medicine Line into Canada, where native groups had long sought safe haven. Though a bluff, Sully's threat had the desired effect, as the startled headmen promised to do all in their power to curb the depredations, return stolen livestock, and kill or capture Owl Child's gang. Heavy Runner was so alarmed by Sully's warning that he asked for a note of safe passage attesting to his cooperation with the whites. Sully gave the chiefs two weeks to meet his conditions.

Unbeknownst to the Indians but suspected by Horace and Nathan Clarke and other Montana whites, the gears of the U.S. war machine were already turning, and just five days after Sully's meeting with the chiefs, Major Eugene M. Baker and four companies of the Second U.S. Cavalry moved out from Fort Ellis (near Bozeman) to Fort Shaw, to be within striking distance of Blackfeet camps if ordered to attack. When Sully's deadline passed without the Indians' compliance, Baker led his men into the teeth of a particularly severe Montana winter, crossing broken, snow-covered terrain in plunging temperatures. On the fourth day the troops discovered a large Piegan encampment at the Big Bend of the Marias River, and deployed quietly in a skirmish line on the bluffs overhead. Among the dozens of concerned citizens who tagged along were the two Clarke brothers.[4]

The carnage that ensued on that bitter morning has been lost not only to the public but to most historians as well, eclipsed by a handful of more infamous army slaughters of Plains Indian peoples. Whereas the atrocity at Sand Creek, Colorado, in 1864 has become a byword for white brutality, and Wounded Knee in South Dakota in 1890 is notable as the last major engagement of the Indian Wars, the Marias (or Baker) Massacre, as it came to be known, soon slipped into relative obscurity, despite the immediate, if momentary, storms of protest it aroused in the East and the reforms in Indian affairs that it engendered.[5] The Piegans, however, never forgot, and neither did Horace Clarke, who lived forever in the shadows cast by the bloody events of 23 January 1870.

Itomot´ahpi Pikun´i

Though white Montanans had endured numerous Piegan assaults throughout the late 1860s, the killing of Malcolm Clarke caused unprecedented levels of anxiety and outrage in the territory. To be sure, other prominent citizens had fallen victim to ambush by the Piegans, most notably John Bozeman, a pioneer who blazed an eponymous trail to Montana Territory before his murder in 1867. And yet, according to conventional wisdom, Clarke of all people should have been safe, given his marriage to a Piegan woman and the location of his ranch so close to the perceived security of the settlement at Helena.

Newspapers throughout Montana mixed their reporting of Clarke's death with impassioned pleas for military support. Just three days after the murder, a writer for the *New North-West* maintained, "The war cloud lowers. It is not conjecture or imagination. There is too much reality in flowing blood." At the same time the editorialist held out little hope of imminent relief from the U.S. troops stationed in Montana. Indeed, the combined strength of the territory's two posts—Forts Ellis and Shaw—was fewer than five hundred men. With these figures in mind, the writer lamented that "until some great massacre awakens the Government to a general retaliation under a good officer . . . we may expect continued and yearly recurrences of the horrors."[6]

Such alarmists found a sympathetic ear in Alfred Sully, who had arrived in Montana in May 1869 as a sort of exile. Despite valiant service in the Union army, Sully had seen his career stall in the late 1860s after he ran afoul of General Philip H. Sheridan. While serving under Sheridan on the southern Plains during the fall of 1868, Sully had clashed bitterly with Lieutenant Colonel George Armstrong Custer, a Sheridan favorite. The following spring Sheridan retaliated by placing Sully on the unassigned list, a humiliation that left the forty-eight-year-old lieutenant colonel in professional limbo as a field officer without a command. In the end he was effectively banished to Montana, becoming one of many soldiers forced into civilian positions by the military drawdown after the Civil War.[7]

Sully was receptive to the aggrieved Montana settlers because he was well versed in the hazards faced by white frontiersmen and their families. From his earlier postings throughout Indian country, Sully recognized the waylaid freighters, the pillaged ranchers, and especially the terrified pioneers who now implored him for assistance. Throughout the tense summer of 1869, he dutifully conveyed their apprehensions to federal officials in Washington, who in turn transmitted his communiqués to the headquarters of the U.S. Army's Division of the Missouri (to which Montana belonged), commanded by none other than Sully's former antagonist Phil Sheridan. While emphasizing in these messages the dangers faced by Montana whites, in advocating for military intervention Sully also adopted a classic bureaucratic pose, noting that the Indians' livestock thefts "will make an expensive claim against the government."[8]

Not all observers shared Sully's dire assessment, however. For instance, Alexander Culbertson, who had far greater firsthand knowledge of Montana than Sully had, argued that the recent depredations, including the murder of his friend and protégé Malcolm

Colonel Philippe Régis de Trobriand, 1862. De Trobriand's reputation among white Montanans soared after Baker's slaughter on the Marias, which many residents of the territory hailed as a fitting "chastisement" for Piegan attacks on homesteads and wagon trains. Photograph in author's collection.

Clarke, were the work of "a portion of the young rabble, over whom the chiefs have no control." Drawing on his four decades of experience with the Piegans, Culbertson blamed some of the trouble on the nonratification of recent treaties and suggested to Sully that provisioning the natives, who faced a growing subsistence crisis with the disappearance of the bison, could help calm tensions.[9]

More important was the opinion of Colonel de Trobriand, who, unlike Sully, placed little faith in the breathless reports of the territory's settlers, sharing Culbertson's belief that only a few Indians were responsible for the unrest and that they had escaped across the border to Canada, anyway.[10] Though he scorned the hysteria of Montana's whites, he nevertheless tried to soothe their fears, as is evident in his patient reply to an October petition from Helena citizens demanding cavalry protection. With Gallic charm, de Trobriand wrote that while it was both his duty and his desire to defend all residents of Montana, "there is actually *no Indian war* in the territory." He promised his correspondents that he would transmit their concerns to Washington, but tempered their expectations with an old French saying: "'the prettiest girl can give but what she has.' So with any military commander."[11] His would not, however, be the last word on the matter.

As THE WINTER of 1868–69 settled in over the southern Plains, small parties of area Indian tribes straggled into Fort Cobb in the western part of Indian Territory (now present-day Oklahoma). They were starving, and many traveled on foot because U.S. troops under the direction of Lieutenant Colonel Custer had incinerated their food supplies and killed their horses. Having eaten the last of their dogs, the natives came to the army outpost seeking relief from General Sheridan, the very officer who had masterminded the devastating campaign against them. Leading one such group was Tosawi, a noted Comanche headman who had treated for peace with federal officials the year before at Medicine Lodge Creek. When he was presented to the general at Fort Cobb, the chief introduced himself by saying in broken English, "Tosawi, good Indian."[12] Sheridan supposedly replied with a glib and chilling rejoinder that he made famous and that haunted him ever after: "The only good Indians I ever saw were dead."[13]

This was the man who in the spring of 1869 became lieutenant general of the U.S. Army and assumed control of implementing military policy in the Division of the Missouri, a sweeping expanse of more than a million square miles of western territory that included the Great Plains and Rocky Mountains. Sheridan's ascent was meteoric—just eight years earlier he had been a lowly first lieutenant; now he answered only to William T. Sherman, the commanding general of the army. A powerful mix of ambition, bravery, luck, and political savvy had propelled him upward, despite his almost comical appearance. "Little Phil" stood at just five feet five inches tall, which was merely the most immediate of his physical shortcomings. Abraham Lincoln famously cataloged the others in describing the general as "a brown, chunky little chap, with a long body, short legs, not enough neck to hang him, and such long arms that if his ankles itch he can skratch them without stooping."[14] Sheridan's fitness as a commander was beyond question, however, displayed especially in the fall of 1864 as he led his troops in laying waste to Virginia's Shenandoah Valley, foreshadowing the destruction in Georgia wrought later that year by Sherman during his fabled March to the Sea.[15]

Critics of Sheridan's prosecution of the Indian Wars denounced him as a garden-variety racist, but this was an oversimplification. To be sure, he harbored the reflexive prejudice toward native peoples characteristic of his time and place, but he did not seek the Indians' extermination. Rather, like many of the eastern reformers who loathed him, Sheridan hoped to see Indians Christianized and settled on reservations, where they could learn the skills and habits of white Americans. But he diverged from the humanitarians on the question of how to reach this goal: while the former emphasized schooling and moral suasion, Sheridan insisted that natives who raided and plundered had to feel the hard hand of war, and not merely the velvet glove.[16] It was precisely this strategy that he employed in subjugating the Indians of the southern Plains in 1868 and bringing admired men like Tosawi to their knees.

Given Sheridan's temperament and inclination, the conflicting reports from Montana that arrived at his Chicago headquarters in the waning months of 1869 placed him in an awkward position. On the one hand, the Piegan depredations roiling the territory seemed to call for just the kind of punishment Sheridan advocated, and yet from prior experience he deeply distrusted Alfred Sully, the source of this information. On the other hand, Régis de Trobriand—whom Sherman knew and commended to Sheridan for his reliability— downplayed the violence in his district and urged restraint in pursuing the Indian offenders, advice that ran contrary to Sheridan's naturally aggressive instincts.

In the end, Sheridan's decision was made for him in October, as Secretary of the Interior Jacob D. Cox—on Sully's behalf—urged the War Department to send troops against the Piegans. Responding later that month to the directives from Washington, Sheridan outlined his strategy: "I think it would be the best plan to let me find out exactly where these Indians are going to spend the winter, and about the time of a good heavy snow I will send out a party and try and strike them."[17] Sherman endorsed the scheme two weeks later, no doubt because such tactics had worked to so-called perfection in Indian Territory the year before, giving Sheridan the signature victory of his campaign on the southern Plains. On 27 November 1868 Lieutenant Colonel George Armstrong Custer, the yellow-haired boy wonder, led the Seventh U.S. Cavalry in a surprise attack against the winter camp on the Washita River of Black Kettle, a Cheyenne chief who had survived the Sand Creek Massacre four years earlier. Though Custer's recklessness contributed to the deaths of a score of U.S. troops, the Indians suffered more than a hundred casualties, including Black Kettle and one of his wives, who were shot in the back while trying to escape.[18]

The Battle of the Washita held another lesson for Sheridan: beware the public reaction. When word of Custer's victory seeped out, harsh condemnation quickly followed from humanitarians and reformers. Though a few members of Black Kettle's camp were no doubt responsible for some of the attacks on white settlements between the Platte River and Red River, the headman himself was known as a peace chief. Moreover, some Americans recoiled at the tactically sound but morally repugnant slaughter of the natives' ponies and the destruction of their foodstuffs in winter, which mirrored the scorched-earth policy Sheridan had employed in the Shenandoah. Though he vigorously defended the actions of his troops, Sheridan never again trusted in the good will of an adoring but fickle public, explaining that "those very men who deafen you with their cheers today are capable tomorrow of throwing stones and mud at you."[19] With such thoughts in mind, he proceeded cautiously in formulating his plan for Montana.

THOUGH MUCH IMPROVED since the steamboat era, travel from the eastern or central United States to Montana Territory was still no easy feat in the late 1860s. For Colonel James A. Hardie, inspector general of the Division of the Missouri and a loyal Sheridan confidant, the arduous journey from Chicago to Fort Shaw took twelve days. Leaving division headquarters in Illinois on 27 December, Hardie crossed the stark and frozen Great Plains on the Union Pacific, which just eight months earlier had linked with the Central Pacific to complete the nation's first transcontinental line. At Corinne, in Utah Territory, Hardie boarded a stagecoach for the second and much less comfortable leg of his trip, arriving at Fort Shaw (via Helena) on 7 January 1870.

Colonel Hardie was no stranger to difficult missions like this one. After all, it was he who on the eve of the Battle of Gettysburg had carried orders from Washington, D.C., to western Maryland transferring command of the Army of the Potomac from Joseph Hooker to George Meade. His present assignment, however, was less straightforward. Mindful of the public backlash following the incident on the Washita, Sheridan wanted to make certain that if he sent troops into the field against the Piegans no friendly Indians would be harmed, inadvertently or otherwise. He thus dispatched Hardie to make a full report on the conditions in Montana.

From the moment he arrived at Fort Shaw, Hardie understood that the situation—as he described it with characteristic understatement—had experienced substantial "modification." But it was much more than that, a complete chiasma. In conferring with de Trobriand on 7 January, Hardie was astonished to learn that the colonel now favored a strike against the Piegans, as quickly as it could be mounted. When the inspector general asked why, after more than three months of opposing such a plan, de Trobriand had changed course so abruptly, the Frenchman cited a rash of Indian depredations in December and especially the unexpected return of Mountain Chief's band from Canada to the U.S. side of the line, affording a prime opportunity to assail them. In order to confirm the Indians' whereabouts, Hardie immediately dispatched Joe Kipp, the mixed-blood son of the famous trader who served as an army scout, to reconnoiter along the winding Marias River.[20]

While waiting on Kipp's report, Hardie exchanged a series of telegraph messages with Alfred Sully in Helena. If de Trobriand's volte-face had surprised him, the inspector general was even less prepared for Sully's change of heart. The man who throughout the summer and fall had consistently urged military action against the Piegans now counseled restraint, insisting that, although his New Year's Day meeting with the chiefs had not yielded results, "no blood should be shed." Instead, Sully suggested that U.S. troops attempt to kidnap Mountain Chief and half a dozen of his men, holding them hostage until the Indians produced Owl Child's gang and the stolen livestock. Hardie was nonplussed and could only guess at the reasons behind Sully's second thoughts.[21]

Joe Kipp returned on 12 January to report that he had found various Blackfeet groups dispersed in winter camps along the Marias, with Mountain Chief's band among them. The next day, Hardie wrote to division headquarters to offer his assessment. The inspector general was intelligent, a thorough and careful man who presented the cases made by Sully and de Trobriand with evenhandedness. But in the end he endorsed the Frenchman's perspective, and urged Sheridan to deploy Major Eugene Baker—who was already en route to Fort Shaw with four companies of the Second U.S. Cavalry—against the Indians. Sheridan wrote back by telegraph two days later with his instructions: "If the lives and property of citizens of Montana can best be protected by striking Mountain Chief's band of Piegans, I want them struck. Tell Baker to strike them *hard*."[22] Sheridan's emphasis on the final word was deliberate and offered a clear indication of what was in store.

THE SECOND U.S. CAVALRY traces its origins to May 1836, when it was established to defend the nation's borders and facilitate westward expansion. Known until 1861 as the Second Dragoons, the regiment developed a lasting reputation for valor on the battlefield and liquor-fueled unruliness in the garrison. Though the unit earned laurels in combat against Seminoles and Mexicans during the 1840s, it secured immortality in the crucible of the Civil War. That conflict produced luminaries like General John Buford, who served as "the *beau ideal* of later generations of cavalrymen" for his heroic performance at Gettysburg, in which he seized the high ground for the Union on the battle's first day and refused to surrender it.[23]

The troops of the Second Cavalry exhibited similar fortitude in the opening weeks of 1870, when the United States was engaged in a battle against another internal foe: the native peoples of the trans-Mississippi West. Few were tested quite like the detachment that marched nearly two hundred miles from Fort Ellis to Fort Shaw in eight days, arriving on 14 January. Like most of the army's western outposts, the fort—named in honor of Colonel Robert Gould Shaw of Massachusetts, who had died leading one of the first black regiments during the Civil War—was little more than a collection of squat adobe buildings ringing a small parade ground. Given the inadequate shelter for both the men and their animals, the soldiers pitched their field tents outdoors and tried to keep warm, despite the most unforgiving winter weather seen in Montana in more than a decade. At such times troops often wore everything they had: several layers of shirts and underclothes, two pairs of pants, and an overcoat of buffalo or bearskin. Sometimes even these measures were insufficient: one contemporary observer estimated that frostbite blackened the faces and extremities of more than 10 percent of soldiers stationed on the northern Plains.[24]

Commanding this squadron was Major Eugene M. Baker, a thirty-two-year-old native of rural upstate New York with extensive military experience in the West. Though he had muddled through the USMA without drawing much notice, Baker had developed into an accomplished officer during the Civil War. In fact, while leading a cavalry regiment during Sheridan's ravaging of the Shenandoah Valley, he had so impressed the general that five years later Sheridan handpicked him to lead the expedition against the Piegans. Baker was equally popular with his subordinates, who marveled at his stature (tall, strong, and thickly bearded—the epitome of an American frontier soldier) and delighted in his common touch, born of a humble upbringing. However, as one member of the Second Cavalry remembered, these qualities also had a sanitizing effect, as they "did much toward bringing [the troops] into forgetfulness [of] some of the reprehensible traits of his character," which included alcoholism and the loose exercise of authority.[25]

Joining the Second Cavalry at Fort Shaw were 130 soldiers of the Thirteenth U.S. Infantry (55 mounted troops and 75 foot soldiers) as well as a few dozen civilians, none more important than the two scouts, Joe Kipp and Joe Cobell. The twenty-year-old Kipp was an obvious choice, given his earlier work at the post and especially his familiarity with both the landscape and the Blackfeet, who called him Choe Keepah. The selection of Cobell, an Italian immigrant who had come to the Upper Missouri as a fur trader in the 1850s, was more surprising, because his marriage to one of Mountain Chief's sisters should have raised concerns about his partiality.[26]

Eugene M. Baker, ca. 1859. Baker's class photo from his time at West Point shows a young officer on the rise. The Empire State native became a personal favorite of General Phil Sheridan's during the Civil War, but Baker's destruction of Heavy Runner's camp in 1870 shattered the reputations of both men and hastened Baker's retreat into alcoholism. Courtesy of the U.S. Military Academy Archives, class album collection.

Barracks, Fort Shaw, 2007. While some members of the force that traveled to the Big Bend of the Marias bunked here in January 1870, many others had to pitch tents on the parade ground and brave the winter weather, which was brutal even by Montana's standards. Photograph by the author.

By contrast, there was no doubting the motives of two other civilians preparing to ride out with the Second Cavalry. Having received de Trobriand's permission to join the expedition, Horace and Nathan Clarke joined Baker and his men when the cavalry passed through the Prickly Pear Valley on its way to Fort Shaw.[27] De Trobriand probably struggled with the decision; the boys' desire to avenge their murdered father would no doubt add an unpredictable element to the mission. Moreover, Horace—though fully recovered—was still only a few months removed from his brush with death. In the end the Frenchman may have regretted his acquiescence, as Horace rashly spilled the particulars of the campaign to a newspaper reporter; that scuttled de Trobriand's best efforts to keep all military preparations secret, lest the Indians get warning from liquor traders eager to protect their best customers.[28]

Nevertheless, by the time this story appeared in print on 21 January 1870, it proved too late to warn the Piegans. Two days earlier, Baker had taken advantage of a slight break in the weather to lead

his party, swollen now to nearly four hundred men, away from Fort
Shaw and on toward the Indians' winter camps along the Marias
River, seventy-five miles to the north. De Trobriand's simple orders
to Baker left much to the discretion of the commanding officer. But
on one thing he (and especially his superiors in Chicago) had steadfastly insisted: the troops were not to molest in any way the friendly
camps of Heavy Runner and the other Piegan chiefs who had met
with Sully on New Year's Day. Phil Sheridan was determined that
this victory would be as clean as it was decisive, denying the humanitarians who had fulminated against him after the Washita battle the
chance to wring their hands or shake their fists.[29]

THE SUN RIVER rises in the Rocky Mountains and then flows in a
southeasterly course through north-central Montana, traveling 130
miles before emptying into the Missouri at the present-day city
of Great Falls. The Piegans called the stream Natoe-osucti, which
means "sun" or "medicine" river, the latter referring perhaps to the
extraordinary purity of its cold waters. In the 1860s, as whites began
to pour into the region, the Sun River provided another sort of medicine, serving as a de facto boundary between the Blackfeet and the
newcomers. South of the river lay the mines and the major American
settlements, Helena chief among them, but north of the stream was
Indian country, stretching out 120 miles to the Canadian border.

At around ten in the morning on Thursday, 19 January 1870,
Major Eugene M. Baker and his troops splashed across the icy Sun as
they moved out to the north from Fort Shaw.[30] The few men remaining behind in the garrison stood at attention as the band played a musical salute, but these gestures probably did little to cheer the outbound
soldiers. Though the weather had warmed a bit in the morning light,
the mercury still registered a blistering thirty degrees below zero, and
adding to the troopers' discomfort, no doubt, were the unknown
dangers ahead. If the U.S. military had won several victories over

Plains Indian groups in recent years, it had also tasted some wrenching defeats, like the Fetterman Massacre of December 1866, in which a combined force of Arapahos, Cheyennes, and Sioux ambushed a detachment of U.S. soldiers near Fort Phil Kearny in what is now north-central Wyoming, killing all eighty of the soldiers, including twenty-seven members of Company C, Second U.S. Cavalry.[31]

Baker's column on that mid-January morning was formidable, a long procession of men, horses, and supply carts threading across the valley. To ward off the chill, the soldiers wrapped their torsos in blankets and their feet in burlap, casting them as dark figures that stood out in high relief against the pale background of the snowy terrain. Their visibility worried Baker, who wanted to preserve the element of surprise, not only for his advantage on the battlefield but also to prevent his Indian quarry from fleeing to safer realms in Canada. Baker thus settled on a strategy that, while reasonable, only added to his detachment's misery: after the first day's march, the column would lay up during daylight hours and push onward through the night. The soldiers made twenty miles before darkness fell on 19 January, at which point they pitched their camp in the shadow of Priest Butte, a 4,100-foot summit near the Teton River. Despite the brutal cold, the few fires that Baker allowed were kept small in order to preclude detection.

The next day was full of little else but waiting. Because the men would not move out until nightfall, they huddled for warmth in the frozen camp, tending their horses and checking their equipment while trying to ward off the strange emotional twins typical of a military campaign: anxiety and boredom. Some of the troops may have turned to the bottle for comfort, as was later claimed by one member of the company, who remembered that throughout the mission the soldiers "tried to keep their spirits up by taking spirits down."[32] This charge—to which Baker was highly susceptible, given his widespread reputation as a drunk—would prove particularly damaging in the aftermath of the operation.

As light faded on the evening of 20 January, the column resumed its march, following the south bank of the Teton River in a north-easterly direction for twenty-two miles. With the first fingers of dawn on the next morning, Baker ordered another halt, and the soldiers bivouacked at the mouth of Muddy Creek. There was no rest for Joe Cobell and Joe Kipp, however, as Baker dispatched his scouts to reconnoiter the area and make certain that the column's intended route was clear of Indians and whiskey traders who might alert the enemy to the advancing troops.

At dusk on 21 January the men once again broke camp, though now they left the Teton and traveled north across open country, right into the heart of the Blackfeet winter campgrounds. The ter-rain in this part of Montana is perilous: undulating plain fractured by hundreds of coulees, steep gulches that run dry in the summer but fill with snow during the colder months and thus pose a consider-able hazard for travelers, especially those on horseback. After twenty exhausting miles, the column struck the dry fork of the Marias River around daybreak on 22 January and set up camp. This time Baker forbade the making of any fires, for he was certain that the Piegan hostiles were close at hand. His shivering men had no choice except to bundle themselves against the piercing chill and to stave off their hunger with cold food.

As the sun slipped behind the Rockies that afternoon, the column shoved off once again, moving to the northeast along the riverbed toward its intersection with the Marias. Sometime that night, after the soldiers had traveled about eleven miles, Baker's intuition was rewarded—his scouts located a small group of five Piegan lodges pitched near the juncture with the Marias. The troops quickly sur-rounded the encampment and awakened the sleeping inhabitants. From the terrified Indians, Baker learned that the camp belonged to a headman named Gray Wolf, but that Mountain Chief and two other wanted Indians—Big Horn and Red Horn—were settled together five to ten miles downstream, at the Big Bend.

With this news, Baker swung into action. First, he sent a small detachment twenty miles upriver to the North West Company fur post under the command of a trader named Riplinger. (De Trobriand had written such instructions into Baker's orders, so that in the event of Indian retaliation the dozen or so employees there would have protection.) Next, he broke off the supply train from the main column, leaving the wagons, their drivers, and a squad of infantrymen to keep watch over Gray Wolf and his followers. Baker then directed the balance of his troops to move rapidly downriver, following a wide trail that ran parallel to the river. He hoped to reach the camp before daybreak.

IN THE GLOAMING, Bear Head worked his way through the timber in search of his horses. The boy was frustrated, for he had planned to go out with a hunting party the day before but had been unable to locate his mounts, which had drifted off into the woods above the camp at the Big Bend. Still, the young Piegan was determined to join the buffalo hunters, even if it meant an arduous ride to overtake them. Though he was only fourteen years old, many people depended upon him. Two years earlier, Owl Child had killed Bear Head's father in a dispute, leaving the boy to care for the dead man's four wives as well as their daughters. Hence the boy's desperation to bring food back to the campsite, where his leader, Heavy Runner, had settled his smallpox-ravaged band in mid-January after Mountain Chief abandoned the location in favor of another spot a few miles downriver.[33]

Just as Bear Head spotted his horses on that frigid morning, a throng of soldiers apprehended him. He recalled years later, "I was so astonished, so frightened, that I could not move." One of the troops, who the boy guessed was an officer because of the yellow metal stripes on his uniform, seized Bear Head by the arm and touched his finger to his lips. Still clutching the boy, the soldier advanced toward the camp, dragging Bear Head behind him. When they arrived at the edge of a bluff overlooking the Big Bend, the boy was petrified to see dozens of soldiers stretched out in a line to his right. Despite the troops left upriver and the fact that every fourth man on the bluffs that morning was a horse holder, Baker still had nearly two hundred guns trained on the thirty-seven lodges below.

In the camp all was quiet, as the Piegans—mostly women, children, and old men, given the recent departure of the hunters—slept, some of them fitfully, as their bodies tried to fight off the dreaded "white scabs" disease burning through the village. Whatever concerns they might have had during that bleak midwinter, a surprise attack by U.S. soldiers was probably not among them, considering their chief's well-known status as a friend to the whites. But just before dawn, the barking of the Indians' dogs suggested that something was amiss.

At Heavy Runner's lodge, located in the middle of the camp, a visitor rousted the headman with news that soldiers had been spotted nearby. Citing his good relationship with the *napikwans*, the chief attempted to calm his panicked followers, insisting that there was nothing to fear. With that, he took his "name paper" (Alfred Sully's note of safe passage), opened his tent, and began walking purposefully toward the bluffs, waving the document high over his head.[34]

Up on the ridge, Joe Kipp had broken the stillness demanded by Baker. As the sun rose higher in the sky, the scout had recognized to his horror that the markings on the central teepee were those of Heavy Runner, and not of Mountain Chief, as Kipp had anticipated. Realizing his mistake and the disaster about to ensue, Kipp shouted frantically to Baker that the unsuspecting encampment below was the wrong target; in fact, it was one of the villages the troops were expressly ordered to avoid. Baker, however, hissed at Kipp to fall silent and placed him under guard.

At that moment Heavy Runner emerged from the camp below, brandishing his paper and, according to some accounts, a peace medal as well. Before he could reach the troops and establish his identity, the chief was hit by a single shot and fell to the snow, clutching Sully's note to his chest. Years later a relative of Joe Cobell's stated that Cobell himself had confessed to cutting down Heavy Runner, and for deeply personal reasons: the scout knew that if fighting broke out at the Big Bend, Mountain Chief's band, into which Cobell had intermarried, would have sufficient time to strike their campsite and head for safety beyond the Medicine Line.[35]

Following the initial blast, the other soldiers on the bluffs opened fire immediately. Most of the men were armed with Springfield rifles or Sharps carbines, both of which used a heavy, .50-70 caliber brass cartridge, an earsplitting charge strong enough to bring down buffalo and other heavy game.[36] The soldiers aimed not only at the sides of the fragile skin tents but shot also at the bindings attached to the lodge poles, so that some of the teepees collapsed on the cooking fires within, suffocating or incinerating their smallpox-ravaged inhabitants. Though virtually no resistance came from the camp, firing continued unabated for almost an hour before Baker called a halt to the shooting and then loosed his cavalrymen upon the Piegans. The troopers swept down from the ridge and charged into the defenseless camp with pistols or sabers drawn, shooting and slashing indiscriminately as the Indians sought cover among the few lodges still standing. The foot soldiers were right behind them, however, cutting their way into the teepees and dispatching those hiding inside.[37] Other troops, who had forded the river just before the shooting began, rounded up captives and corralled the Indians' sizable horse herd. It was all over before midday.

With the end of the skirmish, Bear Head, whom his captor had dragged all the way to the village, was finally released. The dazed boy picked his way among the smoldering ruins of the camp until he found his own tent, which like the others had been utterly destroyed. He stood before the carnage and felt sick. "In the center of the fallen lodge," he remembered, "where the poles had fallen upon the

fire, it had burned a little, then died out. I could not pull up the
lodge-skin and look under it. I could not bear to see my mother, my
almost-mothers, my almost-sisters lying there, shot or smothered to
death." In time he was joined by a handful of survivors, who wept at
the soldiers' terrible cruelty and mourned the violent deaths of those
who had done no wrong.[38] Thereafter the Blackfeet called the Big
Bend Itomot´ahpi Pikun´i—Killed Off the Piegans.[39]

IN THE AFTERMATH of the fight, Major Baker conferred with his officers and scouts. From Kipp and Cobell he received definitive word via
Indian survivors that the annihilated camp was indeed that of Heavy
Runner, the one headman Baker had been explicitly instructed to
avoid. Mountain Chief, Baker learned, had moved his village a few
miles down the Marias. Baker hurriedly adjusted his plans, ordering
Lieutenant Gus Doane and F Company to remain at the Big Bend
while the major himself led the rest of the troops downriver in search
of the other encampment.

Though best known for his role in escorting the Washburn-
Langford expedition through the Yellowstone region in the fall of
1870 (a 10,500-foot mountain in the park is named for him), Gustavus Cheyney Doane was also a magnificent field soldier.[40] Born
in Illinois in 1840, the tall, powerfully built cavalryman—easily recognizable by his long, waxed mustache—was held in high esteem
by his comrades, who admired his courage and integrity. For those
reasons, Baker tasked him with a grim assignment: burning all of the
Piegans' supplies and tallying the dead. That afternoon the lieutenant counted 173 Indians killed in action, later reported by Baker
to have consisted of 120 able-bodied men and 53 women and children (numbers strenuously debated afterward).[41] Though Joe Kipp
claimed to have seen 217 bodies, Doane's became the official figure; the lieutenant deemed the engagement the "greatest slaughter
of Indians ever made by U.S. troops."[42] Baker's men, by contrast,

suffered only one fatality in the battle: Private Walton McKay, a twenty-four-year-old Canadian who was shot through the forehead when he peered into an Indian tent after the cavalry charge.[43]

Meanwhile, Baker's trip downriver took longer than expected. By the time he arrived that afternoon, the Indians had fled, leaving behind a hastily abandoned camp of seven lodges. As Baker expected, Mountain Chief, Owl Child, and some of the other wanted men had crossed to safety beyond the forty-ninth parallel, marked at that time simply by mounds of dirt or stone cairns but representing a haven from the vengeful Americans. There would be no satisfaction for either Horace Clarke or Bear Head, both of whom had lost their fathers at the hand of Ne-tus-che-o: the Indian renegade supposedly died several days later of smallpox, thus depriving the sons of the murdered men of an opportunity to exact their vengeance. Baker and his detachment camped at the site that evening and then burned the deserted lodges the following day.

The killing at the Big Bend, however, had not ended completely when the soldiers' guns fell silent. That evening eight warriors taken prisoner tried to escape, and after their recapture an enraged Lieutenant Doane ordered the Indians dispatched. When some enlisted men reached for their rifles, Doane barked, "No, don't use your guns . . . Get axes and kill them one at a time." Bear Head claimed to have overheard this conversation, and the ensuing horror. He recalled, "I hear[d] a sound as if some one was cutting up meat with an axe and a Grunt[.] I looked around and could see by the firelight one of the . . . Indians lying on the ground with his head split open."[44]

When Baker returned to the Big Bend on the morning of 24 January, Doane explained that the Indians had been killed in the act of escape (which apparently went unquestioned), and then he informed his commanding officer of a most unfortunate discovery: Heavy Runner's camp was beset with smallpox, which though not much of a danger to the soldiers (who were vaccinated) was sure to complicate the fallout with Baker's superiors as well as a skeptical public. In light of this news, Baker ordered the 140 captives freed at once, although he commandeered all of the Piegans' three hundred horses, insisting that most of them had been stolen from whites in the first place.[45] So that they might not starve, Baker left the Indians a few cases of bacon and hardtack. And then the soldiers departed, gone almost as quickly as they had appeared on the morning before.

THE SITUATION FACING the survivors now became desperate. They had no shelter, no transportation, insufficient foodstuffs, and dozens of wounded. Many others were stricken with disease. Some of the Indians found shelter with friendly bands nearby, but others decided to make the arduous, seventy-five-mile trek to Fort Benton (even though many whites there loathed native people). The members of Heavy Runner's family composed one such group. As Spear Woman, the dead man's daughter—who was just a little girl in 1870—recalled many decades later, she and her mother and three siblings (one of them an infant) followed the soldiers' tracks for a time, scavenging any of the column's discarded food and supplies that they found along the way. After a few days they reached Fort Benton, but not before the baby perished.[46]

Baker and his men arrived at Fort Shaw on Sunday, 29 January. There the troops were met by the exuberant Colonel de Trobriand, who three days earlier had received unofficial word of the incident on the Marias. De Trobriand joyously telegrammed to his superiors, "The result of the expedition shows how well it has been conducted by [Baker], and I am Confident that peace and safety is secured for a long time to the Territory."[47] In fact, the colonel was so pleased that a few weeks later he wrote again to his commanders to praise Baker for his "activity, energy, and judgment" while recommending him for a brevet.[48]

For his part, Baker simply wanted to return to Fort Ellis, given the space constraints at Fort Shaw that had inconvenienced his men

Officers of the Second U.S. Calvary at Fort Ellis, 1871. This photo depicts Baker (ninth from left, leaning with his left hand on the fence post) and some of his officers, the year after the Marias Massacre. Lieutenant Gustavus Cheney Doane is fourth from left. Courtesy of the Montana Historical Society.

on the outbound leg of their campaign. Thus on 31 January he led his troops southeast to Fort Ellis, where they arrived on 6 February, precisely one month after their expedition began. All told, the soldiers had traveled more than six hundred miles, and—as Baker explained in his initial report—"in the coldest weather that has been known in Montana for years."[49] Yet even as his troops recuperated from their travails, a storm of a different sort was gathering and would soon break upon the major. In time this tempest would come to engulf not only Phil Sheridan but also William Sherman himself.

The Spoils of Victory

News of the incident on the Marias reverberated throughout Montana and the larger Rocky Mountain West, trumpeted with a jingoistic fervor and greeted with elation by area whites. On 2 February the *Helena Daily Herald* ran a story that began, "The deed is done: the murder of Malcolmb Clark has been avenged; the guilty Indians have been punished, and a terrible warning has been given to others of our red-skinned brethren, who may be inclined to live by murdering and plundering the white man."[50] Meanwhile, the *New North-West* published a resolution submitted by citizens of the Deer Lodge Valley stating, "That we do most heartily and sincerely indorse the manner of treaty then and there made [on the Marias] with those and all others of our red brethren who inhabit the soil of Montana."[51] Neither broadsheet, however, matched the vitriol of Idaho Territory's *Owyhee Avalanche*, which defended Baker by invoking alleged Indian atrocities and suggested hyperbolically that henceforth the army should "[k]ill and roast [the Indians] as they do the pale face. Kill the squaws so the accursed race may cease to propagate. Kill the pappooses."[52]

Expressions of gratitude poured in for Sherman, Sheridan, and Baker from all corners of Montana.[53] There were even scattered encomia for Colonel de Trobriand, who just a few months earlier had elicited jeers from the territory's white residents for his refusal to dispatch the cavalry against the Piegans. The Frenchman explained in a smug missive to his daughter in late January, "The settlers haven't raised a statue to me," though he expressed confidence that they would fondly remember him after he departed for his next posting in Utah.[54] Sure enough, on a visit to Helena a few weeks later, de Trobriand was flattered when during dinner at a local restaurant the maître d'hôtel threw open the windows facing the street so that grateful residents of the city might serenade him (even as they mauled the pronunciation of his last name).[55]

Sherman, however, was far less sanguine. He warned Sheridan in late January to "look out for the cries of those who think the Indians are so harmless, and obtain all possible evidence concerning the murders charged on them."[56] In the end, the general of the army was right to worry about a backlash, although he probably never imagined that it would originate from within his own ranks.

On 6 February, Lieutenant William B. Pease, the Indian agent for the Blackfeet, wrote Alfred Sully to describe a recent visit he had made (on Sully's orders) to an Indian camp containing some survivors of the massacre. Those Piegans who had witnessed Baker's attack gave Pease a very different account of the native casualties suffered at the Big Bend. They explained that smallpox was rife in the camp and that only 33 men were among the dead. The rest of the 140 victims were women and children, all of the latter under the age of twelve "and many of them in their mothers' arms." Pease added that in the aftermath of the slaughter most of the Piegans had fled across the forty-ninth parallel into Canada, and that those Blackfeet remaining in Montana were terribly frightened "and not disposed to retaliate upon the whites for the death of their friends."[57]

Four days later Sully transmitted Pease's report to Ely Parker, a Seneca Indian who had served as Ulysses S. Grant's military secretary during the Civil War and in that capacity drafted the terms of surrender signed by Robert E. Lee at Appomattox; as president, Grant had appointed Parker commissioner of Indian affairs in 1869. Realizing the incendiary nature of the agent's allegations, Sully insisted in his cover letter that by forwarding the dispatch he was not taking sides in the matter; rather, he was simply giving the Indians a fair hearing, which he believed was his duty "as their only representative."[58] This distinction, however, had disappeared by the time Lieutenant Pease's account became public later that month. During debate over an army appropriations bill in the U.S. House of Representatives on 25 February, a letter from Vincent Colyer, secretary of the Board of Indian Commissioners, was read aloud to the chamber. In his missive Colyer cited the dispatch of Lieutenant Pease in referring to the "sickening details of Colonel Baker's attack," adding that these "facts" were "indorsed by General Sully, United States Army."[59] A heated discussion of the subject quickly ensued, as congressmen rose both in defense and in condemnation of Colyer's accusations.

Such indignation was not confined to the halls of government. The *New York Times*, which had received an advance copy of Colyer's letter, published a scathing editorial on 24 February. Noting that it had supported a series of recent strikes against native peoples, including Custer's raid on Black Kettle's encampment in November 1868, the *Times* insisted that on this occasion there could be no defense of such "butchery" and called for an official investigation.[60] Likewise, the editors at *Harper's Weekly* suggested to their 100,000 readers that the Marias massacre was just the latest episode in "our Indian policy of extermination," an ugly pattern that stretched back more than two centuries to the colonial period. The piece ended with a flourish, wondering whether instead of killing Indians "the army should not rather be directed against our own people, whose endless cheating and lawlessness rouse their victims to revenge."[61]

Colyer's letter had a chilling effect within the military establishment, which was anxious to avoid the sort of public chastisement it had absorbed in the wake of the Washita debacle. On 26 February, Sherman's office sent a telegram fraught with concern to General Sheridan, requesting Baker's official report of the incident, which had not yet been received in Washington. Sheridan replied that he would furnish the information as soon as it was available, but then gave over the greater part of his letter to a scorching denunciation of Colyer, whom the general condemned as a tool of the so-called Indian ring, a nebulous web of supposedly corrupt individuals who profited from government contracts made through the Bureau of Indian Affairs. Sheridan went on to recount the base horrors he had seen in the West perpetrated by native peoples—rapes, thefts, and murders. He added, "It would appear that Mr. Vincent Colyer wants this work to go on."[62] Little Phil's rage was understandable: the hero of the Shenandoah knew he was facing one of the greatest political crises of his career.

THOUGH INCENSED BY the affront to his reputation, Sheridan was also vexed by the timing of the controversy, which could not have broken at a more inopportune moment. As it happened, in January 1870 the House of Representatives began debate on legislation that had as one of its key provisions the transfer of the Indian Bureau from the Department of the Interior back to the Department of War, where it had originally resided from the founding of the United States until 1849. The military had sought to regain control of Indian affairs ever since and seemed poised to score a decisive victory that spring. The uproar over Baker's campaign, however, went right to the heart of the explosive post–Civil War dispute over federal Indian policy and threatened to derail the transfer initiative.[63]

At issue in the larger conversation about the "Indian problem" was the best method for avoiding native-white conflict, especially on the Great Plains. With the resumption of American westward expansion after 1865, most evident in the frenzied pace of railroad construction, the trans-Mississippi region had convulsed with spasms of horrific violence. None was more controversial than the Sand Creek Massacre of November 1864, in the midst of the Civil War no less, when militiamen under the command of Colonel John Chivington murdered more than 150 pacific Cheyennes and Arapahos in eastern Colorado and later displayed their scalps and severed genitalia in a Denver theater.[64] The slaughter and other army-Indian clashes throughout the late 1860s caused escalating public outrage, so that when President Ulysses S. Grant took office in March 1869 he vowed to make sweeping changes in the management of Indian affairs. Grant's "peace policy," as it came to be known, emphasized "conquest through kindness" and featured the use of religious groups to Christianize Indians as part of the "civilizing" process.[65]

Like most military men, Grant favored the transfer of Indian affairs to the War Department, for he believed that army officers were less prone to the corruption and ineptitude typical of civilian bureaucrats at the Department of the Interior. Grant did not surrender this conviction when he took up residence in the White House; rather, he reserved the overwhelming number of Indian agency appointments for military officers, giving only a few such positions to Quaker missionaries. Sherman and especially Sheridan were even more adamant than the president about transfer; Sheridan testified before Congress that the use of army personnel in these roles would save untold sums of money while also protecting native peoples from the vicious designs of the unscrupulous Indian ring.[66]

The generals and their backers, however, faced stiff opposition from the Department of the Interior. Among the most outspoken of their opponents was Nathaniel Taylor, the commissioner of Indian affairs and also the chairman of the Peace Commission, an eight-member body established by Congress in July 1867 to treat with native peoples in the hopes of averting additional bloodshed on the Plains. Writing for the commission in January 1868, Taylor enumerated eleven key reasons why the Interior Department should retain control of Indian affairs, including the inability of the War Department to handle such vast administrative responsibilities and the inherent dangers to civil liberty posed by the maintenance of a large standing army. The crux of Taylor's opposition, however, was the glaring contradiction between promoting peace with native peoples while simultaneously investing the War Department with total authority over them.[67]

Advocates of transfer were undeterred by these arguments or the fact that they had failed to achieve their goal of military oversight of Indian affairs on several previous occasions in the postbellum period. One such failed attempt in 1867 had even been spearheaded in the Senate by John Sherman of Ohio, the general's younger brother, but to no avail. And yet by decade's end the ground seemed to have shifted in favor of the War Department, in large part because of renewed native-white hostilities on the southern Plains in the summer and fall of 1868. That violence led to Sheridan's winter campaign and also caused some members of the Peace Commission to reconsider the wisdom of extending the olive branch to recalcitrant Indian bands.

Thus supporters of transfer pushed the issue vigorously as an amendment to the army appropriations bill before the House of

Representatives in the early months of 1870. Surely, they thought, with Grant in office its passage was guaranteed. The partisan *Army and Navy Journal*, so often disappointed in the outcome of previous debates on the issue, expressed optimism in late February that victory was finally at hand, and that with the transfer Indian affairs would at last be overseen by "a set of officers not only respected for their integrity and professional honor, but necessarily subjected to responsibility and accountability, such as the civil service never can furnish."[68]

Such hopefulness proved unfounded. The conflagration over the Piegan affair consumed the proposed legislation as congressmen opposed to the transfer used the scandal to cudgel the military's supporters. Few were more enthusiastic in this regard than Indiana's Daniel Voorhees, "the tall sycamore of the Wabash," who, after hearing the contents of Vincent Colyer's letter, rose before the chamber and declared in regard to Baker's strike, "It cannot be justified here or before the country; it cannot be justified before the civilization of the age, or in the sight of God or man. . . . I shall not vote for one dollar of an appropriation that upholds such a system of warfare as the indiscriminate massacre of all ages and both sexes, the innocent as well as the guilty."[69]

In the face of such passionate opposition, even the bill's sponsor, John Logan of Illinois, disavowed the transfer amendment. The *New York Times* explained that "after [Logan] had read the account of the Piegan massacre his blood ran cold in his veins, and he wanted to ask the Committee to strike out that section [regarding transfer] and let the Indian Bureau remain where it is, and the Committee had agreed to that."[70] On 26 March, one month to the day after it had written with such hope about War Department control of Indian affairs, the *Army and Navy Journal* bemoaned the timing of the news from Montana and its calamitous effect, saying of the transfer proposal that "it seems to have been stricken out by general consent, and it had no friends to say a word for it."[71]

Nevertheless, the transfer movement survived throughout the

1870s, being raised periodically by military supporters in Congress but failing on each occasion and dying out altogether before the end of the decade. By that time even some of its most ardent proponents, like the representative and future president James A. Garfield of Ohio, conceded that sweeping reforms in the Indian Bureau had made the switch unnecessary. But as Garfield had also acknowledged several years earlier on the House floor, victory on the transfer issue was within his grasp in the spring of 1870, but "while we were expecting it to become a law, the Piegan massacre occurred which shocked the sensibilities of the whole nation . . . and it of course failed to become a law."[72]

As IT TURNED OUT, the contretemps over the transfer issue was merely the opening act in a larger drama concerning the Marias massacre. And if the actors in the first scene were politicians and bureaucrats, succeeding them on the national stage were humanitarians and reformers, many of them battle-tested veterans of the abolitionist cause. To the extreme vexation of Sheridan and Sherman, they were cast once again as the fools.

It stood to reason that, with the end of the Civil War and the ratification of the Thirteenth Amendment, some antislavery activists would turn their attention to the plight of native peoples.[73] After all, the mistreatment of Indians had long been an abolitionist concern, dating at least to the anguished debates over Indian removal during the 1820s and 1830s. Indeed, during the presidency of Andrew Jackson, a young William Lloyd Garrison inveighed against Old Hickory's forced deportation of the Cherokees and the Creeks, among others, likening their ejection from the South to the proposed schemes for African colonization.[74] The gaunt-faced Garrison accordingly linked the suffering of native peoples and the enslaved in the nameplate of his newspaper, the *Liberator*, which depicted Indian treaties crushed underfoot by slave auctioneers.[75]

Perhaps the leading figure from the abolitionist movement to take up the Indian cause was Lydia Maria Child.[76] Born in Massachusetts in 1802 and probably best remembered for her Thanksgiving song "Over the River and through the Wood," the prim and serious Child played such crucial roles in various nineteenth-century reform efforts, from antislavery to women's suffrage, that Garrison christened her "the first woman in the republic." While some of her earliest published work in the 1820s dealt with the injustices heaped upon native peoples by white Americans, for most of the antebellum period Child dedicated her energies to the eradication of human bondage, even serving as editor of the *National Anti-Slavery Standard* from 1841 to 1843.[77]

When Child, by then in her sixties, returned to the Indian question in the aftermath of the Civil War, she did so in typically provocative fashion. Her April 1868 essay "An Appeal for the Indians," written in response to the report of the Peace Commission published earlier that year, outlined a gradual plan for native acculturation that, in time, would allow Indians to fully assimilate into mainstream American society. But Child devoted most of her commentary to a blistering indictment of federal Indian policy, placing the preponderance of blame for the Indian Wars on the shoulders of the U.S. government and its white citizens, who she argued were the true barbarians.[78]

Whatever its strident tone, "An Appeal for the Indians" was positively temperate by comparison with Child's full-scale literary assault on the military establishment in the wake of the Piegan massacre. Published in the *Standard* in May 1870, "The Indians" read more like a sermon than a piece of journalism, invoking the infamous British slaughter of some thirty-eight Scottish Highlanders at Glencoe in 1692, which—like Baker's attack on the Marias—caused the deaths of women and children from exposure after they were turned out of their homes. Insisting that unvarnished racism had animated the butchery in Montana, Child wrote, "Shame on General Sheridan for perpetrating such outrages on a people because they were poor, and weak, and despised! Shame on General Sherman for sanctioning it! They have tarnished their laurels and disgraced the epaulets they wear."[79]

Child's was hardly the lone humanitarian voice on the matter. At an 18 May 1870 meeting of the U.S. Indian Commission (which, despite the name, was a private group established in 1868 by the New York philanthropist Peter Cooper), a letter from the prominent Boston abolitionist Wendell Phillips was read to the audience. In his letter Phillips insisted that "[e]very American ought to blush at this nation's treatment of the Indians" and that "[t]he hands of Sheridan are foul with Indian blood, shed by assassins who acted under his orders and received his approval." Not to be outdone, William Lloyd Garrison, Phillips's fellow abolitionist and sometime adversary, sent his own note, maintaining that if the humanitarian response "be loud, the language explicit, the action uncompromising . . . these [protests] will not be in vain."[80]

For their part, the embattled generals pushed back strenuously against their detractors. In a lengthy public missive to Sherman, Sheridan tried to explain away the deaths of Piegan noncombatants with a Civil War analogy: "Did we cease to throw shells into Vicksburg or Atlanta because women or children were there?" And yet by the end of the note Little Phil seemed resigned to his fate, explaining that with the onrushing tide of white settlers, Indians—for the safety of both parties—had to move to reservations and remain there, by force of arms if necessary.[81] Sherman, meanwhile, took his critics head-on, in a letter to the same meeting of the U.S. Indian Commission where the messages from Phillips and Garrison had been read. While praising the good intentions of those gathered in New York, the wizened general patiently explained that "the Indian question is a practical one, and not one of mere feeling," and that if the humanitarians truly wished to appreciate the complexities of the situation, he would be happy to meet them "where the Indians are," in Kansas, Wyoming, or Dakota Territory.[82]

In the end, though, in the battle for public opinion it was the frail and bespectacled agitator who prevailed over the grim-visaged warrior. The unyielding "remonstrances" urged by Garrison took their toll during the spring and summer of 1870; they led eventually to a defeat far more painful than the orphaning of the transfer amendment for Sherman and his military brethren. The final version of the House army appropriations bill signed into law on 15 July 1870 forbade officers from holding positions in the civil service, thus ending the practice of installing soldiers as Indian agents.[83] Not only did this prohibition accelerate the military's lessening influence over native affairs, but it also deprived the army of much-needed patronage jobs, which now went exclusively to Christian missionaries. Thus began a new era of sweeping Indian reform, one grounded in religious education and moral suasion, an approach first proposed in 1864 by none other than Alfred Sully.

Ironically, the new legislation cost Sully and William Pease— both labeled as whistle-blowers—their jobs in Montana, and having incurred the hatred of their superior officers they saw their military careers stall abruptly. Lieutenant Pease, whose report of the massacre ignited the scandal in the East, soon found himself barred by Colonel de Trobriand from making social calls to Fort Shaw, and threatened with forced ejection if he returned to the post on anything other than official business.[84] In December, Pease rejoined his infantry regiment, but would not receive a promotion to captain for thirteen years, the rank at which he retired in 1887. Sully, whom Sherman accused to Sheridan of "doing an unofficerlike and wrong act" by transmitting Pease's account to Washington, may have suffered even more, for he bounced from one assignment to the next and grew more bitter with each new posting, before dying in Washington Territory in April 1879, at the age of fifty-seven.[85]

Fittingly, perhaps, it was Eugene Baker who fell the hardest. Despite Sheridan's unwavering support throughout the spring and summer of 1870, Piegan Baker, as the major came to be known, was unable to recapture even a glint of the promise he had shown during the Civil War. Though he remained a beloved figure among white Montanans, his bonhomie could not mask an ineluctable slide into alcoholism. In fact, his drinking nearly cost the lives of dozens of men under his command when, during a Sioux ambush in eastern Montana in the summer of 1872, Baker was so drunk that he was "inclined to treat the whole alarm as a groundless fright." Only the quick thinking of his subordinates averted disaster.[86] Thereafter Baker drifted about the northern Plains on various assignments, interrupted by frequent sick leaves (characterized on one occasion as a "disorder of [the] spleen and liver, splenic pain and jaundice"—sure signs of alcoholism) and at least one court-martial. By the time he died "of chronic gastritis," in December 1884 at Fort Walla Walla, he had exhausted the patience of the army: the government contributed $150 for his casket but refused to pay the cost of transporting his body for burial on the unceremonious return voyage from the Pacific Northwest to upstate New York.[87]

De-tan-a-ma-ka

On a sunny afternoon in June 1926, Horace Clarke, then seventy-seven, eased into a chair at his home in East Glacier Park to recount the story of his life.[88] His interviewer that day was Martha Plassmann, an old friend from an established Montana family who, having outlived two husbands, had devoted her later years to socialist causes and especially to historical writing. Since Clarke was among the most knowledgeable authorities on the state's colorful frontier past, Plassmann had eagerly traveled the 140 miles from her home in Great Falls in order to chat with him, and they spent several hours talking in Clarke's comfortable, book-lined study.

Clarke—whom Plassmann described for her readers as "a small man with keen black eyes and hair," with a dark complexion "indicative of his Indian blood" and features resembling those of the Japanese—was in a fine mood on this occasion, springing to his feet to emphasize key points in his story and revealing admirable sharpness of mind for a man approaching eighty.[89] Plassmann must have struggled to keep up, as Clarke veered from one subject to the next and sprinkled his ramblings with provocative observations. For instance, he explained that the Blackfeet were the "cleanest" of all native peoples but confessed that he harbored deep skepticism of the typical mixed-blood (though one himself), who he felt relied too heavily on government handouts. He told Plassmann the meaning, if not the provenance, of his Indian name, De-tan-a-ma-ka, which translated as "the Man Who Stands Alone with His Gun." And he mentioned that an official in the Department of War had once asked his sister Helen to write a history of the state, but she had demurred, explaining that if "she confined herself to actual facts they would not be digestible."[90]

During the interview, however, Clarke was more reticent about the two central incidents in his life: his father's murder and the military campaign that followed. (Plassmann, on the other hand, stressed precisely this pair of events in the cover letter to her publisher pitching the resulting article.)[91] Still, Clarke did not sidestep the topics

Horace Clarke, ca. 1910s. Though nearly killed the night of his father's murder, Horace Clarke survived to avenge him at the Marias in 1870, accompanied by his younger brother, Nathan. Horace lived into his eighties and served often as a mediator between the Piegans and federal officials. Courtesy of Joyce Clarke Turvey.

altogether. Sandwiched between his description of a real estate deal and memories of a visit to Canada was a strange and haunting story about a trip he had made to Seattle years before. While en route via steamboat, Clarke became incapacitated by seasickness. He refused medical attention, but his condition worsened after he disembarked, so that he began to hallucinate as he walked the city's crowded streets. In this delusional state he imagined a meeting with a Piegan named Fog Eater, whose jaw had been shot away during the Marias Massacre. As Clarke told Plassmann, the grinning Indian said to him, "You fool. Go back home." And so after his recovery, Clarke quickly returned to Montana.[92]

His unsettling encounter, dreamlike as it was, provides a neat allegory for his enduring relationship to the Baker Massacre. Clarke spent most of his adult life pushing memories of the slaughter to the very margins of his conscience, hoping to downplay or even forget the details of that terrible day. This approach worked well for nearly half a century, until the ghosts of January 1870 caught up with him and forced their way into his consciousness in the twilight of his life.

JOE KIPP, BY contrast, would have been happy with shadowy visits from the occasional phantasm; instead, he lived forever in the harsh daylight of the massacre's aftermath, battered by his own guilt and the Piegans' scorn. Many Blackfeet held Kipp accountable for the deaths of their loved ones as well as for the inauguration of a desolate epoch for the Blackfeet, one marked by hunger, illness, and privation. Stunned that any foe would strike so viciously against the sick and frail in the dead of winter, Piegan chiefs abandoned all plans for retaliation within weeks of the slaughter and pressed for peace with the U.S. government through Jesuit intermediaries.[93] The shift in the natives' fortunes were so stark thereafter that on the tenth anniversary of Baker's campaign, a Montana writer observed, "Ever since January 1870, the Blackfeet tribes . . . have been peaceable

Historical marker, Fort Shaw, 2007. Although the Marias Massacre belongs in any discussion of the worst atrocities committed by American military forces against native peoples, it is largely forgotten today. Note that it does not merit even a passing mention on this placard commemorating Fort Shaw, the staging ground for the expedition against the Piegans in 1870. Photograph by the author.

and quiet, and it has been safe to travel all over their country."[94] In other words, the carnage at the Big Bend had secured the white conquest of the northwestern Plains. And for the Piegans, Joe Kipp—more than anyone except Baker himself—became the reification of all blame for the massacre.

Aside from his obvious responsibility in leading the troops to Heavy Runner's camp, there were other reasons why Kipp was an easy target for Piegan frustrations. For one thing, regardless of his two decades among the Blackfeet, Kipp, in the final analysis, was not one of them: his Indian heritage was Mandan. Moreover, after 1870 he developed a reputation as one of the most successful liquor traders

Joe Kipp, 1889. Born around 1850 to James Kipp, a prominent AFC trader, and a Mandan named Earth Woman, Kipp was one of two army scouts in Major Baker's employ. He mistakenly led the Second U.S. Calvary to the camp of Heavy Runner, who had been guaranteed safe passage just three weeks earlier by Lieutenant Colonel Alfred Sully. Courtesy of the Montana Historical Society.

in the Montana–Alberta borderlands, an unsavory vocation in a place ravaged by native alcoholism and its attendant social disorders.

In later years Kipp won over at least some of his detractors, aided no doubt by the intimate ties he developed with the Piegans. In one of the more poignant, if unusual, developments in the wake of the Marias Massacre, Kipp married Double Strike Woman (known also as Martha), one of Heavy Runner's daughters, and then adopted several other of the slain chief's offspring. According to a friend, Kipp doted on the children and strove to give them every advantage.[95] Nonetheless, his betrayal was so indelible that even today some on the Blackfeet Reservation who carry his name have nothing but contempt for the man. One such individual said in 1995, "I'm not about to do an Honor Dance around Joe's grave."[96]

HORACE CLARKE FARED much better, suffering little of the enmity that dogged Kipp. For instance, he explained to Plassmann that during the attack on Heavy Runner's camp, one of his own uncles had fled into the river and then turned and shot at him. When Clarke explained that he had returned fire, Plassmann asked whether he had ever regretted it: "'No,' he replied. And I am convinced he meant what he said. Ties of blood are not considered in war time."[97] Furthermore, as Clarke insisted, once he realized that the troops had ambushed the wrong camp that morning he tried to protect the embattled Indians, "but one could do little with soldiers after they had tasted blood."[98]

For their part, most Piegans seemed to give Clarke a pass, thinking that his participation in the slaughter was somehow justified by a desire to avenge his father's murder. And Clarke was reasonably insulated against native skepticism by his Piegan blood and particularly his elevated social status, which derived from his father's prominence as well as from his own entrepreneurial ventures after 1870. Whereas Kipp became a whiskey runner, dodging the law and at least once killing an obstreperous Indian customer, Clarke took a more respectable path.[99] In the mid-1870s, having sold his father's ranch in the Prickly Pear, he moved to north-central Montana near the Highwood Mountains, where he raised cattle with his wife, Margaret, a Piegan woman known by her people as First Kill.[100] Then, in 1889, he and his family moved to the small town of Midvale, later renamed East Glacier Park, just east of the Rocky Mountains, where he acquired a homestead after the allotment of the Blackfeet Reservation. With the establishment of Glacier National Park in 1910, Clarke sold a portion of his land to the Great Northern Railway, which then erected the magnificent Glacier Park Lodge, a soaring, chalet-style resort, on Clarke's former property, though Clarke himself did not became wealthy from this transaction.[101]

To be sure, Clarke knew his own share of heartache and tragedy. Of the eight children born to him and Margaret between 1876 and 1883, four died in infancy of scarlet fever and only two—John (1881–1970) and Agnes (1883–1973)—outlived their parents. Perhaps it was the agony caused by these untimely deaths that contributed to the marital strife between him and Margaret, leading to a lengthy separation followed by divorce. Margaret remarried in the 1890s, but he did not.[102] Still, by the early years of the twentieth century, Clarke appeared to have weathered better than most mixed-bloods, and certainly all Blackfeet, the sweeping changes that had utterly transformed Montana since the buffalo days of his youth. With the influence of his sister Helen, the home they shared at East Glacier Park became a literary salon, of sorts, for those visiting the magnificent lodge next door. And it was there that the ghosts of 1870 at last caught up with him, conveyed to his doorstep, if indirectly, by Joe Kipp.

On 8 February 1913 Kipp, aged sixty-three and in deteriorating health, gave a statement about his role in the Baker Massacre to Arthur McFatridge, Indian agent to the Blackfeet. Kipp's description of that fratricidal attack more than four decades earlier was concise and matter-of-fact, differing from the military's accounts on only two main points: Kipp insisted that he himself had tallied 217 dead Indians at the Big Bend (and not the 173 reported by Baker), and that afterward the U.S. soldiers had rounded up an estimated 5,000 horses (as opposed to the army figure of 300), one-tenth of which belonged to Heavy Runner alone. Kipp added that he had been only fifty or sixty yards distant from the headman when he fell, and that upon discovering Heavy Runner's note of safe passage, the troops hurriedly buried the chief in the ground (violating the Indian custom of placing the deceased in trees), presumably to conceal the evidence.[103]

While Kipp's testimony might have been an effort to clear his conscience before he died later that year, there was also a practical reason for his statement. Joe's adopted son Richard (usually called Dick), along with two of Richard's half siblings, Emma Miller and William Upham (born to one of Heavy Runner's other wives), had enlisted McFatridge to assist them in winning compensation from the federal government for the chief's murder and the theft of his horses. And it was no small sum the Indians were after: $75,000. Why the claimants decided to act at that particular moment is unclear; perhaps Joe's accelerating decline gave them a sense of urgency, or maybe McFatridge was more sympathetic to their cause than previous agents had been. In any event, McFatridge forwarded their inquiry to the commissioner of Indian affairs the very same day that he took Kipp's statement.[104]

After almost a year had passed with no answer from Washington, McFatridge wrote again in January 1914, and then in a third letter sent two months later he threw his own weight behind the Indians' petition: "There is no question but that this massacre took place as was described by Joseph Kipp . . . and it appears to me that these people do have a just claim against the government." He added that Dick Kipp and William Upham were contemplating a trip to the East in order to present their case in person, which surely would have caused embarrassment on Capitol Hill.[105]

Whether or not the threat of a visiting Indian delegation caught the attention of federal bureaucrats, a staffer at the Department of the Interior within three weeks of receiving McFatridge's third letter asked the War Department for all available information on Baker's campaign and any subsequent government investigation.[106] Meanwhile, Heavy Runner's heirs solicited and sent to Washington additional testimony from survivors of the massacre. In one deposition Bear Head described his capture by soldiers on the morning of the fight as he rounded up his horses.[107] Kills-on-the-Edge, known by whites as Mary Monroe, remembered how she and her wounded mother had fled the Big Bend and taken shelter in another Piegan camp.[108] And for good measure, the claimants also attached a statement by Alf Hamilton, a white trader, who testified to the number of Heavy Runner's mounts in 1870, noting, "In those days an Indian would not be considered a chief unless he had several hundred head of horses."[109]

And yet it was not enough. Though the Indians won the backing of Senator Harry Lane of Oregon, who in February 1915 introduced a bill on their behalf, officials at the Interior Department refused to endorse the legislation.[110] In justifying the decision, the office of Secretary Franklin K. Lane (no relation to the senator) explained, "It is impossible to reconcile the statements of Joseph Kipp with reports which the military authorities made shortly after the events transpired," adding that the passage of time complicated the gathering of sufficient evidence to overturn the original government version of the incident.[111] Senator Lane tried again in December with a new bill, but received precisely the same reply from the Interior Department. The plaintiffs, however, were undeterred and attempted to strengthen their hand by interviewing other Piegan eyewitnesses to the slaughter.[112] Dick Kipp even made a visit to the Big Bend in December 1916, recovering two six-shooters and posting a notice declaring that it was the site of the battle.[113] But Secretary Lane remained steadfast in his opposition to their claim, withholding his support for similar bills proposed in 1917 and 1920.

At this point the Indians approached Horace Clarke, although his appearance in the record at this time—seven years after Heavy Runner's heirs had initiated their case—invites scrutiny. Presumably, Clarke's testimony would have been invaluable from the start, considering his role in the slaughter and his status as a mixed-blood (which meant that his voice would carry more weight in Washington than that of deponents of pure Indian ancestry). And unlike Joe Kipp, Clarke could provide key information about the military perspective on the engagement unalloyed by any obvious conflict of interest. Given the dogged efforts of the plaintiffs in marshaling evidence to support their claim, perhaps Clarke both received and rebuffed prior requests for his involvement. At the very least, it seems that he did not volunteer any assistance before 1920.

Whatever the circumstances behind its origin, Clarke's brief statement—sworn before a notary public at East Glacier Park on 9 November 1920—was remarkable for its candor. Clarke began by acknowledging his participation in "the Baker fight," as he called it, and moved quickly to stress the injustice of the killings that day, explaining, "[I] personally knew Heavy Runner, a good Indian and a friend of the white people." If the numbers Clarke gave in his statement that day were unhelpful to the plaintiffs (he cited 150 dead Indians and only 1,300 confiscated horses), he nevertheless bolstered their allegation that the army's attack upon their father's camp was a tragic mistake. As proof, he stated for the record what had long been merely rumored: "It is an undeniable fact that Col. Baker was drunk and did not know what he was doing. The hostile camp was Mountain Chief's, and it was the camp we intended to strike, but owing to too much excitement and confusion and misinformation the Heavy Runner camp was the sufferer and the victim of circumstances."[114]

The claimants undoubtedly thought their case stronger than ever. After all, with Clarke's deposition they now had the support of a man who had stood on the bluffs at the Big Bend that awful morning and fired into the sleeping camp, a man who was not looking for absolution and who in fact had reason to despise the Piegans, even if their blood was his own and he had lived among

Horace Clarke et al. 1923. Taken in a Helena studio after their reenactment of a footrace from some fifty years before, this photograph shows Horace Clarke (seated at right) and David Hilger (standing at right), along with two other friends, a reminder that for Montana's old-timers the boundaries of race were more elastic than for later white arrivals. Courtesy of the Montana Historical Society.

them all his adult life. Armed with the new information, Senator Thomas J. Walsh of Montana, soon to become famous for leading the investigation into the Teapot Dome scandal, wasted no time in putting a bill before his chamber, introducing S. 287 just five months later, on 12 April 1921. Nevertheless, the result this time was worse than before: the proposed legislation was not even referred to the Interior Department for consideration.[115] For those who had lost the most on the darkest day in Blackfeet history, there would be no restitution, no apology, not even an acknowledgment of their suffering.

FOR THE HEIRS of Heavy Runner, the unsuccessful claim against the government perhaps brought an official closure to the Baker Massacre, but the suit marked a new beginning of sorts for Horace Clarke. In the last decade of his life, he engaged with the slaughter's aftermath, at least publicly, in a way he never had before. Of course, there was his lengthy interview with Martha Plassmann, but a more symbolic and touching moment came three years earlier.

In September 1923 Clarke traveled from East Glacier Park to Helena in order to meet an old friend, David Hilger, who had recently moved back to the capital after an absence of four decades. The two were joined there by Andrew Fergus—who, like Hilger, was descended from a prominent white family with deep roots in the state—as well as William "Billy" Johns. During their reunion, the men reenacted a celebrated footrace they had run nearly fifty years before, although the youngest among them (Hilger) was now sixty-five. Afterward they took a photograph together in a local studio.[116]

The highlight of the men's gathering, however, was a side trip they made to the former Clarke ranch in the Prickly Pear Valley.[117] It had been so long since Horace had last visited the place that the wooden fence surrounding his father's burial site had long since decayed. Struck by the poor condition of the grave, Clarke—with the

Marias Massacre commemoration, 2006. Each year, students and faculty from the Blackfeet Community College in Browning travel to the site of the Marias Massacre, where they remember those killed on 23 January 1870. Courtesy of Harry Palmer.

assistance of Hilger, newly appointed librarian for the Montana Historical Society—arranged for the construction of a sturdy, wrought iron enclosure the next year.[118] As for a headstone, Clarke left it for the people of the state to erect a suitable monument commemorating, as he put it, "one of the greatest of Montana pioneers and a kind and good father."[119]

The fence around the grave of Malcolm Clarke still stands today, even if worn and rusted, but the only memorial is a small stone tablet, suggesting perhaps that by the 1920s the citizens of Montana preferred to forget the brutal events that had preceded them by half a century. Likewise, there is no historical marker at the Big Bend, though for many years now a group of faculty and students from Blackfeet Community College have made the sixty-five-mile trek from Browning to the site of the massacre each 23 January. On one occasion they placed 217 stones in a circle to commemorate those who died at this now somnolent patch of land, where the dark waters of the Marias form a graceful horseshoe before running east again.[120]

4

The Bird That Comes Home

O n a midwinter day in 1911, Helen Clarke wrote a most unusual
fan letter to Edwin Milton Royle, then a noted American playwright. At the time Royle was nearing the apex of his career. His
most famous piece, *The Squaw Man*, had just concluded its third
run on Broadway, and three years later it would be made into Hollywood's first feature-length film, marking the directorial debut of a
struggling former actor named Cecil B. DeMille.[1]

Clarke, however, was not writing to lavish praise on *The Squaw
Man* or even as a devotee of the theater (though she had once
enjoyed a brief but acclaimed New York stage career herself). Rather,
she sought out Royle to share her powerful reaction to the play's
sequel, a novel published in 1910 titled *The Silent Call*, which for her
had captured so well the complexities of life on an Indian reservation. This feat was no accident. While Royle was a Princeton graduate and a longtime resident of the East Coast, he was, in his words,
a "Western man," raised near Kansas City, Missouri. To honor his
roots, he even named his sprawling estate in Darien, Connecticut,
the Wickiup (another word for wigwam). In short, Royle knew the
West intimately.

Helen P. Clarke, 1895. This studio portrait, taken in New York between her stints as an allotting agent in Indian Territory, gives a sense of Helen Clarke's commanding presence, which fueled her brief but acclaimed stage career in the 1870s. Courtesy of the Montana Historical Society.

From her own life experiences, Clarke recognized the characters and themes in *The Silent Call*: the corrupt Indian agent, the caring but naïve missionary, and particularly the simmering tensions between native peoples and their white neighbors who coveted the Indians' natural resources. Especially poignant for Helen was the dilemma of the novel's protagonist, Hal Calthorpe. Like Helen, Hal was the mixed-blood child of a noted white man and his Indian wife and, like Helen, had enjoyed a remarkable career for someone of such lineage. Most of all, just like Helen, Hal had felt the sharp sting of racial prejudice. Indeed, in one of the novel's most memorable scenes, Hal recoils when assaulted with the epithet "half-breed."

As Clarke explained in her letter to Royle, she hoped that his book might alert others to the plight faced by mixed-blood individuals. But she was doubtful, given the attitudes of "the poor white trash and the half civilized Westerners who believed that [an] Indian could be called good only when dead." She marveled that such vitriol was matched by a toxic combination of ignorance and hypocrisy, which allowed "the so-called American, a mixture of so many breeds [and] nationalities [to] sit in the seat of the scornful and arrogate to himself a pureness of blood, a superiority, something of which he is so unworthy an exponent."[2]

In a prompt and generous reply, Royle likened racial prejudice to superstition, but acknowledged that "we are all more or less tainted with it," noting ruefully that his own grandfather had been a slave owner. Still, he saw cause for optimism, insisting that the progress of the age—steam, electricity, the telephone—would bring people closer together and thus erode, however slowly, the fear and hatred stemming from perceived human difference. To boost her spirits, he even recommended a recent book by a French writer that attacked the notion of fixed racial inferiority.[3]

Regardless of his mollifying words and thoughtful reading suggestions, Royle could not do for Clarke what he had for Hal Calthorpe: provide a happy ending. All turns out well for the hero of *The Silent Call*: Hal secures his father's vast landholdings on the northern Plains, wins the affections of a beautiful Indian girl, and even earns the lasting respect of local whites. Clarke, on the other hand, could only dream of such a tidy resolution. For a mixed-blood woman, even one as arresting and accomplished as Helen Clarke, the racial, gender, and social politics at the turn of the twentieth century—an era she bitterly denounced as "the Age of Tribes"—produced far more ambiguous resolutions.

Aspasia of the Wilderness

The 1860s were bruising years for Edwin Booth, scion of America's most prominent theatrical family. First, his beloved wife, the actress Mary Devlin, became ill in February 1863, and Booth, then starring in New York in *Richard III*, was too drunk to return to their Boston home before she died. Two years later, his younger brother, John Wilkes, assassinated President Abraham Lincoln at Ford's Theatre in Washington, D.C., bringing eternal disgrace upon the family name. Finally, in March 1867, Booth's own playhouse, the Winter Garden, fell victim to the scourge of nineteenth-century theaters, when an errant spark ignited a fire that burned it to the ground, sparing "not even a wig or a pair of tights," as Booth glumly observed.[4]

Booth responded to this latest calamity with typically dramatic flair, by commissioning the most majestic playhouse New York had ever seen. When finished, Booth's Theatre occupied almost an entire city block at the intersection of Twenty-Third Street and Sixth Avenue. And it had just the extraordinary effect the actor had sought. Three towers soared 120 feet above street level while flags fluttered from the mansard roof. The inside was better yet, as a lobby of Italian marble gave way to the domed auditorium, festooned with busts, carvings, and frescoes and illuminated by an enormous gaslight chandelier. The real wonders, however, were hidden from view: hydraulic rams that raised and lowered the scenery flats and boilers capable of producing enough steam to power an engine. Booth's Theatre opened to rave architectural reviews on 3 February 1869, and a heartbreaking decade for the great tragedian thus ended on a triumphant note.[5]

Booth's was not, of course, the only great playhouse of the age. Many others were clustered half a mile to the southeast in the city's first true theater district, the area around Union Square. Among the grandest venues were Wallack's Theatre (at Broadway and Thirteenth Street), the Academy of Music (at Fourteenth Street and Irving Place), and the Union Square Theatre (at Broadway and Fourth Avenue). Before taking in a performance featuring a star such as Maurice Barrymore or Ellen Terry, theatergoers could dine at one of the countless restaurants that lined the streets—the Maison Dorée for the well-heeled, oyster houses or German *Weinstuben* for those of more modest means. The area also boasted a variety of ancillary businesses that served the theater industry: printing offices, costume shops, photography studios, and publishing houses. In the period immediately following the Civil War, the neighborhood became one of Manhattan's most vibrant communities, with a dazzling swirl of entertainment and commerce.[6]

This was the intoxicating milieu discovered by Helen Clarke in the early 1870s, a far cry from the quiet and stately Minneapolis home of her aunt Charlotte, to which she had temporarily retreated after her father's murder.[7] Precisely when and how she arrived in New York is unknown; like the Winter Garden Theatre, most of Clarke's personal papers, which included a hefty scrapbook documenting her acting career, were lost to fire.[8] Still, a glimpse of her time on the Manhattan stage survives in the recollections of friends and relatives and the occasional newspaper account.

If the details of her stay in New York are elusive, her fitness as a performing artist was obvious to all who knew her. For one thing, her flowing hair and willowy stature drew attention: one acquaintance remembered her as "5 feet and 10 inches of magnificent womanhood," while another recalled her "strong aquiline nose and sharp black eyes that could sparkle at a joke or become tender at a recollection."[9] In fact, no less a figure than Thomas Meagher, acting governor of Montana Territory, declared her "a singularly amiable and very prepossessing young lady in appearance" when he visited the Clarke ranch in the fall of 1865.[10] But it was her "wonderful, deep, thrilling voice, unusually deep and strong for a woman," that gave her such presence when on the boards.[11]

Only a sketchy record exists of the theatrical roles Clarke played, but it is clear that she preferred the dramatic fare of the antebellum era—Shakespeare and other classical pieces in the English tradition—to the contemporary melodramas obsessed with the social concerns of the Gilded Age. One of her favorite parts was Meg Merrilies, the soothsaying gypsy in the playwright Daniel Terry's *Guy Mannering*, an 1816 drama adapted from the eponymous novel by Sir Walter Scott. Perhaps she was even typecast, for the character required an actress who was, according to a reviewer of the time, "impassioned, awful, and irresistible . . . [an] indefinable being, tinged with melancholy, clothed with fierce grandeur, and breathing prophecy."[12] Who better to play a mysterious, vengeful nomad than a young woman who had witnessed her father's horrific slaying and then fled the scene? Clarke enjoyed the part so much that she was still reprising it for friends in Montana more than a decade after she left New York.[13]

She may also have performed in Europe; reportedly, her scrapbook contained press clippings lauding her work in theaters from London to Berlin, as well as congratulatory notes from royal luminaries no less than Germany's Kaiser Wilhelm I and Sophie of Württemberg, Queen of the Netherlands.[14] She may even have shared the stage in a supporting role with the French theatrical star Sarah Bernhardt, widely regarded as "the most famous actress the world has ever known."[15] These claims are difficult to verify. What is sure is that by the fall of 1875, at the age of twenty-seven, Clarke had returned to Montana, although the reasons why she abandoned New York are unclear. One oft-told story relates that she went broke trying to repay the hospitality shown to her by Bernhardt during the Frenchwoman's first American tour, treating the actress and her producer, Daniel Frohman, to dinner at Louis Sherry's legendary restaurant.[16] Given Clarke's lifelong financial troubles, this account possesses the ring of truth. And yet upon closer inspection it is almost surely apocryphal: Bernhardt did not make her U.S. debut until 1880 (at Booth's Theatre, no less), the year before Sherry opened his doors.

More plausible is an explanation allegedly offered by Clarke herself, though its provenance cannot be fixed with certainty. In this telling she explained, "I was too much of self to become great. I could not forget that I was Helen Clarke and become the new being of imagination."[17] If such insecurity clings naturally to a performer, it is particularly easy to imagine its grasp upon Clarke; after all, she was a single woman of mixed ancestry from the rural Upper Missouri, on her own in North America's brightest metropolis. Like Hal Calthorpe in *The Silent Call*, who visits England only to experience greater alienation on the London streets than he had ever known in the West, her New York sojourn proved that, whatever its painful associations, Montana was home.

THE MAN WHO BECAME Clarke's patron upon her return to Montana was Wilbur Fisk Sanders, an outsize character who had served with an Ohio volunteer regiment in the Civil War before moving west with his family in 1863. By the end of that year he had secured an enduring spot in Montana lore, successfully prosecuting George Ives for homicide and thus delivering to the hangmen of the Montana Vigilance Committee their first victim.[18] Though renowned for his combativeness and obstinacy, Sanders had a softer side; one friend remembered him as a champion of the downtrodden, citing his pro bono defense of a young Indian charged with murder and another instance in which he won an injunction against a labor union seeking to exclude Chinese workers, perhaps the most despised—and thus most vulnerable—population in the West.[19]

Whether it was his reflexive support for the underdog or unyielding loyalty to his friend Malcolm Clarke, with whom he and ten other leading citizens had incorporated the Historical Society of Montana in February 1865, Sanders recruited Helen to lead a classroom in the Helena grade school in the spring of 1876.[20] To be sure, she was exceptionally well prepared for the job, thanks to her education at Catholic institutions in Cincinnati and Minneapolis and especially her recent stint in charge of the one-room adobe schoolhouse at Fort Benton, a post she had assumed upon her return from New York the preceding autumn. Such strengths, however, were likely beside the point, since she met an even more fundamental qualification for work as a teacher: in Montana and elsewhere throughout the rural West, women were the backbone of the educational system because of their supposed civilizing influence, not to mention the fact that they commanded lower wages than men.[21]

There was more to Sanders's machinations on Clarke's behalf, however, than the dictates of either empathy or benefaction. In truth, he and his wife, Harriet, who were parents to five sons, embraced Helen as the daughter they never had. A glance at the capital city's residential directory says as much: for the next thirteen years, Clarke orbited the Sanderses' mansion like a satellite, renting rooms in boardinghouses never more than a block or two from the family's splendid Victorian home at 328 N. Ewing Street. And she was a frequent visitor, whether stopping by for dinner and a hand of whist, giving dramatic readings in the parlor, or opening presents around the hearth on Christmas Day. She was such a fixture in the Sanders household that their eldest son, James, noted once in his journal— without a trace of irritation—that while visiting Montana on a break from his legal studies at Columbia University, he dropped in on his parents and found "Miss Clarke . . . here as usual."[22]

Obviously, close association with a leading family had tangible benefits for Clarke, but it is also just as evident that she craved the wisdom and affection of "Mr. Sanders," as she forever called him, who became a surrogate father. This is not to say that she turned her back on her own blood relatives; rather, upon her return from the East Coast, the Sanders family was easily the more proximate, and not only in geographical terms. Horace had married and started a family on a ranch near Highwood, more than a hundred miles away. Their younger sister, Isabel, lived there, too, and both siblings were preoccupied with caring for their mother, who as Horace recalled years later never recovered from the shock of witnessing her husband's murder and thus lived a broken life until her passing in June 1895.[23]

Of course, the main reason Helen had so much time for Wilbur and Harriet Sanders is that she had no immediate family of her own, a subject of intense interest to friends and gossips alike. Her single status, however, was hardly for lack of suitors, as is revealed by a sole surviving love letter found among her personal papers.[24] Little is known about her paramour, except that his name was Henry and that he wrote to "Nellie," as she was called by those closest to her, from San Francisco in January 1884. The six-page note speaks to an intense and intimate relationship, as the author repeatedly refers to himself as her "lover," and in closing calls Helen his "darling Pio-topowaka" (her Indian name, which means "the Bird That Comes Home").[25] What became of their relationship thereafter is a mystery. Or maybe not. Rumor had it (though nothing in Clarke's own hand confirms such speculation) that she remained forever unmarried by choice, because she would not wed an Indian and believed that no white man would ever treat her as an equal.[26] What she thought of mixed-blood men as potential romantic partners is unknown.

MANY OTHERS IN Montana, however, had clear feelings about the suit-ability of mixed-blood men as husbands; that led to another Clarke family catastrophe in the fall of 1872. On 16 September, Nathan Clarke, who in the aftermath of Malcolm's murder had sworn to avenge his father, was stabbed to death by James Swan during a drunken brawl. At issue was Swan's daughter: the nineteen-year-old Clarke wanted to court her, but Swan was determined that she marry a white man instead. At the time of the murder Joe Cobell, who had helped guide the Second U.S. Cavalry to Heavy Runner's slumber-ing camp on the Marias two and a half years earlier, lived just across a coulee from Clarke's homestead and thus took on the grim task of collecting the victim's bloody clothes and interring his corpse at the base of the bluff where he had perished.[27]

That the Swans were of mixed blood only compounded the tragedy, highlighting that at least some people of mixed ancestry had imbibed the racial prejudice of the day, however self-loathing, which held that white skin bestowed privileges reserved for those of unalloyed racial purity. Such bigotry was gaining ground on Helen Clarke, too. In February 1880 Elizabeth Chester Fisk, a prominent white woman married to the editor of the *Helena Herald*, the state's leading Republican mouthpiece, pulled her children from the city's school, in part because of her dissatisfaction with Clarke. Though Fisk justified her behavior by citing Clarke's allegedly sour disposition, she noted that Clarke was "a half-breed Indian," suggesting that race had contributed to her decision. Ironically, Lizzie Fisk was a well-known supporter of various reform causes, and her husband used his journalistic perch to advocate (if fleetingly) for black suffrage in Montana. Evidently, the Fisks saw no inconsistency in taking up the cause of African Americans while refusing instruction for their children by individuals of mixed ancestry.[28]

Several factors explain the increasingly precarious circumstances facing mixed-blood peoples in Montana in the 1870s and after. First was a surge in native-white violence in the middle of the decade, as the territory's Indian wars lurched fitfully to a bloody conclusion. On a blistering day in June 1876, Lieutenant Colonel George Armstrong Custer plunged the Seventh U.S. Cavalry into an enormous Indian encampment on the Little Bighorn River in southeastern Montana. Nearly 275 men in Custer's command were killed, in fighting, according to one Indian participant, that lasted "no longer than a hungry man needed to eat his dinner."[29] The following summer Chief Joseph and his fugitive Nez Perces engaged the U.S. Army in a series of costly battles along the Montana–Idaho border, before surrendering just miles from the safety of the Canadian boundary.[30] Such conflict and the instability it engendered mobilized white rage against all Indians, a category that by virtue of their heritage extended to many mixed-blood people, too, especially those who "looked" native.

More important were Montana's rapidly changing demographics, which in the space of a decade remade the territory as a white man's country. Whereas in 1870 Montana's native and non-native populations were roughly equal, at approximately 20,000 people each, by 1880 the number of whites had doubled even as the native population had begun a dramatic slide. Complicating matters, these white newcomers, like Lizzie and Robert Fisk, who arrived in 1867, had no sense of the relative racial accommodation that had characterized the fur trade era. Instead, as had happened on each successive American frontier—from the Appalachians to the Great Lakes, from Colorado to Texas—white emigrants looked with revulsion upon the mixed-blood communities they discovered, seeing in them a combination of the worst elements of both races: white dissipation on the one hand, and native ignorance on the other. "Half-breed" was perhaps putting it too delicately; in the words of one late nineteenth-century white Montanan, such individuals were "sons of a degenerate ancestry."[31]

Insults like these inflicted lasting psychic wounds on their victims, all the more painful for the reminder that to be only part white was in fact to be nonwhite, and maybe something worse. After all, many race scientists of the day believed that pure-blooded individuals, even those of supposedly second-rate stock, like Africans and Asians, were biologically superior to the racially amalgamated offspring of mixed marriages.[32] No less a figure than Joe Kipp, who spent his entire adult life serving as an intermediary between Indians and whites (often to the detriment of Montana's native peoples), suffered grievously from such slights. In a poignant eulogy, a white friend remembered, "Above all things, Kipp hated the word 'breed,' generally prefixed by the expletive 'damn,' so often used by the ignorant and thoughtless. . . . None know better than I how hard he tried to live so as to ever have the respect and friendship of the whites, and what fits of terrible depression overcame him when he heard his kind mentioned in terms of contempt or derision."[33]

TO HIS MANY DETRACTORS, Wilbur Fisk Sanders was the "Mephistopheles of Montana politics." While he may have looked the part, with his dark complexion and piercing black eyes, it was his vigorous leadership of the territory's beleaguered Republican Party that earned Sanders the hatred of his foes. In Montana as in many other western locales, Democrats enjoyed a tenuous majority, having opted to ride out the ideological discomforts of the Reconstruction era as far as geographically possible from the reaches of the federal government. Sanders and his fellow partisans worked tirelessly to stymie their opponents' best-laid plans. Add to that his natural belligerence and hardball tactics, and it is no wonder that Sanders lost four elections—in 1864, 1867, 1880, and 1886—to serve as the territory's lone delegate to the U.S. House of Representatives.[34]

He tasted victory, if by proxy, in a historic 1882 campaign. Capitalizing on recent territorial legislation that extended to women the right to vote as well as to stand for election in various school-related contests, Sanders used his influence with the Republican Commission of Lewis and Clark County to get Helen Clarke on the ballot as their candidate for superintendent of schools.[35] Local Democrats were so impressed with her qualifications that they set aside their animosity toward Sanders, if only for a moment, and withdrew their own candidate, who promptly endorsed Clarke as "a lady well qualified and eminently worthy of the position."[36] On 7 November 1882 Helen Clarke thus became the first woman elected to public office in the history of Montana Territory (though she shared the distinction with Alice Nichols, who won the same post in Meagher County).

By all accounts Clarke excelled in her position. In his annual reports, Montana's superintendent of public instruction singled her out for special mention, praising her zeal and efficiency in managing the school system of the territory's largest and wealthiest county.[37] And the job clearly suited Clarke, starting with the $1,000 annual salary, which gave her a welcome measure of financial independence.[38] Her success did not stop the Democrats from running their own candidate against her in 1884, but she easily dispatched Edmund O. Railsback, principal of the Helena Business College, winning with 55 percent of the vote.[39] She was elected to a third term in 1886.

Clarke's triumphs proved that, even if the fortunes of Montana's mixed-blood peoples were fading by the 1880s, they were not yet in total eclipse. To be sure, hers was an exceptional case. After all,

Clarke was unusually talented and had a commanding presence. She was descended from a leading (white) figure of the territory's celebrated pioneer days and counted another such individual (however divisive) as a patron. Moreover, as an unmarried woman in a world defined by male preeminence, she posed no threat to Montana's new social and political order.

As if to illustrate the singularity of her experience, a local newspaper dubbed Clarke the "Aspasia of the wilderness," likening her to the famous woman from ancient Greece whose wit and charm allowed her to move with ease in a society normally closed to those of her sex.[40] The analogy was apt in another, unintended sense as well. Aspasia was hounded in her own time by rumors that she was a prostitute, slanders spread by those who resented her influence with Pericles, the renowned Athenian statesman as well as the father of her illegitimate son.[41] Clarke had her own chorus of detractors, the Lizzie Fisks of Montana's emerging white middle class, to bully her.

Eventually, such calumnies wore her down, so that by the close of the decade she, too, was defeated by the rising tide of prejudice that had vanquished the territory's other mixed-blood people. Like Joe Kipp, she bore her wounds internally, and perhaps her suffering went unnoticed by even some of her closest white friends. This emotional distress intensified over time and, according to one newspaper, ultimately drove her away from Montana, where the new binary racial calculus left little room for people in between. "Though endowed with much beauty," the correspondent wrote, "Miss Clarke was known to be the daughter of a Piegan Indian woman, and this fact caused her to be looked down upon socially . . . the gilded doors of Helena's social realm were closed to her by the four hundred."[42] Who comprised the "four hundred" (a shorthand then in vogue referring to the social elite of Gilded Age Manhattan, adapted for use elsewhere) and how exactly they ostracized Clarke is a mystery. But by the close of 1889 she had once again turned her back on Montana in search of a brighter future elsewhere.

Children as They Are

Perhaps the best that could be said of Senator Henry L. Dawes's political career was that he remained a staunch Republican Party loyalist. After graduating from Yale College in 1839, he held a number of state offices in his native Massachusetts before winning election to the House of Representatives in 1857, where he served without earning much notice for the better part of two decades. Dawes's so-called big break came in 1874, when he was plucked from obscurity to fill the Senate seat left vacant by the death of Charles Sumner, the radical reformer beloved by many (and hated by others) for his vociferous opposition to slavery. Dawes, in fact, delighted in showing visitors to the Senate chamber the gashes left in Sumner's desk by Preston Brooks, the South Carolinian who, incited by a speech Sumner gave in 1856, had savagely thrashed the Massachusetts senator with a heavy cane, nearly killing him.[43] Sumner's wounded desk seemed about as close to greatness, or even relevance, as Henry Dawes was likely ever to get.

Yet for all his apparent mediocrity, Dawes came to write one of the most significant pieces of legislation enacted during the nineteenth century. Signed into law by President Grover Cleveland in February 1887, the General Allotment Act transformed federal Indian policy and governed U.S. relations with its native peoples for the next half century. Known more familiarly as the Dawes Severalty Act, its improbable sponsor achieved a kind of immortality, joining a select group of lawmakers—including men like Representative Justin Morrill (father of the land-grant college act) and Senator John Sherman (the noted trustbuster)—whose last names became synonymous with their landmark statutes. For a political hack who had discovered "the Indian question" only the decade before, Dawes's lasting fame was a stunning personal triumph.

While his name may be forever linked with allotment, Henry Dawes did not with a mere flick of a wand create the idea, which, in fact, dated back as far as the colonial era. Still, in the post–Civil War period allotment became practically an obsession of Indian reformers, who seized upon the concept as a way to remake natives as "brown white people" by forcing them to assimilate into mainstream Anglo-American society. The humanitarians' goal was straightforward: to break up communally held reservations and install native families on individually owned plots of land, with any surplus made available for purchase by non-Indians. Although the government would hold title to the Indians' homesteads for a twenty-five-year waiting period, the humanitarians believed that native experience with private property would teach them thrift and self-sufficiency while encouraging the abandonment of what they perceived as abhorrent cultural traditions. Years later President Theodore Roosevelt, who was no friend to native peoples, noted admiringly that the Dawes Act had served "as a mighty pulverizing engine to break up the tribal mass."[44]

The blunt paternalism of the Dawes Act, combined with the Indians' staggering loss of land—some 86 million acres between the passage of the bill and its repeal in 1934—have made the law a deserving target of scorn.[45] Yet the legislation was very much a product of its time, and its provisions grew from a fervid belief by "friends of the Indian" that such measures were in the best interests of America's native peoples, a tragic instance of loving not wisely but too well. Surely this was true of the reformers who lobbied for allotment, the legislators who codified it, and the men and women, including Helen Clarke, who implemented the policy on reservations throughout the land.

HELEN CLARKE OWED her surprising career as an allotment agent to the most famous institution that emerged from the same assimilationist impulse that spawned the Dawes Act. Established in 1879, the Carlisle Indian School was the brainchild of Richard Henry Pratt, a retired military officer who had carried out a fascinating experiment four years earlier. Charged with relocating seventy-two native prisoners from Indian Territory to Florida, Pratt decided to try and "civilize" his captives once the group had reached its destination at St. Augustine. His efforts, which included instruction in Christian dogma as well as the English language, wrought such a profound makeover in the natives that Harriet Beecher Stowe, who by then spent winters in Florida, trumpeted Pratt's achievement to her readers. Because of their model behavior, the Indian prisoners were released in 1878, and the following year federal authorities approved Pratt's request to convert some abandoned army barracks in central Pennsylvania to the nation's first off-reservation boarding school.[46]

Like most humanitarians, Pratt had genuine affection for Indians but also believed that their cultures belonged to the Stone Age. At Carlisle, Pratt thus sought, as he famously put it, to "kill the Indian, [and] save the man." Before-and-after photographs offer stark visual evidence of his maxim. Perhaps the best-known set features a young Navajo named Tom Torlino, who enrolled at the school shortly after it opened. Taken in 1880, the first picture shows Torlino as he arrived in Pennsylvania, with flowing locks, gold hoop earrings, and an extravagant necklace—in short, looking every bit the "savage" whom Pratt hoped to transform. The second picture was taken three years later and shows the "civilizing" effects of instruction in white mores: Torlino dressed in a coat and tie and sporting tightly cropped hair.[47]

Helen Clarke had the opportunity to look in on Pratt's human laboratory in January 1890, when she arrived at Carlisle with a pair of her nephews in tow. Eager to escape Montana's stifling social hierarchy, she had volunteered to deliver two of Horace's sons—thirteen-year-old Malcolm and eleven-year-old Ned—to Pratt's care, and then to remain indefinitely in the East, perhaps working again in the theater. No descriptions of the place are found in her papers, but it is easy to imagine her ambivalence as she ambled about the campus.

Richard Henry Pratt (center), with students and teachers at the Carlisle Indian School, 1879. Helen Clarke delivered two of her nephews to Pratt's institution in central Pennsylvania in 1890 and was a frequent visitor thereafter, delighting audiences with readings and dramatic performances. Citing her mixed ancestry, Pratt held her up as a model of achievement for his students. Courtesy of the National Anthropological Archives, Smithsonian Institution.

On the one hand, a woman known to her lover by her Indian name could scarcely have endorsed Pratt's extremist sentiments about the eradication of native culture. And yet in most other respects, Clarke embodied the outlook of the typical female reformer of the day, with whom she shared virtually everything else except race.

In the end, if indeed she had reservations about Pratt's methods, they did not keep her away from Carlisle; she made frequent trips to central Pennsylvania from Washington and New York to check on her nephews, whom Pratt's mouthpieces at the school unfailingly described as "bright little boys." As reported in various school publications, a visit by Helen Clarke was an occasion to be savored, for it usually featured a performance of some sort by the former actress: a poem by Longfellow, a lesson in elocution, or a parable about moral uplift.[48] Pratt was thrilled, seeing in his guest, who was "part Indian herself," as the school newsletter proudly noted, a stunning role model for the boys and girls he hoped to refashion.[49]

Considering his close association with the leading architects of federal Indian policy, it is possible that Pratt encouraged Clarke to seek work in the Indian Service. More likely, however, she took her inspiration from Alice Fletcher, the first—and besides Clarke, the only—female allotment agent during the nineteenth century. As it happened, Fletcher and Pratt had become good friends through their mutual interest in native peoples, and the reformer promoted the school to lawmakers and potential students nationwide. Between 1889 and 1892, Fletcher's companion Jane Gay sent dozens of letters to Pratt describing their work in allotting the Nez Perce Reservation in Idaho Territory. Many of these dispatches were reprinted in the *Red Man*, the school's newspaper, precisely when Clarke was a regular visitor to Carlisle.[50]

Although there is no evidence that the two ever met, Helen Clarke and Alice Fletcher had much in common: both were well-educated, unmarried women of middle age, who worked for personal satisfaction but also out of economic necessity. And yet their lives were hardly identical: while Fletcher was descended on her father's side from an old New England family, Clarke was of mixed ancestry, a fact that played an indispensable role in her appointment in the fall of 1890. Earlier that year Congress had targeted several reservations in Indian Territory for division, including lands held by some of the tribes most opposed to the Dawes Act. In assessing this thorny situation, Commissioner of Indian Affairs Thomas J. Morgan wrote to the secretary of the interior, "It has occurred to me that Miss Helen P. Clark[e] . . . would be a proper person to make those allotments. . . . Being identified with the Indian race, it is probable that she would be able to exert a greater influence with them than one who is not so identified."[51] President Benjamin Harrison signed her commission on 4 October 1890.[52]

IN THE EARLY DECADES of the twentieth century, north-central Oklahoma became not only famous but also rich thanks to its dark oceans of petroleum, reflected aboveground in stately mansions that dotted the grassy landscape. One of them, the Italianate "Palace on the Prairie" built by the oil baron E. W. Marland, boasted fifty-five rooms and 45,000 square feet—fitting for a man who at one time controlled a tenth of the world's known oil reserves.[53] No such luxury awaited the Otoe-Missouria Indians who moved to the area in 1881. Instead, they eked out a living on their small reservation, enduring malarial summers and icy winters, all the while pining for the homes they had left behind. Increased white migration after 1850 had crowded them off their traditional lands along the Kansas–Nebraska border, and so they had reluctantly agreed to head south.[54] In 1890 they were faced with a fresh indignity: the breakup of their tribal land under the new Dawes Act.

Sharing their anger were the Poncas, their neighbors to the north, who had suffered even more grievously at the hands of the federal government. After all, unlike the Otoe-Missourias, the Poncas had never consented to their removal. Because of a stupefying bureaucratic mistake in 1868, their supposedly permanent homeland in northern Nebraska had been ceded by the federal government to their bitter enemies, the Sioux, in that year's Treaty of Fort Laramie. For a time the Poncas clung to their ancestral land, even in the face of withering Sioux aggression, until a U.S. military detachment herded them to Indian Territory in 1877 in what became known as the Ponca Trail of Tears. One of their chiefs, Standing Bear, was so distraught by the move that he led a small group back to Nebraska in 1879 and fought a determined and ultimately victorious legal battle

Helen P. Clarke in Indian Territory, ca. 1890s. Despite her rustic surroundings in the field, she nevertheless managed to cultivate an air of refinement during her stay in present-day Oklahoma, with impeccable table settings and, in her own quarters, a writing desk stacked with books. Courtesy of Joyce Clarke Turvey.

to remain there.[55] By contrast, for the Southern Poncas who stayed behind, the proposed allotment of their lands marked Washington's latest and most devastating betrayal.

When she arrived in July 1891 to break up the communal lands of both peoples, Helen Clarke was well aware of the natives' recalcitrance, but she had reason for cautious optimism, buoyed by her recent success in allotting the sixty-eight members of the Tonkawa tribe, whose postage-stamp reservation bordered the Poncas' tract. Clarke had completed her efforts there in less than two months, with little resistance from the Indians. Of course, this was not to say that the work itself was easy; she sweated for her eight-dollar per diem, from "early morn to dewy eve," as she put it, and often without taking a single day of rest for weeks at a time.[56] Moreover, she and her three- or four-man crew (surveyor, interpreter, and one or two chain-men) moved about constantly, hauling heavy stones to be used as monuments and fretting about the attendant strain upon their horses.

A handful of rare photographs from her time in the field speak at once to the poverty of Clarke's surroundings and to her gritty resourcefulness. Though living for weeks on end in canvas tents pitched directly onto the bare ground, Clarke still preserved at least a dash of her characteristic refinement. One picture shows her at meal-time, joined by two others at a table covered with a crisp white cloth and arrayed with a complete place setting or two. Another image reveals the intimate details of her sleeping quarters, which boasted a heavy, wicker-backed rolling chair, a writing desk, several photo-graphs, and, as always, a collection of books. As any of her friends could attest, Helen Clarke was a woman equally at home on the frontier, in the schoolroom, or on the Broadway stage.

IF THE TONKAWAS had given no trouble, and according to their agent "seem to be satisfied with the new order of things," the same could not be said for the Otoe-Missourias, who vigorously contested Clarke's efforts from the moment she arrived.[57] One of their spokesmen, Mitchell Deroin, explained that the Indians believed, not incorrectly, that if allotted they would lose much of their reservation. "We would rather be naked and go hungry," Deroin said, "than to take allot-ments and to have that land go out of our hand at some future time. . . . [I]f we take allotments we will not have a home."[58] Haunted by the possibility of such an outcome, the natives threatened to kill the first member of their tribe who accepted a homestead, and then set about ripping up the stones carefully laid by Clarke and her team to mark out individual plots.[59]

Yet it was not merely the prospect of allotment that agitated the natives: as Indian Inspector Arthur Tinker explained, they "complained of the Great Father, for sending a woman . . . they say they are men, and want a man to transact business with them, not a woman."[60] To Clarke's chagrin, the Indians were not the only ones guilty of chauvinism: Clarke believed that federal officials had hinted to tribal leaders that she was not qualified for the work, which the Indians took to mean that her allotments had no legal standing.[61] Her concerns were hardly the stuff of fantasy: years later, in reference to her case, an official conceded the "disadvantages under which even the most talented woman labors while engaging in allotment work."[62] Most women employed by the Indian Service (and by the early twentieth century there were many) served as teachers or field matrons, traditionally "female" positions less likely to antagonize skeptics; Alice Fletcher and Helen Clarke, on the other hand, belonged to a tiny and thus beleaguered vanguard.[63]

While her sex proved a liability as an allotting agent, Clarke's race conferred no benefit, as Commissioner Morgan had hoped when he first made her appointment. By the end of November 1891, after almost five months among the Otoe-Missourias, Clarke had completed only 122 allotments, representing less than half the tribe. Nevertheless, if it was no help in persuading Indians to accept their individual tracts, her background did incline her to sympathy for the natives. As she explained to her superiors, "The question of allotment is a stupendous one—he [the Indian] has not been able to grasp it fully. . . . The Indian's future depends upon this choice and this privilege I trust may not be denied him even if he be not as prompt to act as the Department and I would wish."[64]

Admirable as it was, Clarke's patience with the Indians reflected the paternalism of most white reformers. She considered the natives prone to superstition and found them—"like children, as they are"— moody and unreliable.[65] This dim but largely benign assessment took on a darker hue in the winter of 1891–92, when her work among the Otoe-Missourias stalled completely and she moved on to allot the Poncas, who proved even less tractable. Clarke confessed in a plain-

Helen P. Clarke greeting Otoes in Indian Territory, ca. 1890s. Although she sympathized at first with the reluctance of many Indians to accept allotments, in time Clarke grew impatient with their obstinacy, which she attributed to ignorance and superstition. Courtesy of the Montana Historical Society.

tive note to her patron, Wilbur Fisk Sanders, "I feel utterly alone in their Territory—and I long for a home face and for encouragement." In a cryptic aside, she added that her "tents were burned," suggesting, perhaps, that the Poncas had taken matters into their own hands in order to check her progress.[66] Nevertheless, she set to work, alternating between the Ponca Reservation and the Otoe-Missouria Reservation for the next two years.

By the summer of 1894, however, Clarke's deep well of forbearance had all but dried up. Although she had persuaded 410 of 759 Poncas and 175 of 352 Otoe-Missourias to select plots, the natives' unceasing antagonism had worn her down, and she despaired of ever seeing the job through to completion. She vented to Daniel M. Browning, Morgan's successor, "I scarcely think the Indian Office realizes the situation here. I am working among a people whose very

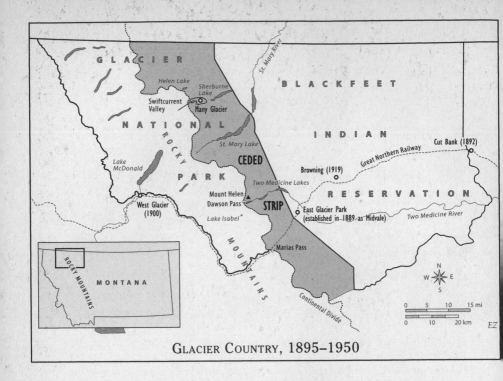

GLACIER COUNTRY, 1895–1950

soul abominates anything tending towards civilization, and they are bright enough to see that *allotments* mean civilization ultimately. And because of this fact they have shown a bitterness unparalleled."[67] She concluded her report by recommending that federal officials impose a deadline by which the Indians must select homesteads or have assignments made for them—a total reversal from her earlier position urging patience and understanding.

As it happened, Browning warmed to her idea of an ultimatum, and thus in August 1894 he ordered Clarke to give the Indians thirty days to make their selections. In a sense, her suggestion worked too well: by the middle of December, she had finished her task and now faced unemployment for the first time in her life. This was an especially worrisome prospect for a member of "the class that destiny has ordered to win bread and butter for himself or herself," as she put it.[68] With no job prospects in Indian Territory, Clarke disposed of her horses and equipment and, true to her Piegan name, set off like a migratory bird making the return journey home. She arrived that spring to find her mother's people locked in their own bitter land dispute with the Great Father.

DURING THE CRETACEOUS period, about 100 million years ago, an enormous slab of rock—hundreds of miles wide and several miles thick—heaved upward and slid east for nearly fifty miles. This geologic event helped form the Rocky Mountains while dragging the ecosystems of the Pacific Northwest all the way inland to the edge of the northern Great Plains.[69] And yet, for all its fascinating biological diversity as well as the dramatic effects of glaciation, which in the process created hanging valleys, sculpted peaks, and aquamarine pools, the area's scenic attractions held little interest for the white visitors who began showing up in droves in the late nineteenth century. Instead, the newcomers were lured to this remote and serene location by persistent rumors of mineral wealth.

An obstacle, however, stood between the would-be prospectors and their golden dreams: the land they coveted was part of the Blackfeet Reservation. Hoping to open the area for mining operations, federal officials dispatched a three-man team in September 1895 to negotiate with the Indians for its purchase. Although many of the natives were hesitant, the commissioners—a group that included the naturalist and ethnographer George Bird Grinnell, a longtime friend of the tribe—held the upper hand. At the time, the Blackfeet were only a decade removed from horrific starvation, brought on largely by government negligence; at its worst moments, the Indians had been reduced to stripping cottonwood trees and eating the bark.[70] Therefore, when in 1895 the Blackfeet requested three million dollars for the land in question, the commissioners responded by threatening to dock their rations until they consented to a lower price.[71]

As it turned out, though, Helen Clarke had just returned to Montana following her assignment in Indian Territory, and the Piegans sought her advice on the matter. Though no record exists of the counsel she gave, it seems certain that, considering her recent allotting experience and the outcome of the deliberations, she urged the Blackfeet to accede to the commissioners' wishes.[72] After all, she knew well the coercive power of the federal government, because she had just deployed it herself against the Poncas and the Otoe-Missourias. In the end, the Indians agreed to sell the "ceded strip" for $1.5 million in exchange for supposedly permanent usage rights, but these promises proved fleeting: when no minerals were found, the government set the land aside as Glacier National Park in 1910 and soon imposed severe restrictions on Blackfeet access, limiting their ability to use the land for hunting and recreation.[73]

Looking back on the treaty from the perspective of the twenty-first century, Darrell Robes Kipp, a leading Piegan intellectual, has characterized the objections of some of his contemporaries, asking rhetorically, "You [all] sold the mountains for $1.5 million on the installment plan? Was that a good deal?" He adds that skeptics might also wonder why Helen Clarke or others did not intervene to insist upon better terms for the Indians. But in explaining, if not necessarily defending, the outcome, Kipp says, "If you were [one of the Indian elders] and you were sitting there watching children starve, you realize, okay, what's the mountains? What's anything worth? The only thing of worth is letting our children live. At their darkest moment—at their bleakest moment—they chose survival." Thus in assessing Clarke's role in the negotiations, Kipp concludes that by recommending the sale, she did not act out of expediency or insensitivity. "No," he says, "[she] did it out of love."[74]

IN THE EARLY MONTHS of 1896, even as Congress was putting the finishing touches on a bill transferring the ceded strip from the Blackfeet to the United States, another document concerning Indian affairs was making the rounds on Capitol Hill. In March the Otoe-Missourias sent a petition to the secretary of the interior insisting that they did not approve of the allotments made for them by Helen Clarke. To be sure, the secretary had received the schedules she had forwarded the preceding December, but thus far he had declined to endorse them, primarily because—as the Indians' agent explained—many of the natives had simply ignored her assignments and settled together in camps (as in the old days of communal living) the moment she left for Montana. Vexed by their insubordination, the Department of the Interior ordered Clarke back to Indian Territory in the autumn of 1897, with instructions to "adjust the existing difficulties."[75]

While surely exasperated by the impermanence of her prior efforts, Clarke was delighted to have the work. The time since her return to Helena had been difficult, and she had gotten by only with help from the Sanders family. So bleak, in fact, were her prospects that in April of that year she had enlisted several well-placed friends to nudge along her reappointment as an allotment agent. To one of her advocates, Senator Thomas H. Carter of Montana, a Republican Party stalwart, she emphasized her good record as well as her "Indian blood," before adding a sharply partisan appeal. Noting the recent election of fellow Republican William McKinley as president, she wrote, "[I]f to the victor belongs the spoils, why *we* who were on the right side should be remembered."[76]

The tribes, of course, did not welcome her reappearance, and as Clarke soon discovered, the natives had grown even more implacable in her absence. Barely a month after her arrival in Indian Territory, the Otoe-Missourias drafted yet another petition to the government detailing their objections to allotment, culminating in a hard truth: "The Indians of the said tribes believed they owned these lands and that they would be allowed to have the undisturbed possession of same, and would not be molested without their consent."[77] The Poncas were equally adamant, and in council with a visiting official from the Bureau of Indian Affairs they attacked Clarke personally. An Indian named Thick Nail declared, "I never did like Miss Clarke;

Miss Clarke came down here and allotted these Poncas without their knowing anything about it . . . ; you white people must like people who tell lies." Even a pro-allotment chief noted that though he had done all that the government had asked, "today we are hungry, we are starving."[78]

If the recent contretemps between Washington and the Blackfeet caused Clarke to reconsider the allotment policy, she did not say. Instead, she worked diligently to complete her task and indicated in an anxious letter to James Sanders, the eldest of Wilbur's children, "I want to remain in this work of allotting lands until I can save enough to live on in my old age."[79] She was even more direct in a missive she sent to the commissioner of Indian affairs in the spring of 1899, declaring the fulfillment of her duties: "After [April 30] I shall be without work. . . . I am a struggling woman without fortune . . . [and] keenly feel the necessity for making every possible provision for the rainy day which comes to all of us who survive the storms of life sufficiently long. I therefore beg you sincerely not to let me remain idle."[80] This time, however, there would be no encore with the Indian Office, perhaps because, as Clarke told James Sanders, "there is a prejudice always at a woman holding any sort of position that pays." Though she remained on the active rolls of the Interior Department until 1904, she was never again summoned to do the bidding of the Great Father.[81]

Grim as it was, Clarke's outlook at the turn of the century was still much brighter than the one facing the Indians living in what became Kay and Noble Counties in north-central Oklahoma. Rapacious whites, especially those who founded the 101 Ranch, began to buy up Ponca lands as soon as the Indians gained their titles. Today the tribe itself owns only 785 of the 101,000 acres that formerly constituted its reservation.[82] Their neighbors, the Otoe-Missourias, may have fared even worse. With the discovery of oil underneath their land, Washington waived the twenty-five-year trust period and forced "independence" upon many of the allottees, hoping that developers would secure the mineral rights. The Indians lost so much of their territory and in such short order that, in an ironic twist, in 1922 their leaders asked the government—with which the tribe had been at odds over allotment for more than four decades—to step in and reassert control over their dwindling patrimony.[83]

Woman with the Shadow Eyes

Like his good friend Theodore Roosevelt, George Bird Grinnell was an experienced outdoorsman, a very model of the strenuous life. Born in 1849 into a wealthy Brooklyn family and raised in upper Manhattan on the former estate of the artist John James Audubon, Grinnell was an easterner who felt most at home on the far side of the Missouri River. By his early thirties he had served Lieutenant Colonel George Armstrong Custer as a naturalist during Custer's controversial 1874 expedition into the Black Hills, helped inaugurate a campaign to save the American bison from extinction, and assumed the editorship of *Forest and Stream*, the nation's premier recreational magazine.

And yet, for all his experience in the West and the reticence born of his genteel upbringing, George Grinnell gushed like a smitten lover in the fall of 1885 after he made his first visit to the backcountry of northern Montana. Near the end of a vigorous two-week camping trip, Grinnell crested a mountain ridge and beheld the transfixing panorama of the Swiftcurrent valley below him: "An artist's palette, splashed with all the hues of his color box, would not have shown more varied contrasts . . . on the mountain side foaming cascades, with their white whirling mist wreathes, gray blue ice masses, and fields of gleaming snow."[84] Grinnell spent much of the next twenty-five years marshaling support to have the "Crown of the Continent," as he called it, set aside as a national park.

In the early twentieth century Grinnell's crusade received an enormous boost from Louis Hill, a railroad magnate who in 1907 had assumed the presidency of his father's Great Northern Railway.

Glacier Park Lodge, 2010. Built in 1913 by the Great Northern Railway on lands that once belonged to Horace Clarke, the hotel catered to well-heeled tourists visiting Glacier National Park, which was established three years earlier. Photograph by the author.

Snaking like a steel thread across the upper Great Plains, from St. Paul, Minnesota, to Seattle, Washington, Hill's line passed just below the southern boundary of the region that had so captivated Grinnell. Inspired by the Northern Pacific's success in promoting the Yellowstone area since the 1870s, and the attendant spike in passenger traffic on its rails, Hill threw his support behind Grinnell's scheme, and the two men rejoiced when in 1910 Congress established Glacier National Park as the nation's tenth such preserve.[85]

The incompatibility of the two men's interests was soon apparent. Whereas Grinnell hoped that the creation of the park would safeguard its natural treasures, Hill wanted to lure thousands of visitors by advertising those very same attractions. To that end, Hill adopted "See America First" as his company's slogan, borrowing the phrase from a recent tourist promotion that sought to recapture for the U.S. market some of the $150 million spent annually by Americans traveling to Europe. Central to Hill's vision was the construction of several Swiss-style chalets meant to evoke the Old World; that was in keeping with the growing reputation of the Glacier area as the "American Alps." The first and grandest of these structures was the Glacier Park Lodge, which opened its doors in 1913 and stood just a few hundred yards from the railway's Midvale station (soon renamed in honor of the park).

While early visitors to Glacier—among them Mrs. Isaac Guggenheim, Mrs. George W. Vanderbilt, and Theodore Roosevelt himself—may have marveled at the view of the Rocky Mountains from the hotel terrace, Hill was just as proud of the interior. In the lobby, guests could stock up on fancy cigars and fashionable hats, warm themselves around an open campfire, or enjoy tea service provided by a Japanese couple, all underneath a canopy of sixty-foot Douglas fir timbers that supported the soaring edifice.[86] For their part, the Piegans, some of whom Hill recruited to set up teepees nearby or perform ceremonial dances to provide a splash of local color, gave the place a simple but perfect name: Omahkoyis, meaning "Big Tree Lodge."

HELEN CLARKE HAD an unimpeded view of the construction work on the grand hotel, which went up directly across the road from the small frame house she had shared with her brother since 1902. Though modest, their two-story bungalow neatly encapsulated the siblings' divergent personalities: running the length of the front was a long, covered porch, a perfect spot for the voluble Horace to smoke a pipe and regale guests with his trademark yarns; the inside, meanwhile, featured an impressive library stocked with works of fiction, drama, and sociology, where, according to one friend, Helen spent hours "communing with the gifted minds that are the glory

Helen and Horace Clarke, ca. 1910s. After her permanent return to Montana in 1902, Helen shared her brother's small frame house at the edge of the Blackfeet Indian Reservation. Their home became a regular stop for artists and intellectuals visiting Glacier country in the early twentieth century. Courtesy of Joyce Clarke Turvey.

of our literature."[87] The defining feature of their property, however, was invisible: a boundary that marked the end of their land, which was on the extreme western edge of the Blackfeet Reservation, and the beginning of Hill's, which sat at the eastern entrance to the park.

Helen Clarke's path back to Montana had been a circuitous one. Following the conclusion of her work in Indian Territory, she had passed through Midvale on the way to San Francisco, where she lived from 1900 to 1902, teaching elocution and, ever the student, learning to speak French. In California she received nearly $2,500 from the government (an indemnity for property she lost during Owl Child's raid on her father's ranch in 1869), but that was far less than the $20,000 she had requested, and at any rate was equal only to a year's salary as an allotment agent.[88] For a woman nearing sixty, with neither spouse nor children to look after her in old age, combining domestic forces with her brother at Midvale—where he had lived since 1889—seemed her best bet for a secure retirement.

Even if it was not a decisive factor in her return, Clarke was also motivated by a desire to set the record straight about her supposed ostracism at the hands of the "four hundred." Not long after she arrived from the West Coast, she sat with a journalist for an interview in which she refuted numerous details printed in that earlier story, especially those concerning her lineage. "Now, as a matter of fact," she told the writer, "I am far from being ashamed of my origin, but on the other hand am proud of both my father and mother," adding, "I had always numbered the very best people of Helena among my friends, and so the statement that I had been ostracised was ridiculous."[89] Maybe so. But bypassing the capital city, where she had lived her entire adult life while in Montana, in favor of the reservation was no way to end such tongue wagging. In any event, after thirty years aloft, Piotowopaka had come home for good.

Like her sojourn in 1895–96, her arrival in 1902 came at a serendipitous moment for the Piegans. With a reservation population of approximately 2,200, the Indians were still on a slow climb back from the abyss of the starvation years nearly two decades before, and had also endured catastrophic administrative instability as Indian agents came and went, five of them between 1897 and 1900 alone. Unfortunately, the man who broke that pattern, James H. Monteath, believed that the surest way to force assimilation upon the Blackfeet was to withhold rations from anyone who, in the agent's estimation, was able-bodied. During his ruinous tenure between 1900 and 1905, Monteath slashed the ration rolls from more than 2,000 names to fewer than 100. In terms of privation, at least, Monteath's self-described "New Policy" must have had a very familiar feel to the Blackfeet.[90]

Clarke orchestrated a campaign in the fall of 1903 to have Monteath removed, alleging "maladministration," which included the proliferation of alcohol on the reservation. The ensuing battle was fought largely in print in two rival newspapers from Great Falls, the most sizable nearby town, as the *Daily Leader* backed the Clarke faction while the *Tribune* sided with Monteath. Through a proxy, the agent insisted that "the breeds are responsible for any dissatisfaction there may be on the reservation," a common allegation by Indian agents who believed that peoples of mixed ancestry like Helen and Horace fomented dissension by manipulating their supposedly slow-witted relatives of pure blood.[91] On another occasion Monteath wrote the commissioner of Indian affairs to complain, "I really believe that Helen and Horace Clarke are crazy," adding gratuitously that "their mother was insane before her death."[92] Though the Clarkes outlasted Monteath, who was replaced in early 1905, their victory was pyrrhic: Horace spent time in the reservation jail, and Monteath blacklisted Helen with federal officials, a factor that in the opinion of an ally prevented her reappointment with the Indian Office.[93]

Monteath's vindictiveness may thus explain why, when the Blackfeet Reservation was allotted beginning in 1907, Helen Clarke was not selected for the job. Certainly she was an obvious and qualified candidate, given her extensive work in Indian Territory. Moreover, if federal authorities had once believed that her mixed ancestry gave her an advantage in dealing with native peoples, how could it be anything but a help with the Piegans, who shared her blood and trusted her counsel? Leaving nothing to chance, the Blackfeet even sent a petition signed by two hundred individuals (representing almost one-tenth of the reservation population) to the commissioner of Indian affairs recommending Clarke for the post, but to no avail; Charles Roblin, a white man who had valuable allotting experience of his own, would see the Piegans through the complex transition to a new way of life.[94]

Compounding Clarke's frustration, no doubt, was her required participation in a humiliating charade: proving her native bona fides in order to secure a homestead. Though that was a standard procedure in the allotting process, her personal history was already well known to the government. Nevertheless, on an April day in 1909, an elderly and respected chief named Little Dog shuffled into agency headquarters and testified to Roblin that Clarke's mother was a full-blood Piegan, thus entitling her daughter to 320 acres of Montana soil.[95] Clarke must have appreciated the irony. After spending most of a decade badgering native peoples to accept allotments in Indian Territory, she had come to rely upon an Indian—and, if judged by Little Dog's traditional dress, an unreconstructed one at that—to vouch for her native ancestry. Thus endorsed by the chief, Clarke became allottee number 283.

GUESTS STAYING AT New York's brand-new McAlpin Hotel in the summer of 1913 could be forgiven if they overlooked some of the building's state-of-the-art amenities, which included Russian and Turkish baths as well as a striking subterranean bar decorated with polychrome terra-cotta murals depicting the city's maritime history.[96] Instead, their attention would have been drawn to the rooftop of the building, located at the intersection of Broadway and Thirty-Fourth Street, where a group of visiting Blackfeet Indians had pitched their teepees, because—in the words of their chief, Three Bear—"my people want air . . . [a] hot room [is] no good. [We] want plenty [of time] outdoors." Louis Hill had brought the natives to New York to promote Glacier National Park, and before they left, the Blackfeet took in sights like the Brooklyn Bridge, the Bronx Zoo, and that quintessential feature of modern city life, the new subway system, then in its infancy.[97]

Hill's publicity stunt had the desired effect, as Helen and Horace Clarke watched scores of well-dressed easterners disembark from the Great Northern's Oriental Limited during the hotel's inaugural season. These visitors then spent vast sums of money at the lodge or on a variety of recreational activities, from hunting and fishing to touring the park's backcountry on horseback with an expert guide. As the air turned chilly and the leaves began to fall, bringing the curtain down on the lodge's spectacular debut season, the Clarkes could see clearly that Glacier National Park offered economic opportunity for them as well.

In truth, they needed extra income. If in their twilight years both enjoyed good health, their finances were not nearly so robust. Like many mixed-blood people on the reservation, who by this time constituted nearly half its total population, the Clarkes ran a few cattle and grew hay. Such ventures, however, were becoming increasingly difficult to sustain, as the allotment process continued to carve up tribal lands and thus reduce common grazing space.[98] More to the point is a recollection by one of Helen's friends: "Neither of them had much business ability so they never made much money."[99]

Some sense of the Clarkes' economic hardships emerges in a series of letters between Helen and J. H. Sherburne, who was the licensed Indian trader on the Blackfeet Reservation. Born in Maine in 1851, Sherburne as a young man had migrated west in search of work and wound up eventually in Indian Territory, where in 1876 he started a trading post. There he met Helen Clarke and was so inspired by her "stories of the great west, and especially Montana . . . [that] we turned our thoughts to the big open spaces in the land of the great mountains."[100] In the end, her encouragement of Sherburne served as a Trojan horse of sorts; according to one observer, by the early 1920s the trader had devoured huge portions of the reservation by buying up the land patents of impoverished Indians.[101]

Although Helen and her brother were not as destitute as many of their neighbors, her correspondence with Sherburne indicates that they were nevertheless on intimate terms with privation. For instance, in one letter she requested a package of rat poison, as "my house is alive with mice." In another, scribbled during a brutal cold snap, Helen asked about a shipment of goods that had not yet arrived. Noting that she had only enough heating oil to get her through the night, she wrote, "We are in a sad plight—no oil . . . and soon no butter . . . send goods so soon as you can."[102] These missives, however, were probably easier to draft than the many concluding with apologies like this one, from January 1916: "Wish we could have paid more on old note—but a little is better than nothing."[103]

In this bleak economic milieu the aging Clarke siblings formed a plan to develop a portion of their land, hoping to capitalize on the Glacier National Park tourist trade. Helen explained in October 1913, "We intend to build chalets and bungalows and induce others to do likewise which will not only benefit the public but enhance the value of our own lands."[104] It was a fine idea, but implementing it was not nearly so simple as she described. After all, as allotted Indians, the Clarkes had first to secure title to their property, which was held in trust by the federal government according to the terms of the Dawes Act. Helen's subsequent navigation of the federal bureaucracy reveals much about the status of mixed-blood peoples at the turn of the century.

While in many cases the government was eager to grant outright ownership to such individuals, thus obviating the need to support them, the unique circumstances of Helen's career helped facilitate her application. From the moment her inquiry arrived in Washington, officials in the Indian Service fast-tracked the paperwork; one of the commissioner's assistants noted that, though the schedule of Blackfeet allotments had not yet been approved by the president, the Clarkes' case "will be taken up specially, and this Office will make a recommendation to the Department [of the Interior] that the allotments be approved."[105]

In other crucial respects, however, her petition was treated like that of any Indian seeking to gain title to allotted land, highlighting the racist assumptions of the day concerning those of native ancestry. To begin with, she needed an endorsement from the reservation's Indian agent. More disheartening was a questionnaire designed to gauge her personal competency, which asked among other things her degree of Indian blood and whether or not she used intoxicants. For a woman who had traveled widely, been the first of her sex to win elected office in Montana, and served the government for nearly a decade as an allotting agent, Helen must have been incredulous as she wrote tersely in another letter, "[W]e know we are capable of handling our own affairs."[106]

Though the Clarkes' applications were approved in the spring of 1914, their desire for financial security did not materialize after they took ownership of the land. The siblings managed to find willing renters, but their timing could hardly have been worse: the sharp economic downturn following World War I caused many of their tenants to default on their payments. As one Sherburne associate explained to Helen, "It is most awful hard to collect a Dollar from any body on any thing [at] these present times." That realization did not stop the trader from trying to collect on Helen's debt, which by the end of the decade had ballooned to nearly $1,500.[107]

IF IT DID NOT bring her riches, Clarke's proximity to Glacier Park brought her visitors instead. In time, the house she shared with her brother became renowned as something of a rustic literary salon, where guests sat for hours with her in order to learn more about the Piegans, who thanks to Louis Hill had became famous nationwide as "the Glacier Indians." However well meaning, her white visitors tended to exoticize their hostess, emphasizing—intentionally or otherwise—her racial difference. Of course, that seems to have been what drew many to her in the first place. Take, for instance, a letter from the prominent Montana suffragist Mary O'Neill, who in 1910 wrote ostensibly to invite Clarke to a statewide gathering of women's organizations. "How are you, Woman with the Shadow eyes?" she began, before arriving at the true purpose of her letter: "One thing I want to see [is] if you and I can collaborate on a book of the Mystic lore of the Indians—and no one could know it better than you."[108] And if these were the sentiments of a suffragette, one can only imagine the extent of the racial caricatures drawn by people who were not so well meaning.

Even her closest friends tended to fetishize Clarke's hybridity. One of them, Helen Fitzgerald Sanders, daughter-in-law of Clarke's most loyal patron, spent extensive time with the Clarke siblings while researching her novel *The White Quiver*. Published in 1913, the book, according to its author, "is a story of the Piegan Indians before they felt the influence of the white man." In this way Sanders's volume resembled the contemporary pictures of the photographer Edward S. Curtis or the paintings of the Taos Society of Artists (whose most senior member, Joseph Henry Sharp, visited Clarke at Glacier), with their romantic and noble visions of an uncorrupted native past. Helen and Horace had been Sanders's portal to that world, which the author acknowledged in her dedication: "To Helen P. Clarke, 'Pi-o-to-po-wa-ka,' in whose noble character mingles the best of the white race and the red."[109]

What Clarke made of such patronizing oblations, however generous and heartfelt, is hard to assess. She was hardly a stranger to this kind of purple language, but it is easy to imagine that she experienced less internal conflict when visited by a second group of guests: needy Piegans. In later years "Aunt Helen," as she was known, became a trusted source of emotional and financial support for Indians on the reservation, especially the elderly, who had experienced the most trouble in conforming to the assimilated ideal set forth in the Dawes Act. According to one friend, it was this generosity, more than any absence of business acumen, that explained the poverty of Clarke's later years.[110]

Helen P. Clarke. Clarke struggled to walk in both white and native worlds, dismissed by some as a "half-breed" but fetishized by others for her in-between-ness. Courtesy of the Montana Historical Society.

On 4 March 1923 a Catholic priest named Father Halligan was called to the Clarkes' home. The old woman, now seventy-five, was failing, and since she had always been a devout member of the church, someone—likely Horace—knew she would take great comfort in having a clergyman nearby. It was pneumonia, "the old man's friend," that had pushed her to the brink of death, an ironic fate, given that it was her lungs that had animated her most defining feature, the sonorous voice that had once thrilled audiences and, more recently, heralded bleak tidings for the Poncas and the Otoe-Missourias.

As he and a small group kept a bedside vigil throughout the night, Father Halligan noticed that, toward the end, Helen "was reviewing her whole life." Because of her weakened condition the priest could make out very little of what she said, but he clearly heard these words, which he shared at her eulogy a few days later. "Children," she had whispered, "should have nothing but the greatest admiration[,] the greatest respect, [and] the greatest love and reverence for their teachers." Halligan explained to the mourners who gathered at her grave site

Headstone at the grave of Helen P. Clarke, 2007. If the dates are incorrect (she was born in 1848), it is certain that Helen P. Clarke was "a pioneer." As the first woman to hold elective office in Montana and one of the very few to serve as an allotting agent, she was an exceptional woman and will be inducted into the Gallery of Outstanding Montanans in 2015. There she will join her nephew John, who was so honored in 2003. Photograph by the author.

(a short walk from the house Helen and Horace had shared for more than two decades) that these "golden words of wisdom" harked back to the "best and happiest years of her life," when she had taught the young children of the territory.[111]

Perhaps the priest was right, that at the hour of her death Clarke thought only of her students at Fort Benton and Helena (and maybe even San Francisco). Yet there is another possible interpretation of her last words, one in which she is still the teacher but her students are the native peoples to whom she devoted so many years. To be sure, such an equation would leave Clarke open to unsettling charges of condescension and self-aggrandizement. Nevertheless, at least according to one acquaintance, this alternative reading may be closer to the truth: "Whatever her own opinions, she could only serve her people by counseling them to submit, make the best of the situation and so educate themselves that they might meet the whites on their own ground and possibly, finally, to obtain justice."[112]

In the summer of 1915 James Willard Schultz, a white man who had married a Piegan woman and lived with the tribe for years, sat with a group of elders around a campfire just outside the boundaries of Glacier National Park. The men feasted on roasted elk ribs and shared a pipe, reminiscing about the old days. After a time the conversation turned serious, with one of the men railing against "the most recent wrong put upon us by the whites." The headman was referring not to the creation of the park, or even to the efforts of federal authorities to exclude the Blackfeet from its premises, but rather to the white outsiders' renaming of the features of the landscape. The group concluded that "the whites' names should at once be wiped out and our names restored to the maps of the region."

Ten years elapsed before Schultz and two respected Piegan elders, Curly Bear and Takes-Gun First, had the chance to realize their plan, but they took to it with tremendous enthusiasm. Over the course of a week in June 1925, the men methodically renamed the sites one by one. In this way, Florence Falls became Pai-ota Oh'tôkwi, or "Flying Woman Falls," named for a sacred holy woman, and the Sherburne Lakes were rechristened Kai'yoîks Otsitait'ska O'mûksîkîmîks, or "Fighting Bears' Lakes," in honor of a tussle between two grizzlies.

Toward the end of their work the group paused to consider Helen Lake, a cerulean glacier-fed pool located in the north-central portion of the park, not far from the spot where George Bird Grinnell had experienced his epiphany forty years earlier. Although they changed the name of the lake, they did not change the person to whom it referred, calling it Pai'ota-pamakan O'mûksîkîmî, or "Came Running Back Lake," both variations of Helen's Indian moniker. In explaining its significance, Schultz wrote that "Miss Clark was a woman of high education, and was a teacher in various Montana schools." He and his friends were particularly proud to claim her as a Piegan.[113]

Today, because of Helen Lake's remote location and the poor campsite nearby, it receives fewer visitors than many other parts of Glacier National Park. Those who do stop at its shores, however, are well rewarded. Enclosed on three sides by soaring mountain walls, backpackers can revel in a sense of total isolation, broken only by the bleat of a mountain goat or the sight of a grizzly seeking refreshment from the impossibly blue waters. If they think of it at all, hikers who reach this lovely spot might wonder about its supposed namesake, the daughter of a white engineer with the U.S. Geological Survey who mapped the area in the early twentieth century.[114] The Piegans, to whom the land originally belonged, maintain that it honors someone else, a complex woman of many talents who, for a time, managed to walk between two increasingly divided worlds.

5

The Man Who Talks Not

Nearly seven decades after Helen Clarke's death, the Montana Historical Society (MHS) mounted a lavish retrospective in 1993 featuring the work of her nephew John L. Clarke, a woodcut artist with a remarkable biography. Descended from one of the state's oldest pioneer families, Clarke had overcome the inability to hear or speak and established a career as an internationally acclaimed sculptor, known especially for his extraordinary renderings of western wildlife. As one admirer recalled, "When John L. Clarke finished carving a bear, you could just smell it."[1]

Highlighting the Helena exhibition was the unveiling of a splendid bas-relief frieze. Carved from a one-ton block of cottonwood, *Blackfeet Encampment* captures the essence of the tribe's lifeways in the period before Montana's absorption by the United States. Accompanied by their dogs, a group of Indians on horseback arrives at a small stand of teepees, whose residents emerge from their lodges to greet the newcomers. A herd of ponies grazing in the distance speaks to the prosperity of the camp, while a kettle suspended over an open fire holds the promise of nourishment for the weary travel-

John L. Clarke and *Blackfeet Encampment*, ca. 1950s. Clarke carved his master-piece on-site at the Montana Historical Society, using both traditional and contemporary tools. Courtesy of Joyce Clarke Turvey.

ers. It is a moving scene, conveying the unmistakable impression that all is right with the world.

The panel had a curious history. It was commissioned in the early 1950s for the MHS, and Clarke executed the frieze on-site, using modern tools (electric drills) as well as more traditional ones (hammer and chisel). When it was completed in 1956, however, its size—thirteen feet long and four feet high—exceeded the display space, and so the MHS lent it to the University of Montana in Missoula. There it hung in the campus field house for the next three decades, presiding over boxing matches, college basketball games, and even a concert by the Grateful Dead, before finding a second home in Great Falls at the Montana School for the Deaf and Blind. Seven years later the MHS reclaimed the panel as the centerpiece for the planned retrospective. Ever since, it has welcomed visitors from its perch just inside the building's entrance.[2]

The peregrinations of *Blackfeet Encampment* stand in marked contrast to the permanence of its creator. Except for short stints at several boarding schools during his childhood and adolescence, John Clarke spent virtually his entire life on the Blackfeet Reservation and its immediate environs. Even as his artworks impressed American and European audiences and found homes in the personal collections of President Warren G. Harding and John D. Rockefeller Jr., Clarke himself remained rooted firmly in place.

There were, of course, compelling reasons for him to stay put. For one thing, his deafness, coupled with his sustained poverty, imposed significant limitations. For another, he was deeply attached to the environment of northern Montana, which inspired his artistry and furnished unparalleled opportunities for outdoor recreation. Indeed, one photo from his youth neatly captures these twin passions: Clarke, rifle in hand, posing proudly outside a log cabin in the dead of winter, with a landscape painting and two carved bears resting on a ledge nearby.

There was likely another reason behind Clarke's persistence in East Glacier Park, however. It had become harder for peoples of mixed ancestry to negotiate life beyond the reservation boundaries. What had been a permeable membrane for his aunt Helen, one through which she passed often if not always easily, had thickened as the twentieth century wore on. The gulf between the races was perhaps most obvious at the edges of the Blackfeet Reservation, in places like Cut Bank, the nearly all-white town on the eastern side whose residents and shopkeepers looked upon Indian visitors with withering hostility. In time the difference between full and mixed-blood peoples held meaning primarily on the reservation itself; to whites living nearby, anyone with obvious native ancestry was simply "Indian."[3]

In truth, such distinctions based on degree of blood seem to have meant little to John Clarke, who considered himself a Piegan. This is not to say that he denied his Anglo ancestry or showed antipathy

John L. Clarke, ca. 1910s. This photo captures Clarke's twin passions: hunting and art. The one pursuit informed the other, as his adventures in Glacier country allowed him to observe closely the wildlife he later rendered in cottonwood. Courtesy of Joyce Clarke Turvey.

toward whites; quite the contrary—he married a white woman, with whom he adopted a white daughter. And he had numerous white benefactors, patrons, and friends. Nevertheless, his life and career suggest that, in the end, he identified more with Coth-co-co-na's people than with Malcolm Clarke's, and thus chose to walk primarily in one world, not two.

A World of Muffled Sound

Until the twentieth-century advent of antibiotics like penicillin, scarlet fever was a childhood scourge. Parents of afflicted youngsters had little warning of the horrors about to ensue—perhaps a complaint of slight malaise or a passing chill. Yet when the disease took hold, terrifying symptoms appeared in rapid succession: convulsive vomiting, powerful spasms, and then a fever rising to 105 degrees or beyond. Usually by the second day, victims bore the telltale rash (the result of toxin released by the bacteria), a constellation of red dots emanating from the neck and chest and spreading eventually over the patient's entire body.

Though not as lethal as smallpox, scarlet fever still exacted its own grim toll. In the late nineteenth century the Boston City Hospital reported a mortality rate of nearly 10 percent for patients afflicted with the disease, and a rate two to three times higher during especially severe outbreaks. Though adults were also susceptible, children, particularly those under the age of six, were the principal victims. In the absence of any known treatment, anguished parents could do little except alleviate the discomfort and pray for recovery, which could take weeks.[4]

Horace Clarke and his wife, Margaret, called First Kill by the Piegans, of whom she was a full-blooded member, knew intimately the terrors of scarlet fever. During the 1880s the sickness passed through their modest ranch in Highwood, Montana, like the angel of death. Though it spared their children Malcolm, Ned, and Maggie, it carried off four other boys all under the age of five. And it ravaged another, John, destroying his ability to hear.[5]

The malady seized John in the autumn of 1883, when he was two and half years old. The timing was typical of the disease, which tended to strike in spring and fall, as were its side effects. A leading medical sourcebook from the time identified scarlet fever as a chief cause of deafness in children, owing to the spread of inflammation from the throat to the middle ear, which in acute cases led to permanent hearing loss. Though it could not have seemed so at the time, John was actually among the fortunate, for he escaped other dire complications such as kidney failure and meningitis.[6]

Margaret must have played some role in her son's care, which probably involved swabbing his feverish body with a wet cloth and moisturizing his skin as it began to slough off after the rash subsided, but she would have been limited by her pregnancy with Maggie, who was born on Christmas Eve 1883. Thus, responsibility for John probably fell to Horace's mother, Coth-co-co-na, and especially to Horace's sister Isabel, who had recently returned from her aunt Charlotte's Minneapolis home, where she had spent the decade after their father's murder. The siblings were close; in fact, knowing Isabel's love of music, Horace sometime around 1880 arranged for the shipment of a piano upriver from St. Louis.[7]

How the family initially reacted to John's impairment is unknown, but for the little boy with black hair and dark complexion, it must have been frightening to be suddenly unable to hear the timbre of his parents' voices or the gentle lowing of the family cattle. Moreover, John's deafness sharply ended his acquisition of speech at just the moment that many children experience rapid linguistic development. Supposedly, he was capable of only one sound—an alarmed yell—and as a child he was prone to violent tantrums when he could not make himself understood.[8] Still, he could see with perfect clarity as adults conversed around him, as his aunt Isabel delighted visitors with her piano playing and, most poignantly, as his older brothers left with their aunt Helen for the Carlisle School in Pennsylvania.

John, by contrast, had no access to proper education until he was a teenager, because the closest Indian school at Fort Shaw, on the other side of Great Falls, made no accommodation for students with disabilities.[9] Presumably, he spent the majority of his time at Horace's side, tending the Clarke livestock and, after the family moved to Midvale around 1889, accompanying his father on hunting and fishing trips into the wilds that later became Glacier National Park. Such excursions stimulated his other senses—the smell of pine, the taste of wild berries, the sting of glacier-fed streams. But the sight of fauna left the deepest impression upon John: playful grizzly bears and sleek mountain lions, proud bighorn sheep and sure-footed mountain goats.

This idyll, if that it was, came to an abrupt conclusion in the fall of 1894 when John left for the bleak hamlet of Devil's Lake, some seven hundred miles distant, to attend the North Dakota School for the Deaf. Why his parents chose that institution is uncertain, especially since Montana had established its own such facility just south of Helena the year before. Perhaps it was the NDSD's strong academic reputation and its visionary superintendent that swayed them, or the handsome new schoolhouse made of brick and featuring amenities like wood-burning stoves and oil lamps. By contrast, the fledging Montana school operated in a leased two-story house.

If the choice of North Dakota was unusual, the timing was probably not, for John's world began unraveling in the early 1890s, starting with the breakup of his parents' marriage. After some fifteen years together, Horace and Margaret "quit each other," in the parlance of the day. While in times past John might have turned to his aunts for comfort, they were largely unavailable as this family crisis unfolded: Helen was working in Indian Territory, and in 1891 Isabel had married Tom Dawson, the mixed-blood son of a prominent American Fur Company trader. His grandmother Coth-co-co-na was in failing health and died the following summer, leaving John effectively alone, at age thirteen, to confront the dissolution of his home life. Little wonder, then, that his parents chose that moment to ship him off to school.

FORMAL INSTRUCTION FOR the deaf in the United States began in 1817 with the establishment of the American School for the Deaf in Hartford, Connecticut, the first permanent institution of its kind in the nation.[10] By the end of the nineteenth century such institutions could be found across the country, although rural areas remained chronically underserved, a problem that preoccupied Anson Rudolph Spear, a twenty-nine-year-old deaf Minnesotan. Spear had studied briefly at Gallaudet College, founded in 1864 in Washington, D.C., and later worked at the Census Bureau before returning home to the Twin Cities in the early 1880s. In particular, he worried that deaf children in the new state of North Dakota—admitted to the union in 1889 and bordering Minnesota immediately to the west—would suffer from limited learning opportunities.

During North Dakota's inaugural legislative session, Spear became a fixture in the halls of the state capital at Bismarck, lobbying members of the house and the senate to remember the most disadvantaged of their constituents. His efforts paid off when on the very last day of the session the legislature overrode the veto of the state's parsimonious governor and endorsed a bill providing for the creation of the NDSD. Housed originally in a vacant bank building, the school opened its doors in the fall of 1890, welcoming twenty-three students. Spear became the first superintendent, thought to be the youngest leader of a state-run educational institution anywhere in the country.[11]

From the beginning the NDSD was a family operation. Spear's deaf wife, Julia, a handsome woman with sandy hair worn in a bun, served as the school's matron, handling all the cooking and cleaning and assuming her husband's administrative duties when illness incapacitated him. Julia's younger sister, Clara Halvorson, who could hear, accepted an appointment as the NDSD's first teacher. And the Spears had a dog, an enormous Saint Bernard named Kent who, true to the popular image of the breed, loved to frolic in the snow, a trait that forever endeared him to the children.

This welcoming atmosphere eased the inevitable homesickness and anxiety that students experienced, which must have been particularly acute for John Clarke when he arrived just before Thanksgiving in 1894. After all, the boy was much farther from home than most of his fifty-odd classmates and stood out as perhaps the only one among them with native ancestry. Maybe the Christmas party that year, described lovingly in the school newspaper, lifted his spirits: "The pupils' dialogues were done in sign language. The Christmas tree was prettily decorated with colored candles. . . . Promptly at 7:30 P.M. Santa Claus rapped on the window. What followed can only be imagined."

John soon learned that while such merriment had its place at the NDSD, it was secondary to the academic aims promoted by Anson Spear. Photos of the bespectacled superintendent suggest that he was aptly named—thin and sharp, with dark, piercing eyes. And he was utterly devoted to his work. Central to Spear's educational vision was his belief in manualism, which placed him on one side of a contentious and enduring debate. Advocates of this approach favored the teaching of American Sign Language (ASL), which was thought to unite the deaf by a common means of communication and, by extension, a similar set of cultural experiences.[12]

After the Civil War, however, another instructional method gained momentum, one that emphasized lipreading and the acquisition of speech. These oralists insisted that deafness was a handicap to be overcome on the road to inclusion in mainstream society, and that reliance upon hand signs imposed unnecessary and humiliating segregation on the deaf. Especially with the establishment in 1867 of the Clarke School for the Deaf in Northampton, Massachusetts, proponents of oralism made significant inroads in American deaf education, and by century's end they had achieved rough parity with the manualists.[13]

Spear, however, remained doggedly committed to manualism and the larger goal of building a national deaf community. To that end, he incorporated vocational instruction into the NDSD curriculum, so that graduates emerged with self-reliance and a firm set of job skills, insulating them against potential prejudice from the hearing. Thus, in addition to instruction in basic subjects like reading, writing, and mathematics, girls learned sewing and needlework while boys like John trained as printers on a small, foot-powered press.

The two and a half years John Clarke spent at the NDSD had profound implications for the rest of his life. For one thing, Spear's devotion to manualism meant that John never learned to lip-read, a fact that in later years surprised some of the visitors to his art studio. On the other hand, John became fluent in ASL during his time in North Dakota, which he augmented with Plains Indian Sign Language (PISL), a centuries-old form of communication that developed among the many Great Plains tribes, which shared no mutual spoken tongue (ASL and PISL are lexically similar but linguistically unrelated).[14]

John's time in North Dakota helped, too, in the acquisition of the skills he needed to communicate with those inexpert in signed communication. Shortly after his arrival in the fall of 1894, John composed the first missive he ever sent, which contained the letters of the alphabet, a handful of words he had learned, and the transcription of a sentence. His father was deeply moved, and wrote in reply, "My Dear, Dear Son, How thankful I am that a kind Providence has provided you the means to make known your thoughts. I trust that by spring you will be able to write understandingly and intelligently. This letter of yours being the first, I will cherish and keep always."[15]

As important as the development of literacy and communication skills was the hardy work ethic that Spear preached and modeled and that took root in John. In his adulthood, Clarke treated woodcarving as a vocation, laboring at it almost every day and using his skills to support himself and his family, precisely the self-reliance that Spear had envisioned. Clarke was so dedicated to his craft that he packed carving tools among his personal effects when he entered the hospital for what turned out to be the last time. And yet a life of such purpose and creativity was scarcely imaginable in June 1897 when he left Devil's Lake for home and an uncertain future.

A RECURRING THEME in the legend of John L. Clarke is that he was discovered sometime before World War I by Louis W. Hill, the president of the Great Northern Railway. According to a contemporary newspaper article, after a guided hike through the backcountry of Glacier National Park, Hill noticed his Indian escort intently sketching a lovely panorama of Glacier's Two Medicine Falls using a lead pencil and a piece of rough board. When Hill asked the young man what he was drawing, Clarke communicated that he was "just putting down what Great Spirit heap up hisself."[16]

The railroad magnate was sufficiently impressed that, upon returning to his home in St. Paul, he shipped some proper materials to Clarke so that the prodigy might execute the scene in oil. Shortly after Christmas, Hill opened a package from Montana and "was suddenly taken back to 'God's Own Country,' as he expressed it . . . clothed in all the radiance of its gorgeous, natural garb." The tableau enjoyed prominent display in the family mansion for years thereafter.

Central to this account is the notion that Clarke "was a born artist and came into the light of things artistic with nature as his only teacher." A catalog for one of his art exhibits many years later was even more explicit in making this point: "Nearly full blooded, [Clarke] takes the natural Indian's delight in hunting and fishing and to this he adapted his early carving in wood."[17] Though it conjures up the hoary stereotype of the "ecological Indian" who lives in perfect harmony with his surroundings, there was at least some truth in this telling.[18] As Clarke himself explained much later, he began experimenting with forms at a tender age: "When I was a boy I first used mud that was solid or sticky enough from any place I could find it," including the riverbanks near his home.[19]

Even if John showed creative promise early in his youth, it is inaccurate to suggest that he was entirely self-taught, a claim that others, including his wife, made occasionally but that he himself never did. As it happened, two brief yet critical interventions around the turn of the twentieth century harnessed his abilities and propelled him into a career as a woodcut artist. The first of these took place just after Christmas 1898, when John left his father's home at Midvale, where he had lived since returning from the NDSD eighteen months before, and traveled two hundred miles south to the small town of Boulder, Montana.

Established in the early 1860s as a stagecoach stop between Fort Benton and the goldfields of the territory's southwestern corner, Boulder took its name from the huge rocks cluttering the small valley where it nestled. The settlement rose to local prominence in the 1880s, thanks to some nearby hot springs and especially its designation as the seat of Jefferson County. The town fathers capitalized on this momentum to lure a range of state institutions during the early years of the next decade, among them the Montana Deaf and Dumb Asylum.

Located originally in a rented home, the school upgraded to an extraordinary new facility on the town's east side just months before John Clarke's matriculation. Fashioned from vermillion-colored bricks and combining the Italianate and Renaissance Revival styles that were popular at the time, the structure boasted a gabled roof, cantilevered granite stairways, maple floors, a glazed tile fireplace, and other flourishes. One reporter who happened to be deaf and "semi-mute" himself wrote, "Anyone taking the time to visit this school will go away with the feeling that this is a mighty good world to live in, especially the section called Montana, since she treats her unfortunates in such a splendid manner."[20]

For the eighteen-year-old Clarke, it was not the majesty of the schoolhouse but what took place inside that made all the difference. He recalled, "While I attended the Boulder School for the Deaf, there was a carving class. This was my first experience in carving. . . . I carve because I take great pleasure in making what I see that is beautiful."[21] Though the course was probably vocational in nature, Clarke was less interested in making decorative plaques and other items manufactured in shop classes of the period.[22] Rather, as he explained, "When I see an animal I feel the wish to create it in wood as near as possible."

Though a pivotal interlude in his artistic development, his stay in

John L. Clarke in his studio, 1920s. Described by one visitor as a "scene from the animal kingdom," Clarke's studio at East Glacier Park was crowded with carvings in various stages of completion. Note the Rocky Mountain goat, his signature subject, at the center. Courtesy of Joyce Clarke Turvey.

Boulder was nevertheless a short one: nine months later he was back at his father's Midvale home in time to be counted in the September 1899 census on the Blackfeet Reservation. Such brevity suggests that Clarke may have attended the Montana Deaf and Dumb Asylum specifically to take the carving class he so enjoyed. In any event, he did not tarry long with his family, leaving at some point that autumn for one last round of schooling, this time in St. Francis, Wisconsin, just outside of Milwaukee.

Like those of his enrollment at the NDSD, the moment and especially the choice of location invite scrutiny. And once again it seems that Clarke family dynamics were involved, with Aunt Helen playing perhaps a decisive role. Certainly the two crossed paths in

Midvale in the summer of 1899, as Helen had returned from her allotment work in Indian Territory just as John, then eighteen, concluded his studies in Boulder. It is easy to imagine the boy's aunt, a former teacher, encouraging her nephew to continue his education and, given her devout Catholicism, suggesting a parochial institution despite its location fifteen hundred miles to the east.

If indeed the appeal of religious instruction was a key variable in the decision to send John to Wisconsin, Helen, or whoever urged such an outcome, could hardly have chosen a better environment for the teenager. The village of St. Francis owed its existence to the Catholic church, for it was founded in 1849 by eleven Franciscan laypeople from Bavaria who had immigrated, at the behest of Milwaukee's first archbishop, to minister to the city's growing German population. Seven years later the group built a seminary on the shores of Lake Michigan, cementing the importance of the little town in the religious life of the greater Milwaukee area.

St. John's School for the Deaf opened in the late nineteenth century about a mile inland from the seminary complex and soon became the hub of Milwaukee's small but cohesive deaf community.[23] Though archdiocese records indicate that Clarke enrolled on 4 November 1899, no record of his initial impression survives. But Milwaukee must have impressed him: with nearly 300,000 residents it was the fourteenth-largest city in the United States, and easily the most imposing urban agglomeration he had ever seen. While he could not distinguish their unusual accents, he surely registered the diversity of the city's many immigrant groups in other ways: the colorful ethnic dress of various eastern European peoples; austere Scandinavians, their faces toughened by years of hard farm labor; and the unintelligible signs adorning German breweries, leather shops, and grocery stores.[24]

The school's director recognized his new student's creative abilities right away. "John had great talent for drawing," he remembered, "and was the most wonderful penman." Still, he wanted him, like all his charges, to develop a marketable skill, and thus he pushed wood-working instead. The director also emphasized the spiritual compo-nent of Clarke's education, noting proudly that during Clarke's time at St. John's, he "acquire[d] a good religious training and firmer character."[25] While the director considered these two pursuits of equal importance, his student apparently did not: John carved for the rest of his life, but evinced little interest in organized religion.[26]

Clarke studied at St. John's until late 1904, leaving just before Christmas to board in Milwaukee, where the school had found him a job making furniture and sculpting church altars.[27] There was no shortage of work for the young man or others of his trade in those heady days, as the city's population swelled during the early twenti-eth century, augmented especially by fresh waves of European immi-grants who crowded into the ethnic neighborhoods on the South Side. However, unlike these foreign-born men and women who came to Milwaukee seeking new and better lives, Clarke after a few years (when exactly is unknown) opted to return to the old country of northern Montana, where he remained for the rest of his days.

Cutapuis

By the early twentieth century, the artist Charles Marion Russell was easily the most beloved figure in Montana, known throughout the United States and even overseas for his vivid paintings of the Ameri-can West. Born in 1864 to a prominent St. Louis family, Charlie in his youth devoured the adolescent pulp fiction that became popular after the Civil War and that bred in him an insatiable curiosity about the frontier. Thinking that a stretch of manual labor on a western ranch might disabuse their son of his dreamy notions, his exasper-ated parents underwrote the boy's trip to Montana in the summer of 1880. The plan backfired. Charlie never returned to his hometown, except for occasional visits.[28]

After spending several years in the saddle as a ranch hand, Russell had by the late 1880s turned his attention from working the range to capturing it with his paintbrush, an urgent task given that the Old West, as most thought of it, was quickly disappearing in the face of relentless modernization. His deeply romantic portraits of frontier subjects thus had broad appeal, earning him fame and wealth. Coupled with his legendary skills as a raconteur, Russell's good nature won him the enduring affection of white Montanans, who considered "the Cowboy Artist" one of their own. Even today, the iconic buffalo skull icon he used as an imprimatur appears on many of the state's automobile license plates.[29]

Considering Russell's popularity and especially his reputation as an artist, John Clarke was surely ecstatic when he received a letter from Russell in May 1918 in response to a missive Clarke sent earlier that spring. The note is classic Russell: replete with misspellings and unorthodox punctuation, but nonetheless filled with charm and generosity. Apparently, Clarke had written seeking advice about the art market, and Russell offered his help, explaining, "[T]here is onley one Art store here [in Great Falls, where he lived] and I know they would be glad to handle your worke but whether they could sell it I couldint say . . . if you send aney here I will boost fore you."[30]

That the two had never met and were at far different stages in their careers raises the question why Russell took an interest in Clarke. There are several reasons, not least among them Russell's characteristic liberality. For another, Clarke's personal circumstances probably aroused the older man's curiosity and compassion. Unlike most of his contemporary white Montanans, Russell evinced a sincere concern for the state's native peoples and lamented the federal government's duplicity in its dealings with them. Moreover, just two years prior to his correspondence with Clarke, he had taken on a protégé, Joe De Young, a fellow Missourian who, after contracting spinal meningitis on the Arizona set of a Tom Mix western, had lost his hearing.[31]

Most of all, Russell championed Clarke because he admired the younger man's work. As Clarke's wife, Mamie, recalled, after that first exchange of letters, Russell dropped in at her husband's studio every summer except his last, in 1926, when Russell's failing health prevented even a short trip to East Glacier Park. "His visits were of greatest possible moments to John," Mamie explained, adding, "Mr. Russell would . . . look at all of my husband's work, sculpture and landscape (oil) and praise it, encouraging just enough and not too much. He was so understanding, deeply sympathetic and in all wholly lovable."[32] The men traded stories and ideas in PISL, which Russell had picked up from some of his native friends.

Charlie Russell was not the only prominent individual who admired John Clarke's early artwork. Louis Hill, who had first noticed Clarke's skill with a brush, came to appreciate his carving, too, so much that he commissioned Clarke to provide a number of sculpted wooden bears to serve as bases for the table lamps that illuminated the Glacier Park Lodge. For good measure, Clarke also supplied Hill with a hundred small carvings of Rocky Mountain goats, which sold for a dollar or two in the lodge's gift shop.[33]

Clarke, however, received no compensation for the most important, and lasting, job he did for Hill. In 1921 the Great Northern Railway adopted the Rocky Mountain goat as the company logo, and emblazoned an image of the shaggy animal—based on a Clarke carving—on its trains and promotional materials. Despite claims to the contrary, Clarke was never credited with the design or paid a royalty for its use, perhaps because of a lingering debate over its provenance. And yet the cover of the railroad's own magazine from May 1927 appears to resolve the matter, for it features a young woman posing with a two-foot sculpture of a Rocky Mountain goat executed by John Clarke.[34]

Word of Clarke's abilities seeped beyond the borders of the Treasure State during World War I, aided in no small measure by Mary C. Wheeler, chair of the art department of the Helena Woman's Club. In 1916 Wheeler had invited Clarke to debut his work as part of a larger exhibition, and she was so impressed by an animal grouping featuring a bison bull and cow that she sent the piece to W. Frank Purdy, director of the School of American Sculpture in New York City. Purdy shared Wheeler's enthusiasm and thus arranged for showings of Clarke's work throughout the eastern United States. Their good judgment was vindicated in 1918 when Clarke won his first major award, a gold medal presented by the Pennsylvania Academy of Fine Art for his carving of a bear.[35]

Bolstered by these successes, Clarke expanded his operations. Since his return from Wisconsin, he had lived with his father and Aunt Helen until 1913, when he established a studio on the main thoroughfare in East Glacier Park. The small clapboard house was situated on the east side of the railroad tracks, just a few yards from the Great Northern depot, assuring a steady stream of visitors during the busy summer months. Following his triumph in Pennsylvania and an attendant spike in sales, Clarke opened a second studio—really more of a rustic retreat, with its cramped interior and unfinished stone walls—in Many Glacier, fifty miles northwest in the Swiftcurrent valley. Although Louis Hill built a resort there in 1915, this one a Swiss chalet, Many Glacier's distance from the train station as well as its location inside the eastern boundary of the park offered Clarke unfettered access to wildlife, whether hunting game or merely observing animal mannerisms and behavior, all the better for rendering them in wood.

As he entered his late thirties, John Clarke was not only an accomplished artist but also a deaf man with considerable personal independence who moved comfortably within the nondeaf community as well, thanks in part to his fluency in PISL. Though little is known about his relationship with his siblings, surely he took note of the achievements of his older brother Malcolm, who made the most of the educational opportunities offered him at the Carlisle Indian School, even becoming something of a poster child for the place, reporting on his accomplishments as a rancher and as a leader among the mixed-blood people on the Blackfeet Reservation.[36] Against great odds, John had equaled his sibling. In coming years he would take his place as perhaps the most celebrated member of this remarkable family.

DESPITE THE GOOD FORTUNE that visited John Clarke in 1918—a budding relationship with Charlie Russell, professional accolades, and a new studio—the most important development in his life that year had nothing to do with woodcarving. On 6 May, John wed Mary Peters Simon—known by her friends as Mamie—at Whitefish, a lakeside town on the Great Northern Railway located two dozen miles west of Glacier National Park. Although their wedding day dawned cold, with a touch of frost on the ground, the late spring sun "turned the morning into a bright, mud-puddle day."[37]

Mamie was not a native Montanan, having come west sometime in the early twentieth century with her family, which had roots in the sprawling farm country along the Illinois–Indiana border south of Chicago. She had met John in the summer of 1916, when he was working for his brother-in-law guiding tours through the park and Mamie was cooking for the Bar X Six, a saddle horse ranch headquartered just outside Babb, in the far northwestern corner of the Blackfeet Reservation.[38] That John fell hard for Mamie is easy to imagine, given her broad, handsome face and crystalline eyes. For her part, neither John's

John and Mamie Clarke, ca. 1920s. The couple married in 1918; Mamie, an expert signer, assumed the business responsibilities for John's artistic career. Courtesy of Joyce Clarke Turvey.

race nor his deafness seemed to give her pause, perhaps because as a divorcée, Mamie was no stranger to social bias. Whether she knew sign language beforehand or became fluent after the marriage, she was an expert signer, no small feat for a hearing person. As one friend recalled, "she could sign so fast, you couldn't keep up with her."[39]

By all accounts theirs was a happy marriage, reflecting perhaps the gratitude of two people in their late thirties who had despaired of ever finding life partners (the median age of first marriage at the time was twenty-five for men and twenty-one for women). And yet the union between artist and spouse can be a fraught one, as the marriage of Charlie and Nancy Russell illustrated. In that relationship, the painter's friends resented the supposed meddling of his much younger wife, who kept him out of the saloon and at his easel, determined to push him to still greater creative heights (and earnings).

Mamie played a similar if less controversial role in John's career, serving as his "interpreter, his press secretary, his correspondent, [and] his business manager," though unlike Nancy Russell she never earned a reputation as a harridan. This was in part because of her winning personality, but also because John, though unfailingly described as gentle and patient, resisted any steering. Mamie once explained, with perhaps a hint of loving exasperation, "John does what he pleases, when he pleases. Right now he has abandoned sculpturing for a while to build a boat for fishing on Two Medicine Lake. He has become nearly exhausted building that boat. That is the way he works with everything."[40]

Many outsiders, however, attributed John's accomplishments almost entirely to Mamie, as if a deaf Indian man were incapable of caring for himself or orchestrating his own successful career. Take, for example, a newsletter story from 1927. Describing the fits and starts of John's early years, the writer explained, "Perhaps he might have given up the struggle had not destiny decreed that a white girl should love him, should become his wife and appreciate his ability."[41] While such sentiments were laced with the casual racism of the day (thus the emphasis on Mamie's whiteness), they reflected also the belief that, because of John's deafness, only sustained and compassionate intervention by others could bring his talent to light.

Mamie, of course, was not John's only helper. In the same 1918 letter in which he volunteered to "boost" for Clarke in Great Falls and beyond, Charlie Russell wrote, "[I]f you have an Indian name I think it would be good to use it." Russell's advice was solid, for he knew how valuable his own background as a cowboy had proved in establishing his authenticity with locals and art buyers alike. Up to that point, Clarke had usually signed his pieces "J. L. Clarke," but apparently he warmed to Russell's suggestion and began emblazoning his pieces (usually but not exclusively) with Cutapuis, which in Piegan means "Doesn't Talk," a moniker bestowed upon him as a youth because of his deafness. However authentic, this was also just the sort of touch that would appeal to buyers in the East and elsewhere and help make his sculptures more appealing and valuable.

In time, however, Clarke would go even further in embracing and promoting his native heritage. Like Russell, he often illustrated his correspondence with rough sketches or even full-fledged drawings, and just as Russell had done with the buffalo skull, he began adding an Indian head to his signature. More dramatic still were the changes Clarke made to the façade of his second home-studio, which he opened in the early 1920s on Highway 49, on the opposite side of the railroad tracks and a few hundred yards to the northwest of his previous building, which had burned down sometime after the end of World War I.

Jutting out at a ninety-degree angle on the new building's south side (the side closest to the Glacier Park Lodge, situated just down the road) was a cantilevered sign reading "Indian Sculptor." Clarke also changed the lettering on the placard hanging over the front door. Whereas in the old location the board had read "John L. Clarke" on the top with "art carvings, paintings, and Indian curios" written underneath, he made a slight but intriguing amendment in its new iteration, adding "Navajo Goods" to the lower left-hand corner, below his name.

This was a peculiar bit of advertising, not least because the Navajo Reservation was more than one thousand miles away in the Four Corners area of the American Southwest, which Clarke had never visited. And it is doubtful that he had many, if any, Navajo items on hand. Rather, such marketing tied Clarke directly to the "Indian craze" of the early twentieth century, a moment characterized by the fetishizing of native cultures, especially their handicrafts, by members of the white elite and middle class. These consumers treasured Indian artwork for its perceived "realness" and simplicity, exactly the qualities such people found lacking in the increasingly complex world of urban America. Because of their enormously popular textiles and silver jewelry, "Navajo" became synonymous with "Indian-made," precisely the message Clarke hoped to convey to passersby with his new billboard, even if he was Piegan.[42]

His work from this period appealed to the antimodern aesthetic then in vogue, in form if not necessarily in theme. In the late teens and throughout the twenties, he carved almost exclusively figures of animals encountered in Glacier National Park, often using his favorite medium, cottonwood, which he preferred for its relative softness. If not explicitly "Indian" in terms of their motifs, the lifelike attributes with which Clarke endowed these creations seemed to suggest his distinctive ability, as a person of native ancestry, to commune with such creatures. One reviewer observed in 1926, "[His] cottonwood bears and deer . . . seem to live and have personality. Many a carver has given us realistic textures, but only occasionally does one underlay them with such knowledge of his subject and such life."[43] What Clarke thought about this sort of essentialism remains a mystery, although if it helped sell his carvings, so much the better.

ONE OF THE MOST PROMINENT Americans swept up in the Indian craze of the early twentieth century was John D. Rockefeller Jr., the only son of the Standard Oil tycoon. Junior, as he was known (in order to distinguish him from his father), and his family made four trips to the West between 1920 and 1930, traveling in their own private railcar, valued at $125,000 and costing $50,000 a year to maintain, as well as by automobile and on horseback.[44] On these sojourns Rockefeller and his wife, Abby, became avid collectors of Indian art, and in time their collection boasted pieces by a variety of indigenous peoples, among them the Apaches, the Nez Perces, and the Sioux, not to mention the obligatory Navajo blankets and silver jewelry.

If each of the trips had its special marvels—Mesa Verde, Yellowstone, Grand Teton—Rockefeller's son David insisted that the family's 1924 trip to Glacier National Park stood out in their collective memory because of the time they spent at a Blackfeet encampment. The group loved the painted teepees, and Junior, though nearly fifty, expressed childish delight when a tribal leader bestowed upon him an honorary Indian name, Imata-Koan (Little Dog). After two weeks spent camping and riding in the rolling countryside east of the park, members of the Rockefeller party retired to the more comfortable accommodations of the Glacier Park Lodge, where they were surprised to find many of the same Indians they had met in the field now providing "local color" for the arriving guests.[45]

Sometime during his stay at the lodge, Rockefeller wandered up the road to John Clarke's studio to have a look. To the young mogul, it was quite a sight. Sitting on the front porch were carvings of a bighorn sheep and a Rocky Mountain goat large enough to serve as visitor seating. It was the inside, however—described years later by one newspaper reporter as "a scene from the animal kingdom"— that really impressed, with its cluttered array of carving tools and works in progress. On the occasion of Rockefeller's visit, Clarke may have hung back at first, as he usually took the measure of his guests' interest—if they seemed truly curious, he would then eagerly show them the best pieces.[46]

Junior did not disappoint that summer day; he purchased eight items, including a standing grizzly bear nearly three feet tall, as well as one of the finest carvings Clarke ever executed, *Fighting Buffaloes*, a cottonwood sculpture measuring 11 × 19 × 11 inches that depicts two bison bulls locked in the type of head-to-head combat typical during mating season. Crafted with hammer and chisel, the sculpture exudes an almost tangible power, seen in the animals' twisted bodies and straining legs. The features were so impressive that they led one critic to liken the piece to the *Laocoön Group* from ancient Greece, in which three human figures writhe in agony from strangulation by sea serpents.[47] Today the carving is a prized part of the David and Peggy Rockefeller Collection, where it resides along with masterpieces by luminaries like Manet, Picasso, and Renoir.[48]

If it was a thrill for Clarke to sell pieces to such a famous collector, Rockefeller's purchases marked merely one of Clarke's many triumphs during the 1920s and 1930s. For instance, in 1922 he earned $275, to that point his highest commission for a single piece, from the Pennsylvania Academy of Fine Arts for *Bear in a Trap*. Six years later he won a silver medal from the Spokane Art Association. And in 1932, at a time when Adolf Hitler and his National Socialist German Workers' Party were waiting in the wings to seize power, a group of sculptors from the village of Oberammergau, a world-renowned woodcarving center in Bavaria, spent part of the summer studying with Clarke at East Glacier Park.

Clarke's personal life continued to trump any professional successes. In 1931 he and Mamie traveled to Helena to adopt a two-year-old white girl, whom they named Joyce Marie. Pleased as John was, Mamie might have been even more elated, because she had lost a child during her brief first marriage, and at fifty despaired of ever becoming a mother. Joyce remembers her father as an especially doting parent, which photographs from her youth also suggest. Though he rarely smiled for pictures, many of the images of father and daughter show John beaming, the most touching of which captures the two holding cherished objects: a carved deer in his hand, a rag doll in hers. Like her mother, Joyce became a skilled communicator in sign language.

John and Joyce Clarke, ca. 1930s. Like her mother, Joyce—who was adopted at the age of two—could communicate easily with John in sign language. Here the two pose with treasured objects. Courtesy of Joyce Clarke Turvey.

Despite John's domestic contentment and artistic accomplishments, times were hardly flush at the Clarke household. Big paydays like the commission from the Pennsylvania Academy of Fine Arts or the windfall from the Rockefeller visit were rare; indeed, the economic climate of the time was dire, affecting artists of the 1930s quite profoundly, and he got by mostly selling smaller pieces one at a time. Years later a friend recalled his first encounter with Clarke, during the Christmas season of 1943. That winter John set up a card table in a Helena department store, where he whittled on site and peddled small pieces for "dirt cheap" prices: one dollar for tiny figurines; fifteen to twenty dollars for exquisite six-inch mountain goats and bears.[49] Joyce explained, "Looking back . . . we were poor, but I didn't realize it," in part because she could ride horses every day.[50] Still, as a little girl Joyce treasured visits from a wealthy family friend who lived in Tacoma, because on those occasions she got to dine at the Glacier Park Lodge, an extravagance her parents could never afford.[51]

The challenges facing the Clarkes during the 1930s are under-scored in a series of letters between Mamie and Eleanor Sherman, the great-granddaughter of Thomas Hopkins Gallaudet, founder of the American School for the Deaf as well as the namesake of the national college for the deaf and hard of hearing in Washington, D.C. Sher-man was the curator of the Hispanic Society of America in New York, but as a deaf person herself, she did extensive volunteer work within the deaf community.[52] In this capacity she wrote to John in June 1934 with an invitation to participate in that summer's International Exhibition of Fine and Applied Arts by Deaf Artists, which she was helping to organize. In her pitch to him, Sherman made a nationalist appeal, informed perhaps by the growing tensions on the other side of the Atlantic: "Europe is sending works of art by 53 artists. . . . We Americans can sustain the high standard only through the exhibition of paintings, engravings, and carvings by acknowledged leaders such as yourself."[53]

Mamie wrote back immediately to confirm John's interest, thus initiating a relationship with Sherman that lasted into the next decade. Mamie explained that she would arrange for a number of her husband's pieces to be shipped from Chicago, where they were on loan to another museum. And while she expressed delight that John's work would show alongside the likes of the celebrated etcher Cadwallader Washburn, it was neither fame nor patriotism that held the greatest appeal. Rather, as she observed in a later note, "I am so anxious to sell something; we need money, & that is why I priced [the pieces] so very low."[54]

Though some forty items sold during the three-week exhibi-tion, John's works were not among them. Ever resourceful, Mamie asked that Sherman keep John's entries on hand in New York, in the hope that Sherman might find a display space or even a gallery

John, Joyce, and Mamie Clarke, ca. 1930s. While John achieved professional renown (if not financial security) in the 1920s and 1930s, he found even greater satisfaction in his home life. Courtesy of Joyce Clarke Turvey.

to exhibit them. In an act of great kindness, Sherman agreed and spent much of the next seven years serving the Clarkes informally as John's agent. Understanding their perilous financial situation, she refused to accept any commission, which could amount to over 50 percent of the sale price. Mamie, however, insisted that Sherman take 20 percent.

Sherman worked doggedly on the Clarkes' behalf, exploring multiple sales opportunities, including the submission of a bear carving as a raffle prize and the installation of some pieces in a display at the Abercrombie and Fitch flagship store, then at Madison Avenue and Forty-Fifth Street in Manhattan. The return on her efforts was negligible, however. That led to plaintive letters from Mamie stressing the family's indigence. Consider this typical missive from July 1939: "We need money at present very much. . . . I've been ill *all* spring & summer."[55] In order to augment his meager income, John offered a carving class at Browning High School during the 1936–37 school year, and starting in the 1940s he, Mamie, and Joyce spent several winters in Great Falls, where John taught at the Montana School for the Deaf and Dumb, which, with a slightly amended name, had relocated from Boulder in 1937.

Sherman's relationship with the Clarkes ended amicably but abruptly during the winter of 1940–41, for reasons that are unclear. Perhaps she became too busy at the Hispanic Society or wanted to focus on her recent marriage to Juan Font, a Puerto Rican who served as the art director at various Spanish-language publications. In any event, the rupture surely disappointed John and especially Mamie, who fretted even more about money as her health began to deteriorate. Though praise for John's work was abundant, sales were poor, a contradiction in terms that Charlie Russell observed in his letter to John in 1918: "Your worke is like mine maney people like to look at it but there are few buyers." John could only take cold comfort from that message; admiration was nice, but financial stability was better yet.

An Artist to the Core

By the time he died, in March 1934, John Two Guns White Calf could claim status as perhaps the most famous Indian in America. Known far and wide for his travels on behalf of the Great Northern Railway in promoting Glacier National Park, he also became a Shriner as well as a member of the Methodist Episcopal Church, and counted several U.S. presidents among his personal acquaintances.[56] Most of all, Two Guns achieved renown because of the debatable assertion—supported by legions of Piegan friends—that he was the model for the buffalo nickel minted in 1913, which featured an Indian head on the obverse.[57] Many daily newspapers and even *Time* magazine printed his obituary.[58]

Two Guns, however, had another side, one less visible to those who held him up as the apotheosis of the "white man's Indian."[59] After all, many of his trips to Washington, D.C., culminated with an "oratorical onslaught" regarding the matter of the $1.5 million he believed the government still owed the Piegans for the acquisition of the ceded strip. This was a deeply personal matter for him, because his father, White Calf, had spoken for the Indians in the contentious negotiations in 1895. One correspondent dubbed him the "W[illiam] J[ennings] Bryan of the red race."[60] And though Two Guns passed away before the Piegans debated the Indian Reorganization Act, his half brother, James, was one of the chief opponents of that 1934 legislation, believing that it disadvantaged full-blooded people like the White Calf family.[61]

Still, in his later years, Two Guns commanded enormous respect from native and non-Indian people alike. On the one hand, he thrilled white guests staying at the Glacier Park Lodge by greeting them each morning at the main entrance, accompanied by a group of fellow tribesmen who entertained with song and dance in the hopes of earning an extra dollar or two.[62] Piegans, meanwhile, revered Two Guns for his dedication to the old ways, seen in his traditional dress, his preference for the mother tongue, and his active participation in ceremonial life.

One such admirer was John Clarke, who, as his daughter recalled, held Two Guns in higher esteem than any of the prominent visitors who dropped in at his studio, even John D. Rockefeller Jr. As a tribute to the man, sometime in the late 1920s or early 1930s, Clarke molded a clay bust of Two Guns, for which the Indian almost surely sat, and later cast it in bronze. The sculpture captures the elderly Piegan with uncanny precision: creased face, distinctive nose, set lips, and braided hair. It is one of Clarke's finest pieces, and certainly among the most keenly felt, as is suggested by a picture taken shortly after its completion. In the photo Clarke beholds his creation, so that he and the bronze cast appear to be looking directly at each other, with his right hand resting gently on Two Guns' left shoulder.[63]

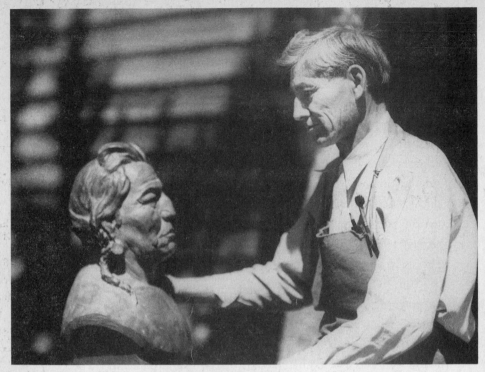

John L. Clarke with bust of Two Guns White Calf, ca. 1930s. Clarke began to explore native themes more explicitly in his midcareer and afterward, as in this sculpture, which depicts a Piegan chief celebrated for his dedication to the tribe's traditional ways. Courtesy of Joyce Clarke Turvey.

Clarke's bust of Two Guns came at a transitional moment in his artistic development, as he began to carve pieces with more explicit native motifs. To be sure, he had portrayed Indian subjects since the earliest days of his career; a photo of his studio from the early twentieth century says as much, revealing a profile sketch of a Piegan warrior tacked to the bottom of his easel. And, of course, he continued to carve animal figures, his stock-in-trade, until the end of his life. Nevertheless, starting in the 1930s Clarke's work clearly reflected a subtle but significant reorientation toward Indian themes.

Several factors help account for this shift. For one thing, some of these new pieces were commissions, which required Clarke to craft works according to the wishes of his patrons, who were often state or federal sponsors. But this alone is insufficient explanation, for in some sense he needed money less than before, especially after 1947, when he lost both of his dependents: Mamie died after a prolonged battle with heart disease, and Joyce graduated from high school and moved to California a few years later to study photography. Thus what little he earned from selling carved goats and bears to guests visiting Glacier Park was probably enough to sustain him, especially considering that his skill with rod and rifle kept food on the table.

It is also possible that by taking up Indian subjects, particularly in the spectacular friezes of his later years, Clarke was looking to secure his legacy as a master sculptor. Even if by the early 1940s one art publication had dubbed him "the best portrayer of western wildlife in the world," he probably understood that a reputation resting mostly on the mass production of animal carvings was unlikely to endure.[64] Conversely, memorializing the native past in grand fashion, especially the romantic and much happier buffalo days before 1880, held the promise of some form of immortality. This was surely the same sort of thinking that led Charlie Russell to choose cowboys, Indians, bison, and gunfights as the narrative subjects for his epic canvases.

Moreover, by midcentury there was a small but growing shift in the broader culture of white America that celebrated native self-determination and social revival. To be sure, overshadowing these gains at the time were the harsh polices of the Termination Era (1945–60), a period in which the federal government ended its supervision and subsidization of many Indian tribes, hoping that such austere measures would speed the assimilation process.[65] Still, even in the depths of that catastrophe can be found the first faint stirrings of a movement that blossomed in the 1960s, in which artists, actors, musicians, and political activists took up the Indian cause and joined forces with native peoples to advance their interests.[66]

And yet perhaps the key reason Clarke embraced Indian themes in his midcareer involves a profound awakening to his own native

John L. Clarke with carvings, ca. 1950s. In another explicit nod to his native ancestry, Clarke in later years often wore a headdress when posing with pieces of his artwork. Courtesy of Joyce Clarke Turvey.

identity. Because nothing in his small collection of personal papers offers conclusive proof of such a transformation, one must look for hints of a more subtle nature. For instance, in older age he often wore a handsome headdress when posing for photographs with his artwork. While a cynic might insist that this was just another affectation meant to appeal to prospective buyers, such a reading seems implausible, or at least incomplete, given that the Indian craze of the early twentieth century was muted during the early years of the Termination Era.

Even more telling were Clarke's efforts to train younger Piegan woodcarvers, among them Albert Racine (1908–84) and especially Willie Weatherwax (1922–98), who loved communicating with

Clarke in PISL. Years later Willie's son Marvin recalled accompanying his father to Clarke's studio when he was a small child. On one such visit, the boy picked up an extraneous piece of wood and carved a horse head. Clarke was so impressed that he urged Willie to instruct his son, and even worked informally with the boy himself. Marvin remembers, "John would take the special time to teach me how to measure with the different joints on my fingers and my hands in order to make sure everything was the right size."[67] In his own quiet way, then, Clarke strove to ensure that Piegan crafts—made by Piegans—would endure even after his own tools fell silent.

FOR MOST AMERICANS at that time and ever since, the human face of the Great Depression belonged to the countless white migrants who fled the Dust Bowl of the central Plains for California, and whose haunted visages are captured in the iconic photographs of Dorothea Lange.[68] Another group of rural people, reservation-bound Indians, suffered at least as much from the economic downturn of the 1930s. In order to alleviate their misery but also to end the disastrous federal polices of the allotment era, President Franklin Delano Roosevelt's commissioner of Indian affairs, John Collier, implemented the "Indian New Deal." Essential to the plan was the restoration of some degree of native self-governance, but Collier aimed also to raise the standard of living among native peoples, and he thus oversaw the construction of new schools and medical facilities.[69]

Few groups embraced the Wheeler-Howard Act of 1934 with the zeal of the Blackfeet, who saw the tangible results of these federal measures when a new hospital for the reservation opened at Browning in 1937.[70] Though backed by federal dollars, the facility was constructed by Indian hands, a reality underscored by three grand friezes carved by John Clarke that flanked the main entrance to the building. Sculpted from Philippine mahogany (which is not mahogany at all, but rather a wood called lauan, prized for its workability and endurance), the pieces depicted Piegan life in the days before Montana's incorporation into the United States.

Clarke's carvings for the Blackfeet Community Hospital were almost surely the result of another New Deal program, the Treasury Section of Fine Arts (TSFA). This initiative, which lasted from 1934 to 1938, drew its inspiration from the Mexican muralists project of the 1920s and early 1930s, in which that nation's federal government paid a variety of painters—most famously José Clemente Orozco, Diego Rivera, and David Alfaro Siqueiros—to decorate public buildings with epic frescoes depicting Mexican history and culture. In the same vein, U.S. officials in Washington, D.C., awarded more than fourteen hundred commissions to American painters and sculptors to produce artworks for government structures, primarily post offices and courthouses but also buildings on Indian reservations, which fell under the purview of federal administration.[71]

Like the Mexican muralists, much of whose work celebrated their nation's indigenous past, many Native American artists who received commissions from the TSFA used their brushes and chisels to celebrate the richness of the country's Indian heritage. Surely such a perspective informed John Clarke's plans for his own award, although the project he executed for the new Blackfeet health facility had been underway for more than a decade prior to the hospital's construction, further evidence of his midcareer embrace of explicitly native themes.

In its loosest form, Clarke's project for the Blackfeet Community Hospital tells the story of the Piegans from the precontact era to the period of U.S. expansion during the nineteenth century, all in a sequence of three eight- by four-foot panels. The first section, which presumably served as a pilaster to the left of the doorway, depicted a Blackfeet *piskun*, or buffalo jump, which many Plains tribes used to kill bison. The sculpture is a swirl of relentless motion: at the top, two Indians drive the doomed beasts toward the edge of a cliff; on the ground below, two other men armed with spears finish off the dying animals. Clarke's scene is a testament to native ingenuity: in the absence of many horses or advanced weaponry, the Indians nevertheless manage to reap a bounty that will yield food, tools, clothing, and shelter.

Located above and to the right of this panel was a horizontal scene, occupying the lintel position over the doorway. This tableau indicates the changes in Piegan life wrought by the widespread acquisition of horses by the Blackfeet in the later eighteenth century. With more and better mounts, the Piegans could pursue game on the open prairie instead of relying on the buffalo jump. Dominating the panorama is an Indian on horseback, bow drawn, racing alongside an enormous and terrified bull. In the distance another rider chases a small group of bison running headlong in the opposite direction, seeking refuge from the human threat. From the sweeping vista of the hill country east of the Rockies to the exquisite features of the desperate action in the foreground, the frieze is arresting.

Completing this narrative arc was a panel on the right side of the entryway portraying what, as it turned out, marked the beginning of the end for the Piegans' traditional lifeways. The frieze shows an Indian encampment—clearly a favorite subject for Clarke—in the Rocky Mountain foothills, with a stand of teepees in the foreground and some grazing horses in the distance. Clarke draws the viewers' eyes to the center-bottom, where two Americans have arrived at the camp. One of the men peers over the shoulders of four Indian women who are preparing a meal, while the other—identified as a soldier by the sword dangling from his belt—accepts what looks to be a pipe from a Piegan warrior bedecked in a flowing headdress. The scene is friendly enough, absent any hint of the future violence that resulted from the collision of these two disparate cultures.

Resplendent as they were to the casual viewer, the panels did not exactly enrich the Clarkes. As Mamie put it ruefully in a letter to Eleanor Sherman, "They [the friezes] are grand . . . but he received only a pittance for the job."[72] It seems doubtful, however, that John

John L. Clarke, frieze for the Blackfeet Community Hospital, ca. 1940. This frieze, one of Clarke's finest, depicts Piegans slaughtering bison in the old way—by running them over a cliff and then piercing the wounded creatures with arrows and spears. Courtesy of Joyce Clarke Turvey.

was too disappointed. After all, the commission was a prestigious one, and given the widespread hardships of the Depression, some income was better than none.

Sadly, not everyone on the reservation held the pieces in such high regard. After several incidents of vandalism, hospital staff removed the friezes around 1965, at which point they were ware-housed at an off-site location. Years later, Clarke's former student Albert Racine lovingly restored the pieces and returned them to the Blackfeet Community Hospital in 1986 on the occasion of the facil-ity's grand reopening after a nearly two-decade (and $9.2 million) effort to improve healthcare on the reservation. At that time the two vertical panels were installed in the hospital's waiting room (though with the sequencing reversed), with the horizontal frieze placed above the receptionist's desk in the main office.[73]

CLARKE HAD SCARCELY put the last touches on his friezes for the Blackfeet Community Hospital when he secured another com-mission for a federal project. In the late 1930s the Works Prog-ress Administration sponsored the construction of two tribally run native arts facilities that would showcase indigenous artifacts and promote craft cooperatives for local artists. First to open was the Sioux Indian Museum in Rapid City, South Dakota, followed shortly by the Museum of the Plains Indian at Browning, Mon-tana, on the Blackfeet Reservation. A third facility, focused on the southern Plains, was established nearly a decade later at Anadarko, Oklahoma.[74] These institutions owed their existence to the work of people like John Collier, who strove to reorient government pol-icy from forced acculturation to cultural self-determination. The embers of such efforts survived the repressive measures of the Ter-mination Era and caught fire in the 1960s.[75]

For the Museum of the Plains Indian, Clarke executed two five-by three-foot wood relief panels, once again in lauan and capturing

John L. Clarke, frieze for the Blackfeet Community Hospital, ca. 1940. Paired with the other frieze (page 230), this carving hints at the transformations wrought in the Piegan world by the arrival of white outsiders. Courtesy of Joyce Clarke Turvey.

scenes from the bygone buffalo days. Placed above the two entry-ways leading into the building, the frieze on the left depicts a group of three Blackfeet men gesturing toward a herd of bison just visible in the distance. Above the opposite door is a domestic counterpart to the hunting party: a mounted warrior in headdress riding into camp trailed by his wife, also on horseback and pulling a travois, as well as the family dog, all looking fatigued from their voyage but heartened by the sight of the teepees up ahead.

While the panels were his most public contributions to the museum, Clarke executed a second project there in the autumn of 1941 that had a different significance. At the close of the tourist season that year, he regularly made the twenty-mile trip between East Glacier and Browning, where he created a series of plaster casts demonstrating the successive steps by which Blackfeet women prepared bison hides in the nineteenth century and before. Each between twelve and eighteen inches high, the monochrome molds showed native women at their labors, whether tanning skins by applying a mixture of brains, liver, and grease or softening the hides by pulling them through a hole in the shoulder blade or against a rope fashioned from animal sinew.[76] Perhaps Clarke was struck by the circularity of his endeavor; a century earlier, his grandmother Coth-co-no-na employed those same time-honored techniques, transforming scores of animal carcasses into goods for use or commodities for exchange.

Clarke's plaster molds were the idea of John C. Ewers, the founding director of the Museum of the Plains Indian. On a superficial level, the two men made an unlikely pair, as Ewers—who was white and more than two decades Clarke's junior—hailed from Cleveland and had studied at Dartmouth College before enrolling in Yale's graduate program in anthropology, where he worked with the famed ethnographer Clark Wissler. After completing his master's degree, Ewers left New Haven to take a curatorial job with the National Park Service, stationed first at Vicksburg, Mississippi, and then in California at Yosemite National Park. Early in 1941 he and his family moved

John L. Clarke, frieze for the Museum of the Plains Indian, ca. 1940s. Besides wildlife, among Clarke's favorite subjects were the buffalo days of the eighteenth and nineteenth centuries. Courtesy of Joyce Clarke Turvey.

to northwestern Montana, where in time Ewers would become the world's foremost non-native authority on the Blackfeet.[77]

Whatever the stark differences in their backgrounds and expertise, Clarke and Ewers bridged such gaps through their mutual fascination with Blackfeet history and culture. Ewers came to Browning already primed with a deep interest in the tribe, kindled in graduate seminars led by Wissler, who himself had undertaken extensive fieldwork among the Blackfeet and other northern Plains groups in the early twentieth century. Thus, almost from the moment he arrived on the reservation, Ewers began cultivating what he called his "Indian informants," members of the tribe in their eighties and nineties who had distinct memories of the buffalo days that so fascinated the young anthropologist. Years later he drew upon these oral histories as he wrote *The Blackfeet: Raiders on the Northwestern Plains,* published in 1958 and still considered the standard academic monograph on the tribe.[78]

Ewers undoubtedly looked to Clarke as an expert on tribal history, even if Clarke was of a slightly later generation than men like Makes Cold Weather (b. 1867) or Chewing Black Bones (b. 1868), both of whom provided Ewers with extensive information about the lifeways of their people. Clarke had gifts the others did not—namely, the ability to shape with his hands what Ewers's elderly informants could only describe with their tongues. Though published years after he had left Browning for an administrative post at the Smithsonian Institution, *The Blackfeet* reveals Ewers's urgency to record the tribe's ancient ways before they slipped into extinction, much as Edward S. Curtis had sought to do with camera and tripod earlier in the century (although Ewers traded much less in the "noble savage" mystique that suffuses Curtis's work).[79] Clarke's carvings and molds fit squarely with Ewers's mission for the Museum of the Plains Indian.

Through it all and up to the very end of his life, Clarke never abandoned his chief artistic pursuit, drawing and sculpting western fauna. In fact, Ewers recalled with poignancy the last time he saw him, in 1969, a little more than a year before the artist's death. Passing through the lobby of the majestic Glacier Park Lodge, Ewers spotted Clarke seated quietly near a stuffed mountain goat on display in a glass case, sketching the creature on a piece of paper. The anthropologist recalled, "I knew that Clarke must have carved scores of mountain goats—perhaps even hundreds—during his long career. But there he was—ever the perfectionist—keeping his hand in drawing that familiar animal from the model."[80] As his daughter put it, Clarke was "an artist to the core."

ERECTED AT THE turn of the twentieth century, the Montana State Capitol is a formidable edifice, built of granite and sandstone and capped by a copper-topped dome that soars 165 feet into the thin alpine sky above Helena. The interior is no less majestic, with beautiful paintings and sculptures that line the quiet marble hallways and preside over formal chambers and meeting rooms. Visitors who follow one of these corridors into the west wing of the building come eventually upon the Gallery of Outstanding Montanans, established in 1979 by the legislature "to pay homage to citizens of the Treasure State who made contributions of state or national significance to their selected fields of endeavor."

On a cold spring day in 2003, officials and assorted guests assembled at the capitol for the induction of John Clarke, who took his place among such illustrious members as the actor Gary Cooper, journalist Chet Huntley, and Clarke's old friend Charlie Russell, all of whom were in the first cohort of honorees. The citation for Clarke recognized not only his professional success but also his triumph over disability; it read in part, "Facing odds that would have deterred lesser men, he crafted a career as a renowned Blackfeet artist. His legacy survives as a worthy inspiration for all Montanans." Kirby Lambert, spokesman for the nominating committee, emphasized the dual nature of Clarke's achievement, adding that of the three dozen individuals so enshrined, "[Clarke] is one of my personal favorites."[81]

That a Clarke should enjoy such recognition seems fitting, in view of the outsize role the family played in the state's history. Moreover, in 1865, Malcolm Clarke, John's paternal grandfather, was among the twelve men who founded the Montana Historical Society, the body that selects new inductees for the hall of fame. And yet the elder Clarke and his associates never intended to honor individuals like his grandson. Rather, they established their organization to celebrate men just like themselves, white pioneers who, in conquering their own set of formidable obstacles—an unyielding physical environment, hostile native peoples—had prepared Montana for its eventual absorption into the United States. Their idol was perhaps Granville Stuart, a miner and rancher as well as a charter member of the MHS, who by the time he died in 1918 was acclaimed as "Mr. Montana" for his lasting contributions to the development of his adopted state, and as such was inducted into the Gallery of Outstanding Montanans in 1985.

It is poignant and not a little ironic that John Clarke and Granville Stuart should share space in the Montana Hall of Fame, given that Stuart effectively renounced his own mixed-blood family in the late nineteenth century. Stuart had long worried that his interracial marriage would hold him back from material and social success, especially after the seismic demographic shift in Montana following the Civil War. Thus in 1890, less than a year and a half after the death of his Shoshone wife, Awbonnie, Stuart married a much younger white woman and four years later secured a prestigious diplomatic appointment as U.S. minister to Uruguay and Paraguay, an unthinkable development had Awbonnie lived, as his biographers note.

His abandoned children did not manage as well, especially two of his sons, who like Horace and Helen Clarke tried to keep their footing in both white and native worlds. Tom Stuart, Granville's oldest boy, worked for a time on his father's ranch, but incurred the older man's wrath in his twenties when he forged Granville's signature on checks and ran up expenses in his father's name. In 1897 a Helena judge ordered Tom confined to the state asylum in Warm Springs, the result of a "threatening and uncontrollable temper" (stemming perhaps from epilepsy). He died there in 1905, just shy of his fortieth birthday. Tom's younger brother Sam fared better, at least for a time, securing a job as a railroad engineer in the mid-1890s and marrying a Swedish woman. In the end he, too, ran afoul of the law and did several stints in prison before dying indigent at the state hospital in 1960.[82]

It is possible, of course, to argue that John Clarke endured his own form of isolation, living on the Blackfeet Reservation during one of the bleakest periods in the history of Native America, when reservations across the country suffered grievously from scarcity and

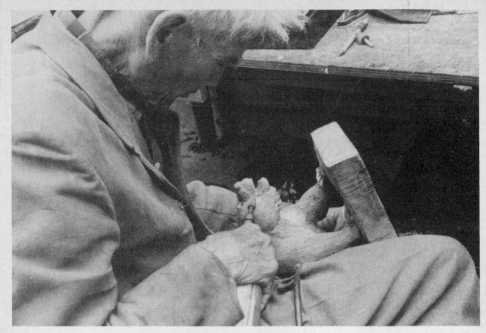

John L. Clarke, blocking out a bear, ca. 1961. Clarke carved almost until the day he died, in November 1970, at the age of eighty-nine, even after his eyes were clouded by cataracts and his hands gnarled by arthritis.

disease. So it was for Clarke, who as one visitor recalled spent his last years in relative poverty, living downstairs in his studio after the roof had burned off in a house fire, "napping on an iron cot, halfway under a tangle of old quilts and accompanied by a puppy or two, while an electric heater buzzed along too close for safety."[83] Evidently, such marginal conditions failed to move everyone who passed by his home; in 1968 some teenagers visiting East Glacier Park broke into his studio and destroyed his tools and sculptures.[84]

John Clarke made little attempt to accommodate himself to the new world forged by Malcolm Clarke and Granville Stuart. He found contentment in the rhythms of his daily life and work. Time and again, close friends and even casual acquaintances remarked on his equanimity, seen in his radiant smile, his unflappable patience, and his humbling generosity. Such was the judgment of Bob Morgan, the curator of the museum at the Montana Historical Society, when he stopped in at Clarke's studio in 1969, shortly before Clarke died. The men had first met nearly three decades earlier, when Clarke had hocked small wood figurines during the Christmas season at the same upscale department store where Morgan, nearly fifty years younger, worked in the advertising and display department, sharing cups of coffee to stave off the bitter winter chill and passing notes back and forth.

On the occasion of their final visit, Morgan was unsurprised to find Clarke hard at work, absorbed in carving a small mountain goat. Clarke looked up and, recognizing his friend, smiled widely and extended his arm. "What a wonderful, gnarled hand to grasp," Morgan recalled, "still strong and resolute." They communicated in the old way, scribbling on a notepad; at one point Morgan, who was an aspiring artist himself, drew a deer head and passed it to John. Clarke replied with his own sketch of a rifle and wrote beneath it "no shells." Stirred, it seems, by the elderly man's circumstances, Morgan slipped him a few dollars, an act of charity that Clarke did not refuse, and wrote "you owe me a steak." Clarke smiled, and they moved on to other subjects before Morgan bought a small bear for five dollars and headed out the door.[85]

Clarke died in November of the following year at the age of eighty-nine, and was interred near Helen and Horace in the small family plot. His home studio languished for several years, until his daughter, Joyce—just like her great-aunt Helen—tired of California and moved, permanently, back to East Glacier. Upon her return to the Upper Missouri, Joyce discovered that her father's home was too dilapidated to preserve but managed nevertheless to save some of the wood from the original building, which she incorporated into the design of the present structure, opened in 1977 as the John L. Clarke Western Art Gallery and Memorial Museum.

Inside, the gallery is warm and inviting, with soft lights and a plush rug that absorbs the footfalls of the many visitors who stop in

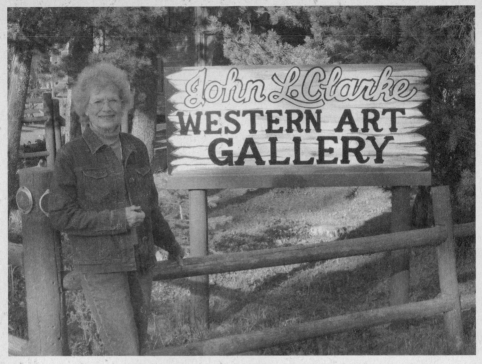

Joyce Clarke Turvey, 2007. John's daughter, Joyce, opened a gallery in 1977 in East Glacier Park that honors her father and displays a small collection of his artwork. Photograph by the author.

during the tourist season, which runs from Memorial Day to the end of September, when the temperatures drop and the snow begins to fall. A few John Clarke originals are on display but not for sale, given Joyce's ongoing attempts to buy back from museums and private collectors those sculptures of her father's that she can locate and afford. In the back of the building, though, are several glass cases that feature a small sample of the artist's tools as well as bronze casts made from miniature Clarke carvings, among them a playful bear cub caught in midstride and a Rocky Mountain goat perched on a ledge, with a muscled back and a shaggy beard. Beneath their alloy veneer and a thin coating of dust, they pulse with the life breathed into them by a master now four decades gone.

Epilogue

In the summer of 1959, not long after John Clarke finished his masterpiece, *Blackfeet Encampment*, occupants of the Blackfeet Reservation noticed a white newcomer in and around Browning. Malcolm McFee was a graduate student in anthropology at Stanford University, but he was hardly a typical academic. Born in Seattle in 1917, McFee had dropped out of the University of Washington during the Depression to take a job selling plumbing supplies. After serving as a copilot on a B-29 during World War II, he returned to the plumbing business, working as an office manager at a Yakima firm until 1955, when—at the age of thirty-eight—he decided to go back to school and complete his undergraduate education. McFee was so taken with his studies that he opted to pursue a doctoral degree at Stanford, even though he was close to forty and had a wife and young son to support.[1]

McFee had come to northern Montana that summer to do field-work among the Blackfeet, as Clark Wissler and John Ewers had before him. The Indians graciously opened their homes to the scholar, who became a virtual fixture among them over the course of the next decade, returning four more times to gather data. McFee dropped in at private residences and public ceremonies, usually armed with a notepad in order to record his observations. His research served as the basis for a scholarly article and a book, both considered classics of cultural anthropology today.[2]

As McFee discovered, the postwar period on the Blackfeet Reservation was a profoundly troubled time, as it was all across Native America during the Termination Era of the 1950s and 1960s. If the Blackfeet did not suffer quite as much as groups like the Klamaths and the Menominees, who faced almost unimaginable poverty and high incidence of disease once federal welfare programs evaporated, conditions at Browning were nevertheless bleak, if not desperate. For instance, statistics from the late 1960s showed that the median annual income for a Blackfeet family was $1700, less than a quarter of the U.S. national average, and McFee reported that numerous Indian homes (especially in outlying areas) had neither electricity nor running water.[3]

While these economic questions interested him, McFee was far more curious about cultural matters among the Blackfeet, to which he devoted most of his attention. What most intrigued him was the Indians' demographic diversity, reflected in tribal enrollment figures from 1960. Those records indicated that of the 4,850 members living on the reservation, 13 percent claimed full-blood status and another 10 percent were less than a quarter Indian, revealing that the vast majority of enrolled Blackfeet were of mixed ancestry, a fact that had struck Ewers, too, just a few years earlier.[4] McFee wanted to know how the Blackfeet in this majority understood their hybrid identity, and after years of interviews and observation he concluded that such persons fell into two basic categories: a "white-oriented" majority and a smaller "Indian-oriented" group.

Divisions between the two populations, he noted, were marked not by biology or appearance but rather by values and behavior. White-oriented people prized hard work and material success, while their Indian-oriented counterparts cherished ceremonies and rituals aimed at preserving the tribe's ancient ways. But, as McFee added in his most enduring assertion, some individuals on the reservation combined traits of both cultural groups. These he called "150% men," explaining that in the case of such a person, "if, by one measure, he scores 75% on an Indian scale, we should not expect him to be limited to a 25% measure on another scale."[5] In other words, one could be powerfully acculturated to both white and native ways simultaneously; the process was not a zero-sum calculation.

McFee's book, *Modern Blackfeet: Montanans on a Reservation*, was praised even before its publication as "without doubt the most definitive piece written on a contemporary American Indian community."[6] But if it was a major contribution to the anthropological literature, in some respects all that the author had done was to illuminate a longstanding demographic phenomenon: the enduring presence of peoples in between, those who were at once both red and white. Such individuals, of course, had existed since the earliest days of colonial America, counting among their number men like Thomas Rolfe, born in Virginia in the early seventeenth century to the English settler John Rolfe and his wife, Pocahontas, a Powhatan Indian. Or, closer in time and space to the Clarkes, consider the life of Jean Baptiste Charbonneau, born during the voyage of the Corps of Discovery to a French Canadian interpreter and his Shoshone wife, Sacagawea. Meriwether Lewis became so enamored of the boy, whom he called "Pomp," that Clark arranged for his education in St. Louis following the expedition.

In a foreword to McFee's book, the series editor hailed the study as a rebuke to "the American mania for cultural uniformity," referring, presumably, to the era that had just passed, the 1950s and early 1960s, a period marked by an apparent spirit of conformism that had flattened difference while imposing stifling orthodoxies.[7] But just as with the concept of the "150% man," the impulse derided by the editor also had a long history in America, emerging in places where Europeans and their descendants achieved social and political dominance, even when they were outnumbered by nonwhite peoples. This process unfolded at different speeds, usually in response to the pace of white settlement—slowly at first in the East, but with blinding swiftness in places like the Rocky Mountain West in the period after the Civil War.

The tale of the Clarkes is so rich and instructive because it captures, in the history of a single such family composed of extraordinary members, the before-and-after qualities attendant to this transformation. Indeed, the world of Coth-co-co-na and Malcolm Clarke—one in which individuals of mixed ancestry stood near the pinnacle of the social order on the Upper Missouri, serving as brokers between white and native societies—was washed away in the course of a single generation. The Clarke children thus inherited a realm in which hybrid peoples were pushed increasingly to the margins by white newcomers, a process laden with physical as well as emotional violence.

And yet the Clarke story also shows that, even as the social space for bicultural people contracted sharply after the end of the fur trade era and the period of rapid national consolidation during Reconstruction, some individuals still found room to maneuver in the quickly dividing worlds of their mothers and fathers. Take the cultural ambidexterity of Horace Clarke, who served on the Blackfeet Tribal Business Council (the tribe's governing body) in the early twentieth century while simultaneously pursuing entrepreneurial ambitions and sustaining close personal relationships with some of Montana's leading white citizens. The same was true for Helen Clarke, seen in her journey from the Broadway stage to elective office to the Indian Service—"white" occupations all—before returning at last to live among the Piegans, whom she counseled and supported to the end of her days, her racial in-between-ness remarked upon frequently (and often favorably) by white residents of the Treasure State. And McFee would surely have identified John Clarke as a "150% man," married to a white woman and with countless non-Indian friends and customers, but dedicated to preserving Blackfeet craft practices and transmitting his knowledge to younger native artists, ensuring that such customs survived even as men like him—born at the tail end of the halcyon buffalo days—grew scarce on the reservation.

Nevertheless, even as the Clarkes and others of mixed Piegan-white ancestry embraced both halves of their heritage, "the mania for cultural uniformity" persists in northern Montana, as it does elsewhere throughout Native America. Visitors today can sense it at either edge of the Blackfeet Reservation, whether in East Glacier Park or Cut Bank, but according to some it has taken root, ironically, among the residents themselves. This "blood-ism" discriminates against those who are actually, or are perceived to be, of lower blood quantum, and it promises to intensify because—with a casino that opened in 2006 and with renewed interest, owing to hydraulic fracturing, in the oil reserves underneath tribal land—there is more at stake now than mere identity.[8] As a result, walking in two worlds—one red, the other white—will continue to pose challenges for those people in between.

Notes

Prologue

1 The best historical treatment of the event is Philip Goldring, "Whisky, Horses, and Death: The Cypress Hills Massacre and Its Sequel," *Occasional Papers in Archaeology and History* 21 (1979): 41–70. More satisfying (though fictional) is Guy Vanderhaeghe's wondrous novel *The Englishman's Boy* (New York: Picador, 1996).

2 James Welch, *Fools Crow* (New York: Penguin, 1986), 156–58.

3 There are, of course, notable exceptions to this general rule, chief among them two works by Gary B. Nash: "The Hidden History of Mestizo America," *Journal of American History* 82, no. 3 (Dec. 1995): 941–64; and *Forbidden Love: The Secret History of Mixed-Race America* (New York: Henry Holt, 1999). See also Thomas N. Ingersoll, *To Intermix with Our White Brothers: Indian Mixed Bloods in the United States from Earliest Times to the Indian Removals* (Albuquerque: Univ. of New Mexico Press, 2005); Theda Perdue, *Mixed Blood Indians: Racial Construction in the Early South* (Athens: Univ. of Georgia Press, 2003); and Theresa Schenck, "Border Identities: Métis, Halfbreed, and Mixed-Blood," in *Gathering Places: Aboriginal and Fur Trade Histories*, ed. Carolyn Podruchny and Laura Peers (Vancouver: Univ. of British Columbia Press, 2010), 233–48. Most recently, Anne F. Hyde's reinterpretation of the nineteenth-century West as a region of families, many of them mixed, has recast our understanding of native-white intermarriage. See her *Empires, Nations, and Families: A History of the North American West, 1800–1860* (Lincoln: Univ. of Nebraska Press, 2011). It is worth noting that there is a fine and growing body of literature that examines the complex legacies of interracial

marriage among peoples of African, Indian, and white ancestry in Oklahoma. See, e.g., Tiya Miles, *Ties That Bind: The Story of an Afro-Cherokee Family in Slavery and Freedom* (Berkeley: Univ. of California Press, 2005); Claudio Saunt, *Black, White and Indian: Race and the Unmaking of an American Family* (New York: Oxford Univ. Press, 2005); and Fay A. Yarbrough, *Race and the Cherokee Nation: Sovereignty in the Nineteenth Century* (Philadelphia: Univ. of Pennsylvania Press, 2007).

4 See David Fridtjof Halaas and Andrew E. Masich, *Halfbreed: The Remarkable True Story of George Bent* (New York: Da Capo Press, 2004).

5 On the Bents and other families of mixed ancestry, see Anne F. Hyde, "Hard Choices: Mixed-Race Families and Strategies of Acculturation in the U.S. West after 1848," in *On the Borders of Love and Power: Families and Kinship in the Intercultural American Southwest,* ed. David Wallace Adams and Crista DeLuzio (Berkeley: Univ. of California Press, 2012), 93–115.

6 I have been inspired in my narrative approach by a number of exemplary works, most especially John Demos, *The Unredeemed Captive: A Family Story from Early America* (New York: Knopf, 1994).

Chapter 1: Cutting Off Head Woman

1 Pierre Clément de Laussat, *Memoirs of My Life to My Son during the Years 1803 and After,* ed. Robert D. Bush (Baton Rouge: Louisiana State Univ. Press, 1978), 88–91, quote p. 90. A nearly identical ceremony took place in St. Louis on 9–10 March 1804, once word of the transfer at New Orleans reached communities upriver following the reopening of traffic after the winter. See Anne F. Hyde, *Empires, Nations, and Families: A History of the North American West, 1800–1860* (Lincoln: Univ. of Nebraska Press, 2011), 1.

2 Numerous volumes deal with these events; this account relies upon George C. Herring, *From Colony to Superpower: U.S. Foreign Relations since 1776* (New York: Oxford Univ. Press, 2008), 101–14, quote p. 106.

3 The literature on the Louisiana Purchase is enormous. Particularly helpful to this telling are Peter J. Kastor, *The Nation's Crucible: The Louisiana Purchase and the Creation of America* (New Haven: Yale Univ. Press, 2004); Roger G. Kennedy, *Mr. Jefferson's Lost Cause: Land, Farmers, Slavery, and the Louisiana Purchase* (New York: Oxford Univ. Press, 2003); and Robert Morgan, *Lions of the West: Heroes and Villains of the Westward Expansion* (Chapel Hill, N.C.: Algonquin Books, 2011), esp. pp. 1–44. For the importance of the Louisiana Purchase in securing American claims to the eastern portion of the continent, especially the Ohio Valley, see François Furstenberg, "The Significance of the Trans-Appalachian Frontier in American History, 1754–1815," *American Historical Review* 113, no. 2 (June 2008): 647–77. See also Eliga H. Gould, *Among the Powers of the Earth: The American Revolution and the Making of a New World Empire* (Cambridge: Harvard Univ. Press, 2012).

4 Adam Arenson, *The Great Heart of the Republic: St. Louis and the Cultural*

Civil War (Cambridge: Harvard Univ. Press, 2011), 12; Jay Gitlin, *The Bourgeois Frontier: French Towns, French Traders, and American Expansion* (New Haven: Yale Univ. Press, 2010), 13–21.

5 Gary E. Moulton, ed., *The Lewis and Clark Journals: An American Epic of Discovery: The Abridgment of the Definitive Nebraska Edition* (Lincoln: Univ. of Nebraska Press, 2004), xiv–xv.

6 Ibid., xxi–xxvi. See also James P. Ronda, *Lewis and Clark among the Indians* (1984; Lincoln: Univ. of Nebraska Press, 2002).

7 See John C. Ewers, *The Blackfeet: Raiders on the Northwestern Plains* (1958; Norman: Univ. of Oklahoma Press, 1983), 3–18; and Oscar Lewis, *The Effects of White Contact upon Blackfoot Culture, with Special Reference to the Rôle of the Fur Trade* (New York: J. J. Augustin, 1942). See also the work of two Canadian scholars: Hugh Dempsey, "The Blackfoot Nation," in *Native Peoples: The Canadian Experience*, ed. R. Bruce Morrison and C. Roderick Wilson (1986; Toronto: McClelland & Stewart, 1995), 381–413; and Diamond Jenness, *The Indians of Canada* (1932; Toronto: Univ. of Toronto Press, 1977), 317–24. Some scholars emphasize also the distinction between North Piegans (living in Canada) and South Piegans (living in the United States).

8 Moulton, ed., *The Lewis and Clark Journals*, l–lii, 340–46, quote p. 345. For the Piegan perspective on these events, see *Two Worlds at Two Medicine*, DVD, directed by Dennis Neary (Browning, Mont.: Going-to-the-Sun Institute and Native Pictures, 2004).

9 In July 2006 a group of Blackfeet held a ceremony commemorating the bicentennial of the event. As the participant George Heavy Runner noted, members of the tribe hoped that U.S. officials might attend and offer an apology, explaining, "That's a way of healing and moving on." *Great Falls Tribune*, 18 June 2006.

10 For excellent surveys of the period, see Charles Sellers, *The Market Revolution: Jacksonian America, 1815–1846* (New York: Oxford Univ. Press, 1991); and Daniel Walker Howe, *What Hath God Wrought: The Transformation of America, 1815–1848* (New York: Oxford Univ. Press, 2007).

11 For the settlement of the trans-Appalachian West, see Stephen Aron, *How the West Was Lost: The Transformation of Kentucky from Daniel Boone to Henry Clay* (Baltimore: Johns Hopkins Univ. Press, 1996). See also Colin G. Calloway, *The Scratch of a Pen: 1763 and the Transformation of North America* (New York: Oxford Univ. Press, 2006).

12 See R. David Edmunds, *The Shawnee Prophet* (Lincoln: Univ. of Nebraska Press, 1983); Gregory E. Dowd, *A Spirited Resistance: The North American Indian Struggle for Unity, 1745–1815* (Baltimore: Johns Hopkins Univ. Press, 1991); and Colin G. Calloway, *The American Revolution in Indian Country: Crisis and Diversity in Native American Communities* (New York: Cambridge Univ. Press, 1995). For recent accounts of that most obscure and overlooked conflict, see Alan Taylor, *The Civil War of 1812: American Citizens, British Subjects, Irish Rebels, & Indian Allies* (New York: Knopf, 2010); and Nicole

Eustace, *1812: War and the Passions of Patriotism* (Philadelphia: Univ. of Pennsylvania Press, 2012).

13 See Robert Martin Owens, *Mr. Jefferson's Hammer: William Henry Harrison and the Origins of American Indian Policy* (Norman: Univ. of Oklahoma Press, 2007).

14 See Howe, *What Hath God Wrought*, 203–42.

15 Quoted in Peter Bernstein, *The Wedding of the Waters: The Erie Canal and the Making of a Great Nation* (New York: Norton, 2006), 319.

16 For the meaning of Napi, see Betty Bastien, *Blackfoot Ways of Knowing* (Calgary: Univ. of Calgary Press, 2004), 226. Bastien explains, "*Napi* is representative of the fallibility of man. He reminds us that to do things that are wrong will result in negative consequences."

17 George Bird Grinnell, *Blackfoot Lodge Tales: The Story of a Prairie People* (1892; Lincoln: Univ. of Nebraska Press, 2003), 203–4; Clark Wissler, "Material Culture of the Blackfoot Indians," *Anthropological Papers of the American Museum of Natural History*, Vol. 5, pt. 1 (New York: Published by Order of the Trustees, 1910), 20–52.

18 For the best description of Plains Indian dependence upon the buffalo, see Andrew C. Isenberg, *The Destruction of the Bison: An Environmental History, 1750–1920* (New York: Cambridge Univ. Press, 2000).

19 L. James Dempsey, *Blackfoot War Art: Pictographs of the Reservation Period, 1880–1920* (Norman: Univ. of Oklahoma Press, 2007), 7.

20 Grinnell, *Blackfoot Lodge Tales*, 227–28. The anthropologist Shepard Krech III offers a more skeptical view of native efficiency in using all parts of slaughtered buffalo in *The Ecological Indian: Myth and History* (New York: Norton, 1999), 123–49.

21 The informant was Saukamappee, a Cree Indian who had lived among the Blackfeet since he was a boy. He told this story to the Welsh fur trader and cartographer David Thompson, who as an employee of the Hudson's Bay Company spent the winter of 1786–87 in a Piegan camp at the base of the Rockies. J. B. Tyrrell, ed., *David Thompson's Narrative of His Explorations in Western America, 1784–1812* (Toronto: Champlain Society, 1916), 334. For more on Thompson's fascinating and tragic life, see D'Arcy Jenish, *Epic Wanderer: David Thompson and the Mapping of the Canadian West* (Lincoln: Univ. of Nebraska Press, 2003). For translation, see Bastien, *Blackfoot Ways of Knowing*, 214.

22 N. Scott Momaday quoted in *The West*, DVD, directed by Stephen Ives (Arlington, Va.: PBS Home Video, 1996).

23 John C. Ewers, *The Horse in Blackfoot Indian Culture, with Comparative Material from Other Western Tribes* (Washington, D.C.: Government Printing Office, 1955), 20. Ewers's book remains the classic account of the transition to equestrianism by Plains Indian societies.

24 Thompson's informant Saukamappee was one of the armed warriors. See Tyrrell, ed., *David Thompson's Narrative*, 330–34; John C. Ewers, *Indian Life on the Upper Missouri* (Norman: Univ. of Oklahoma Press, 1968), 35.

25 For a discussion of such trends considered throughout the Plains, see Pekka Hämäläinen, "The Rise and Fall of Plains Indian Horse Cultures," *Journal of American History* 90, no. 4 (Dec. 2003): 833–62.

26 Grinnell, *Blackfoot Lodge Tales*, 194.

27 Ewers, *The Blackfeet*, 37. Ewers based his estimate on figures provided by Alexander Henry, who—like Thompson—was a fur trader stationed among the Blackfeet in the late eighteenth and early nineteenth centuries.

28 Tyrrell, ed., *David Thompson's Narrative*, 346.

29 Stephen S. Witte and Marsha V. Gallagher, eds., *The North American Journals of Prince Maximilian of Wied* (Norman: Univ. of Oklahoma Press, 2010), 1:421–26.

30 George Catlin, *Illustration of the Manners, Customs, and Condition of the North American Indians* (London: Henry G. Bohn, 1857), 1:30–34.

31 Grinnell, *Blackfoot Lodge Tales*, 143–44.

32 See Mari Sandoz, *The Beaver Men: Spearheads of Empire* (1964; Lincoln: Univ. of Nebraska Press, 2009), 3–21, 313–14.

33 David Hackett Fischer, *Champlain's Dream: The European Founding of North America* (New York: Simon and Schuster, 2008); Carolyn Podruchny, *Making the Voyageur World: Travelers and Traders in the North American Fur Trade* (Lincoln: Univ. of Nebraska Press, 2006); and Eric Jay Dolin, *Fur, Fortune, and Empire: The Epic History of the Fur Trade in America* (New York: Norton, 2010), 13–23.

34 The "HBC point blanket," as it was known, was introduced in 1780 and became popular with native peoples because its white background offered terrific winter camouflage. See "Our History: The HBC Point Blanket," http://www.hbc heritage.ca/hbcheritage/history/blanket/history (accessed 15 Feb. 2012).

35 This is Ewers's interpretation. See *The Blackfeet*, 19.

36 "Henday, Anthony," *Dictionary of Canadian Biography Online*, http://www .biographi.ca/009004 119.01-c.php?BioId=35522 (accessed 14 Feb. 2012).

37 Theodore Binnema argues—rightfully—that sweeping characterizations about differing Blackfeet attitudes toward British, Canadian, and American trappers and traders obscure more complex reasons for the Indians' alternating friendliness and hostility to white newcomers. Still, the historical record clearly supports the generalization that the Blackfeet expressed particular antagonism toward Americans. See Binnema's article "Allegiances and Interests: Niitsitapi (Blackfoot) Trade, Diplomacy, and Warfare, 1806–1831," *Western Historical Quarterly* 37, no. 3 (Autumn 2006): 327–49.

38 For the Canadian fur trade, see two classics: Harold A. Innis, *The Fur Trade in Canada: An Introduction to Canadian Economic History* (New Haven: Yale Univ. Press, 1930); and Arthur J. Ray, *Indians in the Fur Trade: Their Role as Trappers, Hunters, and Middlemen in the Lands Southwest of Hudson Bay, 1660–1870* (Toronto: Univ. of Toronto Press, 1974). For the American system, see David J. Wishart, *The Fur Trade of the American West, 1807–1840: A Geographical Synthesis* (1979; Lincoln: Univ. of Nebraska Press, 1992).

39 Burton Harris, *John Colter: His Years in the Rockies* (1952; Lincoln: Univ. of Nebraska Press, 1993). See also John C. Jackson, "Revisiting the Colter Legend," *Rocky Mountain Fur Trade Journal* 3 (Jan. 2009): 1–19.

40 Moulton, ed., *The Lewis and Clark Journals*, 352–53, 365–66; Harris, *John Colter*, 35–58.

41 For full biographies, see Richard Edward Oglesby, *Manuel Lisa and the Opening of the Missouri Fur Trade* (Norman: Univ. of Oklahoma Press, 1963); and M. O. Skarsten, *George Drouillard: Hunter and Interpreter for Lewis and Clark & Fur Trader, 1807–1810* (1964; Lincoln: Univ. of Nebraska Press, 2005).

42 There are numerous accounts of "Colter's run." The one above is based on the version that his biographer considers the most enduring: John Bradbury, *Travels in the Interior of America in the Years 1809, 1810, and 1811* (1819; Lincoln: Univ. of Nebraska Press, 1986), 44–47. For other versions, see Thomas James, *Three Years among the Indians and Mexicans* (1846; St. Louis: Missouri Historical Society, 1916), 57–64; and Washington Irving, *Astoria, or Anecdotes of an Enterprize beyond the Rocky Mountains* (1836; Lincoln: Univ. of Nebraska Press, 1976), 101–4. Jon T. Coleman offers an intriguing rereading of the episode in *Here Lies Hugh Glass: A Mountain Man, a Bear, and the Rise of the American Nation* (New York: Hill & Wang, 2012), 75–80.

43 For classic histories of the American fur trade, see Hiram Martin Chittenden, *The American Fur Trade of the Far West*, 3 vols. (New York: Francis P. Harper, 1902); Paul C. Phillips, *The Fur Trade*, 2 vols. (Norman: Univ. of Oklahoma Press, 1961); and David Lavender, *The Fist in the Wilderness* (1964; Lincoln: Univ. of Nebraska Press, 1998).

44 James, *Three Years among the Indians*, 80.

45 *Encyclopedia of New York City* (New Haven: Yale Univ. Press, 1995), s.v. "South Street Seaport."

46 Chittenden, *The American Fur Trade*, 1:163–65, quote p. 165. For more on Astor, see James P. Ronda, *Astoria and Empire* (Lincoln: Univ. of Nebraska Press, 1990).

47 Dolin, *Fur, Fortune, and Empire*, 189–222.

48 Gitlin, *The Bourgeois Frontier*, 68.

49 Smoothing this merger was the 1823 marriage of Astor's second-in-command, Ramsay Crooks, to Bernard Pratte's daughter Emilie, who was sixteen years younger than her husband. See Hyde, *Empires, Nations, and Families*, 59.

50 Erwin N. Thompson, *Fort Union Trading Post: Fur Trade Empire on the Upper Missouri* (Williston, N.D.: Fort Union Association, 2003), 3–4. Like many historians of the U.S. fur trade, Thompson notes that while the AFC contained multiple subdivisions, "as far as the general public and the opposition traders were concerned, the whole organization was known as the American Fur Company." See p. 4.

51 For a complete description of the fort as well as some of the archaeological work involved in its reconstruction, see William J. Hunt Jr., "'At the Yellowstone . . . to Build a Fort': Fort Union Trading Post, 1828–1833," in *Fort Union Fur*

Trade Symposium Proceedings: September 13–15, 1990 (Williston, N.D.: Friends of Fort Union Trading Post, 1994), 7–23. There is disagreement in regard to the founding date of Fort Union; some scholars insist that 1829 is the correct year. I have sided with Hunt, one of the leading archaeological experts on the history of the site. For a fascinating account of the controversy attending the fort's partial reconstruction in the years 1985–91, see Paul L. Hedren, "Field Notes: Why We Reconstructed Fort Union," *Western Historical Quarterly* 23, no. 3 (Aug. 1992): 349–54.

52 Catlin, *Illustration of the Manners*, 1:21. For the best history of the post, see Barton H. Barbour, *Fort Union and the Upper Missouri Fur Trade* (Norman: Univ. of Oklahoma Press, 2001). For more on Catlin, see John Hausdoerffer, *Catlin's Lament: Indians, Manifest Destiny, and the Ethics of Nature* (Lawrence: Univ. Press of Kansas, 2009).

53 Unfortunately, no information on the date or artist can be found at the Missouri History Museum, which holds the print. However, it seems probable that the work was executed in the early 1830s, given that McKenzie looks to be in his early thirties (he was born in 1801) and left Fort Union for Europe in 1834.

54 For statistics, see Barbour, *Fort Union*, 36–37.

55 For two similar but not identical accounts, see Annie Heloise Abel, ed., *Chardon's Journal at Fort Clark, 1834–1839* (1932; Lincoln: Univ. of Nebraska Press, 1997), 401–4; and James H. Bradley, "Journal of James H. Bradley," *Contributions to the Historical Society of Montana* (Boston: J. S. Canner, 1966), 3:201–3. See also Ewers, *The Blackfeet*, 56–57.

56 James H. Bradley, "Bradley Manuscript, Book II," *Contributions to the Historical Society of Montana* (Boston: J. S. Canner, 1966), 8:140–41.

57 James H. Bradley, "Bradley Manuscript, Book F," *Contributions to the Historical Society of Montana* (Boston: J. S. Canner, 1966), 8:244–50, quote p. 246.

58 Bradley, "Bradley Manuscript, Book II," 156.

59 Witte and Gallagher, eds., *The North American Journals*, 2:362–65.

60 Frederick Douglass, *Life and Times of Frederick Douglass, Written by Himself* (Boston: De Wolfe & Fiske, 1892), 127.

61 See "Mormon History, Nov. 7, 1833," http://mormon-church-history. blogspot.com/2009/08/mormon-history-nov-7-1833.html (accessed 17 Feb. 2012).

62 Donald W. Olson and Laurie E. Jasinski, "Abe Lincoln and the Leonids," *Sky & Telescope* 98, no. 5 (November 1999): 34–35.

63 Bradley, "Bradley Manuscript, Book II," 134. Lesley Wischmann describes the same event in *Frontier Diplomats: Alexander Culbertson and Natoyist-Siksina' among the Blackfeet* (2000; Norman: Univ. of Oklahoma Press, 2004), 57.

64 Lewis, *The Effects of White Contact*, 36.

65 Clement Augustus Lounsberry, *Early History of North Dakota: Essential Outlines of American History* (Washington, D.C.: Liberty Press, 1919), 144.

66 Catlin, *Illustration of the Manners*, 1:20.

67 William E. Lass, *A History of Steamboating on the Upper Missouri River* (Lin-

coln: Univ. of Nebraska Press, 1962), 13. See also Lass, *Navigating the Missouri: Steamboating on Nature's Highway, 1819–1935* (Norman, Okla.: Arthur H. Clark, 2008); and Michael M. Casler, *Steamboats of the Fort Union Fur Trade: An Illustrated Listing of Steamboats on the Upper Missouri River, 1831–1867* (Williston, N.D.: Fort Union Association, 1999).

68 See Hugh Dempsey, *Firewater: The Impact of the Whisky Trade on the Blackfoot Nation* (Calgary: Fifth House, 2002), 7–25.

69 For more on the consumption of alcohol in the early American republic, see Paul E. Johnson, *A Shopkeeper's Millennium: Society and Revivals in Rochester, New York, 1815–1837* (New York: Hill & Wang, 1978); W. J. Rorabaugh, *The Alcoholic Republic: An American Tradition* (New York: Oxford Univ. Press, 1979); and Ian R. Tyrrell, *Sobering Up: From Temperance to Prohibition in Antebellum America, 1800–1860* (Westport, Conn.: Greenwood Press, 1979).

70 See Peter C. Mancall, *Deadly Medicine: Indians and Alcohol in Early America* (Ithaca: Cornell Univ. Press, 1995); and William E. Unrau, *White Man's Wicked Water: The Alcohol Trade and Prohibition in Indian Country, 1802–1892* (Lawrence: Univ. Press of Kansas, 1996). From the earliest days of the United States, federal officials had tried to keep alcohol out of Indian country, as with the Trade and Intercourse Act of 1790. See Francis Paul Prucha, *The Great Father: The United States Government and the American Indians* (Lincoln: Univ. of Nebraska Press, 1984), 1:98–102.

71 Bradley, "Journal of James H. Bradley," 221–26. See also Clyde D. Dollar, "The High Plains Smallpox Epidemic of 1837–38," *Western Historical Quarterly* 8, no. 1 (Jan. 1977), 15–38; and Ewers, *The Blackfeet*, 65–66. For an account of the epidemic at Fort Union, see Charles Larpenteur, *Forty Years a Fur Trader on the Upper Missouri: The Personal Narrative of Charles Larpenteur, 1833–1872* (1898; Lincoln: Univ. of Nebraska Press, 1989), 109–112. Perhaps the best single description of the event is Abel, ed., *Chardon's Journal at Fort Clark*, 121–45. It is worth noting that there were other outbreaks of the disease on the nineteenth-century Plains, such as an epidemic among the Pawnees in 1831, but nothing as intense farther north until 1837. My thanks to David Wishart for pointing this out. Earlier epidemics had, of course, exacted their own grim toll, with devastating consequences for groups like the Arikaras and the Mandans. See, e.g., Elizabeth Fenn, *Encounters at the Heart of the World: A History of the Mandan People* (New York: Hill & Wang, forthcoming). On the challenges of combating the disease in portions of the twentieth-century developing world, described by the architect of that strategy, see William H. Foege, *House on Fire: The Fight to Eradicate Smallpox* (Berkeley: Univ. of California Press, 2011).

72 For Maximilian's description of the battle, see Witte and Gallagher, eds., *The North American Journals*, 2:393–98.

73 This, of course, is speculation. However, given that a huge Piegan camp of two hundred lodges (approximately 1,600 people) had visited just two weeks before and remained camped nearby at the time of the attack (many of its war-

riors joined the fight), it seems plausible that the girl and her family were in the vicinity of Fort McKenzie, either camped at the post itself or at the much bigger village.

74 Two other dates—1823 and 1827—have been proposed as the year of Coth-co-co-na's birth, but since her age is listed as forty-five on the 1870 federal census, 1825 seems the safest bet. See Ninth Census of the United States, 1870, Montana Territory, National Archives (microfilm), roll M593, p. 225. Though almost always identified as Under Bull, her father has also been listed as Big Snake or Owl Child. For the former see undated document, Montana Historical Society, Helen P. Clarke Papers, SC 1153, folder 3; for the latter see Roxanne DeMarce, ed., *Blackfeet Heritage, 1907–1908* (Browning, Mont.: Blackfeet Heritage Program, 1980), 68.

75 Clark Wissler, "The Social Life of the Blackfoot Indians," *Anthropological Papers of the American Museum of Natural History*, vol. 7, pt. 1 (New York: Published by Order of the Trustees, 1912), 16–18.

76 Grinnell, *Blackfoot Lodge Tales*, 185.

77 Wissler, "Material Culture of the Blackfoot Indians," 63–64; and Ewers, *The Blackfeet*, 109–10.

78 J. N. B. Hewitt, ed., *Journal of Rudolph Friederich Kurz* (1937; Lincoln: Univ. of Nebraska Press, 1970), 79. To be sure, white indignation about perceived gender inequality among the Indians was a major driver of liberal criticism in eastern Indian policy, too.

79 Katherine M. Weist, "Beasts of Burden and Menial Slaves: Nineteenth-Century Observations of Northern Plains Indian Women," in *The Hidden Half: Studies of Plains Indian Women*, ed. Patricia Albers and Beatrice Medicine (Lanham, Md.: Univ. Press of America, 1983), 29–52. See also David D. Smits, "The 'Squaw Drudge': A Prime Index of Savagism," *Ethnohistory* 29, no. 4 (1982): 281–306.

80 For Blackfeet marital customs, see Wissler, "The Social Life of the Blackfoot Indians," 9–14; and Ewers, *The Blackfeet*, 98–101.

81 For more on the Sun Dance, which was celebrated by many Plains Indian peoples, see Clark Wissler, "The Sun Dance of the Blackfoot Indians," *Anthropological Papers of the American Museum of Natural History*, vol. 16, pt. 3 (New York: Published by Order of the Trustees, 1918).

82 Witte and Gallagher, eds., *The North American Journals*, 2:432.

83 Other factors, of course, drove intermarriage throughout the Western Hemisphere. For instance, the Spanish conquest of indigenous empires in the New World brought them inevitably into close and intimate proximity with Indian peoples. The far less numerous French, by contrast, depended upon such interracial relationships to expand the reach of their colonies and to cement critical military alliances with Indian groups, essential in checking the ambitions of other European powers. For the Spanish case, see, among others, J. H. Elliott, *Empires of the Atlantic World: Britain and Spain in America, 1492–1830* (New Haven: Yale Univ. Press, 2006), and David J. Weber, *Bárbaros: Spaniards and Their Savages in the Age of Enlightenment* (New Haven: Yale

Univ. Press, 2007). On the French, see Richard White, *The Middle Ground: Indians, Empires, and Republics in the Great Lakes Region, 1650–1815* (New York: Cambridge Univ. Press, 1991); and Alan Greer, *The People of New France* (Toronto: Univ. of Toronto Press, 1997).

84 Jennifer S. H. Brown and Theresa Schenck, "Métis, Mestizo, and Mixed-Blood," in *A Companion to American Indian History*, ed. Philip Deloria and Neal Salisbury (Malden, Mass.: Blackwell, 2002), 329.

85 William B. Parker, ed., *Thomas Jefferson: Letters and Addresses* (New York: A. Wessels, 1907), 190. For more on Jefferson's views, see Reginald Horsman, *Expansion and American Indian Policy, 1783–1812* (East Lansing: Michigan State Univ. Press, 1967), 104–14; and Anthony F. C. Wallace, *Jefferson and the Indians: The Tragic Fate of the First Americans* (Cambridge: Harvard Univ. Press, 1999).

86 Quoted in Annette Gordon-Reed, *The Hemingses of Monticello: An American Family* (New York: Norton, 2008), 343.

87 Joseph Ellis, *American Sphinx: The Character of Thomas Jefferson* (New York: Random House, 1998), 201.

88 See Sidney Kaplan, "Historical Efforts to Encourage White-Indian Intermarriage in the United States and Canada," *International Social Science Review* 65, no. 3 (Summer 1990): 126–32.

89 For classic treatments of the subject (though in the Canadian context), see Sylvia Van Kirk, *Many Tender Ties: Women in Fur Trade Society* (Norman: Univ. of Oklahoma Press, 1980); and Jennifer S. H. Brown, *Strangers in Blood: Fur Trade Company Families in Indian Country* (Vancouver: Univ. of British Columbia Press, 1980). See also Clara Sue Kidwell, "Indian Women as Cultural Mediators," *Ethnohistory* 39, no. 2 (Spring 1992): 97–107; Ewers, *Indian Life on the Upper Missouri*, 57–74; and "Intermarriage and North American Indians," a special issue of *Frontiers: A Journal of Women Studies* 29, nos. 2–3 (2008).

90 For the relationship between Culbertson and Natawista, see Wischmann, *Frontier Diplomats.*

91 Kenneth McKenzie may have had several Indian spouses, though their names are unknown. For his part, James Kipp eventually abandoned his Mandan wife, Earth Woman, when he returned to Missouri. For more information on the contours of native-white intermarriage on the Upper Missouri, see John Mack Faragher, "The Custom of the Country: Cross-Cultural Marriage in the Far Western Fur Trade," in *Western Women: Their Land, Their Lives*, ed. Lillian Schlissel, Vicki L. Ruiz, and Janice Monk (Albuquerque: Univ. of New Mexico Press, 1988), 199–225; Michael Lansing, "Plains Indian Women and Interracial Marriage in the Upper Missouri Fur Trade, 1804–1868," *Western Historical Quarterly* 31, no. 4 (Winter 2000): 413–33; and William R. Swagerty, "Marriage and Settlement Patterns of Rocky Mountain Trappers and Traders," *Western Historical Quarterly* 11, no. 2 (April 1980): 161–80.

92 Hewitt, ed., *Journal of Rudolph Friederich Kurz*, 155.

93 For more on the benefits and costs of fur post life for Indian women, see Van Kirk, *Many Tender Ties*, 75–94.
94 Author interview with Darrell Robes Kipp, Oct. 2006.
95 Ewers explains, "Adventurous young men hunted the powerful grizzly bear for its claws, which they proudly displayed in the form of necklaces. However, most Blackfoot Indians feared and avoided this dangerous beast. They regarded it as a sacred animal of great supernatural as well as physical power." See *The Blackfeet*, 85.
96 There are several accounts of the marriage, including Culbertson's, which is reflected in the telling above and which Wischmann finds most plausible. See *Frontier Diplomats*, 92–95. The Bloods, meanwhile, have a much more romantic version, recorded by James Willard Schultz, a white man who married a Piegan woman and lived among the Blackfeet for several decades in the late nineteenth century. See his book, *Signposts of Adventure: Glacier National Park as the Indians Know It* (Boston: Houghton Mifflin, 1926), 111–17. In any event, the union effectively ended in 1870, when Natawista returned—without Culbertson—to live among her own people.

Chapter 2: Four Bears

1 Charles Dickens, *American Notes and Pictures from Italy* (1842; New York: Oxford Univ. Press, 1987), 218–19.
2 On West Point, see Stephen Ambrose, *Duty, Honor, Country: A History of West Point* (Baltimore: Johns Hopkins Univ. Press, 1966); James L. Morrison Jr., *"The Best School in the World": West Point, the Pre–Civil War Years, 1833–1866* (Kent, Ohio: Kent State Univ. Press, 1986); and George S. Pappas, *To the Point: The United States Military Academy, 1802–1902* (Westport, Conn.: Praeger, 1993).
3 For Poe's brief West Point career, see Ambrose, *Duty, Honor, Country*, 156–57.
4 Report of Proceedings in the Case of Cadet E. Malcolm Clark, 16 April 1835, Montana Historical Society (cited hereafter as MTHS), Heavy Runner Records (cited hereafter as HRR), Records of the War Department, Office of the Judge Advocate General, Court Martial CC-48, MF 53a.
5 For more on Jackson's interference at West Point, see Ambrose, *Duty, Honor, Country*, 106–24; and Pappas, *To the Point*, 224.
6 The details concerning this second fight are elusive. For the fullest account, see LeRoy R. Hafen, ed., *The Mountain Men and the Fur Trade of the Far West* (Glendale, Calif.: Arthur H. Clarke, 1971), 8:69–72. For Clarke's class rank, see *Register of the Officers and Cadets of the U.S. Military Academy, June 1836*, 14.
7 The painting hangs in the rotunda of the U.S. Capitol. For more on Thomas Seymour, consult J. Hammond Trumbull, ed., *Memorial History of Hartford County, Connecticut, 1633–1844* (Boston: Edward L. Osgood, 1886), 1:193.

For more on the importance of the battle, see Richard M. Ketchum, *Saratoga: Turning Point of America's Revolutionary War* (New York: Henry Holt, 1997).

8 For more on Nathan Clarke's military record, see Reuben G. Thwaites, ed., *Collections of the State Historical Society of Wisconsin*, vol. 11 (Madison: State Printer, 1888), 362–63.

9 Nathan Clarke is much harder to track than his wife. There are different accounts for both the date (1788 or 1789) and place (Connecticut, Massachusetts, or Ohio) of his birth, though 1788 in New England seems the likeliest scenario. For more on Clarke, see Thwaites, ed., *Collections of the State Historical Society of Wisconsin*, 362–63; Doane Robinson, "A Comprehensive History of the Dakota or Sioux Indians," *South Dakota Historical Collections*, vol. 2 (Pierre: State Historical Society, 1904), 155; and E. F. Ellet, "Early Days at Fort Snelling," *Collections of the Minnesota Historical Society*, vol. 1 (St. Paul: Minnesota Historical Society, 1872), 421.

10 Charlotte Ouisconsin Van Cleve, "A Brief Story of the Life of Charlotte Seymour Clarke," Dec. 1873, unpublished manuscript, Minnesota Historical Society, Horatio P. Van Cleve and Family Papers, box 152.E.5.8F, 4.

11 For more on the Northwest and its history of conflict, see R. David Edmunds, *The Shawnee Prophet* (Lincoln: Univ. of Nebraska Press, 1983); Eric Hinderaker, *Elusive Empires: Constructing Colonialism in the Ohio Valley, 1673–1800* (New York: Cambridge Univ. Press, 1997); and Robert M. Owens, *Mr. Jefferson's Hammer: William Henry Harrison and the Origins of American Indian Policy* (Norman: Univ. of Oklahoma Press, 2007).

12 For a concise history of the settlement during this period, see Brian Leigh Dunnigan, "Fortress Detroit, 1701–1826," in *The Sixty Years' War for the Great Lakes, 1754–1814*, ed. David Curtis Skaggs and Larry L. Nelson (East Lansing: Michigan State Univ. Press, 2001), 167–86.

13 Van Cleve, "A Brief Story," 4–5.

14 Lea VanderVelde, *Mrs. Dred Scott: A Life on Slavery's Frontier* (New York: Oxford Univ. Press, 2009), 18.

15 Before he received permission to build a small private house outside the walls, Lieutenant Clarke and his growing family lived only a few yards from the quarters later inhabited by Dred Scott, a slave owned by the post's surgeon who sued (unsuccessfully) for freedom on the basis, in part, of his residence between 1836–38 at Fort Snelling, which was in free territory. For a consideration of Dred Scott's time with his wife at Fort Snelling, see VanderVelde, *Mrs. Dred Scott*.

16 Charlotte Ouisconsin Van Cleve, *Three Score Years and Ten: Life-Long Memories of Fort Snelling, Minnesota, and Other Parts of the Far West* (Minneapolis: Harrison and Smith, 1888), 148.

17 Scott was killed in 1847 in the Battle of Molino del Rey, one of the bloodiest engagements of the Mexican-American War, moments—allegedly—after boasting that, "the bullet is not run that is to kill Martin Scott." J. F. Williams,

"Memoir of Capt. Martin Scott," *Collections of the Minnesota Historical Society*, vol. 3 (St. Paul: Minnesota Historical Society, 1880), 180–87; Van Cleve, *Three Score Years and Ten*, 29.

18 Van Cleve, *Three Score Years and Ten*, 148; Henry Snelling, unpublished manuscript (courtesy of Nancy Cass), 75.

19 For more on this relationship, with particular attention to the Sioux, see Gary Clayton Anderson, *Kinsmen of Another Kind: Dakota-White Relations in the Upper Mississippi Valley, 1650–1862* (Lincoln: Univ. of Nebraska Press, 1984).

20 Van Cleve, *Three Score Years and Ten*, 63–67. That the Indian boy was Ojibwa (and not Dakota) is a guess based on the verbal greeting with which Clarke hailed him.

21 There are numerous accounts of this episode. My version relies primarily upon Van Cleve, *Three Score Years and Ten*, 74–79, supplemented by Marcus Lee Hansen, *Old Fort Snelling, 1819–1858* (Minneapolis: Ross & Haines, 1958), 119–24, and Willoughby M. Babcock Jr., "Major Lawrence Taliaferro, Indian Agent," *Mississippi Valley Historical Review* 11, no. 3 (Dec. 1924): 370–71.

22 Hansen, *Old Fort Snelling*, 124.

23 Van Cleve, *Three Score Years and Ten*, 78.

24 Ibid., 80.

25 Ibid., 99–101.

26 Rachel Jackson died quite unexpectedly three days before Christmas 1828, plunging the president-elect into a state of bewildered grief. Along with the other military officers stationed in Nashville, Nathan Clarke traveled to Jackson's splendid country estate, the Hermitage, to pay his respects and attend the funeral. Ibid., 80–86.

27 For this correspondence, see Records of the War Department, Office of the Adjutant General, U.S. Military Academy Applications, Egbert M. Clarke 17–32, MTHS, HRR, MF 53a.

28 Van Cleve, *Three Score Years and Ten*, 105–9; and Van Cleve, "A Brief Story," 14–15.

29 For recent histories of the Texas Revolution, see H. W. Brands, *Lone Star Nation: How a Ragged Army of Volunteers Won the Battle for Texas Independence—and Changed America* (New York: Doubleday, 2004); James E. Crisp, *Sleuthing the Alamo: Davy Crockett's Last Stand and Other Mysteries of the Texas Revolution* (New York: Oxford Univ. Press, 2005); and William C. Davis, *Lone Star Rising: The Revolutionary Birth of the Texas Republic* (New York: Free Press, 2004).

30 It is an indication of his celebrity that Crockett was the inspiration for the lead character in Knickerbocker James Kirke Paulding's popular 1831 play *The Lion of the West*. Crockett quoted in Davis, *Lone Star Rising*, p. 208.

31 James L. Haley, *Sam Houston* (Norman: Univ. of Oklahoma Press, 2002).

32 It is worth noting that the Texans also cried "Remember Goliad!," which referred to the massacre of 350 rebel prisoners by Mexican soldiers on 27 March 1836, just three weeks after the fall of the Alamo.

33 E. M. Clarke, claim no. 5914, 19 Dec. 1837, Texas State Library and Archives, Republic Claims, reel 18, 48–49.

34 An oft-told story suggests that Clarke led a mutiny on board the steamship that ferried him from New Orleans to Galveston, because of poor treatment by the captain. According to this tale, Houston himself pardoned Clarke after hearing the details of the insurrection, and Malcolm was carried through the streets as a hero. See Van Cleve, *Three Score Years and Ten*, 153.

35 *Register of the Officers and Cadets of the U.S. Military Academy, 1835*, 21, 23.

36 Van Cleve, *Three Score Years and Ten*, 154–55; "Lindsay S. Hagler," Handbook of Texas Online, http://www.tshaonline.org/handbook/online/articles/fha08 (accessed 17 Dec. 2012).

37 Volunteers who arrived in Texas prior to 1 Oct. 1837 were eligible for bounty claims, entitling the holder to a free section of land in Texas. Alternatively, bearers could sell the grant for cash. Though Clarke arrived in Texas before the cutoff date, for reasons that are unclear he seems not to have applied for such compensation. Lindsay Hagler, however, requested and received 1,280 acres in Atascosa County in Dec. 1837, and likely an additional 640 acres in Frio County in March 1839. Thanks to John Molleston of the Texas General Land Office for assistance with this research. For more information, see Thomas Lloyd Miller, *Bounty and Donation Land Grants of Texas, 1835–1888* (Austin: Univ. of Texas Press, 1967), esp. 313–14, for Hagler's grant(s).

38 Letter from Joel Poinsett to John Miller, 31 Dec. 1838, Records of the War Department, Office of the Judge Advocate General, Court Martial CC-48, MTHS, HRR, MF 53a.

39 Maria R. Audubon, *Audubon and His Journals* (1897; New York: Dover, 1960), 2:87–89. Lesley Wischmann provides an excellent account of Audubon's time at Fort Union in *Frontier Diplomats: Alexander Culbertson and Natoyist-Siksina' among the Blackfeet* (Norman: Univ. of Oklahoma Press, 2004), 98–107.

40 Nathaniel P. Langford, "A Frontier Tragedy," Yellowstone National Park Research Library, catalog 7492-7499, ACC 262, 5. A typescript copy of the manuscript can be found at the MTHS, Nathaniel P. Langford Papers (cited hereafter as NPL), SC 215, folder 2.

41 Letter from [unknown correspondent] to Malcolm Clarke, 11 May 1841, Records of the War Department, Office of the Judge Advocate General, Court Martial CC-48, MTHS, HRR, MF 53a.

42 Van Cleve, *Three Score Years and Ten*, 155.

43 Stephen S. Witte and Marsha V. Gallagher, eds., *The North American Journals of Prince Maximilian of Wied* (Norman: Univ. of Oklahoma Press, 2010), 2:357–61, quote p. 360.

44 William R. Swagerty, "A View from the Bottom Up: The Work Force of the American Fur Company on the Upper Missouri in the 1830s," *Montana: The Magazine of Western History* 43, no. 1 (Winter 1993): 18–33. Swagerty's wage

figures are from the 1830s, the closest available date to Malcolm Clarke's arrival.

45 Helen P. Clarke, "Sketch of Malcolm Clarke," *Contributions to the Historical Society of Montana* (Boston: J. S. Canner, 1966), 2:257–58.

46 Charlotte Ouisconsin Van Cleve, "A Sketch of the Early Life of Malcolm Clark," *Contributions to the Historical Society of Montana* (Boston: J. S. Canner, 1966), 1:93. In the late 1820s and early 1830s, Malcolm attended Alexander Kinmont's Academy for Boys, which emphasized the study of religion, mathematics, and the classics. For more, see Charles Frederic Goss, *Cincinnati, the Queen City: 1788–1912* (Chicago: S. J. Clarke, 1912), 2:381–82.

47 John E. Sunder, *The Fur Trade on the Upper Missouri, 1840–1865* (1965; Norman: Univ. of Oklahoma Press, 1993), 87.

48 Charles Larpenteur, *Forty Years a Fur Trader on the Upper Missouri: The Personal Narrative of Charles Larpenteur, 1833–1872* (1898; Lincoln: Univ. of Nebraska Press, 1989), 142.

49 Ibid., 142–43.

50 There are multiple accounts of the so-called Fort McKenzie massacre. See, e.g., among others, James H. Bradley, "Journal of James H. Bradley," *Contributions to the Historical Society of Montana* (Boston: J. S. Canner, 1966), 3:235–37; Larpenteur, *Forty Years a Fur Trader*, 187–89; Wischmann, *Frontier Diplomats*, 111–13; and John G. Lepley, *Blackfoot Fur Trade on the Upper Missouri* (Missoula, Mont.: Pictorial Histories Publishing, 2004), 135–39. Chardon, who was nearly as dissolute as Harvey, was in charge of the post only because Culbertson was downriver at Fort Union hosting John James Audubon.

51 Bradley, "Journal of James H. Bradley," 232. Though Bradley's account suggests a date of 1840, he was almost certainly off by one year. See Wischmann, *Frontier Diplomats*, 83, n. 22.

52 The two best sources on the episode are Hiram Martin Chittenden, *The American Fur Trade of the Far West* (New York: Francis P. Harper, 1902), 2:696 97; and Sunder, *The Fur Trade on the Upper Missouri*, 88–90. See also Larpenteur, *Forty Years a Fur Trader*, 194–96. While they likely crossed paths again—though vast, the Upper Missouri was also intimate—Clarke and Harvey never faced off a second time, and Clarke no doubt breathed much easier in 1854 when he learned of Harvey's death of illness. Sadly, the court case Sunder uses to such great effect, *U.S. v. James Lee, Jacob Berger, and Malcolm Clark*, Case No. 393, is now missing from the National Archives branch at Kansas City.

53 See May G. Flanagan, "The Story of Old Fort Benton," MTHS, May G. Flanagan Papers, SC 1236. For the definitive study of the post, see Joel Overholser, *Fort Benton: World's Innermost Port* (Helena, Mont.: Falcon Press, 1987).

54 Lepley, *Blackfoot Fur Trade*, 128. For a sense of the Culbertson-Clarke working relationship, see letter from Malcolm Clarke to Alexander Culbertson, 5 Nov. 1849, Missouri History Museum, Chouteau Family Papers, Chouteau-Papin Collection.

55 Letter from Nicolas Point to James Van de Velde, 5 July 1847, Archives of

the Society of Jesus, St. Louis, Missouri, AA:415 (my thanks to Beth Vosoba for the translation from the French). For his portrait of Clarke, see Nicolas Point, *Wilderness Kingdom: Indian Life in the Rocky Mountains, 1840–1847: The Journals & Paintings of Nicolas Point, S.J.*, trans. Joseph P. Donnelly (New York: Holt, Rinehart and Winston, 1967), 215. For Clarke's donation, see Cornelius M. Buckley, *Nicolas Point, S.J.: His Life & Northwest Indian Chronicles* (Chicago: Loyola Univ. Press, 1989), 383. As befitting someone who earned three times as much, Alexander Culbertson gave Point fifteen dollars. See also Howard L. Harrod, *Mission among the Blackfeet* (Norman: Univ. of Oklahoma Press, 1971).

56 Alexander Culbertson's younger brother, Thaddeus, spent a week in Clarke's company in the summer of 1850 when he took a break from his studies at Princeton Theological Seminary. He came away so impressed with Clarke's deft maneuvering among the Blackfeet that he wrote, "[I]t is my opinion that in order to [have] a proper appreciation of the Indian, a long residence among them is necessary." Thaddeus A. Culbertson, *Journal of an Expedition to the Mauvaises Terres and the Upper Missouri in 1850* (Washington, D.C.: Government Printing Office, 1952), 116. Sadly, Thaddeus died less than a month after he returned to Pennsylvania from his trip. Another trader described Clarke this way: "[He is] a veteran of over twenty years' experience, and thoroughly versed in all the wiles and mysteries of Indian trading. Clark wears a blue blanket capote, and displays a tobacco-sack of scarlet cloth beautifully garnished with beads, the handiwork of his Blackfoot wife." Henry A. Boller, *Among the Indians: Eight Years in the Far West, 1858–1866* (1868; Chicago: Lakeside Press, 1959), 13–14. Boller credited Clarke with three years more than he had actually been on the Upper Missouri.

57 Clarke, "Sketch of Malcolm Clarke," 256.

58 Clarke's whereabouts during the mid-1850s are difficult to track. It appears that he quit the AFC around 1855, perhaps because of a dispute over wages, though one historian speculates that it was because his temper and reputation for violence had thwarted his advancement within the company. See Lepley, *Blackfoot Fur Trade*, 128. After his return from the Midwest, he joined in a limited partnership with Charles Primeau, another former AFC man, and operated from two small posts at Forts Campbell and Stewart (near Forts Benton and Union, respectively). Their fledgling outfit did well enough that the AFC absorbed it "under pressure" in the spring of 1860, with Clarke subsequently assigned to Fort Union as its bourgeois. He lived there until 1862, when, with the fur trade nearly extinct, he moved with his family into the adobe ruins of the defunct Fort Campbell. For information on Clarke's activities as an independent trader, see "The Fort Benton Journal, 1854–1856" and "The Fort Sarpy Journal, 1855–1856," *Contributions to the Historical Society of Montana* (Boston: J. S. Canner, 1966), 10:1–99, 100–187. Clarke appears sporadically in these pages, usually as a visitor to Fort Union (even after leaving the AFC, Clarke maintained friendly relationships with Alexander Culbertson

and Andrew Dawson). See also Sunder, *The Fur Trade on the Upper Missouri*, 213–14, 238.

59 Barton H. Barbour, *Fort Union and the Upper Missouri Fur Trade* (Norman: Univ. of Oklahoma Press, 2001), 130. It is worth noting that Kipp remained in touch with his native family until the end of his life. See, e.g., letter from James Kipp to Joseph Kipp, 15 Aug. 1878, MTHS, James Kipp Papers, SC 936.

60 Quoted in Clarke, "Sketch of Malcolm Clarke," 259. Alexander Culbertson was also an exception to this rule. In the mid-1850s he settled his family in Peoria, Illinois, where they lived in high style for more than a decade before extravagant spending drove him into bankruptcy, precipitating a move back to Montana. See Wischmann, *Frontier Diplomats*, 272–84.

61 The birth dates for Nathan and Isabel are known with certainty, but some confusion exists in the cases of Helen and Horace. The dates above are those given by Horace's granddaughter and Helen's great-niece, Joyce Clarke Turvey. Author interview with Joyce Clarke Turvey, Oct. 2006.

62 Quoted in Clarke, "Sketch of Malcolm Clarke," 258, 255.

63 Martha Edgerton Plassman, "A Double Heritage," MTHS, Martha E. Plassman Papers, MC 78, box 4, folder 18.

64 Peggy Pascoe, *What Comes Naturally: Miscegenation Law and the Making of Race in America* (New York: Oxford Univ. Press, 2009), 19–22, 94–104. It is worth noting, however, that as racial boundaries hardened in the later nineteenth century, several states—including Maine and the Carolinas in the East as well as Arizona, Idaho, Nevada, and Oregon—outlawed marriages between whites and Indians. See also Karen M. Woods, "A 'Wicked and Mischievous Connection': The Origins of Indian-White Miscegenation Law," in *Mixed Race America and the Law: A Reader*, ed. Kevin R. Johnson (New York: New York Univ. Press, 2003), 81–85.

65 See David D. Smits, "'Squaw Men,' 'Half-Breeds,' and Amalgamators: Late Nineteenth-Century Anglo-American Attitudes toward Indian-White Race-Mixing," *American Indian Culture and Research Journal* 15, no. 3 (1991): 29–61; and Clark Wissler, *Indian Cavalcade; or, Life on the Old-Time Indian Reservations* (New York: Sheridan House, 1938), 217–36.

66 Jennifer Brown and Theresa Schenck, "Métis, Mestizo, and Mixed Blood," in *A Companion to American Indian History*, ed. Philip Deloria and Neal Salisbury (Malden, Mass.: Blackwell, 2004), 329. For more on the difficulties facing such families in the period following the Mexican-American War, see Anne F. Hyde, "Hard Choices: Mixed-Race Families and Strategies of Acculturation in the U.S. West After 1848," in *On the Borders of Love and Power: Families and Kinship in the Intercultural American Southwest*, ed. David Wallace Adams and Crista DeLuzio (Berkeley: Univ. of California Press, 2012), 93–115.

67 Walt Whitman, "The Half-Breed: A Tale of the Western Frontier," in *Walt Whitman: The Early Poems and the Fiction*, ed. Thomas L. Brasher (New York: New York Univ. Press, 1963), 257–91, quoted passages on pp. 258 and 272. See also Thomas C. Gannon, "Reading Boddo's Body: Crossing the Borders

of Race and Sexuality in Whitman's 'Half-Breed,'" *Walt Whitman Quarterly Review* 22, nos. 2–3 (Fall/Winter 2004), 87–107; Kenneth M. Price, *To Walt Whitman, America* (Chapel Hill: Univ. of North Carolina Press, 2004): 9–36; and William J. Scheick, *The Half-Blood: A Cultural Symbol in 19th-Century American Fiction* (Lexington: Univ. Press of Kentucky, 1979), 36–38. Whitman's attitude toward native-white miscegenation seems to have softened by the mid-1850s, as is suggested by the passage from "Song of Myself" that affectionately describes the marriage of the trapper and "the red girl." See Walt Whitman, *Complete Poetry and Selected Prose*, ed. James E. Miller Jr. (Boston: Houghton Mifflin, 1959), 31. The same year that Whitman's novella appeared, the historian Francis Parkman offered his own withering assessment of peoples of mixed ancestry in his celebrated travelogue, *The California and Oregon Trail*. Describing a group of *voyageurs* he encountered on the Platte River in eastern Wyoming, he wrote, "They were a mongrel race . . . in a few, indeed, might be seen the black snaky eye of the Indian half-breed, and one and all, they seemed to aim at assimilating themselves to their savage associates." Parkman, *The Oregon Trail* (1849; New York: Penguin, 1982), 118.

68 Two accounts of the family's history center on the experiences of George Bent, son of William Bent and his Cheyenne wife, Owl Woman. See David Fridtjof Halaas and Andrew Edward Masich, *Halfbreed: The Remarkable True Story of George Bent, Caught between the Worlds of the Indian and the White Man* (Cambridge: Da Capo Press, 2004); and George E. Hyde, *A Life of George Bent, Written from His Letters* (Norman: Univ. of Oklahoma Press, 1968). See also Elliott West, *The Way to the West: Essays on the Central Plains* (Albuquerque: Univ. of New Mexico Press, 1995), 85–125.

69 There is an extensive literature on this subject. Particularly useful are Adele Perry, *On the Edge of Empire: Gender, Race, and the Making of British Columbia, 1849–1871* (Toronto: Univ. of Toronto Press, 2001); and Ann Laura Stoler, *Carnal Knowledge and Imperial Power: Race and the Intimate in Colonial Rule* (Berkeley: Univ. of California Press, 2002). See also Sarah Carter, *The Importance of Being Monogamous: Marriage and Nation Building in Western Canada to 1915* (Edmonton: Univ. of Alberta Press, 2008).

70 The woman was the wife of Joseph La Barge, a steamboat captain, and she came upriver on the *Martha*, piloted by her husband. See Hiram Martin Chittenden, *History of Early Steamboat Navigation on the Missouri River: Life and Adventures of Joseph La Barge* (New York: Francis P. Harper, 1903), 1:183. She did not stay long, however, and Fort Benton did not have a sizable community of white women until the 1870s.

71 Howard R. Lamar, *The Trader on the American Frontier: Myth's Victim* (College Station: Texas A&M Univ. Press, 1977), 33.

72 For the Great Lakes, see Lucy Eldersveld Murphy, *A Gathering of Rivers: Indians, Métis, and Mining in the Western Great Lakes, 1737–1832* (Lincoln: Univ. of Nebraska Press, 2000); Susan Sleeper-Smith, *Indian Women and French Men: Rethinking Cultural Encounter in the Western Great Lakes* (Amherst:

Univ. of Massachusetts Press, 2001); and Richard White, *The Middle Ground: Indians, Empires, and Republics in the Great Lakes Region, 1650–1815* (New York: Cambridge Univ. Press, 1991). For the Lower Missouri, see John Mack Faragher, "'More Motley than Mackinaw': From Ethnic Mixing to Ethnic Cleansing on the Frontier of the Lower Missouri, 1783–1833," in *Contact Points: American Frontiers from the Mohawk Valley to the Mississippi, 1750–1830*, ed. Andrew R. L. Cayton and Fredrika J. Teute (Chapel Hill: Univ. of North Carolina Press, 1998), 304–26; and Tanis C. Thorne, *The Many Hands of My Relations: French and Indians on the Lower Missouri* (Columbia: Univ. of Missouri Press, 1996).

73 See Lyndel Meikle, ed., *Very Close to Trouble: The Johnny Grant Memoir* (Pullman: Washington State Univ. Press, 1996); and Gerhard J. Ens, ed., *A Son of the Fur Trade: The Memoirs of Johnny Grant* (Edmonton: Univ. of Alberta Press, 2008). To be sure, Grant was also leery of imminent tax increases as Montana became more populated. Author correspondence with Lyndel Meikle, 5 March 2009.

74 There has been considerable debate among scholars concerning the most accurate way to render the term "Métis." Some prefer the lowercase *m*, and still others choose to omit the accent mark over the *e*. For more on this discussion, see Jacqueline Peterson and Jennifer S. H. Brown, eds., *The New Peoples: Being and Becoming Métis in North America* (1985; Winnipeg: Univ. of Manitoba Press, 2001), 3–16. I have chosen "Métis," but preserved the spelling used by other scholars where appropriate. The literature on the Red River Métis is enormous. Two indispensable works are Sarah Carter, *Aboriginal People and Colonizers of Western Canada to 1900* (Toronto: Univ. of Toronto Press, 1999), esp. 62–82; and Gerhard J. Ens, *Homeland to Hinterland: The Changing Worlds of the Red River Metis in the Nineteenth Century* (Toronto: Univ. of Toronto Press, 1996). See also Nicole St. Onge, Carolyn Podruchny, and Brenda MacDougall, eds., *Contours of a People: Metis Family, Mobility, and History* (Norman: Univ. of Oklahoma Press, 2012). For a local study of such persons in Montana, see Martha Harroun Foster, *We Know Who We Are: Metis Identity in a Montana Community* (Norman: Univ. of Oklahoma Press, 2006).

75 Letter from Robert Morgan to Andrew Dawson, 15 March 1864, MTHS, Andrew Dawson Papers, SC 292.

76 For more on the couple, see Isabel's obituary in the *Great Falls Tribune*, 5 April 1935.

77 David J. Weber, *The Spanish Frontier in North America* (New Haven: Yale Univ. Press, 1992), 23.

78 For statistics, see Andrew C. Isenberg, *Mining California: An Ecological History* (New York: Hill & Wang, 2005) 23. See also Albert L. Hurtado, *John Sutter: A Life on the North American Frontier* (Norman: Univ. of Oklahoma Press, 2006); and Susan L. Johnson, *Roaring Camp: The Social World of the California Gold Rush* (New York: Norton, 2000).

79 Elliott West, *The Contested Plains: Indians, Goldseekers, and the Rush to Colorado* (Lawrence: Univ. Press of Kansas, 1998).

80 Kent Curtis argues persuasively that the Montana gold rush (like others in the West) "was not the result of gold discovery, it was produced by the efforts of national boosters and the expensive work of expansionism" that facilitated the harvesting of the metal. See his "Producing a Gold Rush: National Ambitions and the Northern Rocky Mountains, 1853–1863," *Western Historical Quarterly* 40, no. 3 (Autumn 2009): 275–97.

81 James H. Bradley, "Bradley Manuscript—Book II: Miscellaneous Affairs at Fort Benton," *Contributions to the Historical Society of Montana* (Boston: J. S. Canner, 1966), 8:127–28. It is hard to pinpoint the date of the first discovery of gold in Montana. Reputedly, François Finlay, a veteran of the California diggings, made the first find in 1852 at Gold Creek. Six years later, the brothers James and Granville Stuart made what is often considered the first recorded discovery of gold in Montana when they panned in the vicinity of Finlay's strike. See Clyde A. Milner II and Carol O'Connor, *As Big as the West: The Pioneer Life of Granville Stuart* (New York: Oxford Univ. Press, 2009), 56–58.

82 W. A. Clarke, "Centennial Address: On the Origin, Growth and Resources of Montana," *Contributions to the Historical Society of Montana* (Boston: J. S. Canner, 1966), 2:50.

83 It is worth noting that western Montana (the portion including the Rocky Mountains) passed successively from Oregon Territory (1848–53) to Washington Territory (1853–63) and to Idaho Territory (1863–64) before becoming part of Montana Territory in 1864. For more, see Mark Stein, *How the States Got Their Shapes* (New York: Collins, 2008), 163–67.

84 K. Ross Toole, *Montana: An Uncommon Land* (1959; Norman: Univ. of Oklahoma Press, 1984), 72; Michael P. Malone, Richard B. Roeder, and William L. Lang, *Montana: A Tale of Two Centuries* (1976; Seattle: Univ. of Washington Press, 1991), 97.

85 The vigilantes, who counted among their number some of the most important men in the territory, including the future U.S. senator Wilbur Fisk Sanders, are still revered by many in Montana today. For the best volume on the subject, see Frederick Allen, *A Decent, Orderly Lynching: The Montana Vigilantes* (Norman: Univ. of Oklahoma Press, 2004).

86 For population estimate, see *Annual Report of the Secretary of the Interior, 1860*, 36th Cong., 2nd sess., 308.

87 Author interview with Darrell Robes Kipp, Oct. 2006.

88 *Annual Report of the Secretary of the Interior, 1859*, 36th Cong., 1st sess., 487–88.

89 For the complete text of the treaty, see the Institute for the Development of Indian Law, *Treaties and Agreements of the Pacific Northwest Indian Tribes* (Washington, D.C.: Institute for the Development of Indian Law, 1974), 51–55. For more on the treaty's significance, see John C. Ewers, *The Blackfeet:*

Raiders on the Northwestern Plains (1958; Norman: Univ. of Oklahoma Press, 1983), 205–25.

90 Albert John Partoll, ed., *The Blackfoot Indian Peace Council: A Document of the Official Proceedings of the Treaty between the Blackfoot Nation and Other Indians and the United States, in October, 1855* (Missoula, Mont.: State Univ., 1937), 10.

91 Kurz goes on to note that while McKenzie missed from time to time, he had little doubt that he "has the skill to shoot 12 cows in 1 mile if his runner should come up with that number." J. N. B. Hewitt, ed., *Journal of Rudolph Friederich Kurz* (1937; Lincoln: Univ. of Nebraska Press, 1970), 194.

92 Ibid.

93 There are numerous accounts of the episode, though none provide much detail. The most reliable is probably Sunder, *The Fur Trade*, 250–51. See also Larpenteur, *Forty Years a Fur Trader*, 298; Chittenden, *History of Early Steamboat Navigation*, 233–34; E. W. Gould, *Fifty Years on the Mississippi* (St. Louis: Nixon-Jones, 1889), 422–25; Martha Edgerton Plassman, "The Killing of Owen McKenzie," MTHS, Martha E. Plassman Papers, MC 78, box 3, folder 1; and *Annual Report of the Secretary of the Interior, 1863*, 38th Cong., 1st Sess., 290.

94 Chittenden, *History of Early Steamboat Navigation*, 234.

95 Clarke, "Sketch of Malcolm Clarke," 258.

96 In the short time between McKenzie's murder and the establishment of his ranch, Clarke finagled an appointment as the chief government farmer at the Blackfeet Indian Agency on Sun River. However, during the extended absence of the Indian agent Henry Reed, Clarke turned the farm, which was intended to model agricultural techniques to the natives, into a hotel and trading post, capitalizing on its excellent location to provision miners and settlers disembarking at Fort Benton. According to at least one source, Clarke may even have operated a brothel at the farm location. Author interview with Carol Murray, Oct. 2006. When Reed's successor, Gad E. Upson, arrived in Oct. 1863, he was so scandalized by the state of affairs at the farm that he promptly fired Clarke. *Annual Report of the Secretary of the Interior, 1864*, 38th Cong., 2nd sess., 438.

97 Gary E. Moulton, ed., *The Lewis and Clark Journals: An American Epic of Discovery: The Abridgment of the Definitive Nebraska Edition* (Lincoln: Univ. of Nebraska Press, 2004), 153–54.

98 Known today as the Sieben Ranch, the 75,000-acre property (nearly 120 square miles) belongs to John Baucus, the brother of U.S. Senator Max Baucus. See MTHS, Sieben Ranch, vertical file. See also MTHS, Edith Grimes Waddell Reminiscence, SC 1669. Born in Ireland to a wealthy merchant family, Meagher had immigrated to the United States in 1852. He served gallantly during the Civil War, leading the famed Irish Brigade into battle first at Antietam and then at Fredericksburg, where he suffered a serious leg wound from a cannonball. Meagher came away from his visit to Clarke's ranch deeply impressed

with the owner, whom he described as a "highly intelligent and adventurous gentleman" who possessed "some of the very best horses in Montana." Clarke surely rose in Meagher's estimation when he poured a nice bottle of champagne at dinner. But the acting governor reserved his most flattering remarks for Clarke's daughter Helen—"a singularly amiable and very prepossessing young lady in appearance"—recently returned to Montana after completing her education at a Cincinnati convent. Reprinted in Thomas Francis Meagher, "A Journey to Benton," *Montana: The Magazine of Western History* 1, no. 4 (Oct. 1951): 49. For more on Meagher's fascinating life see Paul R. Wylie, *The Irish General: Thomas Francis Meagher* (Norman: Univ. of Oklahoma Press, 2007).

99 See Pierre-Jean De Smet, *Life, Letters, and Travels of Father Pierre-Jean De Smet, S.J., 1801–1873*, ed. Hiram Martin Chittenden and Alfred Talbot Richardson (New York: F. P. Harper, 1905), 4:1512; Sandoval Family Genealogy (photocopy in author's possession); William R. Swagerty, "Marriage and Settlement Patterns of Rocky Mountain Trappers and Traders," *Western Historical Quarterly* 11, no. 2 (April 1980): 167–68.

100 "Act of Incorporation," *Contributions to the Historical Society of Montana* (Boston: J. S. Canner, 1966), 1:16–17.

101 For more on the roots and ideology of the herrenvolk, see George M. Frederickson, *White Supremacy: A Comparative Study in American and South African History* (New York: Oxford Univ. Press, 1981).

102 *Annual Report of the Secretary of the Interior, 1864*, 38th Cong., 2nd sess., 441.

103 Tom Stout, *Montana, Its Story and Biography: A History of Aboriginal and Territorial Montana and Three Decades of Statehood* (Chicago: American Historical Society, 1921), 339. See also Hugh A. Dempsey, *The Amazing Death of Calf Shirt and Other Blackfoot Stories: Three Hundred Years of Blackfoot History* (1994; Norman: Univ. of Oklahoma Press, 1996), 47–58.

104 Lyman E. Munson, "Pioneer Life in Montana," *Contributions to the Historical Society of Montana* (Boston: J. S. Canner, 1966), 5:214–16.

105 For the full text of the treaty, see the Institute for the Development of Indian Law, *Treaties and Agreements*, 70–74.

106 A thorough discussion of these events can be found in Ewers, *The Blackfeet*, 236–53.

107 U.S. Congress, *Piegan Indians*, House Executive Document 269, 41st Cong., 2nd sess. (1870), 4.

108 This account relies on the events described in Clarke, "Sketch of Malcolm Clarke," 259–68, with additional information in Langford, "A Frontier Tragedy."

109 Author interviews with Darrell Robes Kipp, Oct. 2006; Carol Murray, Oct. 2006; and Darrell Norman, June 2007.

110 There are differing accounts of the Indians who accompanied Owl Child. This version reflects the telling found in Clarke, "Sketch of Malcolm Clarke."

111 It seems that Coth-co-co-na's mother shared this name with the aunt, though some insist that it was her mother—and not her aunt—who was the one at the ranch to begin with. See, e.g., George Black, *Empire of Shadows: The Epic Story of Yellowstone* (New York: St. Martin's Press, 2012), 221.

112 Clarke, "Sketch of Malcolm Clarke," 266.

113 Ibid., 262, 267–68.

114 Letter and notes by N. P. Langford on the Cullen Treaty with the Blackfoot Indians, 1 Sept. 1868, MTHS, NPL, SC 215, folder 1.

115 Van Cleve, "A Brief Story," 15–16 (emphasis in the original). The news was all the more distressing to Charlotte because she had lost her own Malcolm (Clarke's nephew and namesake) to a murder several years earlier in California.

116 Clarke, "Sketch of Malcolm Clarke," 268.

117 See Elliott West, *The Last Indian War: The Nez Perce Story* (New York: Oxford Univ. Press, 2009).

118 Clarke, "Sketch of Malcolm Clarke," 268. Sherman does not mention this episode in his official report, though he notes that the party stopped twice at Wolf Creek (the location of the ranch, then owned by James Fergus), once for dinner on 24 Aug. and then, on the return from Fort Benton, for breakfast on 28 Aug. See *Reports of Inspection Made in the Summer of 1877 by Generals P. H. Sheridan and W. T. Sherman of Country North of the Union Pacific Railroad* (Washington, D.C.: Government Printing Office., 1878), 84, 86.

Chapter 3: The Man Who Stands Alone with His Gun

1 George Black, *Empire of Shadows: The Epic Story of Yellowstone* (New York: St. Martin's Press, 2012), 239.

2 Letter from Régis de Trobriand to O. D. Greene, 2 Jan. 1870, Montana Historical Society (cited hereafter as MTHS), Régis de Trobriand Papers (cited hereafter as RDT), SC 5, folder 1–2.

3 The name of his second wife, whom Sully met while stationed at Fort Randall, was Sihasapawin (Blackfeet Woman). One of their children was Mary Sully, known also as Akicitawin (Soldier Woman), who, like her father, was an accomplished painter. I am grateful to Phil Deloria (great-grandson of Mary Sully) for this information.

4 For Sully's report on his meeting with the chiefs, see U.S. Congress, *Piegan Indians*, House Executive Document 269, 41st Cong., 2nd session (1870), 36–37. James Welch offers a vivid (if fictional) imagining of this conference in his novel *Fools Crow* (New York: Penguin, 1986), 268–84. It is worth noting that because of their own name for the river, Piegans call the event the "Bear River Massacre."

5 Larry McMurtry spends only four pages on the episode in his catalog of such events, placing much greater emphasis on Sand Creek and Wounded Knee, among others. See *Oh What a Slaughter: Massacres in the American West, 1846–1890* (New York: Simon and Schuster, 2005), 115–19. For a recent study of

another horrific but obscure slaughter of Indians in the nineteenth-century West (though perpetrated not by whites but by a joint force of Mexicans and other native peoples), see Karl Jacoby, *Shadows at Dawn: A Borderlands Massacre and the Violence of History* (New York: Penguin, 2008).

6 *New North-West*, 20 Aug. 1869.

7 See Paul Andrew Hutton, *Phil Sheridan and His Army* (Norman: Univ. of Oklahoma Press, 1985), 60–62; and Langdon Sully, *No Tears for the General: The Life of Alfred Sully, 1821–1879* (Palo Alto: American West Publishing, 1974), 216–18.

8 U.S. Congress, *Piegan Indians*, 7.

9 Ibid., 50–51.

10 For more on de Trobriand's life and career, see Régis de Trobriand, *Military Life in Dakota: The Journal of Philippe Régis de Trobriand*, trans. Lucille M. Kane (1951; Lincoln: Univ. of Nebraska Press, 1982); and Marie Caroline Post, *The Life and Mémoirs of Comte Régis de Trobriand, Major-General in the Army of the United States* (New York: E. P. Dutton, 1910).

11 Letter from Régis de Trobriand to A. S. Simmons et al., 6 Oct. 1869, MTHS, RDT, SC 5, folder 1-2 (emphasis in the original).

12 See Dee Brown, *Bury My Heart at Wounded Knee: An Indian History of the American West* (1970; New York: Owl Books, 2007), 170–72. Tosawi has been rendered in multiple ways, including Toch-a-way, Tosawa, and Toshaway.

13 Though in later years Sheridan vehemently denied ever making much a statement, Captain Charles Nordstrom of the Tenth U.S. Cavalry claimed to have overheard the exchange. See Edward S. Ellis, *The History of Our Country: From the Discovery of America to the Present Time*, 8 vols. (1895; Cincinnati: Jones Brothers, 1900), 6:1483. In time this maxim was shortened to "The only good Indian is a dead Indian," also attributed to Sheridan.

14 Quoted in Hutton, *Phil Sheridan and His Army*, 2.

15 For more, see William G. Thomas III, *The Iron Way: Railroads, the Civil War, and the Making of Modern America* (New Haven: Yale Univ. Press, 2011), 149–73.

16 See Paul A. Hutton, "Sheridan's Pyrrhic Victory: The Piegan Massacre, Army Politics, and the Transfer Debate," *Montana: The Magazine of Western History* 32, no. 2 (Spring 1982): 32–35.

17 U.S. Congress, *Piegan Indians*, 52.

18 The literature on the battle is extensive. See Hutton, *Phil Sheridan and His Army*, 56–114; Jerome A. Greene, *Washita: The U.S. Army and the Southern Cheyennes, 1867–1869* (Norman: Univ. of Oklahoma Press, 2004); and Thom Hatch, *Black Kettle: The Cheyenne Chief Who Sought Peace but Found War* (New York: Wiley, 2004).

19 Quoted in Hutton, *Phil Sheridan and His Army*, 99.

20 For Hardie's report to Sheridan, see U.S. Congress, *Piegan Indians*, 19–34.

21 For Hardie's communications with Sully, see ibid., 43–44.

22 Ibid., 47 (emphasis in the original).

23 See Theophilus F. Rodenbaugh, *From Everglade to Canyon with the Second United States Cavalry* (1875; Norman: Univ. of Oklahoma Press, 2000), 7–13.

24 Douglas C. McChristian, *The U.S. Army in the West: Uniforms, Weapons, and Equipment* (Norman: Univ. of Oklahoma Press, 1995), 22–23. More on the history of Fort Shaw is in a letter from Richard Thoroughman to the author, 3 July 2007.

25 Thomas Marquis, *Custer, Cavalry & Crows: The Story of William White as Told to Thomas Marquis* (Bellevue, Neb.: Old Army Press, 1975), 32.

26 For more on Cobell, see William F. Wheeler, "Personal History of Joe Cobell," MTHS, William F. Wheeler Papers, MC 65, box 1, folder 15.

27 Black, *Empire of Shadows*, 251.

28 *New North-West*, 21 Jan. 1870.

29 For de Trobriand's orders, see U.S. Congress, *Piegan Indians*, 48.

30 There are multiple accounts of the expedition, but this retelling relies primarily on the two best ones: Robert J. Ege, *Strike Them Hard: Incident on the Marias, 23 January 1870* (Bellevue, Neb.: Old Army Press, 1970); and Dave Walter, *Montana Campfire Tales: Fourteen Historical Narratives* (Guilford, Conn.: Globe Pequot Press, 1997), 33–50. It is worth noting that, while Ege's narrative is scrupulously researched, it is also—in the words of its author—"much kinder to Major Eugene M. Baker than most historians have written." See Robert J. Ege to Merrill G. Burlingame, 3 April 1969, Montana State University Library, Merrill G. Burlingame Special Collections, Merrill G. Burlingame Papers, collection 2245, box 36, file 6. See also Ben Bennett, *Death, Too, for The-Heavy-Runner* (Missoula, Mont.: Mountain Press, 1981); Wesley C. Wilson, "The U.S. Army and the Piegans: The Baker Massacre on the Marias, 1870," *North Dakota History* 32, no. 1 (Winter 1965): 40–58; and J. P. Dunn, *Massacres of the Mountains: A History of the Indian Wars of the Far West* (New York: Harper & Brothers, 1886), 509–42.

31 For the best account of the engagement, see John H. Monnett, *Where a Hundred Soldiers Were Killed: The Struggle for the Powder River Country in 1866 and the Making of the Fetterman Myth* (Albuquerque: Univ. of New Mexico Press, 2008). See also Shannon D. Smith, *Give Me Eighty Men: Women and the Myth of the Fetterman Fight* (Lincoln: Univ. of Nebraska Press, 2008).

32 *Great Falls Tribune*, 27 Jan. 1935.

33 Bear Head's account (related in 1935) of the events of 23 Jan. 1870 appears in James Willard Schultz, *Blackfeet and Buffalo: Memories of Life among the Indians* (Norman: Univ. of Oklahoma Press, 1962), 282–305. For a shorter but somewhat different version that he offered in 1915, see deposition of Bear Head, 18 Jan. 1915, MTHS, Heavy Runner Records (cited hereafter as HRR), MF 53.

34 *Billings Gazette*, 3 April 1932. This account was offered by Spear Woman, a daughter of Heavy Runner who was seven at the time of the massacre. More than a decade after her death, Spear Woman's own daughter, Mrs. George Croff, gave her mother's story to the newspaper.

35 Statement by Joe Connelly to Marguerite Marmont in 1931, Glenbow-Alberta Institute (cited hereafter as GAI), Stan Gibson Fonds (cited hereafter as SGF).

36 For more on the military armaments of this period, see McChristian, *The U.S. Army in the West.*

37 See, e.g., deposition of Buffalo Trail Woman, 16 Jan. 1916, MTHS, HRR, MF 53.

38 Schultz, *Blackfeet and Buffalo*, 301–2.

39 Montana place-names in Blackfeet and English, Montana State University Library, Merrill G. Burlingame Special Collections, James Willard Schultz Papers, collection 10, box 6, folder 7.

40 For more on Doane, see Orrin H. Bonney and Lorraine Bonney, *Battle Drums and Geysers: The Life and Journals of Lt. Gustavus Cheyney Doane, Soldier and Explorer of the Yellowstone and Snake River Regions* (Chicago: Sage Books, 1970); and Marquis, *Custer, Cavalry, and Crows*. See also Black, *Empire of Shadows.*

41 U.S. Congress, *Piegan Indians*, 73. Baker did not report specific information on the ages and sexes of the victims until pressed to do so, more than two months after the incident on the Marias. One can only assume that the figures he provided came from Doane's body count.

42 Statement of Joe Kipp, 8 Feb. 1913, MTHS, HRR, MF 53. The Blackfeet recognize Kipp's figure as the correct body count. See *Great Falls Tribune*, 23 Jan. 2007. Doane gave this assessment in 1889 as part of his unsuccessful application for the superintendency of Yellowstone National Park; it is uncertain whether he made this assertion with pride or regret. Quoted in Bonney and Bonney, *Battle Drums and Geysers*, 22.

43 McKay was long mistakenly identified as "Walter." See Stan Gibson to U.S. Army Center of Military History, 14 Feb. 1997, GAI, SGF; and Stan Gibson, notes on Walton McKay, GAI, SGF. It is worth noting that another soldier suffered a broken leg when pitched from his horse, becoming the only trooper wounded in the affair.

44 For an account of this episode see Marquis, *Custer, Cavalry & Crows*, 33. Though Doane is not named, references to "the officer in charge" lead Black, among others, to the conclusion that it was Doane who ordered the executions. For his part, Bear Head believed there were four victims, and they were Bloods who had been in the Piegan camp. See deposition of Bear Head, 18 Jan. 1915, MTHS, HRR, MF 53.

45 For their part, the Piegans insisted that the number of confiscated horses was closer to 5,000. See, e.g., statement of Joe Kipp, 8 Feb. 1913, MTHS, HRR, MF 53. John Ponsford, a member of the expedition, offered a figure of 3,000 horses seized, noting that all but 800 were claimed by their rightful white owners at Fort Shaw, with the balance sold to the highest bidders at an average price of eight dollars each. See John W. Ponsford, Baker Battle, 1870, MTHS, John W. Ponsford Reminiscence, SC 659.

46 *Billings Gazette*, 3 April 1932.

47 Telegram from Régis de Trobriand to O. D. Greene, 30 Jan. 1870, MTHS, RDT, SC 5, folder 1-2.
48 Letter from Régis de Trobriand to O. D. Greene, 18 Feb. 1870, MTHS, RDT, SC 5, folder 1-2.
49 U.S. Congress, *Piegan Indians*, 17.
50 *Helena Daily Herald*, 2 Feb. 1870.
51 *New North-West*, 11 Feb. 1870.
52 *Owyhee Avalanche*, 5 March 1870.
53 See, e.g., the *Daily Rocky Mountain Gazette*, 30 Jan. 1870.
54 Letter from Régis de Trobriand to Marie Caroline Post, 30 Jan. 1870, MTHS, RDT, SC 1201.
55 Letter from Régis de Trobriand to Marie Caroline Post, 9 March 1870, MTHS, RDT, SC 1201.
56 Quoted in Hutton, *Phil Sheridan and His Army*, 192.
57 For Pease's report, see U.S. Congress, *Expedition against Piegan Indians*, House Executive Document 185, 41st Cong., 2nd sess. (1870), 7–8. For more on the exploitation of the forty-ninth parallel by Indians from both sides of the international boundary, see Andrew R. Graybill, *Policing the Great Plains: Rangers, Mounties, and the North American Frontier, 1875–1910* (Lincoln: Univ. of Nebraska Press, 2007), 23–63.
58 For Sully's letter, see U.S. Congress, *Expedition against Piegan Indians*, 6. Sully explained later that he had intended to send a copy of Pease's letter to the War Department at the same time, but that his clerk had forgotten to do so. See *New York Times*, 21 March 1870.
59 *Congressional Globe*, 41st Cong., 2nd sess., 25 Feb. 1870, 1576. Ironically, less than a year earlier Colyer had declared with great optimism that "in less than two years we shall have heard the last of 'Indian outrages.'" See *New York Times*, 15 July 1869. Baker was a brevet colonel, hence Colyer's appellation.
60 *New York Times*, 24 Feb. 1870.
61 *Harper's Weekly*, 19 March 1870. Secretary of the Interior Jacob D. Cox sounded a similar note in a letter to President Grant dated 7 March 1870. Cox insisted that much of the conflict in the West stemmed from U.S. expansion into Indian territory, and he called particular attention to the circumstances in Montana, where, he explained, "the very capital of the Territory is located upon the land to which the Indian title has never been extinguished and which has never been formally opened by the government for settlement." See U.S. Congress, *Appropriations for Certain Indian Treaties*, Senate Executive Document 57, 41st Cong., 2nd sess. (1870), 4.
62 U.S. Congress, *Piegan Indians*, 9–10. Colyer did not allow Sheridan's insult to go unanswered, insisting to the general, "Because I pull aside the curtain and let the American people see what you call 'a great victory over the Indians,' it does not follow that we do not want the *men* who perpetrated the horrid crimes you portray with so much zest, justly punished. Strike, if you must strike, the guilty, not the innocent." *New York Times*, 10 March 1870 (emphasis in the original).

63 The best source for information on the transfer debate (as well as the larger struggle for control of Indian affairs) is Henry G. Waltmann, "The Interior Department, War Department, and Indian Policy, 1865–1887" (Ph.D. diss., University of Nebraska-Lincoln, 1962). See also Donald J. D'Elia, "The Argument over Civilian or Military Indian Control, 1865–1880," *Historian* 24, no. 2 (Feb. 1962): 207–25; and Marvin Garfield, "The Indian Question in Congress and in Kansas," *Kansas Historical Quarterly* 2, no. 1 (Feb. 1933): 29–44.

64 For more on Sand Creek, see Stan Hoig, *The Sand Creek Massacre* (1961; Norman: Univ. of Oklahoma Press, 1977); and Ari Kelman, *A Misplaced Massacre: Struggling over the Memory of Sand Creek* (Cambridge: Harvard Univ. Press, 2013).

65 The literature on Grant's peace policy is extensive. Among the most helpful sources are Henry E. Fritz, *The Movement for Indian Assimilation, 1860–1890* (Philadelphia: Univ. of Pennsylvania Press, 1963); Loring Benson Priest, *Uncle Sam's Stepchildren: The Reformation of United States Indian Policy, 1865–1887* (1942; Lincoln: Univ. of Nebraska Press, 1969); and Francis Paul Prucha, *The Great Father: The United States Government and the American Indians*, 2 vols. (Lincoln: Univ. of Nebraska Press, 1984). For a revisionist perspective, see Henry G. Waltmann, "Circumstantial Reformer: President Grant & the Indian Problem," *Arizona and the West* 13, no. 4 (Winter 1971): 323–42.

66 Hutton, "Sheridan's Pyrrhic Victory," 33–34.

67 *Annual Report of the Secretary of the Interior, 1868*, 40th Cong., 3rd sess., 467–74. It is worth noting that, as a member of the Peace Commission, Sherman signed his name to Taylor's report (along with three other generals). It is doubtful, however, that he endorsed this portion of the document.

68 *Army and Navy Journal*, 26 Feb. 1870.

69 *Congressional Globe*, 41st Cong., 2nd sess., 25 Feb. 1870, 1577. Because Voorhees was a Democrat, his indictment of Grant was surely informed more by the congressman's partisan sensibilities than by a commitment to racial justice; in fact, the historian Kenneth M. Stampp attributed to Voorhees an "intense race prejudice," which no doubt shaped his role as one of the chief Copperheads (northern Democrats who opposed the Civil War and whom Abraham Lincoln lamented as "the fire in the rear"). See his *Indiana Politics during the Civil War* (1949; Bloomington: Indiana Univ. Press, 1978), 211. For more on Voorhees's life and career, see Henry D. Jordan, "Daniel Wolsey Voorhees," *Mississippi Valley Historical Review* 6, no. 4 (March 1920): 532–55.

70 *New York Times*, 11 March 1870. For his part, Sherman was convinced that Logan seized upon any opportunity to thwart him, given that Sherman had passed over Logan when selecting the commander of the Army of Tennessee after the death of General J. B. McPherson in July 1864. See Robert G. Athearn, *William Tecumseh Sherman and the Settlement of the West* (Norman: Univ. of Oklahoma Press, 1956), 254. For more on Logan, who is remembered for conceiving of the idea of Memorial Day, see James Pickett Jones, *John A. Logan: Stalwart Republican from Illinois* (Tallahassee: Univ. Presses of Florida, 1982).

71 *Army and Navy Journal,* 26 March 1870.

72 *Congressional Globe,* 44th Cong., 1st sess., 20 April 1876, 2673.

73 Linda K. Kerber, "The Abolitionist Perception of the Indian," *Journal of American History* 62, no. 2 (Sept. 1975): 271–95.

74 Henry Mayer, *All on Fire: William Lloyd Garrison and the Abolition of Slavery* (1998; New York: Norton, 2008), 138. For the importance of opposition to Indian removal in the strengthening of the antislavery movement, see Mary Hershberger, "Mobilizing Women, Anticipating Abolition: The Struggle against Indian Removal in the 1830s," *Journal of American History* 86, no. 1 (June 1999): 15–40. See also Allison L. Sneider, *Suffragists in an Imperial Age: U.S. Expansion and the Woman Question, 1870–1929* (New York: Oxford Univ. Press, 2008). On the intellectual connections between African colonization and Indian removal, see Nicholas Guyatt, "'The Outskirts of Our Happiness': Race and the Lure of Colonization in the Early Republic," *Journal of American History* 95, no. 4 (March 2009): 986–1011.

75 Robert Winston Mardock, *The Reformers and the American Indian* (Columbia: Univ. of Missouri Press, 1971), 8.

76 For more on Child, see Carolyn L. Karcher, *The First Woman in the Republic: A Cultural Biography of Lydia Maria Child* (Durham: Duke Univ. Press, 1994).

77 For a sampling of these and other pieces, see Lydia Maria Child, *Hobomok and Other Writings on Indians,* ed. Carolyn L. Karcher (New Brunswick: Rutgers Univ. Press, 1986). See also Laura L. Mielke, "Sentiment and Space in Lydia Maria Child's Native American Writings, 1824–1870," *Legacy* 21, no. 2 (2004): 172–92.

78 The article originally appeared in two installments of the *National Anti-Slavery Standard* with the title "A Plea for the Indian," before being reissued in pamphlet form. For a reprint of the essay see Carolyn L. Karcher, ed., *A Lydia Maria Child Reader* (Durham: Duke Univ. Press, 1997), 79–94.

79 Lydia Maria Child, "The Indians," *Standard* 1, no. 1 (May 1870): 2. This periodical, which published only three issues, between May and July 1870, was the successor to the *National Anti-Slavery Standard.*

80 *New York Times,* 19 May 1870.

81 U.S. Congress, *Piegan Indians,* 70–71.

82 *New York Times,* 19 May 1870.

83 U.S. Congress, *Public Acts of the Forty-First Congress,* 2nd sess. (1870), chap. 294, 319. President Grant, apparently, was infuriated by this maneuver, and—according to Sherman—declared to his opponents (who, presumably, hoped to install their own supporters in the Indian agency positions), "Gentlemen, you have defeated my plan of Indian management; but you shall not succeed in *your* purpose, for I will divide these appointments up among the religious churches, with which you dare not contend." Quoted in Waltmann, "Circumstantial Reformer," 334 (emphasis in the original).

84 U.S. Congress, *Second Annual Report of the Board of Indian Commissioners,* Senate Executive Document 39, 41st Cong., 3rd sess. (1871), 90–91.

85 Hutton, "Phil Sheridan's Pyrrhic Victory," 41. See also Sully, *No Tears for the General*, 210–34.

86 James H. Bradley, *The March of the Montana Column: A Prelude to the Custer Disaster*, ed. Edgar I. Stewart (Norman: Univ. of Oklahoma Press, 1961), 55–63.

87 Eugene Mortimer Baker chronology, GAI, SGF.

88 There are two sources for this interview, and they differ slightly on various details: Martha E. Plassmann, notes taken in an interview with Horace Clarke [n.d.], MTHS, Horace Clarke Reminiscence (cited hereafter as HCR), SC 540; and Martha E. Plassmann, "A Double Heritage," MTHS, Martha E. Plassmann Papers (cited hereafter after as MEP), MC 78, box 4, folder 18. I find the first of these more reliable, because the notes were presumably taken at the time of the interview, and because Plassmann confessed to adding "minor touches to render [the article] more salable." See letter from Martha E. Plassmann to James Knapp Reeve, 29 June 1926, MTHS, MEP, MC 78, box 2, folder 24. Plassmann was the daughter of Sidney Edgerton, the first territorial governor of Montana (1864–66).

89 Plassmann, "A Double Heritage." Plassmann stated that Horace was eighty-two, which would place his date of birth in 1844, an impossibility, since that was around the time of his parents' marriage and before the birth of his older sister, Helen.

90 Martha E. Plassmann, notes taken in an interview with Horace Clarke [n.d.], MTHS, HCR, SC 540.

91 Letter from Plassmann to Reeve, 29 June 1926, MTHS, MEP, MC 78, box 2, folder 24.

92 Plassmann, notes taken in an interview with Horace Clarke [n.d.], MTHS, HCR, SC 540. In "A Double Heritage" he remembers the Indian's name as "Big Nose."

93 Letter from Francis Paul Prucha, S.J., to Stan Gibson, 4 Feb. 1997, GAI, SGF.

94 *Helena Weekly Herald*, 1 Jan. 1880.

95 James Willard Schultz, "Joe Kipp," MTHS, James Willard Schultz Papers, SC 721.

96 Letter from Stan Gibson to Jack Hayne, 6 May 1995, GAI, SGF. James Welch paints an unsparing portrait of Kipp in *Fools Crow*, depicting the scout as callous and opportunistic.

97 Martha E. Plassmann, "That Affair on the Marias," Aug. 1934, MTHS, MEP, MC 78, box 4, folder 12.

98 Martha E. Plassmann, "The Baker Massacre," Sept. 1925, MTHS, MEP, MC 78, box 2, folder 15.

99 See Hugh A. Dempsey, *The Amazing Death of Calf Shirt and Other Black-foot Stories: Three Hundred Years of Blackfeet History* (1994; Norman: Univ. of Oklahoma Press, 1996), 47–58.

100 Assessment records from the period show that Clarke was one of the most successful livestock owners in the area, running 125 cattle with an aggre-

gate value of $1,500. See, e.g., Chouteau County Assessment records, 1878, Montana State University, Merrill G. Burlingame Special Collections, WPA Records, collection 2336, box 68, folder 2. Horace and Margaret did not have their union solemnized until 24 April 1883. See marriage license [photocopy] of Horace J. Clarke and Margaretta [*sic*], MTHS, Malcolm Clarke, vertical file.

101 Plassmann, notes taken in an interview with Horace Clarke [n.d.], MTHS, HCR, SC 540.

102 See Margaret Spanish obituary, *Great Falls Tribune,* 29 Sept. 1940.

103 Statement of Joe Kipp, 8 Feb. 1913, MTHS, HRR, MF 53.

104 Letter from Arthur McFatridge to commissioner of Indian affairs, 8 Feb. 1913, MTHS, HRR, MF 53. Regarding the agent's motivations, given his corruption (which led to his removal in 1915), it is possible that he hoped to receive a share of any settlement himself.

105 Letters from Arthur McFatridge to commissioner of Indian affairs, 14 Jan. and 17 March 1914, MTHS, HRR, MF 53.

106 Letter from assistant secretary of the interior to secretary of war, 7 April 1914, MTHS, HRR, MF 53.

107 Statement of Bear Head, 18 Jan. 1915, MTHS, HRR, MF 53.

108 Statement of Mrs. Frank Monroe, 18 Jan. 1915, MTHS, HRR, MF 53.

109 Statement of Joe Kipp, 16 Jan. 1915, MTHS, HRR, MF 53.

110 For more on Lane, who was a strong advocate for Indian rights and a withering critic of government policy toward its indigenous peoples, see Robert D. Johnston, *The Radical Middle Class: Populist Democracy and the Question of Capitalism in Progressive Era Portland, Oregon* (Princeton: Princeton Univ. Press, 2003), 29–45.

111 Letter from first assistant secretary of the interior to Henry F. Ashurst, 20 Feb. 1915, MTHS, HRR, MF 53.

112 See statement of Good Bear Woman, 15 Jan. 1916, and statement of Buffalo Trail Woman, 16 Jan. 1916, MTHS, HRR, MF 53.

113 Letter from Dick Kipp to Senator H. L. Myers, 1 Dec. 1916, National Archives and Records Administration, Bureau of Indian Affairs, Record Group 75, central classified files, 1907–39, PI-163, E-121, Blackfeet, box 93, file 18498-1913-260.

114 Statement of Horace J. Clarke, 9 Nov. 1920, MTHS, HRR, MF 53.

115 See letter from Charles H. Burke to Scott Leavitt, 30 Jan. 1926, MTHS, HRR, MF 53.

116 David Hilger, "An Historical Foot-Race," 4 Dec. 1923, MTHS, David Hilger Papers, SC 854, folder 5.

117 It is worth noting that after Malcolm's murder, James Fergus (Andrew's father) bought the Clarke ranch from Horace and lived there for ten years with his family.

118 Letter from David Hilger to Horace Clarke, 4 Sept. 1924, MTHS, Helen P. Clarke Papers, SC 1153, folder 2.

119 David Hilger, interview with Horace Clarke, 27 Sept. 1924, MTHS, HCR, SC 540.
120 *Great Falls Tribune*, 23 Jan. 2007. For a more extended description of a Blackfeet visit to the Big Bend, see Stan Gibson, "Visit to the Baker Massacre Site," [n.d.], GAI, SGF. See also author interview with Lea Whitford, June 2007.

Chapter 4: The Bird That Comes Home

1 For more on the movie and its reception, see Angela Aleiss, *Making the White Man's Indian: Native Americans and Hollywood Movies* (Westport, Conn.: Praeger, 2005), 19–21. For DeMille's involvement with the film, see Robert S. Birchard, *Cecil B. DeMille's Hollywood* (Lexington: Univ. Press of Kentucky, 2004), 1–13. See also Scott Eyman, *Empire of Dreams: The Epic Life of Cecil B. DeMille* (New York: Simon and Schuster, 2010).
2 Letter from Helen P. Clarke to Edwin M. Royle, 15 Feb. 1911, Montana Historical Society (cited hereafter as MTHS), Helen P. Clarke Papers (cited hereafter as HPC), SC 1153, folder 2.
3 Letter from Edwin M. Royle to Helen P. Clarke, 22 Feb. 1911, MTHS, HPC, SC 1153, folder 2. The book suggested by Royle was Jean Finot, *Race Prejudice* (London: Archibald Constable, 1906).
4 Quoted in Eleanor Ruggles, *Prince of Players: Edwin Booth* (New York: Norton, 1953), 211. Nora Titone explores the rivalry between the brothers in *My Thoughts Be Bloody: The Bitter Rivalry between Edwin and John Wilkes Booth That Led to an American Tragedy* (New York: Free Press, 2011).
5 For the richest description of Booth's Theatre, see William Winter, *Life and Art of Edwin Booth* (New York: Greenwood Press, 1968), 82–90. It is worth noting that the cost of the theater bankrupted Booth, who had to go on tour in order to pay off his debts, a circumstance that kept him working feverishly even into his declining years. Thanks to Tice Miller for drawing my attention to this information.
6 John Frick, "A Changing Theatre: New York and Beyond," in *The Cambridge History of American Theatre*, ed. Don B. Wilmeth and Christopher Bigsby, vol. 2 (New York: Cambridge Univ. Press, 1999), 206–10. For a broader perspective on the U.S. theater scene of the period, see Tice L. Miller, *Entertaining the Nation: American Drama in the Eighteenth and Nineteenth Centuries* (Carbondale: Southern Illinois Univ. Press, 2007).
7 The house (at 603 Fifth St., SE) still stands and is listed in the National Register of Historic Places.
8 The fire (likely caused by faulty wiring) destroyed the East Glacier home formerly occupied by Horace and Helen. At the time of the conflagration the house had passed to Horace's granddaughter Joyce Clarke Turvey and her husband, Irv. *Great Falls Tribune*, 29 April 1962.
9 *Great Falls Tribune*, 15 May 1932; undated reminiscence by Bessie C. Wells, MTHS, HPC, SC 1153, folder 1.

10 Thomas F. Meagher, "A Journey to Benton," *Montana: The Magazine of Western History* 1, no. 4 (Oct. 1951): 49. Meagher had served as acting governor of Montana Territory for less than two years when on 1 July 1867 (under mysterious circumstances) he fell into the Missouri River from a steamboat docked at Fort Benton. His body was never recovered.

11 Undated reminiscence by Bessie C. Wells, MTHS, HPC, SC 1153, folder 1.

12 Quoted in Claire Lamont, "Meg the Gipsy in Scott and Keats," *English* 36, no. 155 (Summer 1987): 139–40.

13 Journal of James Upson Sanders, entry for 17 June 1885, MTHS, James Upson Sanders Papers (cited hereafter as JUS), MC 66, box 2, folder 4.

14 Undated reminiscence by Bessie C. Wells, MTHS, HPC, SC 1153, folder 1.

15 Robert Gottlieb, "The Drama of Sarah Bernhardt," *New York Review of Books,* 10 May 2007, p. 10. The article contains an excellent bibliography of important books about the actress. See also Gottlieb's recent biography, *Sarah: The Life of Sarah Bernhardt* (New Haven: Yale Univ. Press, 2010).

16 *Great Falls Tribune,* 15 May 1932. Lesley Wischmann offers another explanation for the endemic financial problems that plagued former traders and their families; she writes of Alexander Culbertson that "he had become accustomed to the Indian tradition in which a gift given today is reciprocated at some future date. However, in white society, gifts given were often accepted with no sense of future obligation. In all likelihood, Culbertson was deeply in debt before he even realized a problem existed." See *Frontier Diplomats: Alexander Culbertson and Natoyist-Siksina' among the Blackfeet* (2000; Norman: Univ. of Oklahoma Press, 2004), 312.

17 Joyce Clarke Turvey, "Helen Piotopowaka Clarke," in *History of Glacier County, Montana,* ed. Joy MacCarter (Cut Bank, Mont.: Glacier County Historical Society, 1984), 87.

18 For Sanders's role in the trial and its bloody aftermath, see Frederick Allen, *A Decent, Orderly Lynching: The Montana Vigilantes* (Norman: Univ. of Oklahoma Press, 2004), 185–97.

19 A. C. McClure, "Wilbur Fisk Sanders," *Contributions to the Historical Society of Montana* (1917; Boston: J. S. Canner, 1966), 8:25–35. The murder trial involved a Blood Indian named Spopee, or Turtle, who—despite the best efforts of Sanders and his co-counsel, Judge William Chumasero—was convicted of the murder of a white man named Charles Wamesley. Spopee languished in a federal asylum for more than thirty years before he was discovered in 1914 by a Blackfeet delegation visiting Washington, D.C., who then helped him secure a presidential pardon from Woodrow Wilson. Spopee returned to the Blackfeet Reservation, where he died less than a year after his release. For his remarkable story see William E. Farr, *Blackfeet Redemption: A Blood Indian's Story of Murder, Confinement, and Imperfect Justice* (Norman: Univ. of Oklahoma Press, 2012).

20 Letter from Wilbur Fisk Sanders to Helen P. Clarke, 28 March 1876, MTHS, HPC, SC 1153, folder 2.

21 See Jurgen Herbst, *Women Pioneers of Public Education: How Culture Came to the Wild West* (New York: Palgrave, 2008); and Andrea G. Radke-Moss, "Learning in the West: Western Women and the Culture of Education," in *The World of the American West*, ed. Gordon Morris Bakken (New York: Routledge, 2011), 387–417. For instance, in 1886 in Lewis and Clark County, the largest in Montana, male teachers made $100 annually while women earned only $60. See *Eighth Annual Report of the Superintendent of Public Instruction, of the Territory of Montana, for the Year 1886* (Helena: Fisk Brothers, 1887), 28.

22 For Clarke's various residential addresses during this period, see the holdings of the *Helena City Directory* at the MTHS. For her visits to the Sanders home, see journal of James Upson Sanders, JUS, MC 66, box 2, folders 1–5.

23 Martha E. Plassmann, "A Double Heritage," MTHS, Martha E. Plassmann Papers, MC 78, box 4, folder 18.

24 Letter from Henry [last name unknown] to Helen P. Clarke, 11 Jan. 1884, MTHS, HPC, SC 1153, folder 2.

25 A careful consideration of Clarke's Piegan name, including its spelling, pronunciation, and meaning, is in Jack Holterman, "The Homing Bird: The Story of Helen Clarke," unpublished manuscript in author's possession. Another variation offered by the Blackfoot scholar Marvin Weatherwax is "Comes Walking from a Distance." Author interview with Marvin Weatherwax, Oct. 2006.

26 This explanation appears in multiple sources, the earliest of which is an undated obituary (presumably from 1923, the year of Clarke's death) in *The Grass Range Review*, which can be found in MTHS, Helen P. Clarke, vertical file (cited hereafter as HPCVF). See also letter from David Hilger to Mrs. Lou Stocking Stewart, 28 March 1934, HPC, SC 1153, folder 1.

27 For the report of Nathan's death, see letter from George Heldt to Francis [should be Helen?] Clarke, 18 Sept. 1872, MTHS, HPC, SC 1153, folder 2. See also clipping from Isabell Lewis Tabor, *Great Falls Yesterday, Comprising a Collection of Biographies and Reminiscences of Early Settlers* (Helena: Montana Historical Society Library, 1939), found in MTHS, Malcolm Clarke, vertical file; and *Helena Weekly Herald*, 26 Sept. 1872. More than 125 years later, Joyce Clarke Turvey, Nathan's grand-niece, located his grave near the town of Ulm, Mont., and erected a memorial on the site. See *Glacier Reporter*, 17 Dec. 1998.

28 Rex C. Myers, *Lizzie: The Letters of Elizabeth Chester Fisk, 1864–1893* (Missoula, Mont.: Mountain Press, 1989), 107. Helen's devout Catholicism may also have concerned Lizzie Fisk.

29 Geoffrey C. Ward, *The West: An Illustrated History* (Boston: Little, Brown, 1996), 302. For a recent retelling of the engagement, see Nathaniel Philbrick, *Last Stand: Custer, Sitting Bull, and the Battle of the Little Bighorn* (New York: Viking, 2010).

30 See Elliott West, *The Last Indian War: The Nez Perce Story* (New York: Oxford Univ. Press, 2009).

31 Letter from L. W. Cooke to commissioner of Indian affairs, 7 March 1895, National Archives and Records Administration (cited hereafter as NARA), Bureau of Indian Affairs (cited hereafter as BIA), Record Group (cited hereafter as RG) 75, letters received, box 1183, file 13968.

32 See Ariela J. Gross, *What Blood Won't Tell: A History of Race on Trial in America* (Cambridge: Harvard Univ. Press, 2009), 223–30; and Peggy Pascoe, *What Comes Naturally: Miscegenation Law and the Making of Race in America* (New York: Oxford Univ. Press, 2009), 7–8. As Gross explains, some scholars of the day disagreed with this assessment, most notably the pioneering anthropologist Franz Boas, who argued in his 1894 study *The Half-Blood Indian* that hybridization actually produced stronger—not weaker—offspring. For more on the emergence of scientific racism as it applied to Indian peoples in particular, see Brian W. Dippie, *The Vanishing American: White Attitudes and U.S. Indian Policy* (Lawrence: Univ. Press of Kansas, 1982).

33 *Great Falls Daily Tribune*, 5 July 1914.

34 For Sanders's derisive nickname, see Clark C. Spence, "The Territorial Officers of Montana, 1864–1889," *Pacific Historical Review* 30, no. 2 (May 1961), 125. Sanders did achieve his own political success when in 1890 he was appointed to serve as one of Montana's first two senators (though he lost his bid for reelection in 1892).

35 Clark C. Spence, *Territorial Politics and Government in Montana, 1864–89* (Urbana: Univ. of Illinois Press, 1975), 201. Women did not win the vote in Montana until 1914.

36 *Fort Benton River Press Weekly*, 20 September 1882. My thanks to Ken Robison for directing me to this information.

37 See, e.g., the *Seventh Annual Report of the Superintendent of Public Instruction of the Territory of Montana, for the Year 1885* (Helena: Fisk Brothers, 1886), 59.

38 Clarke's salary fluctuated between $750 and $1,000 throughout her time in office.

39 For vote totals, see *Helena Weekly Herald*, 13 Nov. 1884. For his part, Railsback did not go gently, insisting two days after the election that—contrary to reports—he would not concede until his defeat was assured. See *Helena Weekly Independent*, 6 Nov. 1884.

40 Undated newspaper clipping, MTHS, HPCVF.

41 For more on Aspasia and her controversial relationship with Pericles, see Donald Kagan, *Pericles of Athens and the Birth of Democracy* (New York: Free Press, 1991), 181–84; and Anthony J. Podlecki, *Perikles and His Circle* (New York: Routledge, 1998), 109–17.

42 *Monterey New Era*, 1 Jan. 1902. Why this story (which was written by a Helena correspondent) appeared in a California newspaper is unclear.

43 For more on Dawes, see Frederick E. Hoxie, *A Final Promise: The Campaign to Assimilate the Indians, 1880–1920* (1984; Lincoln: Univ. of Nebraska Press, 2001), 28–39. Brooks's uncle was a senator from South Carolina whom Sumner

had ridiculed mercilessly in a stinging condemnation of the Kansas-Nebraska Act.

44 U.S. Congress, *The Annual Message of the President*, House Document 1, 57th Cong., 1st sess. (1901), xlvii.

45 Stuart Banner, *How the Indians Lost Their Land: Law and Power on the Frontier* (Cambridge: Harvard Univ. Press, 2005), 257.

46 For more on Pratt, see David Wallace Adams, *Education for Extinction: American Indians and the Boarding School Experience, 1875–1928* (Lawrence: Univ. Press of Kansas, 1995), 36–55.

47 Multiple dates are given for these photos; I have used those offered by Adams on the dust jacket of *Education for Extinction*. Torlino, who did not graduate from Carlisle, returned to his native Southwest and worked as a farmer. See Peter Iverson, *Diné: A History of the Navajos* (Albuquerque: Univ. of New Mexico Press, 2002), 83.

48 For Clarke's visits, see the *Red Man* (newspaper), vol. 10, no. 1 (Jan. and Feb. 1890); and *Great Falls Leader Daily*, 28 Aug. 1890.

49 *The Indian Helper*, vol. 5, no. 19 (10 Jan. 1890).

50 Fletcher led a remarkable life. In middle age she embarked on a career in the emerging field of ethnography and worked for years at Harvard's Peabody Museum. She also served as president of both the Anthropological Society of Washington and the American Folklore Society. For more on Fletcher, see E. Jane Gay, *With the Nez Perces: Alice Fletcher in the Field, 1889–92*, ed. Frederick E. Hoxie and Joan T. Mark (Lincoln: Univ. of Nebraska Press, 1981); Joan T. Mark, *A Stranger in Her Native Land: Alice Fletcher and the American Indians* (Lincoln: Univ. of Nebraska Press, 1988); and Nicole Tonkovich, *The Allotment Plot: Alice C. Fletcher, E. Jane Gay, and Nez Perce Survivance* (Lincoln: Univ. of Nebraska Press, 2012).

51 Quoted in Berlin Basil Chapman, *The Otoes and Missourias: A Study of Indian Removal and the Legal Aftermath* (Oklahoma City: Times Journal, 1965), 206.

52 Letter from the Office of the Secretary, Department of the Interior, to Helen P. Clarke, 4 Oct. 1890, NARA, BIA, RG 75, letters received, box 667, file 30744.

53 For more on Oklahoma's oil industry, see Brian Frehner, *Finding Oil: The Nature of Petroleum Geology, 1859–1920* (Lincoln: Univ. of Nebraska Press, 2011).

54 The Otoe-Missourias were once separate peoples who banded together in the late eighteenth century. It should also be noted that there was a significant division within the tribe about the move to Oklahoma, though the two sides reconciled in the 1890s. For more on the group, see R. David Edmunds, *The Otoe-Missouria People* (Phoenix: Indian Tribal Series, 1976).

55 For more on the Poncas, see David J. Wishart, *An Unspeakable Sadness: The Dispossession of the Nebraska Indians* (Lincoln: Univ. of Nebraska Press, 1994). For the circumstances surrounding their removal, see Joe Starita, *"I Am a*

Man": Chief Standing Bear's Journey for Justice (New York: St. Martin's Press, 2008).

56 Report of irregular employees in the field, 1 June 1891, NARA, BIA, RG 75, letters received, box 738, file 20061; and Helen P. Clarke to D. W. Browning, 8 Aug. 1894, NARA, BIA, RG 75, special case file 147, box 155, file 30638.

57 *Annual Report of the Secretary of the Interior, 1892,* 52nd Cong., 1st sess., 357.

58 This was part of a speech made by Deroin when he and a tribal delegation visited Washington, D.C., in April 1895. Quoted in Chapman, *The Otoes and Missourias,* 214–15.

59 *Annual Report of the Secretary of the Interior, 1892,* p. 358.

60 Letter from Arthur Tinker to secretary of the interior, 7 Nov. 1891, NARA, BIA, RG 75, special case file 147, box 154, file 40239.

61 Letter from Helen P. Clarke to T. J. Morgan, 7 Sept. 1891, NARA, BIA, RG 75, special case file 147, box 154, file 40239.

62 Quoted in Chapman, *The Otoes and Missourias,* 218.

63 See Cathleen D. Cahill, *Federal Fathers and Mothers: The United States Indian Service, 1869–1933* (Chapel Hill: Univ. of North Carolina Press); Lisa E. Emmerich, "'Right in the Midst of My Own People': Native American Women and the Field Matron Program," *American Indian Quarterly* 15, no. 2 (Spring 1991): 201–16; and Jane Simonsen, *Making Home Work: Domesticity and Native American Assimilation in the American West, 1860–1919* (Chapel Hill: Univ. of North Carolina Press, 2006). Among the Nez Perces, Fletcher may have "aroused more awe than hostility." See Marks, *A Stranger in Her Native Land,* 176–77.

64 Letter from Helen P. Clarke to commissioner of Indian affairs, 12 Dec. 1893, NARA, BIA, RG 75, special case file 147, box 155, file 46539.

65 Letter from Helen P. Clarke to T. J. Morgan, 7 Dec. 1891, NARA, BIA, RG 75, special case file 147, box 154, file 44211.

66 Letter from Helen P. Clarke to W. F. Sanders, 29 Jan. 1892, MTHS, Wilbur Fisk Sanders Papers, MC 53, box 2.

67 Letter from Helen P. Clarke to D. M. Browning, 8 Aug. 1894, NARA, BIA, RG 75, special case file 147, box 155, file 30638 (emphasis in the original).

68 Letter from Helen P. Clarke to General Palmer, 10 April 1897, NARA, BIA, RG 75, special case file 147, box 155, file 22923.

69 Mason Florence, Marisa Gierlich, and Andrew Dean Nystrom, *Rocky Mountains* (Melbourne: Lonely Planet Publications, 2001), 547.

70 John C. Ewers, *The Blackfeet: Raiders on the Northwestern Plains* (Norman: Univ. of Oklahoma Press, 1958), 290–94. See also James Willard Schultz, *The Starving Blackfeet Indians* (Los Angeles: National Association to Help the Indian, 1921).

71 Author interview with Darrell Robes Kipp, Oct. 2006.

72 Evidence of her presence at the negotiations is confirmed by a brief newspaper item: "Miss Helen P. Clark ex-county school superintendent of Lewis and Clarke [*sic*] county and at present special allotting agent of Indian lands,

arrived in this city [Great Falls] this morning and leaves tonight for Helena. She has been in the northwest and was present at the Piegan Indian treaty." *Great Falls Leader Daily*, 16 Oct. 1895.

73 See Mark David Spence, *Dispossessing the Wilderness: Indian Removal and the Making of the National Parks* (New York: Oxford Univ. Press, 1999), 71–100.

74 Author interview with Darrell Robes Kipp, Oct. 2006. Kipp, like many Piegans, is withering on the subject of Grinnell, insisting that he helped strong-arm the Blackfeet into surrendering the land because of his own interest in seeing the area set aside as a national park.

75 For the Indians' petition, see Chapman, *The Otoes and Missourias*, 215–16. For Clarke's instructions, see letter from acting secretary of the interior to commissioner of Indian affairs, 13 Nov. 1897, NARA, BIA, RG 75, special case file 147, box 155, file 48098.

76 Letter from Helen P. Clarke to Thomas H. Carter, 10 April 1897, NARA, BIA, RG 75, special case file 147, box 155, file 22923 (emphasis in the original).

77 Petition to secretary of the interior, 22 Dec. 1897, NARA, BIA, RG 75, special case file 147, box 155, file 914.

78 Transcript of council of Ponca Indians with Thomas P. Smith, 18 July 1898, NARA, BIA, RG 75, special case file 147, box 155, file 34993.

79 Letter from Helen P. Clarke to James U. Sanders, 19 April 1899, MTHS, JUS, MC 66, box 1, folder 4.

80 Letter from Helen P. Clarke to William A. Jones, NARA, BIA, RG 75, special case file 147, box 155, file 18247.

81 Chapman, *The Otoes and Missourias*, 218–19.

82 Joseph H. Cash and Gerald W. Wolff, *The Ponca People* (Phoenix: Indian Tribal Series, 1975), 61–68. This total, of course, does not include the lands owned by individuals.

83 The tribe managed to persuade the federal government to let them keep their surplus lands after the allotment process was complete. In 1906 Congress passed the Burke Act, which provided for the early termination of the trust period in any instance in which the secretary of the interior believed an individual Indian was capable of managing his property. Edmunds, *The Otoe-Missouria People*, 77–80.

84 Quoted in Gerald A. Diettert, *Grinnell's Glacier: George Bird Grinnell and the Founding of Glacier National Park* (Missoula, Mont.: Mountain Press, 1992), 33.

85 For a recent and detailed narrative of Grinnell's efforts, see Andrew C. Harper, "Conceiving Nature: The Creation of Montana's Glacier National Park," *Montana: The Magazine of Western History* 60, no. 2 (Summer 2010): 3–24.

86 An account of Hill's promotional efforts in Glacier is in Marguerite S. Shaffer, *See America First: Tourism and National Identity, 1880–1940* (Washington, D.C.: Smithsonian Institution Press, 2001), 59–92.

87 Transcript of eulogy for Helen Clarke given by Father Halligan, 7 March 1923, MTHS, HPC, SC 1153, folder 4.

88 *Montanian & Chronicle*, 27 June 1902 (clipping found in MTHS, HPCVF); *Monterey New Era*, 26 Sept. 1903.

89 *Montana Daily Record*, 26 Sept. 1903.

90 The most complete account of Monteath's misadventures can be found in Michael F. Foley, "An Historical Analysis of the Administration of the Blackfeet Reservation by the United States, 1855–1950s" (Indian Claims Commission, Docket Number 279-D: 1974), 272–347. See also Thomas R. Wessel, "Historical Report on the Blackfeet Reservation in Northern Montana" (Indian Claims Commission, Docket Number 279-D: 1975), 94–141.

91 *Great Falls Tribune Daily*, 21 Oct. 1903.

92 Letter from James H. Monteath to William A. Jones, 20 Oct. 1903, NARA, BIA, RG 75, letters received, box 2397, file 70531.

93 For Monteath's quarrel with Horace, see NARA, BIA, RG 75, letters received, box 2363, file 56641. Horace unsuccessfully sued Monteath for $5,000, claiming "intent to injure and humiliate." For Monteath's opposition to Clarke, see letter from T. O. Power to commissioner of interior, 12 March 1904, ibid., box 2479, file 18191.

94 Petition from Reservation Blackfeet to commissioner of Indian affairs, 22 Oct. 1907, NARA, BIA, RG 75, central classified files (cited hereafter as CCF), 1907–39, PI-163, E-121, Blackfeet, box 44, file 85710-1907-162; letter from commissioner of Indian affairs to Big Rabbit Woman et al., 31 Oct. 1907, ibid. Anticipating the Piegans' disappointment, the commissioner wrote a private note to Roblin urging him to find some related work for Clarke, perhaps in taking family histories. There is no evidence she was ever thus employed on the Blackfeet Reservation. Letter from commissioner of Indian affairs to Charles E. Roblin, 16 Nov. 1907, ibid.

95 Undated and untitled document [1909?], MTHS, HPC, SC 1153, folder 3. Allottees on the Blackfeet Reservation were entitled to 280 acres for grazing and 40 acres for farming.

96 For a description of the hotel, see *New York Times*, 23 July 1989.

97 Shaffer, *See America First*, 77–78, quote on p. 77.

98 For more on this transitional period, see Paul C. Rosier, *Rebirth of the Blackfeet Nation, 1912–1954* (Lincoln: Univ. of Nebraska Press, 2001), 13–53.

99 *Great Falls Tribune*, 15 May 1932.

100 Letter from J. H. Sherburne to Old Settlers' editor, 20 Sept. 1937, Univ. of Montana Library (cited hereafter as UM), K. Ross Toole Archives (cited hereafter as KRTA), Sherburne Family Papers (cited hereafter as SFP), box 1, folder 14.

101 Schultz, *The Starving Blackfeet Indians*.

102 Letter from Helen P. Clarke to J. H. Sherburne, 1 Dec. 1910, UM, KRTA, SFP, box 10, folder 3.

103 Letter from Helen P. Clarke to J. H. Sherburne, 11 Jan. 1916, UM, KRTA, SFP, box 33, folder 24.

104 Letter from Helen P. Clarke to commissioner of Indian affairs, 4 Oct. 1913, NARA, BIA, RG 75, CCF, 1907–39, PI-163, E-121, Blackfeet, box 132, file 12004-1913-312.

105 Letter from C. F. Hanke to S. B. Hege, 16 Jan. 1914, NARA, BIA, RG 75, CCF, 1907–39, PI-163, E-121, Blackfeet, box 132, file 12004-1913-312.

106 Letter from Helen P. Clarke, application for a patent in fee, 2 Dec. 1913, NARA, BIA, RG 75, CCF, 1907–39, PI-163, E-121, Blackfeet, box 132, file 12004-1913-312; letter from Helen P. Clarke to commissioner of Indian affairs, 4 Oct. 1913, NARA, ibid.

107 Letter from [unknown] to Helen P. Clarke, 31 May 1922, UM, KRTA, SFP, box 40, folder 7; letter from J. L. Sherburne to Helen P. Clarke, 7 Feb. 1919, ibid., box 38, folder 6.

108 Letter from Mary O'Neill to Helen P. Clarke, 28 May 1910, MTHS, HPC, SC 1153, folder 2.

109 Helen Fitzgerald Sanders, *The White Quiver* (New York: Duffield, 1913).

110 *Great Falls Tribune*, 15 May 1932; Warren L. Hanna, *Stars over Montana: Men Who Made Glacier National Park History* (West Glacier, Mont.: Glacier Natural History Association, 1988), 184.

111 Transcript of eulogy for Helen Clarke given by Father Halligan, 7 March 1923, MTHS, HPC, SC 1153, folder 4.

112 Undated reminiscence by Bessie C. Wells, MTHS, HPC, SC 1153, folder 1.

113 James Willard Schultz, *Signposts of Adventure: Glacier National Park as the Indians Know It* (Boston: Houghton Mifflin, 1926), 155.

114 Glacier National Park History: http://www.glacierparkinformation.com/history (accessed 7 Oct. 2010).

Chapter 5: The Man Who Talks Not

1 The quote is attributed to the western artist J. K. Ralston. See Loren Pinski, "John L. Clarke, 'The Man Who Talks Not,' Blackfeet Woodcarver": http://johnclarke.lppcarver.com/clarkearticle.pdf (accessed 11 Jan. 2011).

2 For a history of the panel's travels, see author correspondence with Kirby Lambert, 4 Jan. 2011.

3 Woody Kipp offers a vivid description of such prejudice in his memoir, *Viet Cong at Wounded Knee: The Trail of a Blackfeet Activist* (Lincoln: Univ. of Nebraska Press, 2004).

4 Information on the disease from a nineteenth-century perspective can be found in William Osler and Thomas McCrae, *The Principles and Practice of Medicine* (1892; New York: D. Appleton, 1921), 337–48.

5 Joyce Clarke Turvey, "Clarke History," in *Trails and Tales of the Highwoods*, ed. Highwood Woman's Club (Highwood, Mont.: Highwood Woman's Club, 1988), 84. Contrary to Turvey's assertion, Ned did not perish from scarlet fever before the family's move to Midvale in 1889.

6 Osler and McCrae, *The Principles and Practice of Medicine*, 343.

7 Letter from Helene Dawson Edkins to K. Ross Toole, 10 Oct. 1952, Overholser Historical Research Center, Fort Benton, Mont. My thanks to Ken Robison for help in locating this document. The piano is now on display at the Fort Benton Museum.

8 Judy Clayton Cornell, "An Artist's Vision," *Whitefish: The Magazine of Northwest Montana* 6, no. 2 (Winter and Spring, 1993–94), 28; Dale A. Burk, *New Interpretations* (Stevensville, Mont.: Stoneydale Press, 1982), 165.

9 Multiple sources state that Clarke attended the Fort Shaw Indian School, though his name appears nowhere in that institution's register of pupils, available at the National Archives and Records Administration–Rocky Mountain Regional Archives, Denver, Records of the Bureau of Indian Affairs, Fort Shaw Indian School, vol. 1, 1892–1908, entry 1358. My thanks to Renee Meade for assistance with this research.

10 The institution was originally called the Connecticut Asylum (at Hartford) for the Education and Instruction of Deaf and Dumb Persons. Robert L. Osgood, *The History of Special Education: A Struggle for Equality in American Public Schools* (Westport, Conn.: Praeger, 2008), 28–30.

11 For information on the NDSD, see "North Dakota School for the Deaf History: Early Pioneers and the *Banner*," available at http://www.nd.gov/ndsd (accessed 14 Jan. 2011).

12 Robert M. Buchanan, *Illusions of Equality: Deaf Americans in School and Factory, 1850–1950* (Washington, D.C.: Gallaudet Univ. Press, 1999), 52–68. See also Susan Burch, *Signs of Resistance: American Deaf Cultural History, 1900 to World War II* (New York: New York Univ. Press, 2002).

13 Osgood, *The History of Special Education*, 28–30. For more on the battle between manualists and oralists, see Douglas C. Baynton, *Forbidden Signs: American Culture and the Campaign against Sign Language* (Chicago: Univ. of Chicago Press, 1996).

14 For more on the relationship between the two sign languages, see Jeffrey E. Davis, *Hand Talk: Sign Language among American Indian Nations* (New York: Cambridge Univ. Press, 2010), 99–132.

15 Lilia Bakken, *North Dakota School for the Deaf Chronological History: The Early Years, 1890–1895* (Devil's Lake, N.D.: North Dakota School for the Deaf, 2010), 46. My thanks to Dana Turvey for alerting me to this correspondence.

16 *Daily Missoulian*, 24 March 1912, available at http://fortbenton.blogspot .com/2008/12/john-l-clarkes-first-oil-painting.html (accessed 20 Jan. 2011). Three letters from Hill to Clarke (dated 17 Oct. 1911 and 21 and 28 Feb. 1912) confirm the particulars of the story. All are available in Minnesota Historical Society, Louis W. Hill Papers, letterpress books, outgoing correspondence, 67.C.2.3. My thanks to Eileen McCormack for assistance in locating these items. For another version of this story, which does not identify Hill by name and suggests that Clarke's carving (not painting) attracted notice, see "What Deaf Men Do: Indian Artist," undated typescript, Gallaudet Univ. Library, Deaf Collections and Archives (cited hereafter as GUA), International Exhibition of Fine Applied Arts by Deaf Artists (cited hereafter as IEFAA), MSS 91, box 2, folder 10.

17 Brochure from the Arts Club of Chicago, "Catalogue of our Exhibition of

Sculpture in Wood by John L. Clarke (Cutapuis), 3 to 26 April, 1934," GUA, IEFAA, MSS 91, box 2, folder 10.

18 For more on this concept, see Shepard Krech III, *The Ecological Indian: Myth and History* (New York: Norton, 1999); and Michael E. Harkin and David Rich Lewis, eds., *Native Americans and the Environment: Perspectives on the Ecological Indian* (Lincoln: Univ. of Nebraska Press, 2007).

19 Cornell, "An Artist's Vision," 28.

20 The building was added to the National Register of Historic Places on 10 May 1985, after a strenuous effort to forestall its demolition. John Westenberg, "Montana Deaf and Dumb Asylum," National Register of Historic Places Nomination Form, Montana State Historic Preservation Office, Helena, Mont., 1980; Chere Jiusto, "Trustees for Those Who Come after Us," *Drumlummon Views* 1, nos. 1–2 (Spring/Summer 2006): 177–83, available at http://www.drumlummon.org/images/PDF-Spr-Sum06/DV_1-2_Jiusto .pdf (accessed 24 Jan. 2011), quote p. 180. In 1937 the school moved to Great Falls, where it is still in operation today. Thanks to Kate Hampton for help with this information.

21 Cornell, "An Artist's Vision," 28; notes on life of John L. Clarke [undated], GAU, IEFAA, MSS 91, box 2, folder 11.

22 For more on the woodworking class (including photos) at Fort Shaw Indian School, see John C. Ewers, *Plains Indian Sculpture: A Traditional Art from America's Homeland* (Washington, D.C.: Smithsonian Institution Press, 1986), 214–15.

23 The facility closed in 1983, and has since become Deer Creek Intermediate School in the township of St. Francis, Wisc. For more on the history of St. John's School, see *Milwaukee Sentinel*, 26 March 2006.

24 For more on the demographics of late-nineteenth-century Milwaukee, see Robert Nesbit and William F. Thompson, *Wisconsin: A History*, 2nd ed. (1973; Madison: Univ. of Wisconsin Press, 2004), 341–61.

25 Cornell, "An Artist's Vision," 28.

26 I have found only one exception to this. Cornell claims that on the day of their marriage, John and his fiancée, Mamie Peters Simon, traveled to the nearby town of Whitefish for the ceremony, as "they desired a Catholic wedding." This is the only reference to John's religious observance I have discovered. See ibid., 29.

27 For information on Clarke's attendance at St. John's see author correspondence with Shelly Solberg (archivist of the Archdiocese of Milwaukee), 28 Jan. 2011. Burk, *New Interpretations*, 166.

28 John Taliaferro, *Charles M. Russell: The Life and Legend of America's Cowboy Artist* (Boston: Little, Brown, 1996), 12–28.

29 Ibid., 9.

30 For a photographic reproduction of the letter itself, see Brian W. Dippie, ed., *Charles M. Russell, Word Painter: Letters, 1887–1926* (Fort Worth, Tex.: Amon Carter Museum, 1993), 253.

31 Debate lingers about Russell's attitude toward Indians. For instance, Talia-
    ferro notes in *Charles M. Russell* (p. 79) that the only surviving erotica pro-
    duced by the artist involves cowboys having intercourse with native women.
    Still, the historian Brian W. Dippie, a leading Russell scholar, asserts that "the
    man known as the 'Cowboy Artist' was a sympathetic student of the Indian
    and a vigorous champion of native rights." See Dippie, ed., *Charles M. Rus-
    sell,* 6.

32 "'So Understanding,' Says Wife of the Indian Sculptor John L. Clarke," *Fed-
    eral Illustrator* 9 (Winter 1926–27): 23. Curiously, in an interview not long
    before his death, Horace Clarke insisted that the only Montana artist who
    had true "genius" was Charlie Russell. Whether this was intended as an insult
    directed at his son is uncertain. See Martha E. Plassmann, notes taken in an
    interview with Horace Clarke [n.d.], Montana Historical Society (cited hereaf-
    ter as MTHS), Horace Clarke Reminiscence, SC 540.

33 Larry Len Petersen, *The Call of the Mountains: The Artists of Glacier National
    Park* (Tucson: Settlers West Galleries, 2002), 138. Prices come from Bob Mor-
    gan, "Reminiscences of John L. Clarke," 29 Oct. 1993, courtesy of Joyce
    Clarke Turvey (copy in author's possession).

34 Extensive email correspondence (courtesy of Joyce Clarke Turvey, in author's
    possession) between the editor of *Deaf Life Magazine* and several members of
    the Great Northern Railway Historical Society from Feb. 2007 to July 2008
    produced no conclusive answer on the matter, establishing only that the artist
    who designed "Rocky" (as the logo came to be known) was either John Clarke
    or Joe Scheurele, an Austrian-born painter who was part of Charlie Russell's
    circle. But the cover of the railroad's journal, *The Great Northern Goat* 2, no.
    3 (May 1927), convinced Clarke's daughter that her father deserves the credit,
    an opinion shared by the author. For the changing design of the company
    logo, see Charles R. Wood, *Lines West: A Pictorial History of the Great North-
    ern Railway Operations and Motive Power from 1887 to 1967* (Seattle: Superior
    Books, 1967), 8.

35 *Rocky Mountain Leader* 26, no. 5 (Feb. 1927): 2–3. Although the awarding
    institution is listed in the story as the "American Art Galleries of Philadelphia,"
    I can find no record of such a place and thus assume that the author meant
    the Pennsylvania Academy of the Fine Arts, which exhibited several of Clarke's
    pieces in the teens and twenties.

36 The *Red Man* 3, no. 5 (Dec. 1910): 179. It is worth noting that Malcolm
    Clarke and his wife Ella were part of the delegation of mixed-bloods that dis-
    covered Spopee at St. Elizabeth's hospital and secured his release (see chapter
    4, note 19). Farr, *Blackfeet Redemption,* 169–96.

37 Cornell, "An Artist's Vision," 29.

38 For a thorough history of the ranch (including its complex relationship to
    Blackfeet land claims), see Charles M. Stone, "What Does It Mean to Be at
    Hillhouse? Resolve to Understand," unpublished manuscript in author's pos-
    session.

39 Cornell, "An Artist's Vision," 29. See also author interview with Joyce Clarke Turvey, Oct. 2006.

40 Cornell, "An Artist's Vision," 29.

41 *Rocky Mountain Leader* 26, no. 5 (Feb. 1927), 2.

42 See Erika Marie Bsumek, *Indian-Made: Navajo Culture in the Marketplace, 1868–1940* (Lawrence: Univ. Press of Kansas, 2008); and Elizabeth Hutchinson, *The Indian Craze: Primitivism, Modernism, and Transculturation in American Art, 1890–1915* (Durham: Duke Univ. Press, 2009).

43 Quoted in Ewers, *Plains Indian Sculpture*, p. 216.

44 William Hoffman, *David: Report on a Rockefeller* (New York: Lyle Stuart, 1971), 86. See also David Rockefeller, *Memoirs* (New York: Random House, 2002), esp. 39–49; and Ron Chernow, *Titan: The Life of John D. Rockefeller, Sr.* (New York: Random House, 1998), 641–47. As it happened, David was not among the travelers on the 1924 excursion, which included only his three older brothers—John III, Nelson, and Laurance. David and his brother Winthrop visited Glacier two years later, but did not meet John Clarke at that time. See David Rockefeller to Joyce Clarke Turvey, 14 Aug. 1976 (copy in author's possession).

45 Bunny McBride, *Journeys West: The David & Peggy Rockefeller American Indian Art Collection* (Bar Harbor, Maine: Abbe Museum, 2007; catalog in author's possession). Also author correspondence with Bunny McBride, 17 Nov. 2010 (in author's possession).

46 *The Silent Worker* 2, no. 2 (Oct. 1949): 3.

47 *Artists Monthly*, 5 Dec. 1932 (newspaper clipping in MTHS, John Clarke, vertical file).

48 For a sampling of its bounty, see Museum of Modern Art, *Masterpieces of the David and Peggy Rockefeller Collection: Manet to Picasso* (New York: Museum of Modern Art, 1994).

49 Morgan, "Reminiscences of John L. Clarke."

50 John traded a woodcarving and a horsehair belt for his daughter's first mount. Author interview with Joyce Clarke Turvey, June 2007. See also Gail Jokerst, "The-Man-Who-Talks-Not," *Montana Magazine*, Dec. 1993, p. 30.

51 Author interview with Joyce Clarke Turvey, Oct. 2006.

52 For additional information, see her obituary, *New York Times*, 7 Sept. 1982.

53 Letter from Eleanor Sherman to John L. Clarke, 9 June 1934, GAU, IEFAA, MSS 91, box 2, folder 11.

54 Letter from Mamie Clarke to Eleanor Sherman, 2 July 1934, GAU, IEFAA, MSS 91, box 2, folder 11.

55 Letter from Mamie Clarke to Eleanor Sherman, 24 July 1939, GAU, IEFAA, MSS 91, box 2, folder 11. (Emphasis in the original)

56 See Adolph Hungry Wolf, *The Blackfoot Papers* (Browning, Mont.: Blackfeet Heritage Center, 2006), 4:1411–19.

57 For a recent consideration of the issue, see Don Johnson, "Two Guns White Calf—a Model Indian?" *Piegan Storyteller* 15, no. 1 (Jan. 1990): 1, 3–4.

58 *Time,* 26 March 1934.

59 Robert E. Berkhofer, *The White Man's Indian: Images of the American Indian from Columbus to the Present* (New York: Knopf, 1978).

60 *Hardin Tribune-Herald,* 13 April 1934, quoted in Hungry Wolf, *The Blackfoot Papers,* 4:1415.

61 Paul C. Rosier, *Rebirth of the Blackfeet Nation, 1912–1954* (Lincoln: Univ. of Nebraska Press, 2001), 115–21.

62 *New York Times,* 14 March 1934.

63 Clarke may have learned how to work in bronze from Adrien Alexandre Voisin (1890–1979), an American sculptor born to French parents; he met Clarke in the 1920s during one his many trips to the West. The artist was so charmed by Clarke that in 1929 he made bronze busts of both him and his mother (who was seventy-nine at the time). For additional information as well as photographs of the sculptures, see Bill Harmsen, *Illustrating the Lost Wax Method, Sculpture to Bronze: Featuring the Life and Sculpture of Adrien Alexandre Voisin* (Denver: Harmsen Publishing, 1981), 44–45. My thanks to Mary Scriver for this reference.

64 This assessment appeared in the 1941 edition of *Who's Who in Art.* Quoted in Dana Turvey, "The Man Who Talks Not," *Flathead Living,* July/Aug. 2007, p. 47.

65 Standard works on termination include Donald L. Fixico, *Termination and Relocation: Federal Indian Policy, 1945–1960* (Albuquerque: Univ. of New Mexico Press, 1986); Kenneth R. Philp, *Termination Revisited: American Indians on the Trail to Self-Determination, 1933–1953* (Lincoln: Univ. of Nebraska Press, 1999); and Roberta Ulrich, *American Indian Nations from Termination to Restoration, 1953–2006* (Lincoln: Univ. of Nebraska Press, 2010). For the Blackfeet, see Rosier, *Rebirth of the Blackfeet Nation,* esp. 217–82.

66 See, e.g., Phil Deloria, *Playing Indian* (New Haven: Yale Univ. Press, 1999), and esp. Sherry L. Smith, *Hippies, Indians, and the Fight for Red Power* (New York: Oxford Univ. Press, 2012).

67 Author interview with Marvin Weatherwax, Oct. 2006. For more on Albert Racine, see Burk, *New Interpretations,* 39–44.

68 See Linda Gordon, *Dorothea Lange: A Life beyond Limits* (New York: Norton, 2009).

69 See Kenneth R. Philp, *John Collier's Crusade for Indian Reform, 1920–1954* (Tucson: Univ. of Arizona Press, 1977).

70 See Rosier, *Rebirth of the Blackfeet Nation,* esp. 101–29. The bill was also known by a third name, the Indian Reorganization Act.

71 The TSFA was the successor to the significant but short-lived Public Works of Art Project, which lasted from Dec. 1933 to June 1934. The TSFA itself was absorbed into the Federal Works Agency in 1938, where it remained until 1943, which saw the termination of all New Deal art programs. See Jennifer McLerran, *A New Deal for Native Art: Indian Arts and Federal Policy, 1933–1943* (Tucson: Univ. of Arizona Press, 2009), 161–97.

72 Letter from Mamie Clarke to Eleanor Sherman, 23 March 1937, GUA, IEFAA, MSS 91, box 2, folder 11.

73 *Glacier Reporter*, 27 Feb. 1986. In their present installation indoors, the buffalo jump frieze is on the right and the Indian encampment is on the left, with the horizontal frieze currently nowhere on display in the facility. My thanks to Ken Robison and especially Bob Doerk and Bruce Druliner for confirming the placements of these works.

74 McLerran, *A New Deal for Native Art*, 158.

75 For a broader discussion of this paradigm shift from allotment to revival, with particular attention to the role of non-Indians in facilitating this transformation, see Sherry L. Smith, *Reimagining Indians: Native Americans through Anglo Eyes, 1880–1940* (New York: Oxford Univ. Press, 2000).

76 For a fuller description of such processes, see George Bird Grinnell, *The Cheyenne Indians: History and Society* (1923; Lincoln: Univ. of Nebraska Press, 1972), 1:213–17. Plains Indian peoples used similar techniques in hunting and dressing bison.

77 William Walker, "A Living Exhibition: The Smithsonian, Folklife, and the Making of the Modern Museum" (Ph.D. diss., Brandeis Univ., 2007), 21–29.

78 John C. Ewers, *The Blackfeet: Raiders on the Northwestern Plains* (1958; Norman: Univ. of Oklahoma Press, 1983), ix.

79 For more on Curtis, see Mick Gidley, ed., *Edward S. Curtis and the North American Indian Project in the Field* (Lincoln: Univ. of Nebraska Press, 2003); and Timothy Egan, *Short Nights of the Shadow Catcher: The Epic Life and Immortal Photographs of Edward Curtis* (New York: Harcourt, 2012).

80 Ewers, *Plains Indian Sculpture*, 216.

81 *Montana Senior News* 19, no. 5 (June/July 2003): 56.

82 Clyde A. Milner II and Carol O'Connor, *As Big as the West: The Pioneer Life of Granville Stuart* (New York: Oxford Univ. Press, 2009).

83 Mary Strachan Scriver, *Bronze Inside and Out: A Biographical Memoir of Bob Scriver* (Calgary: Univ. of Calgary Press, 2007), 116; author correspondence with Mary Scriver, 31 Jan. 2011.

84 Burk, *New Interpretations*, 168.

85 Morgan, "Reminiscences of John L. Clarke."

Epilogue

1 McFee taught at the Univ. of Oregon from 1965 to 1982 and died in 1992. See "Assembly Minutes [University of Oregon] 6 Jan. 1993," http://pages.uoregon.edu/assembly/dirassembly/A6Jan93.html (accessed 4 Sept. 2012).

2 Malcolm McFee, "The 150% Man, a Product of Blackfeet Acculturation," *American Anthropologist* 7 (Dec. 1968): 1096–103; and McFee, *Modern Blackfeet: Montanans on a Reservation* (New York: Holt, Rinehart and Winston, 1972).

3 McFee, "The 150% Man," 1097; and McFee, *Modern Blackfeet*, 31.

4 Ewers wrote in 1958, "The most remarkable trend in the history of [the Black-feet] during the first half of this century has been the rapid growth in the mixed-blood element of the population." See *The Blackfeet: Raiders on the Northwestern Plains* (1958; Norman: Univ. of Oklahoma Press, 1983), 326. Rules pertaining to membership in the tribe changed significantly in 1962, when the tribal constitution was amended to limit enrollment to those of at least one quarter Indian descent; before that time there had been no stipulation concerning degree of Indian blood. See McFee, "The 150% Man," 1097.

5 "The 150% Man," 1101. The historian Paul C. Rosier employs McFee's concept in "Joseph W. Brown: Native American Politician," in *The Human Tradition in the American West*, ed. Benson Tong and Regan A. Lutz (Wilmington, Del.: SR Books, 2002), 117–35.

6 Letter from George and Louise Spindler to Malcolm McFee, 4 June 1970, Stanford University Libraries, Department of Special Collections, George and Louise Spindler Papers, SC0943, box 6, folder 7.

7 McFee, *Modern Blackfeet*, vi.

8 For "blood-ism," see author interview with Donald Pepion, Jan. 2008. For the rise of casino gambling and oil development on the reservation, see *New York Times*, 15 Aug. 2012.

Bibliography

Manuscript Collections

Gallaudet University, Deaf Collections and Archives, Washington, D.C.
International Exhibition of Fine Applied Arts by Deaf Artists
Glenbow-Alberta Institute, Calgary, Alberta
Stan Gibson Fonds
Minnesota Historical Society, St. Paul, Minnesota
Louis W. Hill Papers
Horatio P. Van Cleve and Family Papers
Missouri History Museum, St. Louis, Missouri
Chouteau Family Papers, Chouteau-Papin Collection
Montana Historical Society, Helena, Montana
Helen P. Clarke Papers, SC 1153
Helen P. Clarke, Vertical File
Horace Clarke Reminiscence, SC 540
John L. Clarke, Vertical File
Malcolm Clarke, Vertical File
Andrew Dawson Papers, SC 292
May G. Flanagan Papers, SC 1236
Heavy Runner Records, MF 53
David Hilger Papers, SC 854
James Kipp Papers, SC 936
Nathaniel P. Langford Papers, SC 215
Martha E. Plassmann Papers, MC 78
John W. Ponsford Reminiscence, SC 659
James Upson Sanders Papers, MC 66

Wilbur Fisk Sanders Papers, MC 53
James Willard Schultz Papers, SC 721
Sieben Ranch, Vertical File
Régis de Trobriand Papers, SC 5 and SC 1201
Edith Grimes Waddell Reminiscence, SC 1669
William F. Wheeler Papers, MC 65
Montana State University Library, Merrill G. Burlingame Special Collections, Bozeman, Montana
Merrill G. Burlingame Papers, Collection 2245
James Willard Schultz Papers, Collection 10
WPA Records, Collection 2336
National Archives and Records Administration, Washington, D.C.
Records of the Bureau of the Census, Ninth Census of the United States, 1870, Montana Territory, RG 29
Records of the Bureau of Indian Affairs, Central Classified Files, Blackfeet, 1907–39, RG 75
Records of the Bureau of Indian Affairs, Letters Received, RG 75
Records of the Bureau of Indian Affairs, Special Case File 147, RG 75
Stanford University Libraries, Department of Special Collections, Stanford, California
George and Louise Spindler Papers, SC0943
University of Montana Library, K. Ross Toole Archives, Missoula, Montana
Sherburne Family Papers
Texas State Library and Archives, Austin, Texas
Republic Claims

Oral Interviews

Darrell Robes Kipp. Interview by the author, Oct. 2006.
Carol Murray. Interview by the author, Oct. 2006.
Darrell Norman. Interview by the author, June 2007.
Donald Pepion. Interview by the author, Jan. 2008.
Joyce Clarke Turvey. Interviews by the author, Oct. 2006 and June 2007.
Marvin Weatherwax. Interview by the author, Oct. 2007.
Lea Whitford. Interview by the author, June 2007.

Government Documents

Congressional Globe, 41st Cong., 2nd sess., 1870.
Congressional Globe, 44th Cong., 1st sess., 1876.
U.S. Congress. *Appropriations for Certain Indian Treaties.* Senate Executive Document 57, 41st Cong., 2nd sess., 1870.

———. *Expedition against Piegan Indians.* House Executive Document 185, 41st Cong., 2nd sess., 1870.

———. *Piegan Indians.* House Executive Document 269, 41st Cong., 2nd sess., 1870.

———. *Public Acts of the Forty-First Congress,* 2nd sess., 1870.

———. *Second Annual Report of the Board of Indian Commissioners,* Senate Executive Document 39, 41st Cong., 3rd sess., 1871.

———. *The Annual Message of the President.* House Document 1, 57th Cong., 1st sess., 1901.

U.S. Department of the Interior. *Annual Reports of the Secretary of the Interior.* 1859–92.

Newspapers and Periodicals

Army and Navy Journal
Billings Gazette
Daily Missoulian
Daily Rocky Mountain Gazette
Federal Illustrator
Fort Benton River Press Weekly
Glacier Reporter
Great Falls Daily Tribune
Great Falls Leader Daily
Great Falls Tribune
Great Falls Tribune Daily
Harper's Weekly
Helena Daily Herald
Helena Weekly Herald
Helena Weekly Independent
The Indian Helper
Milwaukee Sentinel
Monterey New Era
Montana Daily Record
Montana Senior News
National Anti-Slavery Standard
New North-West
New York Times
Owyhee Avalanche
The Red Man
The Register-Guard
Rocky Mountain Leader
The Silent Worker
The Standard
Time

Online Sources

Dictionary of Canadian Biography Online: http://www.biographi.ca/index-e.html
Glacier National Park History: http://www.glacierparkinformation.com/history
Handbook of Texas Online: http://www.tshaonline.org/handbook/online
Mormon Church History: http://mormon-church-history.blogspot.com/
North Dakota School for the Deaf History: http://www.nd.gov/ndsd
Loren Pinski, "John L. Clarke": http://johnclarke.lppcarver.com/clarkearticle.pdf
University of Oregon: http://pages.uoregon.edu/assembly/dirassembly/A6Jan93
    .html

Published Primary Sources

Abel, Annie Heloise, ed. *Chardon's Journal at Fort Clark, 1834–1839.* 1932; Lincoln: Univ. of Nebraska Press, 1997.

Annual Report of the Superintendent of Public Instruction, of the Territory of Montana. 1885, 1886; Helena, Mont.: Fisk Brothers, 1886 and 1887.

Audubon, Maria. *Audubon and His Journals.* 2 vols. 1897; New York: Dover, 1960.

Boller, Henry A. *Among the Indians: Eight Years in the Far West, 1858–1866.* 1868; Chicago: Lakeside Press, 1959.

Bradbury, John. *Travels in the Interior of America in the Years 1809, 1810, and 1811.* 1819; Lincoln: Univ. of Nebraska Press, 1986.

Bradley, James H. *The March of the Montana Column: A Prelude to the Custer Disaster.* Edited by Edgar I. Stewart. Norman: Univ. of Oklahoma Press, 1961.

Brasher, Thomas, ed. *Walt Whitman: The Early Poems and the Fiction.* New York: New York Univ. Press, 1963.

Catlin, George. *Illustration of the Manners, Customs, and Condition of the North American Indians.* 2 vols. London: Henry G. Bohn, 1857.

Child, Lydia Maria. *Hobomok and Other Writings on Indians.* Edited by Carolyn L. Karcher. New Brunswick: Rutgers Univ. Press, 1986.

Contributions to the Historical Society of Montana. 10 vols. Boston: J. S. Canner, 1966.

Culbertson, Thaddeus A. *Journal of an Expedition to the Mauvaises Terres and the Upper Missouri in 1850.* Washington, D.C.: Government Printing Office, 1952.

Dickens, Charles. *American Notes and Pictures from Italy.* 1842; New York: Oxford Univ. Press, 1987.

Douglass, Frederick. *Life and Times of Frederick Douglass, Written by Himself.* Boston: De Wolfe & Fiske, 1892.

Ellet, E. F. "Early Days at Fort Snelling." *Collections of the Minnesota Historical Society.* Vol. 1. St. Paul: Minnesota Historical Society, 1872.

Ens, Gerhard J., ed. *A Son of the Fur Trade: The Memoirs of Johnny Grant.* Edmonton: Univ. of Alberta Press, 2008.

Gay, E. Jane. *With the Nez Perces: Alice Fletcher in the Field, 1889–92.* Edited by Frederick E. Hoxie and Joan T. Mark. Lincoln: Univ. of Nebraska Press, 1981.

Gould, E. W. *Fifty Years on the Mississippi*. St. Louis: Nixon-Jones, 1889.

Grinnell, George Bird. *Blackfoot Lodge Tales: The Story of a Prairie People*. 1892; Lincoln: Univ. of Nebraska Press, 2003.

Hewitt, J. N. B., ed. *Journal of Rudolph Friederich Kurz*. 1937; Lincoln: Univ. of Nebraska Press, 1970.

Institute for the Development of Indian Law. *Treaties and Agreements of the Pacific Northwest Indian Tribes*. Washington, D.C.: Institute for the Development of Indian Law, 1974.

Irving, Washington. *Astoria, or Anecdotes of an Enterprize beyond the Rocky Mountains*. 1836; Lincoln: Univ. of Nebraska Press, 1976.

James, Thomas. *Three Years among the Indians and Mexicans*. 1846; St. Louis: Missouri Historical Society, 1916.

Karcher, Carolyn L., ed. *A Lydia Maria Child Reader*. Durham: Duke Univ. Press, 1997.

Larpenteur, Charles. *Forty Years a Fur Trader on the Upper Missouri: The Personal Narrative of Charles Larpenteur, 1833–1872*. 1898; Lincoln: Univ. of Nebraska Press, 1989.

Laussat, Pierre-Clément de. *Memoirs of My Life to My Son during the Years 1803 and After*. Edited by Robert D. Bush. Baton Rouge: Louisiana State Univ. Press, 1978.

Marquis, Thomas. *Custer, Cavalry & Crows: The Story of William White as Told to Thomas Marquis*. Bellevue, Neb.: Old Army Press, 1975.

Meagher, Thomas Francis. "A Journey to Benton." *Montana: The Magazine of Western History* 1, no. 4 (Oct. 1951): 46–58.

Meikle, Lyndel, ed. *Very Close to Trouble: The Johnny Grant Memoir*. Pullman: Washington State Univ. Press, 1996.

Miller, Thomas Lloyd. *Bounty and Donation Land Grants of Texas, 1835–1888*. Austin: Univ. of Texas Press, 1967.

Moulton, Gary E., ed. *The Lewis and Clark Journals: An American Epic of Discovery: The Abridgment of the Definitive Nebraska Edition*. Lincoln: Univ. of Nebraska Press, 2004.

Myers, Rex C. *Lizzie: The Letters of Elizabeth Chester Fisk, 1864–1893*. Missoula, Mont.: Mountain Press, 1989.

Parker, William B., ed. *Thomas Jefferson: Letters and Addresses*. New York: A. Wessels, 1907.

Parkman, Francis. *The Oregon Trail*. 1849; New York: Penguin, 1982.

Partoll, Albert John, ed., *The Blackfoot Indian Peace Council: A Document of the Official Proceedings of the Treaty between the Blackfoot Nation and Other Indians and the United States, in October, 1855*. Missoula, Mont.: State Univ., 1937.

Point, Nicolas. *Wilderness Kingdom: Indian Life in the Rocky Mountains, 1840–1847: The Journals & Paintings of Nicolas Point, S.J.* Translated by Joseph P. Donnelly. New York: Holt, Rinehart and Winston, 1967.

Post, Marie Caroline. *The Life and Mémoirs of Comte Régis de Trobriand, Major-General in the Army of the United States*. New York: E. P. Dutton, 1910.

Reports of Inspection Made in the Summer of 1877 by Generals P. H. Sheridan and W. T. Sherman of Country North of the Union Pacific Railroad. Washington, D.C.: Government Printing Office, 1878.

Rodenbaugh, Theophilus F. *From Everglade to Canyon with the Second United States Cavalry.* 1875: Norman: Univ. of Oklahoma Press, 2000.

Sanders, Helen Fitzgerald. *The White Quiver.* New York: Duffield, 1913.

Smet, Pierre-Jean De. *Life, Letters, and Travels of Father Pierre-Jean De Smet, S.J., 1801–1873.* Edited by Hiram Martin Chittenden and Alfred Talbot Richardson. 4 vols. New York: Francis P. Harper, 1905.

Thwaites, Reuben G., ed. *Collections of the State Historical Society of Wisconsin.* Vol. 11. Madison: State Printer, 1888.

Trobriand, Régis de. *Military Life in Dakota: The Journal of Philippe Régis de Trobriand.* Translated by Lucille M. Kane. 1951; Lincoln: Univ. of Nebraska Press, 1982.

Trumbull, J. Hammond, ed. *Memorial History of Hartford County, Connecticut, 1633–1844.* 2 vols. Boston: Edward L. Osgood, 1886.

Tyrrell, J. B., ed. *David Thompson's Narrative of His Explorations in Western America, 1784–1812.* Toronto: Champlain Society, 1916.

U.S. Military Academy. *Register of the Officers and Cadets of the U.S. Military Academy.* West Point, N.Y.: U.S. Military Academy, 1835–36.

Van Cleve, Charlotte Ouisconsin. *Three Score Years and Ten: Life-Long Memories of Fort Snelling, Minnesota, and Other Parts of the Far West.* Minneapolis: Harrison and Smith, 1888.

Whitman, Walt. *Complete Poetry and Selected Prose.* Edited by James E. Miller Jr. Boston: Houghton Mifflin, 1959.

———. "The Half-Breed: A Tale of the Western Frontier." In *Walt Whitman: The Early Poems and the Fiction,* edited by Thomas L. Brasher, 257–91. New York: New York Univ. Press, 1963.

Williams, J. F. "Memoir of Capt. Martin Scott." *Collections of the Minnesota Historical Society.* Vol. 3. St. Paul: Minnesota Historical Society, 1880.

Witte, Stephen S., and Marsha V. Gallagher, eds. *The North American Journals of Prince Maximilian of Wied.* 3 vols. Norman: Univ. of Oklahoma Press, 2008–12.

Secondary Literature

Adams, David Wallace. *Education for Extinction: American Indians and the Boarding School Experience, 1875–1928.* Lawrence: Univ. Press of Kansas, 1995.

Adams, David Wallace, and Crista DeLuzio, eds. *On the Borders of Love and Power: Families and Kinship in the Intercultural American Southwest.* Berkeley: Univ. of California Press, 2012.

Albers, Patricia, and Beatrice Medicine, eds. *The Hidden Half: Studies of Plains Indian Women.* Lanham, Md: Univ. Press of America, 1983.

Aleiss, Angela. *Making the White Man's Indian: Native Americans and Hollywood Movies.* Westport, Conn.: Praeger, 2005.

Allen, Frederick. *A Decent, Orderly Lynching: The Montana Vigilantes.* Norman: Univ. of Oklahoma Press, 2004.

Ambrose, Stephen. *Duty, Honor, Country: A History of West Point.* Baltimore: Johns Hopkins Univ. Press, 1966.

Anderson, Gary Clayton. *Kinsmen of Another Kind: Dakota-White Relations in the Upper Mississippi Valley, 1650–1862.* Lincoln: Univ. of Nebraska Press, 1984.

Arenson, Adam. *The Great Heart of the Republic: St. Louis and the Cultural Civil War.* Cambridge: Harvard Univ. Press, 2011.

Aron, Stephen. *How the West Was Lost: The Transformation of Kentucky from Daniel Boone to Henry Clay.* Baltimore: Johns Hopkins Univ. Press, 1996.

Athearn, Robert G. *William Tecumseh Sherman and the Settlement of the West.* Norman: Univ. of Oklahoma Press, 1956.

Babcock, Willoughby M., Jr. "Major Lawrence Taliaferro, Indian Agent." *Mississippi Valley Historical Review* 11, no. 3 (Dec. 1924): 358–75.

Bakken, Gordon Morris, ed., *The World of the American West.* New York: Routledge, 2011.

Bakken, Lilia. *North Dakota School for the Deaf Chronological History: The Early Years, 1890–1895.* Devil's Lake, N.D.: North Dakota School for the Deaf, 2010.

Banner, Stuart. *How the Indians Lost Their Land: Law and Power on the Frontier.* Cambridge: Harvard Univ. Press, 2005.

Barbour, Barton H. *Fort Union and the Upper Missouri Fur Trade.* Norman: Univ. of Oklahoma Press, 2001.

Bastien, Betty. *Blackfoot Ways of Knowing.* Calgary: Univ. of Calgary Press, 2004.

Baynton, Douglas C. *Forbidden Signs: American Culture and the Campaign against Sign Language.* Chicago: Univ. of Chicago Press, 1996.

Bennett, Ben. *Death, Too, for The-Heavy-Runner.* Missoula, Mont.: Mountain Press, 1981.

Berkhofer, Robert F. *The White Man's Indian: Images of the American Indian from Columbus to the Present.* New York: Knopf, 1978.

Bernstein, Peter. *The Wedding of the Waters: The Erie Canal and the Making of a Great Nation.* New York: Norton, 2006.

Binnema, Theodore. "Allegiances and Interests: Niitsitapi (Blackfoot) Trade, Diplomacy, and Warfare, 1806–1831." *Western Historical Quarterly* 37, no. 3 (Autumn 2006): 327–49.

Birchard, Robert S. *Cecil B. DeMille's Hollywood.* Lexington: Univ. Press of Kentucky, 2004.

Black, George. *Empire of Shadows: The Epic Story of Yellowstone.* New York: St. Martin's Press, 2012.

Bonney, Orrin H., and Lorraine Bonney. *Battle Drums and Geysers: The Life and Journals of Lt. Gustavus Cheyney Doane, Soldier and Explorer of the Yellowstone and Snake River Regions.* Chicago: Sage Books, 1970.

Brands, H. W. *Lone Star Nation: How a Ragged Army of Volunteers Won the Battle for Texas Independence—and Changed America.* New York: Doubleday, 2004.

Brown, Dee. *Bury My Heart at Wounded Knee: An Indian History of the American West.* 1970; New York: Owl Books, 2007.

Brown, Jennifer S. H. *Strangers in Blood: Fur Trade Company Families in Indian Country.* Vancouver: Univ. of British Columbia Press, 1980.

Brown, Jennifer S. H., and Theresa Schenck. "Métis, Mestizo, and Mixed-Blood." In *A Companion to American Indian History,* edited by Philip Deloria and Neal Salisbury, 321–38. Malden, Mass.: Blackwell, 2002.

Bsumek, Erika Marie. *Indian-Made: Navajo Culture in the Marketplace, 1868–1940.* Lawrence: Univ. Press of Kansas, 2008.

Buchanan, Robert M. *Illusions of Equality: Deaf Americans in School and Factory, 1850–1950.* Washington, D.C.: Gallaudet Univ. Press, 1999.

Buckley, Cornelius M. *Nicolas Point, S.J.: His Life & Northwest Indian Chronicles.* Chicago: Loyola Univ. Press, 1989.

Burch, Susan. *Signs of Resistance: American Deaf Cultural History, 1900 to World War II.* New York: New York Univ. Press, 2002.

Burk, Dale A. *New Interpretations.* Stevensville, Mont.: Stoneydale Press, 1982.

Cahill, Cathleen D. *Federal Fathers and Mothers: The United States Indian Service, 1869–1933.* Chapel Hill: Univ. of North Carolina Press.

Calloway, Colin G. *The American Revolution in Indian Country: Crisis and Diversity in Native American Communities.* New York: Cambridge Univ. Press, 1995.

————. *The Scratch of a Pen: 1763 and the Transformation of North America.* New York: Oxford Univ. Press, 2006.

Carter, Sarah. *Aboriginal People and Colonizers of Western Canada to 1900.* Toronto: Univ. of Toronto Press, 1999.

————. *The Importance of Being Monogamous: Marriage and Nation Building in Western Canada to 1915.* Edmonton: Univ. of Alberta Press, 2008.

Cash, Joseph H., and Gerald W. Wolff. *The Ponca People.* Phoenix: Indian Tribal Series, 1975.

Casler, Michael M. *Steamboats of the Fort Union Fur Trade: An Illustrated Listing of Steamboats on the Upper Missouri River, 1831–1867.* Williston, N.D.: Fort Union Association, 1999.

Cayton, Andrew R. L., and Fredrika J. Teute, eds. *Contact Points: American Frontiers from the Mohawk Valley to the Mississippi, 1750–1830.* Chapel Hill: Univ. of North Carolina Press, 1998.

Chapman, Berlin Basil. *The Otoes and Missourias: A Study of Indian Removal and the Legal Aftermath.* Oklahoma City: Times Journal, 1965.

Chernow, Ron. *The Life of John D. Rockefeller, Sr.* New York: Random House, 1998.

Chittenden, Hiram Martin. *The American Fur Trade of the Far West.* 3 vols. New York: Francis P. Harper, 1902.

————. *History of Early Steamboat Navigation on the Missouri River: Life and Adventures of Joseph La Barge.* 2 vols. New York: Francis P. Harper, 1903.

Clayton Cornell, Judy. "An Artist's Vision." *Whitefish: The Magazine of Northwest Montana* 6, no. 2 (Winter and Spring, 1993–94): 27–29, 70–71.

Coleman, Jon T. *Here Lies Hugh Glass: A Mountain Man, a Bear, and the Rise of the American Nation.* New York: Hill & Wang, 2012.

Crisp, James E. *Sleuthing the Alamo: Davy Crockett's Last Stand and Other Mysteries of the Texas Revolution.* New York: Oxford Univ. Press, 2005.

Curtis, Kent. "Producing a Gold Rush: National Ambitions and the Northern Rocky Mountains, 1853–1863." *Western Historical Quarterly* 40, no. 3 (Autumn 2009): 275–97.

Davis, Jeffrey E. *Hand Talk: Sign Language among American Indian Nations.* New York: Cambridge Univ. Press, 2010.

Davis, William C. *Lone Star Rising: The Revolutionary Birth of the Texas Republic.* New York: Free Press, 2004.

D'Elia, Donald J. "The Argument over Civilian or Military Indian Control, 1865–1880." *Historian* 24, no. 2 (Feb. 1962): 207–25.

Deloria, Philip. *Playing Indian.* New Haven: Yale Univ. Press, 1999.

Deloria, Philip, and Neal Salisbury, eds. *A Companion to American Indian History.* Malden, Mass.: Blackwell, 2002.

DeMarce, Roxanne, ed. *Blackfeet Heritage, 1907–1908.* Browning, Mont.: Blackfeet Heritage Program, 1980.

Demos, John. *The Unredeemed Captive: A Family Story from Early America.* New York: Knopf, 1994.

Dempsey, Hugh. "The Blackfoot Nation." In *Native Peoples: The Canadian Experience*, edited by R. Bruce Morrison and C. Roderick Wilson, 381–413. 1986; Toronto: McClelland & Stewart, 1995.

———. *The Amazing Death of Calf Shirt and Other Blackfoot Stories: Three Hundred Years of Blackfoot History.* 1994; Norman: Univ. of Oklahoma Press, 1996.

———. *Firewater: The Impact of the Whisky Trade on the Blackfoot Nation.* Calgary: Fifth House, 2002.

Dempsey, L. James. *Blackfoot War Art: Pictographs of the Reservation Period, 1880–1920.* Norman: Univ. of Oklahoma Press, 2007.

Diettert, Gerald A. *Grinnell's Glacier: George Bird Grinnell and the Founding of Glacier National Park.* Missoula, Mont.: Mountain Press, 1992.

Dippie, Brian W. *The Vanishing American: White Attitudes and U.S. Indian Policy.* Lawrence: Univ. Press of Kansas, 1982.

———. ed. *Charles M. Russell, Word Painter: Letters, 1887–1926.* Fort Worth, Tex.: Amon Carter Museum, 1993.

Dolin, Eric Jay. *Fur, Fortune, and Empire: The Epic History of the Fur Trade in America.* New York: Norton, 2010.

Dollar, Clyde D. "The High Plains Smallpox Epidemic of 1837–38." *Western Historical Quarterly* 8, no. 1 (Jan. 1977): 15–38.

Dowd, Gregory E. *A Spirited Resistance: The North American Indian Struggle for Unity, 1745–1815.* Baltimore: Johns Hopkins Univ. Press, 1991.

Dunn, J. P. *Massacres of the Mountains: A History of the Indian Wars of the Far West.* New York: Harper & Brothers, 1886.

Dunnigan, Brian Leigh. "Fortress Detroit, 1701–1826." In *The Sixty Years' War for the Great Lakes, 1754–1814,* edited by David Curtis Skaggs and Larry L. Nelson, 167–86. East Lansing: Michigan State Univ. Press, 2001.

Edmunds, R. David. *The Otoe-Missouria People.* Phoenix: Indian Tribal Series, 1976.

———. *The Shawnee Prophet.* Lincoln: Univ. of Nebraska Press, 1983.

Egan, Timothy. *Short Nights of the Shadow Catcher: The Epic Life and Immortal Photographs of Edward Curtis.* New York: Harcourt, 2012.

Ege, Robert J. *Strike Them Hard: Incident on the Marias, 23 January 1870.* Bellevue, Neb.: Old Army Press, 1970.

Ellis, Edward S. *The History of Our Country: From the Discovery of America to the Present Time.* 8 vols. Cincinnati: Jones Brothers, 1900.

Elliott, J. H. *Empires of the Atlantic World: Britain and Spain in America, 1492–1830.* New Haven: Yale Univ. Press, 2006.

Ellis, Joseph. *American Sphinx: The Character of Thomas Jefferson.* New York: Random House, 1998.

Emmerich, Lisa E. "'Right in the Midst of My Own People': Native American Women and the Field Matron Program." *American Indian Quarterly* 15, no. 2 (Spring 1991): 201–16.

Ens, Gerhard J. *Homeland to Hinterland: The Changing Worlds of the Red River Metis in the Nineteenth Century.* Toronto: Univ. of Toronto Press, 1996.

Eustace, Nicole. *1812: War and the Passions of Patriotism.* Philadelphia: Univ. of Pennsylvania Press, 2012.

Ewers, John C. *The Horse in Blackfoot Indian Culture, with Comparative Material from Other Western Tribes.* Washington, D.C.: Government Printing Office, 1955.

———. *The Blackfeet: Raiders on the Northwestern Plains.* 1958; Norman: Univ. of Oklahoma Press, 1983.

———. *Indian Life on the Upper Missouri.* Norman: Univ. of Oklahoma Press, 1968.

———. *Plains Indian Sculpture: A Traditional Art from America's Homeland.* Washington, D.C.: Smithsonian Institution Press, 1986.

Eyman, Scott. *Empire of Dreams: The Epic Life of Cecil B. DeMille.* New York: Simon and Schuster, 2010.

Faragher, John Mack. "The Custom of the Country: Cross-Cultural Marriage in the Far Western Fur Trade." In *Western Women: Their Land, Their Lives,* edited by Lillian Schlissel, Vicki L. Ruiz, and Janice Monk, 199–225. Albuquerque: Univ. of New Mexico Press, 1988.

———. "'More Motley than Mackinaw': From Ethnic Mixing to Ethnic Cleansing on the Frontier of the Lower Missouri, 1783–1833." In *Contact Points: American Frontiers from the Mohawk Valley to the Mississippi, 1750–1830,* edited by Andrew R. L. Cayton and Fredrika J. Teute, 304–26. Chapel Hill: Univ. of North Carolina Press, 1998.

Farr, William E. *Blackfoot Redemption: A Blood Indian's Story of Murder, Confinement, and Imperfect Justice.* Norman: Univ. of Oklahoma Press, 2012.

Finot, Jean. *Race Prejudice.* London: Archibald Constable, 1906.

Fischer, David Hackett. *Champlain's Dream: The European Founding of North America*. New York: Simon and Schuster, 2008.

Fixico, Donald L. *Termination and Relocation: Federal Indian Policy, 1945–1960*. Albuquerque: Univ. of New Mexico Press, 1986.

Florence, Mason, Marisa Gierlich, and Andrew Dean Nystrom. *Rocky Mountains*. Melbourne: Lonely Planet Publications, 2001.

Foege, William H. *House on Fire: The Fight to Eradicate Smallpox*. Berkeley: Univ. of California Press, 2011.

Foley, Michael F. "An Historical Analysis of the Administration of the Blackfeet Reservation by the United States, 1855–1950s." Indian Claims Commission, Docket Number 279-D: 1974.

Fort Union Fur Trade Symposium Proceedings: September 13–15, 1990. Williston, N.D.: Friends of Fort Union Trading Post, 1994.

Foster, Martha Harroun. *We Know Who We Are: Metis Identity in a Montana Community*. Norman: Univ. of Oklahoma Press, 2006.

Frederickson, George M. *White Supremacy: A Comparative Study in American and South African History*. New York: Oxford Univ. Press, 1981.

Frehner, Brian. *Finding Oil: The Nature of Petroleum Geology, 1859–1920*. Lincoln: Univ. of Nebraska Press, 2011.

Frick, John. "A Changing Theatre: New York and Beyond." In *The Cambridge History of American Theatre*, vol. 2, edited by Don B. Wilmeth and Christopher Bigsby, 196–232. New York: Cambridge Univ. Press, 1999.

Fritz, Henry E. *The Movement for Indian Assimilation, 1860–1890*. Philadelphia: Univ. of Pennsylvania Press, 1963.

Furstenberg, François. "The Significance of the Trans-Appalachian Frontier in American History, 1754–1815." *American Historical Review* 113, no. 2 (June 2008): 647–77.

Gannon, Thomas C. "Reading Boddo's Body: Crossing the Borders of Race and Sexuality in Whitman's 'Half-Breed.'" *Walt Whitman Quarterly Review* 22, nos. 2–3 (Fall/Winter 2004): 87–107.

Garfield, Marvin. "The Indian Question in Congress and in Kansas." *Kansas Historical Quarterly* 2, no. 1 (Feb. 1933): 29–44.

Gidley, Mick, ed. *Edward S. Curtis and the North American Indian Project in the Field*. Lincoln: Univ. of Nebraska Press, 2003.

Gitlin, Jay. *The Bourgeois Frontier: French Towns, French Traders, and American Expansion*. New Haven: Yale Univ. Press, 2010.

Goldring, Philip. "Whisky, Horses, and Death: The Cypress Hills Massacre and Its Sequel." *Occasional Papers in Archaeology and History* 21 (1979): 41–70.

Gordon, Linda. *Dorothea Lange: A Life beyond Limits*. New York: Norton, 2009.

Gordon-Reed, Annette. *The Hemingses of Monticello: An American Family*. New York: Norton, 2008.

Goss, Charles Frederic. *Cincinnati, the Queen City: 1788–1912*. Chicago: S. J. Clarke, 1912.

Gottlieb, Robert. "The Drama of Sarah Bernhardt." *New York Review of Books*, 10 May 2007, pp. 10–12, 14.

———. *Sarah: The Life of Sarah Bernhardt*. New Haven: Yale Univ. Press, 2010.

Gould, Eliga. *Among the Powers of the Earth: The American Revolution and the Making of a New World Empire*. Cambridge: Harvard Univ. Press, 2012.

Graybill, Andrew R. *Policing the Great Plains: Rangers, Mounties, and the North American Frontier, 1875–1910*. Lincoln: Univ. of Nebraska Press, 2007.

Greene, Jerome A. *Washita: The U.S. Army and the Southern Cheyennes, 1867–1869*. Norman: Univ. of Oklahoma Press, 2004.

Greer, Alan. *The People of New France*. Toronto: Univ. of Toronto Press, 1997.

Grinnell, George Bird. *The Cheyenne Indians: History and Society*. 2 vols. 1923; Lincoln: Univ. of Nebraska Press, 1972.

Gross, Ariela J. *What Blood Won't Tell: A History of Race on Trial in America*. Cambridge: Harvard Univ. Press, 2009.

Guyatt, Nicholas. "'The Outskirts of Our Happiness': Race and the Lure of Colonization in the Early Republic." *Journal of American History* 95, no. 4 (March 2009): 986–1011.

Hafen, LeRoy R., ed. *The Mountain Men and the Fur Trade of the Far West*. 10 vols. Glendale, Calif.: Arthur H. Clarke, 1965–1972.

Halaas, David Fridtjof, and Andrew Edward Masich. *Halfbreed: The Remarkable True Story of George Bent, Caught between the Worlds of the Indian and the White Man*. Cambridge: Da Capo Press, 2004.

Haley, James L. *Sam Houston*. Norman: Univ. of Oklahoma Press, 2002.

Hämäläinen, Pekka. "The Rise and Fall of Plains Indian Horse Cultures." *Journal of American History* 90, no. 4 (Dec. 2003): 833–62.

Hanna, Warren L. *Stars over Montana: Men Who Made Glacier National Park History*. West Glacier, Mont.: Glacier Natural History Association, 1988.

Hansen, Marcus Lee. *Old Fort Snelling, 1819–1858*. Minneapolis: Ross & Haines, 1958.

Harkin, Michael E., and David Rich Lewis, eds., *Native Americans and the Environment: Perspectives on the Ecological Indian*. Lincoln: Univ. of Nebraska Press, 2007.

Harmsen, Bill. *Illustrating the Lost Wax Method, Sculpture to Bronze: Featuring the Life and Sculpture of Adrien Alexandre Voisin*. Denver: Harmsen Publishing, 1981.

Harper, Andrew C. "Conceiving Nature: The Creation of Montana's Glacier National Park." *Montana: The Magazine of Western History* 60, no. 2 (Summer 2010): 3–24.

Harris, Burton. *John Colter: His Years in the Rockies*. 1952; Lincoln: Univ. of Nebraska Press, 1993.

Harrod, Howard L. *Mission among the Blackfeet*. Norman: Univ. of Oklahoma Press, 1971.

Hatch, Thom. *Black Kettle: The Cheyenne Chief Who Sought Peace but Found War*. New York: Wiley, 2004.

Hausdoerffer, John. *Catlin's Lament: Indians, Manifest Destiny, and the Ethics of Nature.* Lawrence: Univ. Press of Kansas, 2009.

Hedren, Paul L. "Field Notes: Why We Reconstructed Fort Union." *Western Historical Quarterly* 23, no. 3 (Aug. 1992): 349–54.

Herbst, Jurgen. *Women Pioneers of Public Education: How Culture Came to the Wild West.* New York: Palgrave, 2008.

Herring, George C. *From Colony to Superpower: U.S. Foreign Relations since 1776.* New York: Oxford Univ. Press, 2008.

Hershberger, Mary. "Mobilizing Women, Anticipating Abolition: The Struggle against Indian Removal in the 1830s." *Journal of American History* 86, no. 1 (June 1999): 15–40.

Hinderaker, Eric. *Elusive Empires: Constructing Colonialism in the Ohio Valley, 1673–1800.* New York: Cambridge Univ. Press, 1997.

Hoffman, William. *David: Report on a Rockefeller.* New York: Lyle Stuart, 1971.

Hoig, Stan. *The Sand Creek Massacre.* 1961; Norman: Univ. of Oklahoma Press, 1977.

Horsman, Reginald. *Expansion and American Indian Policy, 1783–1812.* East Lansing: Michigan State Univ. Press, 1967.

Howe, Daniel Walker. *What Hath God Wrought: The Transformation of America, 1815–1848.* New York: Oxford Univ. Press, 2007.

Hoxie, Frederick E. *A Final Promise: The Campaign to Assimilate the Indians, 1880–1920.* 1984; Lincoln: Univ. of Nebraska Press, 2001.

Hungry Wolf, Adolph. *The Blackfoot Papers.* 4 vols. Browning, Mont.: Blackfeet Heritage Center, 2006.

Hunt, William J., Jr. "'At the Yellowstone . . . to Build a Fort': Fort Union Trading Post, 1828–1833." In *Fort Union Fur Trade Symposium Proceedings: September 13–15, 1990,* 7–23. Williston, N.D.: Friends of Fort Union Trading Post, 1994.

Hurtado, Albert L. *John Sutter: A Life on the North American Frontier.* Norman: Univ. of Oklahoma Press, 2006.

Hutchinson, Elizabeth. *The Indian Craze: Primitivism, Modernism, and Transculturation in American Art, 1890–1915.* Durham: Duke Univ. Press, 2009.

Hutton, Paul A. "Phil Sheridan's Pyrrhic Victory: The Piegan Massacre, Army Politics, and the Transfer Debate." *Montana: The Magazine of Western History* 32, no. 2 (Spring 1982): 32–43.

———. *Phil Sheridan and His Army.* Norman: Univ. of Oklahoma Press, 1985.

Hyde, Anne F. *Empires, Nations, and Families: A History of the North American West, 1800–1860.* Lincoln: Univ. of Nebraska Press, 2011.

———. "Hard Choices: Mixed-Race Families and Strategies of Acculturation in the U.S. West after 1848." In *On the Borders of Love and Power: Families and Kinship in the Intercultural American Southwest,* edited by David Wallace Adams and Crista DeLuzio, 93–115. Berkeley: Univ. of California Press, 2012.

Hyde, George E. *A Life of George Bent, Written from His Letters.* Norman: Univ. of Oklahoma Press, 1968.

Ingersoll, Thomas N. *To Intermix with Our White Brothers: Indian Mixed Bloods in the United States from Earliest Times to the Indian Removals.* Albuquerque: Univ. of New Mexico Press, 2005.

Innis, Harold A. *The Fur Trade in Canada: An Introduction to Canadian Economic History.* New Haven: Yale Univ. Press, 1930.

"Intermarriage and North American Indians." A special issue of *Frontiers: A Journal of Women Studies* 29, nos. 2–3 (2008).

Isenberg, Andrew C. *The Destruction of the Bison: An Environmental History, 1750–1920.* New York: Cambridge Univ. Press, 2000.

———. *Mining California: An Ecological History.* New York: Hill & Wang, 2005.

Iverson, Peter. *Diné: A History of the Navajos.* Albuquerque: Univ. of New Mexico Press, 2002.

Jackson, John C. "Revisiting the Colter Legend." *Rocky Mountain Fur Trade Journal* 3 (Jan. 2009): 1–19.

Jacoby, Karl. *Shadows at Dawn: A Borderlands Massacre and the Violence of History.* New York: Penguin, 2008.

Jenish, D'Arcy. *Epic Wanderer: David Thompson and the Mapping of the Canadian West.* Lincoln: Univ. of Nebraska Press, 2003.

Jenness, Diamond. *The Indians of Canada.* 1932; Toronto: Univ. of Toronto Press, 1977.

Jiusto, Chere. "Trustees for Those Who Come after Us." *Drumlummon Views* 1, nos. 1–2 (Spring/Summer 2006): 177–83.

Johnson, Don. "Two Guns White Calf—a Model Indian?" *Piegan Storyteller* 15, no. 1 (Jan. 1990): 1, 3–4.

Johnson, Kevin R., ed. *Mixed Race America and the Law: A Reader.* New York: New York Univ. Press, 2003.

Johnson, Paul E. *A Shopkeeper's Millennium: Society and Revivals in Rochester, New York, 1815–1837.* New York: Hill & Wang, 1978.

Johnson, Susan L. *Roaring Camp: The Social World of the California Gold Rush.* New York: Norton, 2000.

Johnston, Robert D. *The Radical Middle Class: Populist Democracy and the Question of Capitalism in Progressive Era Portland, Oregon.* Princeton: Princeton Univ. Press, 2003.

Jokerst, Gail. "The-Man-Who-Talks-Not." *Montana Magazine*, Dec. 1993, pp. 28–31.

Jones, James Pickett. *John A. Logan: Stalwart Republican from Illinois.* Tallahassee: Univ. Presses of Florida, 1982.

Jordan, Henry D. "Daniel Wolsey Voorhees." *Mississippi Valley Historical Review* 6, no. 4 (March 1920): 532–55.

Kagan, Donald. *Pericles of Athens and the Birth of Democracy.* New York: Free Press, 1991.

Kaplan, Sidney. "Historical Efforts to Encourage White-Indian Intermarriage in the United States and Canada." *International Social Science Review* 65, no. 3 (Summer 1990): 126–32.

Karcher, Carolyn L. *The First Woman in the Republic: A Cultural Biography of Lydia Maria Child*. Durham: Duke Univ. Press, 1994.

Kastor, Peter J. *The Nation's Crucible: The Louisiana Purchase and the Creation of America*. New Haven: Yale Univ. Press, 2004.

Kelman, Ari. *A Misplaced Massacre: Struggling over the Memory of Sand Creek*. Cambridge: Harvard Univ. Press, 2013.

Kennedy, Roger G. *Mr. Jefferson's Lost Cause: Land, Farmers, Slavery, and the Louisiana Purchase*. New York: Oxford Univ. Press, 2003.

Kerber, Linda K. "The Abolitionist Perception of the Indian." *Journal of American History* 62, no. 2 (Sept. 1975): 271–95.

Ketchum, Richard M. *Saratoga: Turning Point of America's Revolutionary War*. New York: Henry Holt, 1997.

Kidwell, Clara Sue. "Indian Women as Cultural Mediators." *Ethnohistory* 39, no. 2 (Spring 1992): 97–107.

Kipp, Woody. *Viet Cong at Wounded Knee: The Trail of a Blackfeet Activist*. Lincoln: Univ. of Nebraska Press, 2004.

Krech, Shepard, III. *The Ecological Indian: Myth and History*. New York: Norton, 1999.

Lamar, Howard R. *The Trader on the American Frontier: Myth's Victim*. College Station: Texas A&M Univ. Press, 1977.

Lamont, Claire. "Meg the Gipsy in Scott and Keats." *English* 36, no. 155 (Summer 1987): 137–45.

Lansing, Michael. "Plains Indian Women and Interracial Marriage in the Upper Missouri Fur Trade, 1804–1868." *Western Historical Quarterly* 31, no. 4 (Winter 2000): 413–33.

Lass, William E. *A History of Steamboating on the Upper Missouri River*. Lincoln: Univ. of Nebraska Press, 1962.

———. *Navigating the Missouri: Steamboating on Nature's Highway, 1819–1935*. Norman, Okla.: Arthur H. Clark, 2008.

Lavender, David. *The Fist in the Wilderness*. 1964; Lincoln: Univ. of Nebraska Press, 1998.

Lepley, John G. *Blackfoot Fur Trade on the Upper Missouri*. Missoula, Mont.: Pictorial Histories Publishing, 2004.

Lewis, Oscar. *The Effects of White Contact upon Blackfoot Culture, with Special Reference to the Rôle of the Fur Trade*. New York: J. J. Augustin, 1942.

Lounsberry, Clement Augustus. *Early History of North Dakota: Essential Outlines of American History*. Washington, D.C.: Liberty Press, 1919.

MacCarter, Joy. *History of Glacier County, Montana*. Cut Bank, Mont.: Glacier County Historical Society, 1984.

Malone, Michael P., Richard B. Roeder, and William L. Lang. *Montana: A Tale of Two Centuries*. 1976; Seattle: Univ. of Washington Press, 1991.

Mancall, Peter C. *Deadly Medicine: Indians and Alcohol in Early America*. Ithaca: Cornell Univ. Press, 1995.

Mardock, Robert Winston. *The Reformers and the American Indian*. Columbia: Univ. of Missouri Press, 1971.

Mark, Joan T. *A Stranger in Her Native Land: Alice Fletcher and the American Indians*. Lincoln: Univ. of Nebraska Press, 1988.

Mayer, Henry. *All on Fire: William Lloyd Garrison and the Abolition of Slavery*. 1998; New York: Norton, 2008.

McBride, Bunny. *Journeys West: The David & Peggy Rockefeller American Indian Art Collection*. Bar Harbor, Maine: Abbe Museum, 2007.

McChristian, Douglas C. *The U.S. Army in the West: Uniforms, Weapons, and Equipment*. Norman: Univ. of Oklahoma Press, 1995.

McFee, Malcolm. "The 150% Man, a Product of Blackfeet Acculturation." *American Anthropologist* 7 (Dec. 1968): 1096–103.

———. *Modern Blackfeet: Montanans on a Reservation*. New York: Holt, Rinehart and Winston, 1972.

McLerran, Jennifer. *A New Deal for Native Art: Indian Arts and Federal Policy, 1933–1943*. Tucson: Univ. of Arizona Press, 2009.

McMurtry, Larry. *Oh What a Slaughter: Massacres in the American West, 1846–1890*. New York: Simon and Schuster, 2005.

Mielke, Laura L. "Sentiment and Space in Lydia Maria Child's Native American Writings, 1824–1870." *Legacy* 21, no. 2 (2004): 172–92.

Miles, Tiya. *Ties That Bind: The Story of an Afro-Cherokee Family in Slavery and Freedom*. Berkeley: Univ. of California Press, 2005.

Miller, Tice L. *Entertaining the Nation: American Drama in the Eighteenth and Nineteenth Centuries*. Carbondale: Southern Illinois Univ. Press, 2007.

Milner, Clyde A., II, and Carol O'Connor. *As Big as the West: The Pioneer Life of Granville Stuart*. New York: Oxford Univ. Press, 2009.

Monnett, John H. *Where a Hundred Soldiers Were Killed: The Struggle for the Powder River Country in 1866 and the Making of the Fetterman Myth*. Albuquerque: Univ. of New Mexico Press, 2008.

Morgan, Robert. *Lions of the West: Heroes and Villains of the Westward Expansion*. Chapel Hill, N.C.: Algonquin Books, 2011.

Morrison, James L. *"The Best School in the World": West Point, the Pre–Civil War Years, 1833–1866*. Kent, Ohio: Kent State Univ. Press, 1986.

Morrison, R. Bruce, and C. Roderick Wilson, eds. *Native Peoples: The Canadian Experience*. 1986; Toronto: McClelland & Stewart, 1995.

Murphy, Lucy Eldersveld. *A Gathering of Rivers: Indians, Métis, and Mining in the Western Great Lakes, 1737–1832*. Lincoln: Univ. of Nebraska Press, 2000.

Museum of Modern Art. *Masterpieces of the David and Peggy Rockefeller Collection: Manet to Picasso*. New York: Museum of Modern Art, 1994.

Nash, Gary B. "The Hidden History of Mestizo America." *Journal of American History* 82, no. 3 (Dec. 1995): 941–64.

———. *Forbidden Love: The Secret History of Mixed-Race America*, New York: Henry Holt, 1999.

Nesbit, Robert, and William F. Thompson, *Wisconsin: A History.* 2nd ed. 1973; Madison: Univ. of Wisconsin Press, 2004.

Oglesby, Richard Edward. *Manuel Lisa and the Opening of the Missouri Fur Trade.* Norman: Univ. of Oklahoma Press, 1963.

Olson, Donald W., and Laurie E. Jasinski. "Abe Lincoln and the Leonids." *Sky & Telescope* 98, no. 5 (Nov. 1999): 34–35.

Osgood, Robert L. *The History of Special Education: A Struggle for Equality in American Public Schools.* Westport, Conn.: Praeger, 2008.

Osler, William, and Thomas McCrae, *The Principles and Practice of Medicine.* 1892; New York: D. Appleton, 1921.

Overholser, Joel. *Fort Benton: World's Innermost Port.* Helena, Mont.: Falcon Press, 1987.

Owens, Robert Martin. *Mr. Jefferson's Hammer: William Henry Harrison and the Origins of American Indian Policy.* Norman: Univ. of Oklahoma Press, 2007.

Pappas, George. *To the Point: The United States Military Academy, 1802–1902.* Westport, Conn.: Praeger, 1993.

Pascoe, Peggy. *What Comes Naturally: Miscegenation Law and the Making of Race in America.* New York: Oxford Univ. Press, 2009.

Perdue, Theda. *Mixed Blood Indians: Racial Construction in the Early South.* Athens: Univ. of Georgia Press, 2003.

Perry, Adele. *On the Edge of Empire: Gender, Race, and the Making of British Columbia, 1849–1871.* Toronto: Univ. of Toronto Press, 2001.

Petersen, Larry Len. *The Call of the Mountains: The Artists of Glacier National Park.* Tucson: Settlers West Galleries, 2002.

Peterson, Jacqueline, and Jennifer S. H. Brown, eds. *The New Peoples: Being and Becoming Métis in North America.* 1985; Winnipeg: Univ. of Manitoba Press, 2001.

Philbrick, Nathaniel. *Last Stand: Custer, Sitting Bull, and the Battle of the Little Bighorn.* New York: Viking, 2010.

Phillips, Paul C. *The Fur Trade.* 2 vols. Norman: Univ. of Oklahoma Press, 1961.

Philp, Kenneth R. *John Collier's Crusade for Indian Reform, 1920–1954.* Tucson: Univ. of Arizona Press, 1977.

———. *Termination Revisited: American Indians on the Trail to Self-Determination, 1933–1953.* Lincoln: Univ. of Nebraska Press, 1999.

Podlecki, Anthony J. *Perikles and His Circle.* New York: Routledge, 1998.

Podruchny, Carolyn. *Making the Voyageur World: Travelers and Traders in the North American Fur Trade.* Lincoln: Univ. of Nebraska Press, 2006.

Podruchny, Carolyn, and Laura Peers, eds. *Gathering Places: Aboriginal and Fur Trade Histories.* Vancouver: Univ. of British Columbia Press, 2010.

Price, Kenneth M. *To Walt Whitman, America.* Chapel Hill: Univ. of North Carolina Press, 2004.

Priest, Loring Benson. *Uncle Sam's Stepchildren: The Reformation of United States Indian Policy, 1865–1887.* 1942; Lincoln: Univ. of Nebraska Press, 1969.

Prucha, Francis Paul. *The Great Father: The United States Government and the American Indians.* 2 vols. Lincoln: Univ. of Nebraska Press, 1984.

Radke-Moss, Andrea G. "Learning in the West: Western Women and the Culture of Education." In *The World of the American West,* edited by Gordon Morris Bakken, 387–417. New York: Routledge, 2011.

Ray, Arthur J. *Indians in the Fur Trade: Their Role as Trappers, Hunters, and Middlemen in the Lands Southwest of Hudson Bay, 1660–1870.* Toronto: Univ. of Toronto Press, 1974.

Robinson, Doane. "A Comprehensive History of the Dakota or Sioux Indians." *South Dakota Historical Collections.* Vol. 2. Pierre, S.D.: State Historical Society, 1904.

Rockefeller, David. *Memoirs.* New York: Random House, 2002.

Ronda, James P. *Astoria and Empire.* Lincoln: Univ. of Nebraska Press, 1990.

———. *Lewis and Clark among the Indians.* 1984; Lincoln: Univ. of Nebraska Press, 2002.

Rorabaugh, W. J. *The Alcoholic Republic: An American Tradition.* New York: Oxford Univ. Press, 1979.

Rosier, Paul C. *Rebirth of the Blackfeet Nation, 1912–1954.* Lincoln: Univ. of Nebraska Press, 2001.

———. "Joseph W. Brown: Native American Politician." In *The Human Tradition in the American West,* edited by Benson Tong and Regan A. Lutz, 117–35. Wilmington, Dela.: SR Books, 2002.

Ruggles, Eleanor. *Prince of Players: Edwin Booth.* New York: Norton, 1953.

Sandoz, Mari. *The Beaver Men: Spearheads of Empire.* 1964; Lincoln: Univ. of Nebraska Press, 2009.

Saunt, Claudio. *Black, White and Indian: Race and the Unmaking of an American Family.* New York: Oxford Univ. Press, 2005.

Scheick, William J. *The Half-Blood: A Cultural Symbol in 19th-Century American Fiction.* Lexington: Univ. Press of Kentucky, 1979.

Schenck, Theresa. "Border Identities: Métis, Halfbreed, and Mixed-Blood." In *Gathering Places: Aboriginal and Fur Trade Histories,* edited by Carolyn Podruchny and Laura Peers, 233–48. Vancouver: Univ. of British Columbia Press, 2010.

Schlissel, Lillian, Vicki Ruiz, and Janice Monk, eds. *Western Women: Their Land, Their Lives.* Albuquerque: Univ. of New Mexico Press, 1988.

Schultz, James Willard. *The Starving Blackfeet Indians.* Los Angeles: National Association to Help the Indian, 1921.

———. *Signposts of Adventure: Glacier National Park as the Indians Know It.* Boston: Houghton Mifflin, 1926.

———. *Blackfeet and Buffalo: Memories of Life among the Blackfeet.* Norman: Univ. of Oklahoma Press, 1962.

Scriver, Mary Strachan. *Bronze Inside and Out: A Biographical Memoir of Bob Scriver.* Calgary: Univ. of Calgary Press, 2007.

Sellers, Charles. *The Market Revolution: Jacksonian America, 1815–1846.* New York: Oxford Univ. Press, 1991.

Shaffer, Marguerite S. *See America First: Tourism and National Identity, 1880–1940.* Washington, D.C.: Smithsonian Institution Press, 2001.

Simonsen, Jane. *Making Home Work: Domesticity and Native American Assimilation in the American West, 1860–1919.* Chapel Hill: Univ. of North Carolina Press, 2006.

Skaggs, David Curtis, and Larry L. Nelson, eds. *The Sixty Years' War for the Great Lakes, 1754–1814.* East Lansing: Michigan State Univ. Press, 2001.

Skarsten, M. O. *George Drouillard: Hunter and Interpreter for Lewis and Clark & Fur Trader, 1807–1810.* 1964; Lincoln: Univ. of Nebraska Press, 2005.

Sleeper-Smith, Susan. *Indian Women and French Men: Rethinking Cultural Encounter in the Western Great Lakes.* Amherst: Univ. of Massachusetts Press, 2001.

Smith, Shannon D. *Give Me Eighty Men: Women and the Myth of the Fetterman Fight.* Lincoln: Univ. of Nebraska Press, 2008.

Smith, Sherry L. *Reimagining Indians: Native Americans through Anglo Eyes, 1880–1940.* New York: Oxford Univ. Press, 2000.

———. *Hippies, Indians, and the Fight for Red Power.* New York: Oxford Univ. Press, 2012.

Smits, David D. "'The Squaw Drudge': A Prime Index of Savagism." *Ethnohistory* 29, no. 4 (1982): 281–306.

———. "'Squaw Men,' 'Half-Breeds,' and Amalgamators: Late Nineteenth-Century Anglo-American Attitudes toward Indian-White Race-Mixing." *American Indian Culture and Research Journal* 15, no. 3 (1991): 29–61.

Sneider, Allison L. *Suffragists in an Imperial Age: U.S. Expansion and the Woman Question, 1870–1929.* New York: Oxford Univ. Press, 2008.

Spence, Clark C. "The Territorial Officers of Montana, 1864–1889." *Pacific Historical Review* 30, no. 2 (May 1961): 123–36.

———. *Territorial Politics and Government in Montana, 1864–89.* Urbana: Univ. of Illinois Press, 1975.

Spence, Mark David. *Dispossessing the Wilderness: Indian Removal and the Making of the National Parks.* New York: Oxford Univ. Press, 1999.

Stampp, Kenneth M. *Indiana Politics during the Civil War.* 1949; Bloomington: Indiana Univ. Press, 1978.

Starita, Joe. *"I Am a Man": Chief Standing Bear's Journey for Justice.* New York: St. Martin's Press, 2008.

Stein, Mark. *How the States Got Their Shapes.* New York: Collins, 2008.

Stoler, Ann Laura. *Carnal Knowledge and Imperial Power: Race and the Intimate in Colonial Rule.* Berkeley: Univ. of California Press, 2002.

St. Onge, Nicole, Carolyn Podruchny, and Brenda MacDougall, eds. *Contours of a People: Metis Family, Mobility, and History.* Norman: Univ. of Oklahoma Press, 2012.

Stout, Tom. *Montana, Its Story and Biography: A History of Aboriginal and Ter-*

ritorial Montana and Three Decades of Statehood. Chicago: American Historical Society, 1921.

Sully, Langdon. *No Tears for the General: The Life of Alfred Sully, 1821–1879*. Palo Alto, Calif.: American West Publishing, 1974.

Sunder, John E. *The Fur Trade on the Upper Missouri, 1840–1865*. 1965; Norman: Univ. of Oklahoma Press, 1993.

Swagerty, William R. "Marriage and Settlement Patterns of Rocky Mountain Trappers and Traders." *Western Historical Quarterly* 11, no. 2 (April 1980): 161–80.

———. "A View from the Bottom Up: The Work Force of the American Fur Company on the Upper Missouri in the 1830s." *Montana: The Magazine of Western History* 43, no. 1 (Winter 1993): 18–33.

Taliaferro, John. *Charles M. Russell: The Life and Legend of America's Cowboy Artist*. Boston: Little, Brown, 1996.

Taylor, Alan. *The Civil War of 1812: American Citizens, British Subjects, Irish Rebels, & Indian Allies*. New York: Knopf, 2010.

Thomas, William G., III. *The Iron Way: Railroads, the Civil War, and the Making of Modern America*. New Haven: Yale Univ. Press, 2011.

Thompson, Erwin N. *Fort Union Trading Post: Fur Trade Empire on the Upper Missouri*. Williston, N.D.: Fort Union Association, 2003.

Thorne, Tanis C. *The Many Hands of My Relations: French and Indians on the Lower Missouri*. Columbia: Univ. of Missouri Press, 1996.

Titone, Nora. *My Thoughts Be Bloody: The Bitter Rivalry between Edwin and John Wilkes Booth That Led to an American Tragedy*. New York: Free Press, 2011.

Tong, Benson, and Regan A. Lutz, eds. *The Human Tradition in the American West*. Wilmington, Del.: SR Books, 2002.

Tonkovich, Nicole. *The Allotment Plot: Alice C. Fletcher, E. Jane Gay, and Nez Perce Survivance*. Lincoln: Univ. of Nebraska Press, 2012.

Toole, K. Ross. *Montana: An Uncommon Land*. 1959; Norman: Univ. of Oklahoma Press, 1984.

Turvey, Dana. "The Man Who Talks Not." *Flathead Living*, July/Aug. 2007, pp. 46–49.

Turvey, Joyce Clarke. "Helen Piotopowaka Clarke." In *History of Glacier County, Montana*, edited by Joy MacCarter, 87. Cut Bank, Mont.: Glacier County Historical Society, 1984.

———. "Clarke History." In *Trails and Tales of the Highwoods*, edited by Highwood Woman's Club, 84–86. Highwood, Mont.: Highwood Woman's Club, 1988.

Two Worlds at Two Medicine. DVD. Directed by Dennis Neary. Browning, Mont.: Going-to-the-Sun Institute and Native Pictures, 2004.

Tyrrell, Ian R. *Sobering Up: From Temperance to Prohibition in Antebellum America, 1800–1860*. Westport, Conn.: Greenwood Press, 1979.

Ulrich, Roberta. *American Indian Nations from Termination to Restoration, 1953–2006*. Lincoln: Univ. of Nebraska Press, 2010.

Unrau, William E. *White Man's Wicked Water: The Alcohol Trade and Prohibition in Indian Country, 1802–1892*. Lawrence: Univ. Press of Kansas, 1996.

Vanderhaeghe, Guy. *The Englishman's Boy.* New York: Picador, 1996.

VanderVelde, Lea. *Mrs. Dred Scott: A Life on Slavery's Frontier.* New York: Oxford Univ. Press, 2009.

Van Kirk, Sylvia. *Many Tender Ties: Women in Fur Trade Society.* Norman: Univ. of Oklahoma Press, 1980.

Walker, William. "A Living Exhibition: The Smithsonian, Folklife, and the Making of the Modern Museum." Ph.D. diss., Brandeis Univ., 2007.

Wallace, Anthony F. C. *Jefferson and the Indians: The Tragic Fate of the First Americans.* Cambridge: Harvard Univ. Press, 1999.

Walter, Dave. *Montana Campfire Tales: Fourteen Historical Narratives.* Guilford, Conn.: Globe Pequot Press, 1997.

Waltmann, Henry G. "The Interior Department, War Department, and Indian Policy, 1865–1887." Ph.D. diss., Univ. of Nebraska-Lincoln, 1962.

———. "Circumstantial Reformer: President Grant & the Indian Problem." *Arizona and the West* 13, no. 4 (Winter 1971): 323–42.

Ward, Geoffrey C. *The West: An Illustrated History.* Boston: Little, Brown, 1996.

Weber, David J. *The Spanish Frontier in North America.* New Haven: Yale Univ. Press, 1992.

———. *Bárbaros: Spaniards and Their Savages in the Age of Enlightenment.* New Haven: Yale Univ. Press, 2007.

Weist, Katherine M. "Beasts of Burden and Menial Slaves: Nineteenth-Century Observations of Northern Plains Indian Women." In *The Hidden Half: Studies of Plains Indian Women,* edited by Patricia Albers and Beatrice Medicine, 29–52. Lanham, Md.: Univ. Press of America, 1983.

Welch, James. *Fools Crow.* New York: Penguin, 1986.

Wessel, Thomas R. "Historical Report on the Blackfeet Reservation in Northern Montana." Indian Claims Commission, Docket Number 279-D: 1975.

The West. DVD. Directed by Stephen Ives. Arlington, Va.: PBS Home Video, 1996.

West, Elliott. *The Way to the West: Essays on the Central Plains.* Albuquerque: Univ. of New Mexico Press, 1995.

———. *The Contested Plains: Indians, Goldseekers, and the Rush to Colorado.* Lawrence: Univ. Press, of Kansas, 1998.

———. *The Last Indian War: The Nez Perce Story.* New York: Oxford Univ. Press, 2009.

White, Richard. *The Middle Ground: Indians, Empires, and Republics in the Great Lakes Region, 1650–1815.* New York: Cambridge Univ. Press, 1991.

Wilmeth, Don B., and Christopher Bigsby, eds. *The Cambridge History of American Theatre.* Vol. 2. New York: Cambridge Univ. Press, 1999.

Wilson, Wesley C. "The U.S. Army and the Piegans: The Baker Massacre on the Marias, 1870." *North Dakota History* 32, no. 1 (Winter 1965): 40–58.

Winter, William. *Life and Art of Edwin Booth.* New York: Greenwood Press, 1968.

Wischmann, Lesley. *Frontier Diplomats: Alexander Culbertson and Natoyist-Siksina' among the Blackfeet.* 2000; Norman: Univ. of Oklahoma Press, 2004.

316 BIBLIOGRAPHY

Wishart, David J. *The Fur Trade of the American West, 1807–1840: A Geographical Synthesis.* 1979; Lincoln: Univ. of Nebraska Press, 1992.
———. *An Unspeakable Sadness: The Dispossession of the Nebraska Indians.* Lincoln: Univ. of Nebraska Press, 1994.
Wissler, Clark. "Material Culture of the Blackfoot Indians." *Anthropological Papers of the American Museum of Natural History.* Vol. 5, pt. 1. New York: Published by Order of the Trustees, 1910.
———. "The Social Life of the Blackfoot Indians." *Anthropological Papers of the American Museum of Natural History.* Vol. 7, pt. 1. New York: Published by Order of the Trustees, 1912.
———. "The Sun Dance of the Blackfoot Indians." *Anthropological Papers of the American Museum of Natural History.* Vol. 16, pt. 3. New York: Published by Order of the Trustees, 1918.
———. *Indian Cavalcade; or, Life on the Old-Time Indian Reservations.* New York: Sheridan House, 1938.
Wood, Charles R. *Lines West: A Pictorial History of the Great Northern Railway Operations and Motive Power from 1887 to 1967.* Seattle: Superior Books, 1967.
Woods, Karen M. "'A Wicked and Mischievous Connection': The Origins of Indian-White Miscegenation Law." In *Mixed Race America and the Law: A Reader,* edited by Kevin R. Johnson, 81–85. New York: New York Univ. Press, 2003.
Wylie, Paul R. *The Irish General: Thomas Francis Meagher.* Norman: Univ. of Oklahoma Press, 2007.
Yarbrough, Fay A. *Race and the Cherokee Nation: Sovereignty in the Nineteenth Century.* Philadelphia: Univ. of Pennsylvania Press, 2007.

Index

Page numbers in *italics* refer to illustrations.
Page numbers beginning with 247 refer to endnotes.

Sully's conflict with, *108,* 111, 114
 on transfer initiative, 135
Sherman, Eleanor, support of J. L.
 Clarke by, 220–22, 229
Sherman, John, 135, 166
Sherman, William Tecumseh, 103–4,
 108, 130, 275
 accolades for, 131
 as Army commanding general,
 113, 115
 condemnation of, 137, 139–40
 in March to the Sea, 114
 in Marias Massacre debate, 133
Sherry, Louis, 158
Shoshones, 14, 23–26, 243
Side Hill Calf, 17
Sieben Ranch, *98,* 267
sign language:
 of deaf, 203–4, 214, 218, *219*
 Indian, 16–17, 204, 211, 212,
 227
Siksikau ("black foot"; "black feet"),
 28
 three groups of, 14
Silent Call, The (Royle), 153–55, 158
Sioux, 62, 63, 122, 141, 171, 217
Sioux Indian Museum, 231
Siquieros, David Alfaro, 228
slavery, 40, 49, 76, 155
 activists against, 137–41, 275
slave uprisings, 11
smallpox, 2, 43, 126, 128–29, 132,
 199, 254
Smith, Joseph, 40
Snelling, Fort, 60–63, *61, 64,* 67, 258
Snelling, Josiah, 60, 63–65
solar eclipse, 41
Sophie of Württemberg, Queen of the
 Netherlands, 158
South Platte River, gold rush at, 86
Spain, imperialistic goal of, 14, 85
Spear, Anson Rudolph, 201–4

Spear, Julia, 202
Spear Woman, 129
Split Upper Lip, 63–64
Spokane Art Association, 218
Spopee (Turtle), 279, 289
spotted fever, 58
spyglass, 99
squaw man, 81–82
Squaw Man, The (Royle), 153
Squires, Lewis, 72–73
Standing Bear, 171–72
Stanford University, 241
starvation, 113, 177, 178, 180, 185
steamboats, 20, 41–42, 43, 65, 83,
 90–91, 115, 142
stereotypes, 82–83, 190–91, 205
Stowe, Harriet Beecher, 168
Stuart, Awbonnie, 237
Stuart, Granville "Mr. Montana,"
 236–37, 238, 266
Stuart, Sam, 237
Stuart, Tom, 237
Sully, Alfred H., 97, 107–9, *108,* 117,
 269
 diplomatic mission of, 107–9, 117,
 121, 125, *145*
 embitterment, decline and death
 of, 140
 in Marias Massacre debate,
 131–33
 Sherman's conflict with, 111, 114,
 140
Sumner, Charles, 166, 281–82
Sumter, Fort, 67
Sun Dance, 47
Sun River (Natoe-osucti), 121
superstitions:
 bias as, 155
 Indian, 45, 174
surround, in bison hunt, 22
Swan, James, 161
Swiftcurrent valley, 181, 212

About the Author

Andrew R. Graybill was born and raised in San Antonio, Texas, and educated at Yale (B.A.), Trinity (M.A.T.), and Princeton (M.A., Ph.D.) universities. From 2003 to 2011 he taught in the history department at the University of Nebraska, before moving to Southern Methodist University in Dallas, Texas, where he is associate professor of history and director of the William P. Clements Center for Southwest Studies. He is the author of *Policing the Great Plains: Rangers, Mounties, and the North American Frontier, 1875–1910* (2007), and co-editor (with Benjamin H. Johnson) of *Bridging National Borders in North America: Transnational and Comparative Histories* (2010). His current book project is a history of the Taos Revolt of 1847. He lives with his wife and two children in Old East Dallas.